LONGSTREET'S AIDE

THE CIVIL WAR LETTERS OF
MAJOR THOMAS J. GOREE

A NATION DIVIDED
NEW STUDIES IN CIVIL WAR HISTORY

James I. Robertson, Jr.
General Series Editor

Wendy Hamand Venet,
Neither Ballots nor Bullets:
Women Abolitionists and the Civil War

Ervin L. Jordan, Jr.,
Black Confederates and Afro-Yankees
in Civil War Virginia

Thomas W. Cutrer, ed.,
Longstreet's Aide: The Civil War Letters of
Major Thomas J. Goree

LONGSTREET'S AIDE

THE CIVIL WAR LETTERS OF
MAJOR THOMAS J. GOREE

Edited by
THOMAS W. CUTRER

UNIVERSITY PRESS OF VIRGINIA

CHARLOTTESVILLE AND LONDON

THE UNIVERSITY PRESS OF VIRGINIA

Copyright © 1995 by the Rector and Visitors
of the University of Virginia
First published 1995

Library of Congress Cataloging-in-Publication Data

Goree, Thomas Jewett, 1835–1905.
    Longstreet's aide : the Civil War letters of Major Thomas J. Goree
/ edited by Thomas W. Cutrer.
    p.   cm.—(A nation divided)
    Includes bibliographical references and index.
    ISBN 0-8139-1574-0
    1. Goree, Thomas Jewett, 1835–1905—Correspondence.   2. United
States—History—Civil War, 1861–1865—Personal narratives,
Confederate.   3. Confederate States of America.   Army of Northern
Virginia—Biography.   4. Longstreet, James, 1821–1904—Friends and
associates.   5. Soldiers—Confederate States of America—
Correspondence.   I. Cutrer, Thomas W.   II. Title.   III. Series.
E605G664   1995
973.7′82—dc20   94-37521
                                                                                              CIP

Printed in the United States of America

FOR Privates

Edward W. Cutrer,

Irwin E. Cutrer,

Isaac N. Cutrer,

and

Oren B. Cutrer

COMPANY B

SIXTEENTH LOUISIANA INFANTRY

C.S.A.

CONTENTS

ILLUSTRATIONS

LONGSTREET'S AIDE

THE CIVIL WAR LETTERS OF
MAJOR THOMAS J. GOREE

INTRODUCTION

WHEN I WAS A SMALL BOY GROWING UP IN SOUTH LOUISIANA, I WOULD from time to time pester my father with requests for various dispensations. "Dad, if I had so-and-so, I'd be able to do thus-and-such," my argument generally ran. "Yes, and if Longstreet had gotten to Gettysburg on time, we'd still be spending Confederate money," was his habitual reply. Thus I was informed not only that the object of my desire was as remote and unobtainable as Southern independence, but that the legend and controversy surrounding the performance of Lt. Gen. James Longstreet on our most disastrous field still ran deep in the consciousness of the Southern folk, almost one hundred years later.

Although Longstreet occupied a position inferior only to Lee's and Jackson's in the command structure of the Army of Northern Virginia, his popularity with the Southern people has always been eclipsed by theirs. In his famous triptych in Richmond's Battle Abbey, artist Charles Hoffbauer forever fixed the iconography of the army, portraying Lee, Jackson, and Jeb Stuart as its spiritual leaders. Charles R. Wilson rightly argues in his study of the religion of the Lost Cause, *Baptized in Blood,* that Lee, Jackson, and Davis comprised that Holy Trinity in the postbellum South.[1] In a seminal biography historians Hamilton J. Eckenrode and Bryan Conrad attribute Longstreet's fall from grace to his postwar career as a Republican officeholder, friend of Ulysses S. Grant, and apologist for the North's Reconstruction measures. They argue more damningly, however, that Longstreet was a failure as a corps commander and that from the war's opening campaign "he was dissatisfied with a subordinate position, longing for complete authority. That longing "was to grow with time and become one of the elements in the failure of the Southern cause." This breaking of faith with the Southern cause and lèse-majesté toward its most beloved leader and symbol combined to remove Longstreet from the pantheon of Confederate deities and relegate him to the status of a Miltonic Satan.[2]

Longstreet's soldiers, however, revered their corps commander, cheering him wildly when he rode by and never deserting him, even during the dark days of Reconstruction when he seemed to have turned apostate. One of his most loyal minions and articulate advocates was his aide-de-camp Thomas Jewett Goree. Goree's letters from Virginia and Tennessee to his mother and other members of his family in Texas are among the richest and most perceptive of any written from the Army of Northern Virginia. Present at Longstreet's headquarters and able to hear the counsels of Lee and his lieutenants and to observe the personalities of many of the Confederate high command, Goree made shrewd observations on matters of strategy and politics and prepared insightful portraits not only of Longstreet but of Jefferson Davis, P. G. T. Beauregard, John Bell Hood, J. E. B. Stuart, and others of Lee's inner circle as well.

Goree was also attentive to Confederate fortunes beyond the boundaries of Virginia, and his letters contain much discerning analysis of military affairs and personnel in the Army of Tennessee and in the Trans-Mississippi Department. Wartime politics and social change also were the subjects of Goree's observation, and he not only reports on but gives remarkably judicious critiques of such issues as black troops and black servants in the Confederate army, the murderous effect of inflation on the war effort, and the affairs of his numerous and influential extended family throughout the South.

In addition to members of his family, Goree corresponded with such Confederate notables as E. Porter Alexander, George E. Pickett, G. Moxley Sorell, and Micah Jenkins. Also of significance is Goree's travel diary, June through August 1865, describing his trip with Longstreet from Appomattox to Talladega, Alabama. After the war Goree maintained a close relationship with Longstreet, whose letters to Goree shed great light on the old general's postbellum career and his acrimonious debate over his conduct at Gettysburg and elsewhere with such former brothers-in-arms as Jubal Early, John Brown Gordon, and William Nelson Pendleton.

In the years after Appomattox, Longstreet called often upon his former aide for personal recollections that might vindicate his former commander's behavior at Gettysburg. Although at least a few of Goree's replies are now missing, those that remain indicate not only that he remained loyal to Longstreet but that the old general had been dealt with unfairly by his many powerful critics. Goree recounted, for example, an incident during the winter of 1863–64 when Longstreet sent him from East Tennessee with some dispatches to General Lee. On that occasion Lee admitted to Goree that "if he had permitted you to carry out your plans, instead of making the attack on Cemetery Hill, he would have been successful." [3]

Not only do insights into the actions and character of the high command of the Army of Northern Virginia issue from these letters, but their writer, Thomas Jewett Goree, emerges as well as a remarkable individual, worthy of attention on his own account. The eldest child of Dr. Langston James Goree and his second wife, Sarah Williams Kittrell Goree, Thomas Jewett Goree was born in Marion, Alabama, on 14 November 1835. His father, a planter and physician, married Susan Kenner in 1817, and with her had nine children, three of whom, Samuel Escridge, Mary Francis, and Martha Anna, lived to adulthood. Susan Kenner Goree died in 1833, and the following year Goree married for a second time. In 1837 he and his family moved from Orange County, South Carolina, to Marion, where Dr. Goree, with his brother Dr. James Lyles Goree, helped establish the Judson Female Institute, which was chartered on 7 January 1839. The first president of the institute, which is now known as Judson College, was Milo P. Jewett, who was later to become the first president of Vassar College. Thomas J. Goree's middle name honored the president of the Judson

Academy, and the Gorees' fourth son, Edwin King Goree, was named for Gen. Edwin D. King, president of the academy's board. For eleven years Langston Goree served the school as dean and Sarah Goree as matron.

Among Judson Female Institute's earliest graduates was Margaret Moffette Lea, later to become the second Mrs. Sam Houston. From this association sprang a close and cordial friendship between the Goree and Houston families, with Mrs. Goree serving as Mrs. Houston's matron of honor and hostess of her wedding dinner at Marion in 1840.

Thomas Jewett was followed by four brothers who lived to adulthood, Robert Daniel ("Bobby") Goree; Langston James ("Toby") Goree II; Edwin King ("Ed") Goree; and Pleasant Kittrell ("Scrap") Goree; and one sister, Susan Margaret Goree, known to her brothers as "Sudy." All four of Goree's brothers would follow him into Confederate service, three serving in John Bell Hood's redoubtable Texas Brigade.

In December 1850 the Goree family and their forty slaves followed their friends Sam and Margaret Houston to Texas, settling first at Huntsville—some seventy miles north of the city of Houston—where they rented the Houstons' Woodland Home. While at Huntsville the Gorees built their own plantation, Trinity Bend, some thirty miles to the north on the Trinity River in Houston County. There the family engaged in cotton planting until Langston Goree died on 5 July 1853. The next year Sarah Goree moved her family to Moffatsville plantation in Madison County to be near her brother Pleasant Williams Kittrell, and early in 1858 she purchased Raven Hill plantation in Walker (now San Jacinto) County from Sam Houston.[4]

Thomas J. Goree had attended Howard College in Marion, Alabama, and, after the family moved to Texas, received a bachelor of arts degree in 1856 from the Texas Baptist Educational Society, now Baylor University, then at Independence. While attending college young Goree resided with the Houston family and was baptized with Sam Houston by the Reverend Rufus C. Burleson, head of the Baptist Educational Society, on 19 November 1854. "As you may imagine," Goree wrote to his mother, "Mrs. Houston was in ecstasies when the General joined. She could not keep from turning Methodist and shouting a little."[5]

On 1 June 1857 Goree became headmaster of "a male school" at Washington, Texas, while reading law in the office of William P. Rogers. In Washington he boarded with the Rogers family who "treated me as well as I could be treated anywhere," but his venture into pedagogy proved a failure. "I commenced," he wrote to his mother, "taught 2 weeks, and had only twelve or thirteen scholars," and so gave up the business having earned only twenty dollars, "enough to pay my board while at Washington." Goree then entered law school at Independence despite advice to the contrary from a family friend and neighbor, George W. Baines, the grandfather of Lyndon Baines Johnson. "In reference to the law," Goree informed his mother, "I am sorry that Mr. Baines has disturbed your mind about it, but I think that he is better posted up on other subjects than he is on that. For my life I cannot see what there is in law to prevent one from being a Christian. Some of the best of men have been lawyers, and there are, too, a great many lawyers who are very bad men, but that is no reason that all should be such." [6]

At Independence, Goree took rooms with the Burleson family and studied under William P. Rogers and Royall T. Wheeler, then an associate justice of the Texas Supreme Court and later its chief justice. He attended five lectures per week, and "besides being examined on the lectures every day, we have each day from one to two hundred pages assigned us in Blackstone and Kent to read, and on which we are examined. Every Monday we hold a moot court, and try cases just the same as in a regular court." [7] Wheeler, who took a great interest in the young Goree's career, wrote to his mother upon his graduation in 1858 that her son's "uniformly gentlemanly & exemplary deportment has endeared him to us all; especially to my own family who entertain for him the sincerest regard & esteem. He bears with him our best wishes for his prosperity & happiness. We shall cherish an abiding interest in his welfare, & the success in his pursuits which we confidently anticipate." [8]

Upon graduation Goree was admitted to the bar and entered the firm of Rogers, Willie, and Goree. His partners were his old mentor William P. Rogers and James Willie, a former state representative and attorney general under Governor Elisha M. Pease. Goree was assigned to supervise the Montgomery County office of the firm while Rogers and Willie kept offices in Houston. "I think you have made a judicious selection," wrote his former teacher Royall T. Wheeler. "You have a healthy place, & the county is destined to have wealth & business." Although he advised his former student that building a practice would take longer in the more settled Montgomery County than on the frontier, the experience would make him a better lawyer "from the fact that you will have leisure for study & time to master your cases." Goree's partners were excellent attorneys, Wheeler assured him, but he warned his protégé not to rely upon them too much. "Master the law of your cases," he advised, "& then conduct them yourself in the courthouse." Despite such fine prospects and sound advice, however, Goree soon closed the Montgomery office and moved to Houston. [9]

More than the law, politics had become Goree's overriding passion. Although Texans were increasingly hostile toward the growing abolitionist sentiment in the North and fearful of the development of the Republican party, Goree remained fiercely loyal to Sam Houston, a devout Unionist. When "the Old Hero" entered the Texas governor's race in 1857, Goree wrote that, despite his opposition to disunion, "if the General is not a traitor to the South and to his country, I am certain that he has done enough to entitle him to any office he may ask at the hands of the people" and for a time entertained the notion of following him on his electioneering tour of Texas. Although Goree at last determined not to accompany Houston on the campaign, he remained convinced that he "will be triumphantly elected, Modern Democracy to the contrary notwithstanding."[10]

When Houston was elected in 1859, Goree and several of his friends, styling themselves "the National Democracy of Old Montgomery," hosted a formal dinner on 15 October in honor of Houston's "fearless advocacy of the principles of a sound National Democracy." Goree's commitment to the Union was, at that time, as unconditional as that of Houston, and with the other sponsors of the dinner Goree swore to be "ever true to the Union of the States under the Constitution."[11] Long before the fall of Fort Sumter, however, Goree's commitment to the Union had collapsed. "As for myself," he informed his mother on 13 December 1860, "I favor immediate secession," and when the state's secession convention met in Austin in January 1861, Goree expressed the hope that "Texas will promptly secede from a Union which is no longer worth preserving."[12]

With the formation of the Confederate States, and as the inauguration of Abraham Lincoln loomed nearer, the threat of war overwhelmed all else in Goree's mind, leading him to lament that "one day from the news we are led to hope that the revolution will be bloodless, at another time civil war seems to be inevitable." Once the "inevitable" occurred, Goree set out for Virginia in May 1861 in company with Benjamin Franklin Terry, Thomas Saltus Lubbock, and John A. Wharton "with the determination of being in the first battle for Southern independence." Wharton, who later became a Confederate major general, was forced to drop out of the party due to illness, but the others arrived at Manassas Junction and were appointed as independent scouts for the command of Brig. Gen. P. G. T. Beauregard.[13]

On 18 July 1861, the day of the first fighting on Bull Run, Goree was appointed volunteer aide on the staff of Brig. Gen. James Longstreet, who had traveled with the Texans from Galveston. Goree remained on Longstreet's staff as an aide-de-camp for the remainder of the war, ultimately becoming a major and participating in nearly all of the battles of the Army of Northern Virginia: Yorktown, Williamsburg, Seven Pines, and the Seven Days fighting before Richmond during the Peninsula campaign, Second Manassas, South Mountain, Sharpsburg, and Fredericksburg, Longstreet's Suffolk campaign, Gettysburg, Chickamauga, the Knoxville campaign, the siege of Petersburg, and finally the surrender at Appomattox.[14]

The aide-de-camp on a Civil War staff was an ex officio officer, appointed by a general grade officer and reporting directly to him. Army regulations authorized a lieutenant general to employ four aides, a major general two, and a brigadier general one, although this regulation was often breached in practice. The aide's position was one of great responsibility, as he served as an amanuensis to his commander and often personally delivered the general's orders to subordinate commanders and was a liaison to higher echelons of command. On campaign he was required to be thoroughly knowledgeable about troop dispositions, routes of march, and the locations of superior and subordinate officers' headquarters. He was also expected to have a sufficient understanding of tactics and his superior's intentions for conducting battle and campaign that he could modify his commander's orders on the field if circumstances required. As William T. Sherman defined the position, aides should be "good riders, and intelligent enough to give and explain the orders of their general." British military historian Paddy Griffith goes so far as to aver that "when it came to controlling a battle only the adjutant and the ADCs would have a role—the former as the brigadier's right-hand-man and general 'expediter,' the latter as his link with higher commanders or outlying detachments." [15]

Not all aides, of course, filled this ideal description. On the eve of the first battle of Manassas, for example, veteran London *Times* correspondent William Howard Russell visited the headquarters of Union general-in-chief Winfield Scott and was shocked by the poor quality of his aides. "The worst-served English general," Russell recorded in his diary, "has always a young fellow or two about him who can fly across the country, draw a rough sketch map, ride like a foxhunter, and find something out about the enemy and their position, understand and convey orders, and obey them." For these types Russell looked in vain. Instead he found "a few plodding old pedants, with map and rules and compasses, who sit in small rooms and write memoranda" and "some ignorant and not very active young men, who loiter about the headquarters' halls, and strut up the street with brass spurs on their heels and kepis raked over their eyes as though they were soldiers." But among Scott's aides the journalist who had covered the Crimean War and the Great Mutiny in India could find "no system, no order, no knowledge, no dash!" [16]

Goree, however, seems to have had a natural affinity for military service and for staff work. In his own modest way, he never claimed more than to have "served faithfully during the war." Of his services at the second battle of Manassas, however, Longstreet wrote on 10 October 1862, "I am under renewed and lasting obligations" to Goree and the other members of his staff. "These officers, full of courage, intelligence, patience, and experience, were able to give directions to commands such as they thought proper, which were at once approved and commanded my admiration." [17] Longstreet's chief of staff, Brig. Gen. G. Moxley Sorrel, moreover, wrote of Goree: "The General was fortunate in having an officer so careful, observing, and intelligent. His conduct on all occasions was excellent and his intrepidity during exposures in battle could always be counted on." To Longstreet, Goree was always "a gentleman of high position and undoubted integrity." [18]

Goree's commander, James Longstreet, was a native of Edgefield District, South Carolina, spent his youth in Georgia, and was appointed to the West

Point class of 1842 from Alabama. His academy classmates included U. S. Grant, Henry W. Halleck, Irvin McDowell, George H. Thomas, and William T. Sherman. After graduating fifty-fourth in a class of sixty-two, Longstreet was brevetted a second lieutenant in the Fourth United States Infantry and saw duty in Louisiana and Missouri before he was transferred to the Eighth Infantry in Florida. During the war with Mexico, Longstreet served under Zachary Taylor in the Monterrey campaign and under Winfield Scott in the campaign against Mexico City. He was wounded in the storming of Chapultepec and breveted to major. After the war Longstreet served on the Texas frontier until 19 July 1858 when he was promoted to major and transferred to the Paymaster Corps.

Longstreet resigned from the United States Army on 1 June 1861 and was commissioned a brigadier general in the Confederate States Army on 17 June. He sought and expected to receive an administrative assignment but instead was given command of a brigade of infantry which he led at the first battle of Manassas. His skill in that battle led to his promotion to major general on 7 October 1861 and assignment to command of a division. During Joseph E. Johnston's retreat up the Peninsula during the spring of 1862, Longstreet performed well as commander of the Rebel rearguard but badly mishandled his attacks at the battle of Seven Pines. His courage and aggressiveness during the Seven Days battles impressed Robert E. Lee who rewarded him with promotion to lieutenant general and command of I Corps of the Army of Northern Virginia on 1 October 1862. Longstreet's command abilities were shown to advantage at Second Manassas, Sharpsburg, and Fredericksburg, although in each of those campaigns he was prone to disagree with his commanding general and to delay acting on Lee's orders when he believed that his own judgment was superior. This hubris and tendency toward insubordination proved to be Longstreet's greatest character flaw, an affliction to the Confederate cause and the nemesis of his personal reputation after the war.

His failure to win laurels as an independent commander during the fruitless Suffolk campaign in the spring of 1863 did nothing to alter Longstreet's estimate of himself as a better strategist and tactician than his commander, and during the subsequent Gettysburg campaign, he delayed enacting Lee's orders to assault the Federal center on the morning of 2 July 1863. Whether his judgment of the tactical situation was right or wrong, he forever sealed his fate in the minds of Lee's partisans in and out of the army as the man who lost the war.

Transferred with his corps to Georgia in September 1863, Longstreet partially refurbished his tarnished glory at Chickamauga under Braxton Bragg but then failed at a second try at independent command when he proved unable to capture Knoxville in November. He and his troops returned to Virginia in May just in time to perform decisively at the battle of the Wilderness. There they checked Grant's tactical offensive and were on the cusp of crushing the Federal left wing when Longstreet sustained a wound from friendly fire under circumstances that bore an uncanny resemblance to the fatal shooting of Stone-wall Jackson on the same field one year earlier. He returned to command during the siege of Richmond and was at the head of I Corps when it surrendered at Appomattox.

Longstreet was unquestionably a superior corps commander and a fine tactician. Despite his many disagreements with his senior subordinate, Robert E. Lee had a genuine affection and respect for Longstreet, calling him "my old War Horse," and the men of I Corps regarded him with great fondness, referring to him as "Old Pete." With the other senior officers of the Army of Northern Virginia, however, Longstreet fared much less well, especially after Lee's death. His blatant defiance of Lee's authority rankled many who worshiped their old commander. The fact that Longstreet was not of the "Virginia clique" of the Army of Northern Virginia, became a Republican after the war, and held a succession of federal appointments under his personal friend and kinsman by marriage U. S. Grant effectively excluded him from the pantheon of Confederate heroes and has been blamed for setting him up as a scapegoat for the Confederate failure at Gettysburg and the subsequent loss of the war. To such keepers of the flame as Early, Gordon, and Pendleton, in fact, he assumed the aspect of one who would sooner "reign in Hell than serve in Heaven."

Views of the personal character of Longstreet and his staff were as varied as are those of his military reputation, but Goree's observation that "he is some days very sociable and agreeable, then again for a few days he will confine himself mostly to his room, or tent, without having much to say to anyone, and is as grim as you please" seems to have been borne out by other close observers. Francis W. Dawson, an Englishman who served as the general's assistant ordnance officer, wrote that "I cannot say that my connection with General Longstreet had been pleasant to me personally, for the reason that he was disposed to be reserved himself, while the principal members of his staff, with two exceptions, were positively disagreeable." Despite Longstreet's reserve, however, Dawson recalled that "the great American game of poker was played nearly every night." In addition, "there was hard drinking as well as high playing; and it was reported that at the end of one debauch General Longstreet had played horse with one of the stronger officers of his staff, who on all-fours carried Longstreet around and around the tent until the pair of them rolled over on the ground together." To Lt. Col. James Arthur Lyon Fremantle, an officer in Her Majesty's Coldstream Guards on a tour of observation in the Confederate States, I Corps headquarters was a most congenial place. "General Longstreet and his staff at once received me into their mess," he wrote. They were "all excellent good fellows," he recalled, "and most hospitable." Fremantle further remarked that "all the [Confederate] generals are thorough soldiers, and their staffs are composed of gentlemen of position and education, who have now been trained into excellent and zealous staff officers."[19]

Goree appeared to bear a charmed life in battle, but his three brothers in Hood's Texas Brigade were wounded, two being crippled for life. Although he was exposed to constant fire for seven hours in the battle of Williamsburg and his saddle and accoutrements were struck seventeen times, he never received a wound. At Sharpsburg, known to the Confederate gunners as an "artillerists' hell," Goree, Gilbert Moxley Sorrel, John W. Fairfax, Thomas Walton, and Peyton T. Manning saw action as cannoneers with the Washington Artillery after the battalion's gun crews were struck down. "The gunners had fallen by their pieces," wrote Sorrel, "which were temporarily without cannoneers." While other staff members held their horses, those officers "leaped from them to the guns. The position was most important and it would never do for those 'barkers' to be dumb, even for a minute; so at it we went, the improvised gunners, and were afterward cheered by being told we did it well and could always get a gunner's berth when we might want it." None of the staff members was hurt, and as they remounted, with cheerful grins at our sudden adventure," Longstreet, "much pleased, turned his attention to other imperiled points." [20]

Lieutenant Colonel Fremantle, who accompanied I Corps during the invasion of Pennsylvania, wrote that just after the great assault on the Federal center at Gettysburg was broken, Walton was the only officer with Longstreet, for "all the rest had been put into the charge. In a few minutes Major Latrobe arrived on foot, carrying his saddle, having just had his horse killed. Colonel Sorrel was also in the same predicament and Captain Goree's horse was wounded in the mouth." Goree was back at Longstreet's side "just after Pickett's repulse, when General Lee so magnanimously took all the blame of the disaster upon himself." [21]

After Gettysburg, Goree accompanied his chief to Tennessee to take part in the battle of Chickamauga and the sieges of Chattanooga and Knoxville. At Chattanooga, Goree shared a tent with Sorrel, Walton, Dawson, and Frank Vizetelly, a journalist for the *Illustrated London News*. During the siege Goree led a small force of sharpshooters from Longstreet's corps, armed with Whitworth rifles equipped with telescopic sights, in an attempt to disrupt Union communications and break up the enemy's supply trains. Goree posted his detail among the crags of Raccoon Mountain, some twelve miles in rear of the Federal works, overlooking an unguarded stretch of the road on the other side of the Tennessee River. Vizetelly accompanied Goree's party and reported to his newspaper:

Scarcely had we arrived at our destination and got the men hidden behind the rocks, when, far up the gorge, could be heard distinctly the rumbling of approaching wheels. Presently emerged the leading files of an infantry escort, followed by the first waggon. The order was not to fire before the open space of the road in front of us was filled. At last came word, and a

score of sharp cracks leapt in deafening echoes from crag to crag, and a
score of mules, with their riders, went down, creating the most dire confusion. Then came a stampede as was never before seen. The teams in
front endeavoured to gallop on, but were prevented by one or more
mules hanging dead in the traces; others behind made an effort to turn,
but got blocked by those in the rear. Crack! crack! still went the rifles,
until the road was choked with dead and dying men and mules, and over-
turned waggons. The escort, after firing a few shots in return, fled panic-
stricken, followed by the exultant shouts of the Confederate riflemen.[22]

One further bit of information about Goree's activities during this period
comes from the east Tennessee campaign. While Longstreet's corps was quartered near Greeneville, a group of stragglers found their way into the home
of Vice President Andrew Johnson. Johnson's personal property, including his
Masonic paraphernalia, was still in the house, and, according to Moxley Sorrel,
"our fellows thought they had made a find of value and were about starting off
with it." Goree, however, halted them and "had everything carefully repacked
and put in a safe place for the rightful owner."[23]

Goree also served as Longstreet's courier to Robert E. Lee while the I Corps
served in Tennessee, and after Longstreet was severely wounded at the battle
of the Wilderness, Goree was often with him during his recovery at Campbell
Courthouse, Virginia. Edwin King Goree was also gravely wounded at the Wilderness, however, and for two months after Longstreet was removed to Georgia for convalescence, Goree remained with his brother at the hospital at
Lynchburg until his wound was safely healing. In mid-October 1864 Longstreet,
though "crippled," returned to the Army of Northern Virginia, and Goree rejoined his staff.[24]

Not only did Goree's superiors use him as an aide, a courier, gunner, and
sometime troop commander, but Longstreet appreciated his advice as a strategist as well. From his camp near Richmond on 4 October 1864, for example,
Longstreet wrote to General Lee that "in discussing the movements of the enemy, according to newspaper reports, Captain Goree suggested that Sheridan
would probably send his infantry to the relief of Sherman." Longstreet agreed
with his aide that "it is not unlikely that Grant will be obliged to relieve Sherman with some of his troops" and forwarded to Lee Goree's suggestion so "that
you may advise General Early that he may look for it."[25]

After General Lee's surrender Goree accompanied Longstreet to Lynchburg,
Virginia, and from there, in June 1865, the two traveled together to Greensboro,
Alabama, where they parted, Longstreet going to Mississippi and Goree to
Texas. "Finding that there was very little money to be made at my profession,"
Goree returned to Raven Hill, the Walker County plantation that his mother
had purchased from Sam Houston in 1858. There he farmed for two years but,

as he wrote to Col. Edward Dromgoole Nolley of Durant, Mississippi, on 14 November 1867, "on account of excessive rains & worms, have not met with success. I shall attempt planting again next year but necessarily on a reduced scale." Nevertheless, at age thirty-two, Goree was writing to Nolley "upon a very interesting and delicate subject," requesting the hand of his daughter, Eliza Thomas Nolley, in marriage. "I am poor," he confessed to Nolley, "and have very little to offer your daughter but an honest, loving heart, and a willing hand." As personal references Goree offered, in addition to General Longstreet, his partner, Leonard Anderson Abercrombie; Peter W. Gray, a former Confederate congressman from Houston and later a justice of the Texas Supreme Court; and Andrew Barry Moore, former governor of Alabama.

Thomas J. Goree and Eliza T. Nolley were married on 25 June 1868 at the Methodist church at Huntsville.[26] Soon thereafter, after selling Raven Hill in January 1869, the couple moved to the nearby hamlet of Midway where he became a merchant and she opened a small school. In the fall of 1873 they returned to Huntsville where Goree resumed the practice of law in partnership with Leonard Abercrombie, former lieutenant colonel of the Fifth Texas Infantry.[27] That same year Governor Richard Coke appointed Goree to the board of directors of the Texas State Penitentiary at Huntsville, and on 2 April 1877 Governor Richard B. Hubbard appointed him superintendent of the state penitentiary.

In 1881, when Governor Oran M. Roberts consolidated the management of all the state penal institutions, he appointed Goree superintendent of prisons, a title changed to superintendent of penitentiaries in 1883. During the Roberts administration the legislature investigated the conduct of the penitentiary at Huntsville. According to W. L. Hill, a Houston attorney and early historian of the Texas prison system, Roberts told the legislature that it could "pass all the laws you want to, but leave me Goree."[28] Goree served until 1891 under the administrations of Roberts, John Ireland, and Lawrence Sullivan Ross. During his tenure as superintendent, he lived in Huntsville in the Steamboat House, once the home of Sam Houston.

According to Donald R. Walker, the most recent historian of the Texas penal system, "Goree displayed a commitment to his tasks and a sensitivity to the purposes and objectives of confinement unparalleled in any of his associates and contemporaries." He is credited with establishing contact with the National Prison Association and seeking to incorporate into the Texas system such progressive theories of prison management as the indeterminate sentence, abolition of the convict lease system, and a separate institution for juvenile offenders.[29]

In May 1891 newly elected governor James Stephen Hogg chose not to reappoint Goree, however, probably because Goree's nephew Norman Goree Kittrell, a prominent Houston attorney, had failed to support Hogg during the

early months of his campaign. The Austin *Statesman* observed that "the con-
templated change is the topic of general conversation, and is a surprise to a
large number of members of both houses" and a matter of regret to many in
the government. Frederick H. Wines, executive secretary of the National
Prison Association, protested to Hogg that his membership would regard Goree's removal "as a misfortune to the cause of prison reform in the United
States" against which they would protest "if they had the opportunity to do so
and were sure that their protest would be received in the spirit in which it is
offered." Goree, however, seemed little concerned, stating that if he were to be
removed "it was a gratification to him to know, that his administration was
warmly endorsed by both the outgoing and incoming administrations." The
Statesman concluded that the new governor, who had expended so much political capital to have Goree replaced, "will be disappointed in his successor."[30]

After he left the prison system, Goree was appointed general agent for the
New Birmingham Iron and Improvement Company of New Birmingham,
Texas. This community, founded in 1888 in an iron ore–rich area of Cherokee
County, promised a great industrial future and by 1891 boasted two railroads,
a hotel, two blast furnaces, a brick plant, a newspaper, and a population of
3,000. Governor Hogg's Alien Land Law of 1891 dried up much foreign capital,
however, and the burning of one of the two blast furnaces, linked with the
general financial panic of 1893, led to the collapse of the New Birmingham en-
terprise.[31]

In 1892 Goree made a bid for the Democratic nomination for lieutenant
governor on the ticket of former Texas attorney general George Clark but was
defeated by the incumbent Hogg and his running mate, Martin McNulty
Crane. In January 1893, in the wake of the New Birmingham disaster, Goree
became assistant general manager of the Texas Land and Loan Company of
Galveston, which he served until 1900. Thereafter he practiced law, dabbled in
the real estate business, and, according to Moxley Sorrel, enjoyed "good health
and good Confederate memories." Former governor Oran Roberts spoke of
Goree as "well known throughout the state as a public official and an enterprising business man and . . . popular with his comrades of the Confederacy."[32]

For years Goree had urged Longstreet to visit him in Texas, but each time
the old general planned a trip, something forestalled it. Finally, however, in
January 1891 Longstreet arrived in San Antonio where Goree visited him. "The
old comrades in arms had not met for years and the re-union yesterday was
quite affecting." In 1895 Goree invited Longstreet to attend the annual convention of the United Confederate Veterans at Houston, but "as he received no
official invitation, he did not go."[33] Nevertheless, the two old soldiers maintained a fond and frequent correspondence until shortly before Longstreet's
death on 2 January 1904.

Fourteen months later, on Sunday, 4 March 1905, Thomas J. Goree died of pneumonia at his Galveston home. He was buried near his old friend Sam Houston in Huntsville's Oakwood Cemetery. He was survived by his wife, two children, seven grandchildren, three of his brothers, Robert Daniel Goree, Edwin King Goree, and Pleasant Kittrell Goree, and their sister Sudy, then Mrs. Hugh T. Hayes, and their half sister, "Sis Frank," Mrs. Pleasant Williams Kittrell. The three oldest of Goree's five children died in infancy or early childhood. The two survivors were Sue Hayes Goree, who married Dr. John W. Thomason and became the mother of Goree's seven grandchildren including the famed Marine Corps officer, author, and illustrator John W. Thomason, Jr., and Robert Edwin Goree, a Texas attorney and Mississippi planter.[34]

On 7 March 1905 the Texas House of Representatives passed a resolution honoring Goree, and the Texas Senate passed a similar resolution on 10 March and adjourned early in his memory. No testimonial to his character was more affecting, however, than the letter that James Longstreet's widow wrote to the widow of Thomas J. Goree. "I am grieved beyond all words to know of your great loss," wrote Helen D. Longstreet. "Your husband was so dear to General Longstreet that he became dear to me, though I had never looked upon his face. I had hoped to meet him before our journeyings in this world should be over. There is comfort in the thought that he has clasped hands again with his old Commander. I mourn with you, and send you across the miles all my heart's tenderest, most loving sympathy. And I mourn doubly, because I was denied the privilege of knowing personally one who was as great a soldier and citizen, and one whom General Longstreet loved so deeply to the last."[35]

The Goree letters and travel diary, which survived the great Galveston hurricane of 1900, are now located in the John W. Thomason Rare Books and Special Collections Room of the Newton Gresham Library at Sam Houston State University in Huntsville, Texas. They were donated by Thomas J. Goree's granddaughters, Sue Goree Thomason Noordberg of Huntsville and Emily Thomason Peterson of Houston. Goree's letters written during the Second Manassas, Sharpsburg, Fredericksburg, Suffolk, Gettysburg, Chickamauga, and Knoxville campaigns are now missing.

In 1981 the Family Heritage Foundation of Bryan, Texas, issued an edition of the Goree letters—limited to 200 copies, 100 of which were reserved for members and friends of the Goree family—edited by Langston James Goree V, a collateral descendant. That edition, like this one, was largely based on a transcription by Charles Dwyer, former director of the Thomason Room.[36]

The unavailability of decent paper and writing instruments, the difficult circumstances under which Goree wrote some of his letters—"I write on my saddlebags, my seat on the ground," he informed one correspondent—and the inevitable ravages of time have made transcription, in some cases, somewhat problematic, but Goree, who was both highly literate and favored with fine penmanship, made the task of transcription relatively easy. In general Goree's spelling was remarkably good and his punctuation regular; only occasionally does he lapse into such usages as "staid" for "stayed" and "brot" for "brought." Because his letters, more often than not, consist of a single lengthy paragraph, and many of his upper- and lowercase letters seem identical, I have indented paragraphs to indicate a logical transition in thought and capitalized words according to modern usage when Goree's intention was not clear. Proper names are rendered as Goree wrote them, and misspellings—including his use of "Sumpter" for Sumter and "Drainsville" for Dranesville—rare though they are, are pointed out and corrected in notes. I have inserted emendations in square brackets where damage to the original letter has destroyed or rendered illegible the original text. Marginal notes, headnotes, and notations written on envelopes have been treated as postscripts. Ampersands and &c. have been retained, but superscripts have been brought down to the line. Goree only sometimes punctuated his abbreviations of titles, military ranks, and unit designations; I have followed the author, neither adding nor deleting periods to make them standard. All of Thomas Jewett Goree's known Civil War correspondence is included in this edition, and no part of any of his letters has been excised. In short, these letters have required very little editing and are, with few exceptions, exactly as Goree wrote them.

Goree mentioned scores of individuals in his letters, some of whom are well known to Civil War historians and others of whom have been obscured or even obliterated to memory by the passage of time. I have provided biographical information on every individual that I could identify on the first occasion that Goree mentioned him or her. I have cited in the notes the principal sources of this information except for such standard reference volumes as the *Dictionary of American Biography,* Mark M. Boatner's *Dictionary of the Civil War,* Richard N. Current's *Encyclopedia of the Confederacy,* Patricia L. Faust's *Historical Times Illustrated Encyclopedia of the Civil War,* Francis Bernard Heitman's *Historical Register and Dictionary of the United States Army,* Robert K. Krick's *Lee's Colonels: A Biographical Register of the Field Officers of the Army of Northern Virginia,* E. B. Long's *The Civil War Day by Day: An Almanac, 1861–1865,* Jon. L. Wakelyn's *Biographical Dictionary of the Confederacy,* Ezra J. Warner's *Generals in Gray* and *Generals in Blue,* and Ezra J. Warner and W. Buck Yearns's *Biographical Register of the Confederate Congress.*

1861

"I HAVE MADE UP MY MIND TO DO MY DUTY"

TO PLEASANT WILLIAMS KITTRELL

Dear Uncle Pleas:[1]   Houston, April 7th, 1861

Knowing that you feel a very great anxiety in the troubled condition of the country, I have concluded to write you today some of the latest news—which is very exciting.

Yesterday's steamer brought the intelligence that on the 3rd instant an attempt was made, as was supposed, to reinforce Fort Sumpter.[2] A schooner, heavily laden, attempted to pass the outermost battery at Morris Island. A shot was fired across her bows when she ran up the U. S. flag—two other shots were then fired across her bows—but she kept on her way—a shot was then fired amidships, on which she stood out to sea.

Major Anderson[3] sent a messenger to the city, declaring that if the shots were fired with a hostile intention, he should be compelled to open fire on the state batteries. Genl Beauregard[4] was busy giving orders and making preparations for the anticipated fight.

Dispatches from Washington April 3d say that great activity was then prevailing in both the army and navy departments—all the available vessels in port are ordered to prepare for sea. Four or five vessels under command of Com. Stringham[5] are ordered to the mouth of the Mississippi River. The U. S. Govt. is preparing for war—Fort Pickens[6] is to be reinforced—U. S. troops are concentrating on Long Island—it is also said that a protest has been sent to the European govts. against the Confederate States.

Many here yesterday were disposed to doubt the truth of the above—but the steamer this morning (Sunday), two days later, brings news, as I understand, not only confirming the above, but saying that Fort Sumpter was by order of Pres. Davis declared in a state of siege. All communication whatever is forbidden.

I will try and send you a paper, if any comes up this evening. I suppose that now there is no doubt but that the war has commenced—well! be it so. I for one have calculated on nothing else. I advocated Secession, believing that we would have to fight to sustain it. I am ready to do it, and more than willing.

It may be best for us to have war—'Twill unite us at home and force the border states to come with us—I fear nothing else will.

There is but little news of interest besides this—cotton is still advancing—I have not time at present to write more. Give my best love to all.

Your Nephew Aff'ly.,
Thos. J. Goree.

P. S. Reported at Washington that the new Republican mail agent for Virginia has been tarred and feathered.

TO SARAH WILLIAMS KITTRELL GOREE

My Dear Mother:[8]   Brashear City,[7] Berwick Bay, La., June 15th, 1861

I promised when I left to write to you from New Orleans, but have concluded to do so from here, as I may not have time enough when I get there.

We left Houston on Monday evening last, and reached Galveston the next morning. Started at 2 o'clock P.M. on Tuesday in a little schooner (15 by 40 feet) for this place, which we reached just at dark last night.[9]

They promised to make the trip in 30 hours, but we were on the Gulf just 102 hours. We had to stay out on deck all the time, nothing to protect us from the sun or rain.

We were in 3 squalls on the trip, when very often the water would run all over the deck. Though, notwithstanding all this, I enjoyed the trip very much. Was only sick a little the first evening after leaving Galveston. Dr. Woodson[10] was sick all the time. So were several others.

There are now about 20 of us here, bound for Virginia. How we will dispose of ourselves when we get there is as yet uncertain. I think Capt. Lubbock[11] and Col. Terry[12] will be very apt to succeed in getting the authority to raise a company or battalion of guerillas.

We start for New Orleans after dinner today, and will leave there in the morning for Richmond, which place we expect to reach on Thursday next (the 20th).

There has been no fighting of much importance as yet. Several little skirmishes in which the Confederate forces have always been successful. I think that we will get there in time to have a hand in the pie—at least I hope so.

There is no news of importance. I shall write to you again from Richmond, and as often afterwards as I have opportunity. I shall be very anxious to hear from you before I can tell you where to write. When you know where to direct your letters, you must all write very often.

Give my love to all, and kiss the children for me.

Please excuse this short, uninteresting letter, as I have to write it under difficulties—poor pen—ink, and a poor place to write on.

Your aff. son,
Thos. J. Goree

TO SARAH WILLIAMS KITTRELL GOREE

My Dear Mother,   Richmond, Virginia, June 23, 1861

One week ago to day, I wrote you a short letter from Brashear City, La. Today I write you from Richmond. We reached N. Orleans from Brashear on last Sunday evening, and staid there until the next evening when we started for this place which we reached on Friday, the 21st. inst.

The Goree family. *From left to right, seated:* Susan Margaret Goree, Edwin King Goree, portrait of Sarah Williams Kittrell Goree, Langston James Goree, Jr., Thomas Jewett Goree; *standing:* Pleasant Kittrell Goree, portrait of Langston James Goree, Robert Daniel Goree. (John W. Thomason Rare Books and Special Collections Room, Newton Gresham Library, Sam Houston State University)

Our route was through Mississippi, up to Grand Junction in the northern part of the State. From thence through Decatur & Huntsville, in North Alabama, to Chattanooga, then through East Tennessee, & West Virginia to Richmond.

On the route I saw some very pretty country, and a great deal of very poor country. The land on the road through Mississippi did seem particularly poor. North Alabama is a very pretty picturesque country, also the eastern part of Tennessee & West Virginia.

In Louisiana, Mississippi, & Alabama we found a fine state of feeling among the people. Every man, woman & child seemed to be enthusiastic about the war. They seemed to have their whole soul enlisted in the Cause. No state has done more than Mississippi for the Cause, and she is willing to do still more. So is Alabama.

But not so in East Tennessee. There they are yet strong for the Union, a large majority of them. Whenever there was a good seccessionist, you could see a secession flag waving over his house, but as a general thing the men looked sour, mean and grum. But, judging from appearances, I would say that the ladies were almost unanimous for secession & the war. As the cars (which were well filled with soldiers) would pass, they would run to the doors & wave their little secession flags or their handkerchiefs. Not so with the men.

When we passed through Greeneville (the place Cousin Robert Pulliam used to live), the Union men were holding a convention. The cars usually stop in Greeneville 30 minutes for dinner, but the troops and others on board having heard that resolutions were offered in the convention in favor of separation of East Tennessee from the other portion of the State, and also that Maynard, one of the leaders, had advocated open rebellion, they determined, when they stopped, to disperse the convention.

The conductor, finding this out, would make no stop for dinner, but throwed out the mail and passed through, much to the chagrin of most on board. Andy Johnson was not there, but had left a few days before as soon as he found that the letter enclosing a draft from Boston for his services had been intercepted. He left in a close carriage with a guard around him, and swearing that he would return at the head of 20,000 men from the North to resist the secession of Tennessee.

As soon as we crossed the Tennessee & Virginia line, what a change!! At every depot the platform was crowded with men, women & children & negroes to welcome the troops. Every lady, almost, had a bouquet for a soldier. I received several.

In the country as we passed houses, the men would hurrah, and wave their hats, the ladies their handkerchiefs, and the children their flags. The negroes in the field would stop and wave something at us, and were equally as enthusiastic as the whites. Texas is a long way behind the times. You never saw such excitement & enthusiasm in your life as there is here.

Here, nine out of every ten men you see is dressed in a military suit. This is a perfect military camp. Thousands of troops are encamped here. Many are quartered in the different churches, and there are from 2 to 500 arriving daily.

We passed several hundred on the road (among them 2 companies from Eastern Texas) which have not yet reached here. While there are so many coming in, they send others out to the Seat of War. Most of the troops are now being sent to Manassas Gap, some to Yorktown, and some to Harpers Ferry. All seem to be anxious to go where seems the best prospect for a fight.

One cannot hear much more news here than in Texas. Our plans are all kept very secret, and it is impossible to tell what the movements are to be until they are about to be executed. At this time, everything seems to be in "status quo." Each party is awaiting for the other to make the attack.

The Yankees, after their little experience at Bethel, Phillippi & Vienna[13] are not so keen to fight. In every fight and skirmish that has taken place they have ingloriously fled. I have seen men who were in the fight at Bethel, and from what they say the Yankees must have had 500 killed and wounded. At Vienna they had about 20 killed.

At the hotel I am now at, there are two Federal officers who were captured by our men last Wednesday or Thursday. One of them is a Lieut. Col. in a Pennsylvania Regiment. He says that he has seen enough, and will never take up arms against the South again. The other one does not talk so. He says, their cause is just and he intends to fight it out.

I have nearly finished this sheet, and have told you nothing of my future movements. Nor do I know I am yet prepared to give you much information on the point.

Before leaving Texas we had the promise of men enough to come with us for a large company, but when the time came but few of them could raise the money to come on. We then concluded (those who could) to come on, and do all we could to get such a company received, and if successful, to send back for picked men.

Messrs. Lubbock, Terry, & Wharton,[14] together with Messrs. Wigfall[15] & Waul,[16] & Major (now General Longstreet) have called upon Mr. Davis and asked that he receive and mount such a company as we want. They seemed to think that he will do so. He favors the movement and would readily receive them, but he says that he does not know that he has the authority to mount them. That is the only difficulty. He will take time to consider of it, and will give us an answer in a few days. At the last interview he said to Capt. Lubbock, "I must have your men." Messrs. Wigfall and Waul will in the meantime urge the matter upon him.

Major Longstreet, who came on from Galveston with us and who resigned his position in the U. S. Army, has promised us all his influence. He says that he has been in the service 20 years and knows the value of such men. He will have influence, for I have heard today that he has been promoted to the position of Brigadier General in the C. S. Army.

The few of us that have come on have determined for the present to establish a Texas Camp here and remain in it until the President decides. And if he agrees to receive us, then until we send back after more men.

Major Longstreet told me yesterday that if he received the appointment of Brig. Genl., he would establish a camp here, and would give us a tent, and let us place by the side of his. He does this because he wished to organize a command, and have it composed of Texians. Mr. Davis has agreed to receive 20 companies from Texas for the war. They ought to be here in a few weeks. In a day or two there will be 4 or 5 Texas Companies here, one from Polk, one from Tyler Co., one from Harrison, and one from Cass.

Besides these, there are a great many Texans scattered about, who we hope to collect together by establishing the Texas Camp I spoke of. The first man I met after my arrival here was Billy Denson.[17] It was quite an agreeable surprise. He is looking better than I ever saw him. I have been with [him] ever since my arrival until today when he left for Yorktown, the place where his company is established.

William Hume of Huntsville is also here. He belongs to a Mississippi Company. John White of Huntsville is here with an Alabama Company.[18] It is such a long way from Texas here that it is truly gratifying to meet up with anyone from Texas, whether you ever knew them before or not.

Dr. Woodson has not yet reached here. Just before crossing over into Va. he was standing on the platform of the cars taking his watch out to see the time; he dropped it off. The cars stopped for him to get off after it, but would not wait until he got it. He had been off 2 hours before I knew of it. I suppose he will be here tomorrow. The Dr. lost his hat on the Gulf, and his watch off the cars. Ill luck, I believe, attends him.

I will write to you again in a few days. Direct your letters to me at Richmond, Va., and write soon, for I am very anxious to hear from you all. I could write much more but have not time, as I want to send this by a gentleman who starts to Texas very soon.

Give my love to all.

Your aff. Son,
Thos. J. Goree

TO SARAH WILLIAMS KITTRELL GOREE

My Dear Mother,   Fairfax Court House, July 6th, 1861

When I last wrote you from Richmond, I expected to write again in a very few days. And in fact I did write soon after my arrival here, but actually I was not able until yesterday to get 10 cents in silver to mail my letter. So I concluded to write today, and not send the other letter.

Anything in the shape of gold & silver is very scarce here. Paper currency is altogether used. And postage is required to be paid in hard money.

Well! our little Texas Squad has been received as independent Texas Rangers. We are furnished with rations and forage whilst in service and are allowed to quit whenever we feel so disposed. I prefer this, as I do not care to be bound down for the war, although I expect to serve my country as long as the war lasts. But I want to be at liberty to go home when I desire so to do. We had at Richmond about 15 Texans, but only about 5 of that number have yet reached this place. I cannot imagine what detains the others. We need them very much.

I have a very good horse, and have been in active service for 5 or 6 days. We are acting as Rangers or as scouts for this division of the army, and we flatter ourselves that we will render very efficient service to the cause in that way. From what I have seen and know, Texas could render as much, or more, service for the cause in Virginia, by arming and equipping 100 picked, mounted men for each division of the Army than if she were to send one regiment of infantry for each division. These 100 men would not be wanted particularly to act as cavalry (for this country is not very well suited for cavalry to operate in) but they will only want horses to ride into the neighborhood of the enemy and then dismount and bushwhack it. 100 Texans would get up a little fight every day; as it is now, it is very seldom and then accidental that the scouting parties of the two forces meet.

Our scouts consist principally of the Virginia Cavalry, and if you were to think a week you could hardly imagine anything more harmless and inefficient than a company of Virginia Cavalry acting as scouts. A little squadron of 20 went out last Sunday, and they suffered 2 of their men and 4 horses to be taken by the enemy without even firing a shot. Those who were not taken turned and fled, nor did they stop until they reached this place, 5 miles distant. The first evening after we reached here, Messrs. Terry & Lubbock, of our squad, went out with some of the cavalry. When they came in sight of some of the enemy, they made a charge, thinking that they would be followed up by the cavalry—but no, the Virginians stopped and formed as if to receive the attack from the enemy, instead of charging, too. So that Terry and Lubbock made the charge by themselves, running into their picket camp where they had 6 men, 2 of which they captured, together with a horse and Sharpes rifle. They shot twice at another man, and no doubt severely wounded him. They had run within 300 yards of the main camp of the enemy, when they turned, and went back to the Va. cavalry.

I have several times been out scouting, but have never happened to meet any of the enemy. Yesterday we were sent out by Genl Bonham[19] near Fall's Church (where they have 10,000 men) to see if they had made any advance this way. We were inside of their pickets and but a little more than a mile from their camp. We satisfied ourselves that they had made no advance.

Every day nearly, we are within a mile or two of their camp and travel over the same country that their scouts do. And whenever we do meet up with them, they will not have Va. Cavalry to deal with. Our leader (Col. Terry) is a very bold, fearless man, in whose discretion & valor we have the greatest confidence.

We went out on the 4th near Fall's Church with about 600 men under Col. Kershaw[20] of the 2nd S. C. Regiment, with 6 companies of infantry, 2 of cavalry, and one of artillery, with the expectation of drawing the enemy into a fight. We started about midnight and were just getting into position about daylight [with] every thing working admirably, when the Col. of Cavalry started 2 of his men forward to where we were with 2 companies of infantry (about 2 miles in advance) to convey some information. When they got opposite to where the 4 reserve companies of S. C. infantry were stationed, they were going very fast, with pistols drawn. When the South Carolinians mistaking them for the enemy fired upon them, killing 1 of them, both of their horses, wounding one, and killing another man & wounding 3 horses in another part of the field. This broke up the expedition. Genl Bonham, upon hearing of it, ordered us back. If he had permitted us to proceed, we would have had a very pretty fight and would no doubt have taken several prisoners.

I have no idea when a general fight will take place here. You need not be surprised to hear of one at any time. We have in this division of the army about 25,000 men, the larger proportion of them South Carolinians. Genl Beauregard has Manassas very strongly fortified, and new fortifications are being made here every day. I think that the enemy are advancing by degrees upon this place. Falls Church, where they have so many men, is only seven miles from here. Our men are very impatient and anxious for a fight. They don't think of a defeat. In Genl Beauregard they have the greatest confidence, and they believe him invincible. Fairfax Court House is just 12 miles from Alexandria. The Federalists must have about 30,000 men about and on this side of Alexandria. As a general thing, the people here seem very indifferent about the war. There are some few who render every assistance they can, but not one in ten. There are hundreds of tories who we dread much more than the Yankees. The traitors are not native Virginians but Yankees who have settled in here. And they are not a few.

Mother, I have written this scattering letter after having been walking and riding for 2 days and nights. I hardly know what I have written. Hereafter, I will try and write at least once a week. I am very anxious to hear from you all. Write to me here, and direct your letter to the care of Col. B. F. Terry, Fairfax Court House. My health is excellent.

Give my best love to all & write soon.

Your Son Affly.
Thos. J. Goree

TO SARAH WILLIAMS KITTRELL GOREE

My Dear Mother,   Bull Run—Near Manassas, July 20th 1861

When I last wrote you it was from Fairfax C. H. I then intended to have written you again before this, but have not had the opportunity to do so, as I have been in very active service since that time—Have been in one skirmish and one battle. On the morning of the 17th inst. the enemy appeared in great force at Fairfax. The[y] probably numbered over 40,000. We only had 6 or 7000 there, and we thought that discretion was the better part of valor. So we retreated in rather hot haste to a stronger position. We left without firing a gun except 2 that a gentleman and myself who brought up the rear fired at a distance, with what effect I do not know. We placed ourselves in very strong position on a large creek called Bull Run, and will have today about 35 or 40,000 men ready for the fray. We got our positions here on the night of the 17th. Our lines and fortifications extend 5 or 6 miles up and down the river [with] different Genl 's in command at different points: Genl Beauregard in general command until Genl Joe Johnston[21] reaches here, which he probably did last night. The Brig. Genls. are Cocke,[22] Bonham, Longstreet, Jones,[23] Jackson,[24] Ewell.[25]

On the 18th a large body of the enemy made an attack, principally against Genl Longstreet's Command.[26] And he repulsed them most gloriously. We had about 15 men killed and 50 or 60 wounded. The loss of the enemy from all accounts was very large. They have removed many of their dead. I was sent out yesterday by Genl Longstreet with a Company of Cavalry to make a reconnaissance, and found on the battlefield 12 of the enemy's dead, and the whole country for some distance was covered with canteens, blankets and haversacks. I forgot first to say that Genl Longstreet has appointed me one of his aides and that I now rank as *Captain*.[27]

Yesterday the enemy made some demonstrations, but no attack. We are expecting a big battle today, probably 35 or 40,000 men on each side. If we repulse them we will follow them, and try at once to take Washington City. If we do fight today, it will be one of the greatest battles on record. In the fight day before yesterday I was acting on Genl Bonham's Staff. We had several rifle cannon balls to fall in a few yards of us. Times felt quite squally for a while. Cols. Terry & Lubbock have gone back. [28] [*One line illegible.*]

Dr. Woodson has been very sick and has gone to his uncle's beyond Richmond. I am about the only Texan here. I have an excellent position and am well pleased.

Genl Longstreet has me in his mess and is very kind. He is considered one of the best genls. in the army. I have been introduced to Genl Beauregard and most of the other genls. Beauregard is truly a great general.

I would not be surprised if David Scott is not here.[29] He belongs to Genl Johnston's division of the army, the greater part of which was expected here last night. I have met up with young Thos. Moorman[30] a grandson of Aunt Lucy Kenner. He is a *very nice* young man, about 19 or 20. I have also seen Col. Simms, who owns old Uncle Bart. He says Bart is well and on the plantation in Arkansas. I would like to write more, but cannot now. Our headquarters are in the open air in a pine thicket. I write on my saddlebags, my seat on the ground, the Genl and balance of the Staff on the ground around.

I am very tired. Have been on my horse almost all the time since the commencement of the retreat from Fairfax.

Have not had a chance to wash my face for more than three days. You will probably have heard of the big fight before this reaches you. I may not survive it, but if I am killed, it will be in a glorious cause. I hope, though that I may survive it. Almost feel confident of it.

Do not feel uneasy. I will write you again soon.

Write me and direct to Manassas Junction, "Care of Brig. Genl Longstreet, 4th Brigade." Get Uncle Pleas to direct it. I have not heard a word since I left, and you must know my anxiety to hear from you. Write often.

If the fight takes place today, we will not be in the first of it, as our brigade is held in reserve. The two armies, I think, are in about 2 miles of each other. We think the attack will probably be made against Genl Cocke, who has command at the bridge.

I must close. My very best love to all.

Your Son Aff'ly
Thos. J. Goree

P.S. During the fight a cannon ball passed through and knocked over Genl Beauregard's dinner.

TO SARAH WILLIAMS KITTRELL GOREE

My Dearest Mother,   Centreville, Va, July 23d 1861

Ere you receive this you will no doubt hear of the great battle fought and victory won by us on the 21st Inst.[31] And it will be but natural that you feel a great anxiety to know if I came safely out of it. Although a considerable portion of the time I was exposed to a very heavy fire of shell and grape, I am happy to inform you that I did not receive a scratch. But to be honest, I will say that I was pretty badly frightened. And it was time to be when you could constantly see men being killed and wounded in but a few paces of where I was. I wrote you on the 20th of the fight on Thursday, also what disposition I had made of myself. We fully expected an attack all day on Saturday, the 20th, but the day passed off without any. Early, however, on the morning of the 21st we were awakened by the rattling of the enemy artillery wagons. We saddled as soon as possible and placed our brigade in position. We had hardly done so before they commenced throwing their infernal shells at us. Everything indicated that the main attack was to be made against Genl Longstreet. And we were *fully* prepared for them; but it seems that they had seen enough of him on the 18th. We soon saw that the demonstration against us was only a feint and that the main attack would be made at some other point. And so it was. While they were using their artillery against Genl Jones, Genl Longstreet and Genl Bonham, the main body of their forces were moving against Genl Cocke 4 or 5 miles above. They wished to keep us in apprehension of an attack, so as to prevent reinforcements going above. We could hear the fight (which lasted 8 long hours) going on above and were anxious to be in it but were afraid to leave our positions. Genl Longstreet solicited and received, once, permission to advance an attack on the enemy in their rear and to take the batteries which were pouring shell and grape into us all day, but before he crossed his men, the order was countermanded. If this had been done

[*The remainder of this letter is missing.*]

TO PLEASANT WILLIAMS KITTRELL

Headquarters 4th Brigade, Centreville

Dear Uncle Pleas,   August 2nd 1861

I wrote hurriedly to Mother soon after the battle, knowing that she would be very solicitous and anxious to hear of my safety.

Having intended for some time to write to you, I take this opportunity to do so. You all at home no doubt think that I do not write often enough and I confess that I do not; but if you only knew how very difficult it *has* been here to procure writing material, you would very readily excuse me. Since, however, I have become a member of Genl Longstreet's Staff I can no longer have such an excuse, and will consequently try and do better in the future. You can have no idea how very anxious I am to hear from home, never having received one line from any of you since I have been here. I console myself, however, with the thought that you have written but the letters have miscarried.

You have long since heard of the great "Battle of Manassas," and the great victory achieved by our brave soldiers. To you at a distance who do not know the full particulars, it does seem like a great victory, and so it was. But to others (and myself among the rest) it really does not seem so—we cannot enjoy it so much for the simple reason that we *know* it was not complete. There is no good reason why our army should not now be encamped on Arlington Heights or in Washington City as here around the battleground. My descriptive powers are not very good, but still

I will try and give you an account of the occurrences from the time we evacuated Fairfax Court House until the rout of the enemy.

Genl Bonham of S. C.—(a man whom I think is *totally* unfit for a military leader) had command at Fairfax Court House. It had always been the intention of Genl Beauregard to evacuate Fairfax on the approach of the enemy. Early on the morning of the 17th ult. we heard the firing of our pickets, and very soon afterwards they came in. Soon the enemy came in sight about 2 miles distant. Their approach was from two sides, and when I saw them it almost seemed as if there were 500,000 of them. It was then we commenced striking our tents and loading our wagons, which ought to have been done long before, as it was well known on the 16th that they had commenced their forward movement. The consequence was that everything was done very hurriedly, and a considerable amount of property was left behind—consisting of provisions, forage, tents, some guns and ammunition. By the time our wagons had left, the enemy was in about a mile of the town, moving down on it very slowly. Gen. Bonham all the time appeared very much flurried. After moving his troops around and making some demonstrations as if for a fight, he ordered a retreat, which ought to have been done before the enemy was so close. From the number of canteens, knapsacks, blankets, &c. which our men threw away on the road, our retreat no doubt appeared more like a rout than a retreat in good order. By the time we had reached this place, a distance of eight miles, our men were almost broken down. After resting here a few hours, the most of our troops were sent on back across Bull Run, Genl Bonham remaining with one regiment to make a demonstration here. He did not do so, however, for about midnight on the 17th we again commenced our retreat and took position on the other side of the Run.

The enemy came in early next morning and occupied this place. By this time they were in fine spirits: they had come to the conclusion that they would have no fighting to do, and would march direct to Richmond. They did not tarry long here, but Gen. Tyler[32] with his division of 15,000 moved direct on towards Manassas, or rather Blackburn's and Mitchell's Ford on Bull Run. Gen. Longstreet guarding the former and Bonham the latter. Capt. Kemper[33] with his battery had been sent in advance of our forces, and when the enemy made his appearance, the Captain turned loose his guns upon them with considerable effect. After firing several times, he withdrew to his position across the Run.

In the meantime the enemy had opened his batteries upon Capt Kemper and Genl Bonham, and everything seemed to indicate that he would attempt a crossing at Mitchells Ford on the direct road to Manassas. But whilst his batteries were playing upon Bonham, Tyler moved seven regiments of infantry down against Longstreet at Blackburn's Ford. Genl Longstreet had in his brigade which extended up and down the river, the 1st, 11th, and 17th Va. Regiments. The 7th Va. was held in reserve.[34] The attack was made against the points where the 17th was stationed, and 2 companies of the 1st—the whole not amounting to more than 1200 men. While that of the enemy to at least 6000. Our troops had no embankments to fight behind, as has been represented, but fought from the bank of the creek or run. The enemy were just above on a high bluff on the other side of the run. Until it was

Thomas J. Goree led this group of sharpshooters in an attack on the Federal supply route into the besieged city of Chattanooga in December 1863. The scene was described and the sketch drawn by *Illustrated London News* correspondent Frank Vizetelly.

necessary to use the bayonet, the enemy had by far the advantage in position. They made the attack with great vigor and confidence, and it was with great difficulty that our men were persuaded to stand. Some of them started to fall back two or three times, but Genl Longstreet, amid a perfect shower of balls, rode amongst them, with his cigar in his mouth, rallying them, encouraging, and inspiring confidence among them. For several minutes there was one continuous roar of musketry. Three times were the enemy repulsed, and three times did they come back to the attack; finally, Genl Longstreet gave the order for our boys to charge. Only two companies, however, succeeded in crossing the run but these were sufficient to cause the Hessians to flee precipitately. These two companies with their bayonets ran them out of the woods they were in, and made them go in every direction. Then it was that the 7 pieces of our artillery in our rear opened upon them and did terrible execution. Prisoners taken say that our artillery swept their ranks from one end to the other, besides disabling some pieces of their artillery. It was about 2 o'clock when our artillery opened upon their retreating forces. Theirs at the same time opened upon us, and there was a constant fire from both sides until 4 P.M. when the enemy retreated to Centreville—3 miles. Our battery threw amongst them more than 300 shot and shell. Our loss was 15 killed and about 50 wounded. Theirs is estimated at from 500 to 2000 killed and wounded. Some of the prisoners have told me that it *was* about 2000. I know that they left many of their dead on the field, although they had 2 hours under cover of their guns to carry off the dead and wounded.

This fight of the 18th went a great way towards winning the victory of the 21st. For it gave our troops confidence in themselves, and convinced the enemy that we would fight. The disparity in numbers on the 18th was greater than on the 21st. I have given a fuller account of this fight than I would otherwise have done, had I not seen in the papers the credit for it given to Genl Bonham, when his command did not fire a gun. Genl Longstreet alone deserves all the credit. Had he not rode amongst his troops and himself rallied them when they started to fall back, had he not exhibited the coolness and courage that he did, the result of the whole affair might have been very different.

At one time Genl L. was himself exposed to fire from both the enemy and our own troops. He had ordered up his reserve, the 7th Va. Regt. (and fearing that they in their excitement might fire before he was ready for them) he placed himself immediately in front of them. No sooner than they were in position and while the Genl was before them, they commenced firing and the Genl only saved himself by throwing himself off his horse and lying flat on the ground.

The battle of the 21st I cannot describe so particularly as I was farther from it. Before day on Sunday morning we were aroused by the rattling of the enemy's artillery wagons. By sunup they had placed three batteries in about 1 mile of Blackburn's Ford—so as to play on that point—on Genl. Bonham who was just above at Mitchell's Ford—and Genl Jones just below at McLane's Ford.

Genls. Beauregard & Johnston were so certain from all the indications that the attack would again be made at Blackburn's Ford (it also being the weakest point) that they had stationed nearly all the reserve force near that point. The enemy opened their three batteries upon Genls. Bonham, Longstreet and Jones about sunrise and from that time until 4 o'clock they poured the shell and grape in upon us.

This demonstration against us turned out to be only a feint [*two words illegible*] real point of attack was to be made at another point. About 6 O'clock A.M., Col. Frank Terry, who was also acting as Aide to Genl Longstreet, solicited and obtained permission from him to make a reconnaissance. Crossing the run, he ascended a high hill and climbing a tree had a full view. He was the first to discover and gave the information that the enemy was making the attempt to turn our left flank.

When he made his report, Genl Beauregard immediately ordered the reserve up near the Stone Bridge across Bull Run, a distance of 4 or 5 miles. It was never suspected that the enemy would cross the rear above Stone Bridge, and we were not prepared for it. They, however, crossed more than a mile above without being seen, and attacked our left flank.

Then the battle commenced in earnest, from 9 o'clock A.M. until about 4 P.M. it continued. The roar of the artillery for a few moments would be terrific—then it would be hushed and for several minutes we could hear one continuous volley of musketry. During all of that time we below were in an agony of suspense. But whilst all this was going on, and early in the day, Genl Longstreet solicited and obtained orders from Genl Beauregard to assume the offensive against the force which was keeping us in check.

The plan was, and the orders were, for Genl Ewell, who occupied the extreme right, to move forward to Centreville and attack their rear. Genl Jones at the same time was to commence an attack on their right flank. And when they opened the fight Genl Longstreet was to come forward and attack them in front.

In compliance with these orders, Genl Longstreet's Brigade was moved across the run, placed in position and awaited for 2 hours for Genl Ewell to commence the attack. All the time we were exposed to a heavy firing from the batteries on the hill (and I am sorry to say that a portion of the 5th North Carolina Regiment in our Brigade made a pretty fast retrograde movement, but the most of them soon rallied and returned. 2 captains, however, declared that they couldn't stand it and left the field.)

The messenger who was to convey the order to Genl Ewell became frightened and did not carry it. So the movement proposed was abandoned for the time. In the evening however, the order was again given us to make the movement, and this time all received it. But while we were waiting for Ewell and Jones to attack, another order came, countermanding the former order. Genl Longstreet refused to resume his former position without another positive order. Soon it came from Johnston & Beauregard and stated, too, that a large column was moving down from the railroad, which they supposed was Patterson,[35] and that we must not move, but hold ourselves in readiness to cover the retreat of our army.

The same order was given to Genl Jones; but before he received it, he had moved forward and commenced the attack with 1 S. C. Regiment and 2 Mississippi Regiment.

The enemy poured a heavy fire into him of shell & grape, his troops became confused and the Mississippians retreated in considerable disorder.

The next order received was that the enemy were completely routed and for Genl Bonham & Longstreet to start in pursuit, it having fortunately turned out that the column which Johnston feared was Patterson was the brigade of Genl Smith,[36] who had stopped the cars above on the R. R. and marched over direct to the scene of action and who coming up attacked the enemy's flank and commenced the rout.

Our boys, when they received the order to start in pursuit, made the welkin ring with their shouts. I never saw a more jubilant set of troops.

The order was for Genl Bonham (who ranks Genl Longstreet) to take a road leading to the left across the country so as to attack the enemy on the road leading from Stone Bridge to Centreville and about half way between the two points, while Genl Longstreet was to march directly here and attack them. But Genl Bonham instead of taking this crossroad, comes over into our road and orders us to go through the wood to the right which it was impossible for us to do. So we had to fall in just behind his brigade. To have seen Genl Bonham, with his sword drawn and colors, you would have thought he would hardly stop short of New York.

But he had not proceeded far before some scouts (Messrs. Terry & Lubbock whom Genl L. had sent ahead) came in sight of a battery which the enemy had

Eliza Thomas Nolley Goree,
the wife of Thomas J. Goree.
(Editor's collection)

turned to cover the retreat. When they came in sight, it fired 2 rounds of grape at them without effect.

When Genl Bonham heard this firing he turned his Brigade and came back in quick time until he met Genl Longstreet. About this time Messrs. Terry and Lubbock came back and reported to them what they saw.

Genl Bonham said "we must go back, that a glorious victory might (not) be turned into a terrible disaster."

Genl Longstreet and others insisted that we be permitted to proceed. He told him that he would capture that battery without the loss of a man and that we would at Centreville cut off the rear of their army and follow straight into Washington City. But it was of no avail. He ordered us back, and we sullenly retraced our steps to our old position.

Genl Bonham could not realize that the enemy was so completely routed and disorganized, as they were, and he was fearful that they might rally in force and cut us to pieces. But if you can possibly conceive of how *great* the rout was, how utterly *demoralized* the enemy were, you can readily perceive how easy it would have been for 5000 fresh men to [*several words illegible*] (with a full clear moon) and follow them on to Arlington Heights or even into Washington.

I have seen intelligent gentlemen from Washington who said that at any time

on Monday, the 22nd, one regiment could have taken Washington without difficulty. Genl Longstreet, knowing from experience how utterly impossible it was to
rally a demoralized army, was the more anxious to pursue. Genl Bonham (being a
civilian and politician) could not understand it. For these reasons I think I am justi-
fied in saying the victory was not completed. I heard the next day Genl Beauregard
express his regrets to Genl Longstreet that he (Genl Longstreet) was so situated as
not to have his own way about the pursuit. I thought on our return that Genl
Bonham could well be compared to the great French general who marched up the
hill, and then marched down again. It is against military law to complain of the
conduct of our superior officers—but this is only to you all at home, who I feel
anxious should fully understand everything.

I wish Uncle Pleas that you could have ridden along the road (the morning after
the battle) between Stone Bridge and Centreville. The first thing that attracted my
attention when I came into the road was the quantity of muskets scattered on the
roadsides. Many were in the road and the wagons had run over and broken and
bent them in nearly every shape. The next thing were two dead yankees on the
roadside. Then at a creek where then was a bad crossing, were wagons in almost
a perfect jam, some broken to pieces, some overset, and some fastened against
others. The most of them loaded, some with bridge timbers, others with ammunition, one with handcuffs, and others still with a variety of things. Then came cannon abandoned, some because a horse had been killed, some because wheels were
broken, and others because they were too heavy to proceed fast with. Every few
hundred yards along the road a cannon was left. And all along were dead men—
dead horses—muskets, canteens, knapsacks, blankets &c &c. There were also a
fine lot of hospital stores—surgical instruments—also ambulances of the best description.

The Yankees say that the Southerners do not fight like men—but devils. We
were several times very nearly whipped, and nothing but the bulldog pertinacity
of our men saved us. Several times some of our regiments, and even companies,
were disorganized and scattered; but they would fall in with other regiments and
companies and fight on.

Some of the enemy's batteries were taken and retaken several times during the
day. You could easily tell where a fight had occurred over a battery from the great
number of dead men and horses. There is one place on the field where in an area
of 8 or 10 acres there are more than 100 dead horses and I suppose at least double
the number of men. The enemy must have fought well. Ellsworth's Zouaves[37] were
nearly all killed & wounded. On our side the Hampton Legion[38] suffered severely,
also Gen. Bartow's Brigade[39] [and] also a Louisiana Regiment.[40] But none suffered
worse than the 4th Alabama. It and a Louisiana Regiment for nearly one hour bore
the whole brunt of the battle with the enemy firing on them from three sides. The
loss of the 4th Alabama was about 200 in killed & wounded. The proportion,
though, of killed was small. They went into the battle with 600 men.

Judge Porter King's[41] Company lost 15 killed & wounded. I am happy to state
that Cousin David Scott behaved very gallantly and passed through without a
scratch. No one from Perry [County] that I knew was killed. I saw Dave for a few

moments yesterday, the first time I knew certainly he was here. I never could until yesterday find the 4th Alabama, although I had diligently hunted for it.

Dave does not look very well. He has just gotten well of the measles. I did not see Capt. King as he had gone off. Sel Evans is a lieutenant in the company. He is a good looking young man. I shall go over and spend a day with them soon. They belong to Johnston's army and I to Beauregard's. Our field officers all acted very gallantly. Genl Beauregard was in the very thickest of the fight, and at one time led the Hampton Legion for 15 minutes. Genl Johnston also seized a flag and marched at the head of a brigade.

Several amusing incidents are related of the fight and rout. An Episcopal minister had charge of one of our batteries. Whenever he got ready to fire, he would exclaim, "Oh, Lord, have mercy on their Souls, for I will have none on their bodies." It is told of another preacher that he came in close quarters with a Yankee and that drawing his sword he nearly severed the Yankee's head from his body. Then, flourishing his sword in the air, he exclaimed, "The sword of the Lord and of Gideon! *On, boys, on!*" On the 21st the Chaplain of 5th N. C. Reg.—who is a Scotch Presbyterian—acted as Major of the Reg. (the Maj. being sick.) He rallied that portion of the Regiment which ran—In speaking of it afterwards he very penitently remarked to me that "he hoped the Lord would forgive him, but he *had* to swear *once* or *twice* at the boys to make them come back."[42] There was a boy about 16 in the battle, who received 3 slight wounds and had besides 2 other bullet holes through his clothes.

Many senators, congressmen & ladies were at this place to see the fight. Senator Foster[43] of Connecticut is said to have gone from here to Fairfax C. H. on foot and bareheaded. Congressmen outran the soldiers. Lovejoy[44] had hired a man with a 3-minute horse to drive him here. On the return, the man said he went back at full speed but every once and awhile Lovejoy would ask why in the name of God didn't he drive faster.

We had actually engaged in the fight about 20,000 men—The enemy had about 50,000.[45] They selected their own ground, and had every advantage in position. We had no embankments or fortifications and not one *masked* battery. It was a fair field fight.[46]

We had all told at that time 40 or 45,000 men. The enemy first made their advance with 55,000, but after the repulse of the 18th, they reinforced themselves with 15,000 men. Their total number was 70,000. Our loss in killed and wounded is not 2000. Theirs in killed, wounded, & missing according to the N.Y. Herald is 20,000, but I suppose 10,000 will probably cover it. We have a great many prisoners, many of their wounded. They did not pretend to send back to bury their dead. We had two of their surgeons here who we released on parole to attend their wounded— but they not only broke their parole, but left their wounded who are all anxious that they be caught & hung.

We have a very large force now here, say 50,000. What the next movement will be I cannot tell, but my opinion is that as soon as we can get transportation an advance will be made on Washington—Everything tends that way now. But I must close for you are no doubt tired, and so am I.

This letter is long enough for you all, and is so intended. All must answer it—My love to Grandma,[47] Mother & all.

Your Nephew Affly.,
Thoms. J. Goree

I saw Honl. Jacob Thompson[48] yesterday and he sends his kindest regard to Grandma, Mother, & Yourself.

Direct your letters to Capt. Thos. J. Goree
On Genl Longstreet's Staff 4th Brigade
Manassas Junction Va.

TO SARAH WILLIAMS KITTRELL GOREE

My Dearest Mother,   Headquarters 4th Brigade, Centreville, August 8th, 1861

I wrote a few days since a very long letter to Uncle Pleas (but which was intended for you all) which I hardly expected you would read through, it being so very long and uninteresting. But here (there being nothing else talked, or even thought of) one does not know what to write of except things connected with the war and the army. When I commenced that letter, I hardly thought that I would write one sheet, but I believe I filled up as many as three.

You see from this that we are still at Centreville. How long we are to remain here I do not know, but all of us are very impatient and anxious for a movement to be made, that is, if made towards Washington. If a movement be made in that direction very soon, I have no doubt but that Washington can be easily captured, but if delayed too long, it can only be done with very great loss of life.

We are very pleasantly situated though now. Centreville is a very high, healthy place, with a plenty of good water. I believe that I never before saw a place so well supplied with good springs. Nearly every lot about here has one or two good springs in it. Yet, nothwithstanding we are so pleasantly situated, we are all anxious to be in action.

Genl Longstreet has about the best Brigade in the service. It is composed of the 1st, 7th, 11th, & 17th Virginia Regiments (all splendidly drilled) together with one battery, which consists of 4 pieces of artillery, and he has also 3 or 4 companies of horsemen.

It is truly a splendid looking sight to see our brigade out in the evening on drill with our splendid band of music. The 1st (Virginia Regiment) has a band with 10 or 12 drummers and about as many brass instruments, which band makes the most splendid music I ever listened to.

Now just imagine this Brigade in solid column, with Genl Longstreet and his staff (myself amongst the number) in full uniform in advance, then 200 splendidly mounted men with swords drawn just behind us. Next, this splendid band playing soul stirring airs. Then comes the 1st & 17th (Virginia Regiments). After them the

4 pieces of artillery with their caissons, each cannon drawn by 4 horses, and each caisson by 4 horses.

After this comes the 11th and 7th (Va Regts.) We proceed in this way until we reach a point where a Brigade standard bearer has been stationed, when the General and staff take their position behind this standard, and all the officers of the Brigade salute them as they pass.

Whenever we have Brigade drill, it always attracts a large crowd of spectators.

I went over last Sunday and spent the day with David Scott. He is stationed about 10 miles from here between this and Richmond. He was very well. David is very anxious to get a furlough for two or three months so as to move his negroes this fall out to Texas, but I very much doubt if he succeeds in procuring one, as it is a very difficult matter now to get leave-of-absence for two days. He is extremely anxious to see you all. I saw also Capt. King who appeared very glad to meet with me and treated me very kindly. He enquired very particularly after each member of the family, and remarked to me that my father was one of the best friends he ever had. I was very much surprised to see there also and almost grown Cousin Sarah's[49] son, Ed Goree. He is a very good looking boy, and looks very much like his father. He sports a very respectable pair of whiskers.

I also saw George D. Johnston (an old school mate at the Howard)[50] Sad Hinton, Lew Sewell, Sel Evans, and several other boys that I used to know about Marion. Mr. Pleasant that used to live in Marion also has a brother in the company.

I was very much pleased to know that this company behaved very gallantly in the battle of the 21st. For one hour and 1 quarter, the 4th Alabama Regt stood the brunt of the battle. And a part of the time they were exposed to a severe fire from 3 sides. When at last they were relieved and started to retire, they went to a branch to get some water. Just as they were all getting their water, another regiment just in front of them (who they thought were friends) poured a heavy fire into them. They, however, rallied, and dispersed that regiment.

I think that the Colonel, Lieut. Colonel, & Major of the 4th Ala. were all either killed or wounded, and the gallant General of the Brigade (Barnard E. Bee)[51] was mortally wounded whilst at the head of this Regiment. No man's place will be more difficult to fill in this army, than that of Genl Bernard E. Bee. He had no superior in the army, not even Beauregard or Johnston. The 4th Ala. will never have another such general to lead them in battle.

David Scott says that he never felt more playful in his life than when in this fight—that he was laughing & joking the boys all the time, and did not think of being shot.

I have not seen Thomas Moorman since the battle. He belonged to Col. Kershaw's (South Carolina) Regiment, which was also in the thick of the fight. This regt sustained but little loss. It is now in Gen. Bonham's Brigade abut 10 miles in advance of this. I believe that it is generally thought when a movement is made, that Genl Longstreet will be put in advance. I hope this may be so, for it is an honorable position, and I never want Genl Bonham to be in advance of us again.

I cannot imagine, Mother, why it is that I have received no letters from you. Not a word have I received since my departure from Texas. I have sent to the office today, and if a letter does not come I shall feel quite uneasy. I hope that you will all write often, and I will try and do the same. I shall always try and write to you when I find out a movement is about to take place. And after a battle, if I should survive it, will write immediately to relieve your mind of all anxiety. Give my love to all, and remember me in your prayers.

Your Aff. Son,
Thos. J. Goree

TO SARAH WILLIAMS KITTRELL GOREE

Camp Harrison, Fairfax CH, Aug 19th 1861
My Dear Mother,   Headquarters, 4th Brigade, Ist Corp, Army of Potomac

I have not at present much of interest to communicate, but merely write to relieve the anxiety I know you feel about me, and to let you know that I am still in the land of the living and in excellent health and spirit.

I feel that I have been particularly blessed in the enjoyment of such splendid health since my arrival in Va. whilst so many of our army have suffered from sickness & disease. I have been exposed a great deal, but it does not seem to affect me in the least.

It is truly to be regretted that we have now so much sickness in our army. The cause no doubt is owing to the damp rainy weather we are now having and have had since the battle of Manassas. It has been raining and is raining now, nearly all the time. And it makes those who are recovering or have recovered from the measles relapse into a kind of typhoid fever. Many deaths occur daily from this horrible disease. I believe that the South Carolinians and Mississippians suffer more from it than any others.

Our brigade is comparatively healthy, and we must have at least 4 or 500 on the sick list, and some of them seriously ill. From all accounts, though, the enemy is suffering as much, or more, from sickness than we are.

When I last wrote you, it was from Centreville. Since that time we have advanced to this place, a distance of seven miles. We are now very comfortably quartered in a nice, commodious house, which is much more pleasant this wet weather than tents.

Our brigade is now in advance of any other in this direction, though others are being moved forward at different points. I am inclined to think that we will continue in the advance.

Genl Beauregard is expected to remove his headquarters to this place in a few days, when it is more than probable that we will be sent seven miles further forward to a place call[ed] Falls Church, a place where the Yankees were encamped for a long time previous to the battle of Manassas.

We have a picket stationed now at that point, and they have a skirmish with the picket of the enemy nearly every day.

There is a very fine peach orchard just beyond Falls Church over which the two pickets fight nearly every day. I went down there a few days since and started over to that orchard after peaches. When I got about half way, I discovered lurking around two Yankees, one an officer between me and our picket. When they saw me they started off, thinking (I suppose) that I had a company with me (which I had not).

They were about 150 yards off when I ordered them to halt, which they immediately did. I was almost sure then that I had two prisoners, but when they turned around, and saw that I was alone and without my gun, they took to their heels like race horses. How I then wished for my gun to pepper them with, but I had nothing except my 6 shooter, which would not reach so far. One of the Yankees had a sword & pistol, the other a gun, and they could have shot me with all ease had they not been so cowardly.

If we should move to Falls Church, we will occupy a hill from which we can see Washington City, about 10 miles distant. From this place we almost daily hear the cannon there, when they are constantly drilling & practicing. In good weather they must fire their cannon at least 100 times per day. A report from one of our cannon is never heard except in battle.

We are all here becoming very impatient to move forward, for we are fearful that if we delay too long, we will not be able to quarter this winter in Philadelphia.

I think that our generals are only waiting for Genl Lee & Wise[52] to strike a blow in N W Va, so as to move down through Maryland and cooperate with us against Washington.[53]

I have seen David Scott but once since I last wrote you. He was then very well, and I suppose is now. Our camps are now about 20 miles apart, and I do not know when I will have another opportunity to see him, as it is now very difficult for either of us to obtain leave of absence.

Mother, I know that you all must write me from home, and I do not know why your letters do not reach me, but as yet I have not received one from there. I have seen one advertised in Richmond, and have sent for it, but have not received it yet.

Please write often, and maybe I will receive one once in a while. I believe I have told you before how to direct to the care of Genl James Longstreet, 4th Brigade, Ist Corps, Army of the Potomac, Manassas, or probably better to Fairfax Courthouse, Va.

I forgot to tell you that I had made the acquaintance of some very nice young ladies here, who I visit two or three times during the week, and I assure you that the monotony of camplife is very much relieved by it.

Give my love, Mother, to all, Grandma, Uncle Pleas, Sis Frank[54] and the children, and the boys and Sudy,[55] also to my friends and all the negroes.

Your aff. son,
Thos. J. Goree

TO MARY FRANCES GOREE KITTRELL

Dear Sis Frank,   Camp Harrison, near Fairfax CH Aug. 23d 1861.

As I have not yet written to you, and have written once to Uncle Pleas, I have concluded to address this to you, in reply to yours & Uncle Pleas' very welcome letter of the 12th. ult., which I received only two days since. It has been now more than ten weeks since I left Texas. I have tried to make it a point to write home at least once per week, and Uncle Pleas' and your letter is the first and only one I have received in reply.

I not only am ignorant of what is going on at home, but even of the general Texas news. The newspapers seem so much taken up with the war news here that they never publish any Texas news at all.

I feel very anxious to hear the result of the elections in Texas, and more particularly to know if my friend Abercrombie[56] was elected District Attorney. Please inform me on these points in your next.

I am sorry that I have so little news of interest here to communicate. Everything at present seems quiet. How long to continue so, I do not know. I fear that on account of sickness in our army, it will be impossible to make an advance movement soon. There is still a great deal of sickness.

Our Brigade, I suppose, is one of the healthiest in the army, and there are between 4 & 500 on the sick list. In Genl Bonham's Brigade nearby there are about 1500 sick. In Genl Whiting's, the one to which David Scott belongs, are about 1900, and in Col. Forney's[57] Brigade about 2200 on the sick list. A Brigade consists of from 3 to 4,000 men.

The Brigade to which Dave belongs is 4 miles beyond Manassas from here, just about 20 miles distant. I have not been able to see David for two weeks. When I last saw him he was very well. I would go to see him oftener but for the difficulty of obtaining leave. Occupying as we do the advance post, Genl Longstreet does not wish us to be away from our post, as an attack might be made on us at any time, and we may be ordered forward at any hour.

If you wish to write to David, direct to "David B. Scott, Care of Capt. Porter King, 4th Alabama Regiment, Genl Whiting's Brigade, 2nd Corps, Manassas Junction, Va.," but "Whiting's Brigade" without letters are very plainly directed, are very liable to miscarry or be lost. I hope you will write to Dave, as he seemed very anxious to hear from you, & all about his place, etc.

Capt. King is now acting as Lt. Col. of the Regiment, and will probably be regularly promoted to that position. The Lt. Col. of the Regt. was either killed or wounded in the battle.

I am sorry to hear, Sis Frank, that you were having so much sickness at home, and I do trust it will not continue. I was also surprised to hear that we have suffered from drought. Here there has been a great deal of rain, which I think has caused the great amount of sickness in camp.

I do feel very much for the people in this section of the state. They all made excellent grain crops, which have had to rot in the field, because all their horses and wagons have been pressed into the service and they have no way to get it out. Their corn crops too are very fine, but they are just now in roasting ears, and our soldiers are making sad havoc of it. It is impossible to restrain them.[58]

Many of the citizens here too have suffered very severely from the depredations of the Yankees when they were through. The house in which we have our head-quarters belongs to Capt. Ball, who, you recollect, was taken prisoner when Alexandria was evacuated. This house the Yanks seemed to have a peculiar spite at. They broke down the doors and windows, broke open and robbed the trunks and wardrobes, smashed the looking glasses, and I do not think they left a whole piece of furniture in the house.

Miss Ball (a sister of the Capt.) had a very nice piano, which they were ready to cut up with an axe, when someone bought it from them for two dollars, and thus saved it. Many other houses were served in a similar manner.

At Centreville, one of the churches was very much defaced by them. They wrote all kinds of obscene sentences on the wall, & inscribed their names from the top to the bottom. And it seems like a just retribution that the man's name written the oftenest was killed in the battle and buried within steps of the Church which he had so desecrated.

War, as you remark, is truly a horrible thing. God grant that the theatre of it never be in your neighborhood!

Uncle Pleas in his letter said something of Crabb & Shaffer. I think that Mother need feel no uneasiness from any of their threats. They can do nothing except probably to harass her a little.

Genl Longstreeet, since I commenced this letter, has been very busy studying the geography of the country in advance of us; and from some orders which he has stopped me to write, I infer that something is on foot. I know not what. One regiment and another battery has been added to our Brigade. We now have 5 regiments of infantry, 3 companies of cavalry, & 9 pieces of artillery, which is a very nice little army.

Col. Wigfall has reached Manassas with his Texas Regiments. There is nothing else of interest I can think of at present. You must all write often to Fairfax Court House. Give my love to all.

> Your Brother Affly.
> Thos. J. Goree

TO SARAH WILLIAMS KITTRELL GOREE

My Dearest Mother,   Camp Harrison, Fairfax CH, Aug. 27th, 1861

Your kind letter of the 2nd Inst. has just been received to which I hasten to reply.

I had long and anxiously expected a letter from you, and you cannot imagine how delighted I was to receive one from you. I had just the evening before received the 2nd letter from Uncle Pleas & Sis Frank, which I will answer soon. It seems to have been written just after the reception of my letter of the 20th of July, and before any letter from me written after the 21st ult. I have written I think every week, and I hope that my letters come duly to hand. Although I fear that they do not contain much news of interest, yet I know that they will serve to allay your apprehensions and anxiety in regard to my health and safety.

You ask in your letter, Mother, if Dr. Woodson is still with me. I believe that I have before written you that several days before the battle he left here and went to his uncle about 200 miles distant, where he still is. I hear from him occasionally. He says that his health is improving, and he hopes to be on hand at the next fight. The Dr. was very sick when he left here, not able to sit up, and I was very fearful that he would not be able to reach his destination. It was very fortunate indeed that he got off when he did, for if he had been down sick here when the Yankees came he would have stood a very good chance of being taken prisoner on account of the difficulty of procuring at that time any conveyance to escape in.

I am here almost a stranger though I occasionally meet up with some old acquaintance, and have besides formed many very pleasant acquaintances both in the army and amongst the citizens. What few people are left here now, are, I believe, of the best kind. This country has heretofore had a majority of Yankees in it, but they have nearly all left for a more congenial clime. Hereafter I shall be exceedingly loath to place my confidence in one of those "Northern men with Southern feelings," for here not one in ten has proved true. There were some here before the advance of the Northern Army, who it was thought would do to tie to, but as soon as we retreated and the Yankees took possession, they became arrogant and insolent, and the best sort of Union men. Then they supposed the "Grand Army" could not be whipped; but when the grand retreat took place, they packed up and retreated from the country. What few desertions from our army that we have had has been confined to those Yankees who had joined our army, and were no doubt (in profession) strong secessionists.

Until recently the enemy has been almost as well posted about our affairs here as we were ourselves. This has been a great disadvantage under which we had to labor, and under which we still labor.

I have not been able to see Billy Denson since I met with him in Richmond. He is in another part of the state from this, down at Yorktown under Genl Magruder.[59] That is in the southeastern portion of the State. This is the eastern, or, rather, northeastern portion. I should be very much delighted to have Billy Denson near me.

Cousin David Scott is, I suppose, still at Bristow—about 20 miles in the rear of this. I have not seen him for some time, nor do I know when I shall have that pleasure again soon. Occupying (as we are now) the advanced position of the army, it is a very difficult matter to procure leave of absence even for a day or two. Should I ask it Genl Longstreet would without hesitation grant it, but I dislike to ask for it when I know we are likely to be needed at any moment in the day or night.

Within the last 3 or 4 days we have had two false alarms, (the enemy reported advancing) when we have turned out our whole command to meet them. Both on Friday & Sunday the alarm was given, and on each day in the space of three hours

I must have ridden 25 miles in ordering out troops and conveying other orders for the Genl.

On last Friday in two hours from the time the alarm was given Genl Longstreet had about 15,000 men on the march. The advance of the enemy, however, only turned out to be a regiment of infantry, a company of cavalry, & 2 pieces of artilley out on a scout. On Sunday, what was reported as the enemy, was only a large force of our own troops on a scout.

Genl Longstreet now has under his control and subject to his orders in case of an emergency, his own brigade, consisting of 5 regiments of infantry, 3 companies of cavalry, and 8 pieces of artillery. He has besides the following brigades: Genl Bonham's, Genl Ewell's, Genl Elzey's,[60] Genl Jones', Genl Jackson's, & Genl Cocke's, also Col. Stuart's[61] Regiment of Cavalry (14 Companies). His command now (so long as Genls. Johnston & Beauregard remain at Manassas) consists of at least 20,000 men, quite a respectable little army. And Genl Longstreet is fully capable of commanding it.

The most of the other generals permit their staffs to remain idle except in a fight, but Genl Longstreet tries to keep his in employment. One he has to act as quartermaster for the brigade, another as commissary, another as provost marshal, and myself as ordinance officer. Mine is about the easiest position of any.

Genl Longstreet is one of the kindest, best hearted men I ever knew. Those not well acquainted with him think him short and crabbed, and he does appear so except in three places: 1st, when in the presence of ladies, 2nd, at the table, and 3rd, on the field of battle. At any of those places he has a complacent smile on his countenance, and seems to be one of the happiest men in the world.

We have not yet advanced the main body of our forces from here, but have advanced our pickets a mile or two farther in the direction of the enemy. Our advanced pickets are now about 4 or 5 miles this side of Alexandria. We expect every day for the enemy to attempt to drive them back, when we hope to have a little fight. In fact, night before last and yesterday they made several attacks there, but were every time repulsed. We sent over last night two regiments of infantry, & 4 pieces of artillery with the expectation that they would attack with force, but they did not do it.

Genl Beauregard telegraphs to Genl Longstreet to hold our position in front of us at all hazards.

I am very sorry to hear, Mother, that you have had so much sickness, and I do hope that it is over with before now. My health is excellent, and I believe that of the Army is improving. We are still having rain. Do not have more than three fair days in succession. I wish that you had a portion of it in time to have done your cotton crop good. The corn crops here are very fine for this country, but do not begin to compare with ours.

I received, Mother, the gold dollar enclosed in your letter for which I am very much obliged. I send, Mother, my best love to all without particularizing. When I write again I trust to have something of more interest to communicate.

Write soon to your Aff. Son,
Thos. J. Goree

P.S. Tell Langston[62] & Ed[63] that a soldier's life is a hard one, and they must make up their minds to undergo a great many privations & hardships. If in their places, I should prefer serving, I think, in an infantry Co. to a regular cavalry Co.[64]

If they have not gone, supply them well with good blankets, and have them to wear next to their skin red flannel drawers & undershirts, which I think is very conducive to health.

TO DR. AND MRS. PLEASANT WILLIMAS KITTRELL

My Dear Uncle & Sister,

Headquarters 4th Brigade Ist Corp A.P.
Fairfax Court House August 29th 1861

I am fearful that I write home so often on one subject (the war, etc), that my letters have lost or will lose much of their interest; but being at leisure tonight, I have concluded to risk it, and write you a few lines in reply to your very interesting letter of the 3rd inst., which was received a few days since.

I wrote two or three days since to Mother, and gave her most of the news current here. Since that time we have driven in the enemy's pickets, and taken two fine positions occupied by them. The positions are Mason's & Munson's Hills, each about 5 miles this side of Alexandria, and from which Washington, Georgetown & Alexandria are in full view.

We took these hills without any loss on our side, but after taking Munson's Hill day before yesterday, the enemy made a demonstration as if to retake it. A fight occurred between about 100 on each side, which resulted in our driving them back & dispersing them with a considerable loss. Our loss was 4 men killed and 4 wounded.[65] Yesterday in the same neighborhood skirmishing was going on all day, but nobody on our side hurt. Not a day passes without several skirmishes.

On last Friday we marched down with the expectation of meeting a good large body and having a fight, but the main body having retired, we fired our artillery 13 times into a house & barn where there were several Yankees. This had its effect, for it made them believe that we were on the advance, and caused them to withdraw their forces which they had stationed above on the Potomac down near Alexandria. The same night they destroyed some bridges on the railroad which they had but recently reconstructed. This shows that we frightened them very badly. It would seem, too, that they have not much idea of making an advance from their destroying the bridges, but Genl Longstreet last night received information that they had fixed on to-day or tomorrow to make another advance on us. The consequence of which has been a considerable movement amongst our forces today. Genl Longstreet has now command of about 25 or 30,000 men, which command he will retain until Genl Johnston or Beauregard moves up to this place.

I think that Genl Bonham is very much chagrined that Genl L. should be placed over him. But both Genl Johnston & Beauregard have the greatest confidence in Genl L., and he is equal to any emergency. If it is true that the enemy intend making an advance as reported, there will be no retreat from Fairfax, but the fight will be here, and will no doubt be a desperate one. At Manassas we whipped them in an open field fight, and we can do it again.

I believe that I had rather have them advance than for us to make the attack, for Arlington Heights will be very hard to take. It can only be done with a great sacrifice of life.

It is today rumored that Genl Lee has taken Rozencrantz[66] and his command.[67] This lacks confirmation, but I would not at all be surprised if it were so. If so, Lincoln is no doubt shaking in his shoes, and will prepare his cabinet for an exit from Washington. I do not know what is the policy of our generals, but it is no doubt a wise one.

It is raining here nearly all the time, and the roads are very bad. I wish that you had had a portion of it in Texas. Until the reception of your letters, I felt perfectly easy with regard to the crops in Texas, and was very much surprised to hear of the drought. I am sorry to hear of the continued sickness in Texas. There is still a great deal here. Give my love to all, and write often. I would write more, but there is so much noise and confusion that I cannot do so. I have not seen or heard from David Scott since my last.

Yours aff'ly,
Thos. J. Goree

TO SARAH WILLIAMS KITTRELL GOREE

Headquarters, 4th Brigade, Ist Corps, AP
Near Fairfax Court House, September 6th, 1861

My Dearest Mother,

I have delayed writing to you for several days in expectation of receiving a reply to the numerous letters already written by me, but have been disappointed. I do most earnestly request that if you have not done so, that some of you will write to me at least once a week. Yourself, Bob, Uncle Pleas & Sis Frank might very easily enter into an arrangement for one of you to write every week. It would not be much trouble to you all, and it would certainly afford me a great deal of pleasure and satisfaction.

Since I last wrote, nothing of much interest has transpired. We yesterday stormed and took Hall's Hill with the loss of two men wounded. This is one of the same range of hills as Munson's and Mason's, which we are now fortifying. Should the enemy make an advance, it is understood that our pickets will fall back and the fight will be made here. But, from the defensive preparations which they are making, I do not think that they can have much idea of an advance.

I have been twice this week to our lines, and for the first time had a view of the Capitol. The first time (Monday) that I went down was in company with Genls. Beauregard, Longstreet, Jones & Cooke. I went again on Wednesday with Genls. Johnston, Longstreet & Jones. Genl Johnston returned and spent the night with us night before last. So you see that we occasionally have distinguished guests.

Both Genls. Johnston & Beauregard are expected to move up in a few days and make their headquarters at this place. What their plan of operations will be, I do not know. They seem to keep their own counsels. Genl Beauregard has said that if he thought his old coat knew his thoughts & plans, he would cast it from him.

It may be that in a very few days orders will be given to move forward and take Washington by storm. The Yankees are making formidable preparations to resist us. We can see them at about 3 miles distant on the opposite hill from Mason's & Munson's, throwing up strong entrenchments. When we were down on Wednesday, they had a flag raising over this entrenchment. They could be seen very distinctly, throwing up their hats, and were apparently quite jubilant. *They believe in flags* from the way in which they have them floating in every direction. If we take a prisoner (which is done nearly every day) and ask him what he is fighting for, and the invariable answer is "for our flag."

If we do make the attack in front against all these forts and breastworks, the loss of life is bound to be very great. It will be no child's play, I assure you. But if attempted, I think it will be done. I have made up my mind to do my duty regardless of consequences, and I sincerely hope that if I should meet death in the discharge of my duty, I may be prepared to do so with alacrity.

We still have considerable sickness in our army, though there is much less now than a few days since. The weather is still very rainy and unpleasant.

Has our neighborhood become any more healthy than when you last wrote? I have been quite uneasy about you all ever since the reception of your letter. My health is and has been as good as possible. I have not had one day's sickness since I left Texas, for which I trust I feel duly thankful.

Have seen nothing of David Scott since I last wrote you. I wrote him about a week since, but have received no answer. If I *could* get off I would go to see him. I have just seen a gentleman from California who says that he is quite an intimate friend of Cousin Jonathan Kittrell.[68] He saw him in June last, and speaks of him as a very true secessionist.

I have heard nothing from Dr. Woodson for two or three weeks. He was nearly well when I last heard.

Mother, I dislike to make the application, but I am out of money, and would ask that you, if possible, send me $50.00. I have had to pay so extravagantly for everything here that what little I had left after procuring my horse, saddle, pistols, etc., has lasted me but a short time. If you can accommodate me, please enclose a bill or bills in a letter and direct plainly to me care of Genl James Longstreet, Fairfax Court House, Va. I find that it requires money in the army as well as elsewhere.

Mother, please write soon. Give my love to all.

Your aff. Son,
Thos. J. Goree

TO SARAH WILLIAMS KITTRELL GOREE

Headquarters, Advanced Forces, AP
My Dearest Mother,   Fairfax CH, Sep. 12th 1861

I take this opportunity of writing you a few lines, although I have not much news of interest to write. We are still at this place, and I am unable to say when we will move farther. Genl Beauregard will move here today, and he may send Genl Longstreet further in advance.

We had a little fight yesterday which I hoped might bring on a large one, but it has not. We had a picket at a place called Lewinsville, some 6 or 7 miles from Washington. Early yesterday morning the enemy advanced in considerable force, say 1500 or 2000, and drove in our picket, and took possession of the place. As soon as Genl Longstreet heard of it, he ordered Col. Stuart of the cavalry to push forward and drive them back to their entrenchments. The Colonel (who would storm Washington with his regiment alone if ordered to do so) went out yesterday evening with 300 of his men and 2 pieces of artillery, and attacked this force of about 2000, driving them back in the utmost confusion.

His attack on them was so spirited and sudden that they fled without firing a single piece of their artillery, although they had 8 pieces. He did not have a man hurt. The enemy left four dead on the field, and we took 4 prisoners. I hope they will try and retake the place, so as to give us a respectable fight.

I intend going out to our lines this morning with Genl Waul of Texas, who spent the night with me last night. He is anxious to get a view of the Capitol.

I met up yesterday with a relation here which was quite unexpected [to] me. A Mrs. Bates from South Carolina was boarding at a house and she was remarking to someone that she had at home a beautiful pet dog which she had named "Goree" after her relations. When some one sitting by said they had been introduced a few days before to Capt. Goree, she said she knew it must be a relation, and immediately sent a message for me to come and see her.

I called yesterday evening, and found that Mrs. Bates was formerly Miss Hattie Caldwell, about whom I have often heard. Her husband is a Lieutenant in one of the South Carolina Regiments encamped near here. She seemed delighted to meet up with me, and I was equally so to see her, for she is an amiable, elegant lady. She said that she loved the Gorees better than any relations she had in the world. She made many kind enquiries after you all, and expressed a great anxiety to visit you and for her husband to move to Texas.

I have not yet seen her husband, and consequently do not know how I shall like him. She says that Aunt Lucy is alone, and very much distressed that Howson[69] should have left her, but she and Howson's wife did not agree very well. I told her that you were all exceeding anxious that Aunt Lucy should come to Texas and spend the remnant of her days. Cousin Hattie says she thinks that would be better for her than anything she could do. She says that Mr. Bates has been off to the war ever since they were married, and that they have not gone to housekeeping yet, or she would try and persuade her to live with them. Howson, she says, drinks a good deal, which renders his Mother very unhappy.

Fannie Caldwell spends the most of her time in Columbia where she is very much admired.

Cousin Hattie told me to say to Minnie and Bart, etc., that their sister Mary Ann was living with her about 20 miles below Columbia, and was very well. She sends her best love to all.

I have not seen David Scott since I last wrote you. I wrote to him several days since, but he did not reply.

I received a letter from Dr. Woodson a few days since. He expects to come on soon. Give my best love to all.

Your aff. Son,
Thos. J. Goree

TO SARAH WILLIAMS KITTRELL GOREE

Headquarters, Advance Forces
Falls Church, Va., Sept. 27th 1861

My dearest Mother,

I believe that more than a week has passed by since I wrote to any of you at home, and as I feel that it is my duty to write as often as possible, I have concluded to take this opportunity of doing so. While I always take great pleasure in writing to you all, Mother, yet I know that that pleasure would be greatly increased if I could occasionally have some of you to write to me, and have your letters to answer. Since I have been in Virginia I have received only three letters from Texas, one written by Uncle Pleas and Sis Frank to Richmond, another written by you just after the battle of Manassas and before you had heard from me, and the third written by Uncle Pleas & Sis Frank just after they had received mine of the 20th of July. These are the only letters I have received, though I have written time & again. I assure you that it is really discouraging, and I cannot believe that you have all failed to write to me, but am disposed to think that the letters have miscarried. If some of you would only write once a week and say how you all were, I would be better satisfied. But you all are not alone. My other correspondents have treated me the same way. I have written several times to Genl Rogers and he has not replied. Twice have I written to Dave Scott, only 25 miles off, and can hear nothing from him. If I quit writing for a while myself, it will be better, for then I think you may write to know whats the matter. But I dislike to try that expedient.

I am enjoying very fine health as usual. Everything seems to agree with me and I have really become fond of the life. But I assure you, Mother, that while officers may have a very nice time, the privates have quite a rough one. I every day think of Langston & Eddy and wish that they were in some positon in the army that they could live comfortably. Privates do about as well as officers until they get sick, or while it is good, clear weather and they have no long marches to make. I am very anxious to know where the boys are so that I can write to them occasionally. And I beg of you, Mother, that if you never write to me at all, that you will to them often, for you cannot imagine how much good it does a soldier to receive a letter from home.

Since I wrote you last Mother, I have made an application for a commission in the Provisional Army, and think it very possible that I will procure it. If so, and it be a Captain's Commission, it will be worth $120 per month, a part of which sum I intend to send monthly to Langston & Edwin, or either of my other brothers that my be in the field as a private.

Genl Waul told me that if I would apply for a commission that he felt satisfied he could procure it for me. Genl Longstreet told me that he would approve my application. The following is Gen. L's approval, viz:

"Capt. Goree has served on my Staff as Volunteer officer since the 18th of July; the principal part of the time as ordnance officer of the Brigade. He is an industrious, intelligent officer, and well worthy of a position in the Confederate Service. I hope he may receive the position he so well deserves. I would like to have Capt. G. appointed to some position in the Ordnance Department, and remain with me in the position he now occupies."

(Signed) James Longstreet

Now with this flattering endorsement of Gen. Longstreet, and Genl Waul to work for me in Richmond, if I do not get the commission, I will be indeed very much disappointed. If I should be disappointed in this, I will then try for a position in Col. Terry's Regiment, as he promised to save a nice one for me.

Genl Longstreet still has command of the Advanced Forces, but nothing of much interest has transpired since I last wrote. On day before yesterday, it was reported that the enemy were making an advance upon us, or rather in the direction of Lewinsville, a little place four miles above here, from which we whipped them more than two weeks since. We at once loaded all of our wagons and sent them to Fairfax C. H., expecting to have a very severe fight. We then went out to give them battle, and exchanged some 30 cannon shots with them, when they as usual retired without letting us come to close quarters with them. They got some of the best of this fight, as they killed one of our men, and took another prisoner, who rode up to them mistaking them for friends. The enemy, so far as we know, only had one man wounded.

We are making some few fortifications here, but it is not the intention of our generals to make the fight here, but to fall back if the enemy advance, and receive them between this and Fairfax C. H. Gen. Longstreet is anxious to fight them here and to fortify for that purpose, but he is overruled by Genls. Johnston and Beauregard. I think, Mother, that the fight will come off somewhere in a very few days. We will either advance or the enemy will. We heard yesterday from two or three sources that the enemy would make an advance this week. If so, we will be prepared to give them a very cordial greeting. The enemy are still fortifying in front of us very strongly, and will no doubt give us a right hard fight if we attack them behind their works. The truth is that we ought to have [taken] Washington two months since. It could have been done then with but little loss. Somebody is to blame for the delay, and that sombody I am disposed to believe is President Davis. It is reported that he has caused the delay in opposition to the wishes of the Generals for some political reason. Genl L. remark[ed] when he heard it was "that it may be very good politics, but it was very poor fighting."

We are in a very pleasant place here, and I rather dislike leaving it. We are occupying quite a fine large two story house, which belongs to a runaway Yankee. I have an elegant room upstairs to myself. The furniture had all been taken away before we reach[ed] here, but we supplied ourselves with other furniture from some other abandoned Yankee houses. We have very nice sofas, tables with marble tops, washstands, &c &c. We also had at one time as many as 3 elegant cooking stoves which we have given away. If you were in reaching distance, I could supply you with everything of the sort which you might need.

Every day or two we have distinguished visitors, sometimes Genl Johnston, then Gen. Beauregard, then probably some members of Congress, and very often a lot of nice ladies who come down to see us and take a look at Washington & the Yankees on this side. I took our ambulance to Fairfax C. H. last week and brought down Cousin Hattie Bates and 3 other young ladies—They dined with us, and seemed to enjoy themselves very much. Cousin Hattie sends her love to all. I saw Tom Moorman a few days since. He had just recovered from the measles. His father was out. Mr. Moorman sends his kind regards to all. I have not heard from Dr. Woodson or Cousin David since I last wrote.

Give my best love to all, without enumerating.

Your Aff. Son,
Thos. J. Goree

TO MARY FRANCES GOREE KITTRELL

Headquarters Advanced Forces AP.
Dear Sister Frank.   Fairfax Court House. Octr. 5th 1861

Yours of the 30th of August was received only two days since. It was more than a month on the road. I had almost despaired of hearing from you all again, and in my last letters I have complained bitterly at your not writing. I now take it all back, and shall put all the blame on the mails, since I find that you write. At the same time I received your letter, informing me that Langston & Edwin had left Texas for Virginia, I received one from my friend Creed Woodson at Richmond informing me of their arrival there. I was very much pleased to hear it, as I was fearful that their co. would be sent out on the Texas frontier.[70] I yesterday received a letter from Langston. He and Ed were both well, and seemed to be in good spirits. He said they had had quite a disagreeable time between Texas & New Orleans. I do hope that the regiment to which they belong will be sent up here so that we can be near together.

I saw this morning in one of the Richmond papers that one of the Texas regiments was to be sent to northwestern Virginia, and I am afraid it may be the one to which the boys belong. I have just telegraphed to Genl Waul at Richmond to find out. If he is there, I will receive an answer probably before mailing this letter.

I have just written a long letter to Langston & Ed. in which I have endeavoured to give them some good advice about their health, morals, &c. I have also written to Creed Woodson and requested that he would keep a supervision over them. I know that I have always loved my brothers dearly, but I feel as if I love them ten times more than I ever did. I feel desirous that they should be in this division of the army, not only that I may be near them, but also because I think the winter will not be so severe here as in N. W. Virginia. It is very cold there now, while here the weather is very balmy & pleasant. Another reason, I must confess that I have very little confidence in the ability of our generals in that part of the state. We have expected great things of them, and they have accomplished nothing. Floyd[71] is no General. Gen. Lee has quite a reputation, but he has not sustained it. He is a great military man in theory, but he has never had any practice. I very much fear that Rozencrantz will out-general him. I think Gen. Longstreet will soon be made a Major Genl., and if so, I hope the boys may be placed in his division.

I wrote Mother last week from Falls Church, and described to her how pleasantly situated we were there. The very night after I wrote, we recd. an order from Genl Johnston to abandon all our advanced posts, and fall back without delay. The order was recd. just at dark, and before midnight we had abandoned all the splendid positions (Mason's, Munson's, & Upton's Hills) and other splendid positions, which we held in front of the enemy and in sight of the Potomac & Washington. We regretted leaving, not only on account of being so pleasantly situated, but we all liked the excitement which our proximity to the Yankees produced. We moved our troops back 3 or 4 miles, and have again made Head Quarters at Fairfax C. H. The enemy now occupy the positions which we abandoned. I think the move was a strategetic one, made to try and induce the Yankees to make an advance on us and give us battle in an open field; but they do not seem disposed to accommodate us.

President Davis was here a few days since. On day before yesterday he reviewed portions of Genls. Longstreet's, Cocke's, D. R. Jones' and Walker's Brigades. It was quite a display. The line was about a mile & a half in length. The President & Genls. Johnston, Beauregard & Smith, with their aids & escort, rode along the line in front, whilst our bands as they passed were discoursing excellent music. The President would salute each flag as he passed it. After he passed the line, he then took a position, and the line formed into column and passed him, the officers saluting as they passed. Genl Longstreet & Staff headed the column. After the review, Genl Longstreet assembled his field officers and staff, and called on the President at Genl Beauregard's where he introduced us all to him. His greeting was very cordial indeed. He spoke of the honorable positions which we had occupied in the advance. He asked if we could give him a view of the Potomac. I told him we could have done so, a few days since, but could not now. His reply was, "Well, I hope that in a short time we will force a view of it, at the Long Bridge." He has now gone to

Richmond, but expects to return in a few days, when, I think, you may be on the qui vive for stirring events. We have recently erected a battery lower down on the Potomac which I think will effectually blockade the Potomac. This may force the Yankees out. Since the completion of that battery, our genls. have evidently expected an advance, and I fancy are a little disappointed that the enemy will not come.

Your letter to David I forwarded immediately to Manassas near which place I thought he was, but I only learned today that his brigade had been moved down near this battery on the Potomac—which may account for my not hearing from him. I shall write to him by the first opportunity.

Cousin Tom Moorman & Hattie Bates are both well, and send their love to you all. Cousin Hattie will remain here until cold weather drives her home. She has recently heard from Aunt Lucy, who was well. I believe I mentioned in my letter to Mother, that I had met with Mr. Moorman. Cousin Hattie saw him afterwards, and she said that he was perfectly charmed with me. Cousin Hattie thought that I ought to take it as quite a compliment, as he was not given to flattery and very rarely expressed his opinion even if he thought well of any one. I only treated him with the same courtesy that I do any other friends.

You spoke, Sis Frank, of sending me some clothes. I assure you that they would be very acceptable. If there is a chance, I would like for Mother to send me two nice shirts, 2 pairs coarse red flannel drawers & two undershirts—same material— 2 pairs wool socks. These could be placed in a very small package and brought by any one coming out. I was very lucky in regards to coat & pants. Soon after the battle I purchased a beautiful suit of grey for $25.00 (coat & pants). The pants with black stripes down the legs, and the coat with gold braid around the sleeves & collar. The same suit would now in Richmond cost $50.

The day after the battle, an excellent pair of Yankee pants (blue) perfectly new, were brought in, and they fitted me exactly. I took possession of them, and they have done me very fine service.

Dr. Woodson is now in Richmond awaiting the arrival of Col. Terry's Regiment, which is daily expected. The Dr. is in fine health & spirits. His uncle with whom he has been for some time, sends me a very cordial invitation to come and spend some time with him. I am still enjoying fine health—the weather is very fine. You must write often, Sis Frank. Give my love to all.

Your Brother Affectionately,
Thos. J. Goree

TO SARAH WILLIAMS KITTRELL GOREE

Headquarters, 2nd Division, Ist Corps, A.P.

My Dearest Mother,   Near Centreville, Va., Octr. 18th 1861

It gives me very much pleasure to acknowledge the reception within the last two or three days of several very interesting letters from yourself, Uncle Pleas &

Sis Frank. The letters received were two which were written about the time Langston & Edwin left home, and which they mailed me from Richmond. Another was from Uncle Pleas & Sis Frank, written 24th Septr. And yesterday I received your long & interesting letter of the 29th of September. I need not assure you that the perusal of all these letters afforded me very much pleasure and gratification, particularly so as I had almost given up all idea of hearing from any of you at all.

I believe, Mother, that I have allowed more than the usual time to have elapsed without having written to any of you. This is owing to the fact of our moving about a great deal, and being somewhat unsettled. The last letter I wrote was, I think, to Sister Frank after our removal from Falls Church to Fairfax Court House. It is my intention to write every week.

You have no doubt before this, heard of the safe arrival of Langston & Edwin at Richmond. I have only recd one letter as yet from them, written soon after their arrival there and from that they seemed to be in fine spirits, having stood remarkably well their trip from Texas. I have since heard from them though through Creed [Woodson] and Dr. Woodson, having recently received letters from them both. Each of them spoke of the boys being very well. I have written to them to keep a lookout over them and to attend to them in case of sickness, which I have no doubt they will do.

I have also written a long letter to the boys in which I endeavoured to give them all the good advice in my power, both in reference to their health and morals. I have never before felt so much solicitude, both for their temporal & spiritual welfare, as I do now.

I am very sorry to hear that they came off without any preparation for the winter, for I do not know what reason they had to believe that they would be supplied here, as I have heard of no preparation for anything of the sort.

I think it advisable, Mother, that you fix up such things as you think they will need, and send them by first opportunity. You will, no doubt, hear of things being sent from time to time from different places. Have them fixed up in a strong box and plainly marked, directed to them, giving the name of the captain, and the Co., and the number of the regiment, which I believe is the 5th, but I am not certain.

I would suggest that you send them some good blankets (colored if possible) 2 suits each of good strong, warm clothing, some flannel shirts and drawers, socks, a pair of good strong shoes for each (if you can get them), a comforter for the neck, pocket handkerchiefs if they have not a supply, a half dozen or more coarse towels, some soap, and other little comforts as you think they may need.

I have merely enumerated the above articles because I know what things are most generally needed and are most difficult to procure.

And I wish, Mother, if you could have spared any of them, that you had sent with them one of the boys Lloyd, Rob, or Pomp, to have waited on them and cooked for them. It would not have cost anything to have brought one of them, nor to have kept one here, as they would have rations furnished them for him. And you cannot imagine how much assistance it would have been.

For instance, the boys will have to go out on picket duty, march 6 or 8 miles,

and when there, will have to stay out on picket for 24 hours before they are relieved. Now, it would be very pleasant to have someone to cook their meals and
have them ready for them when they come in, to dry their clothes when wet, &
perform all these little offices.

I have seen soldiers on the march throw away all the blankets they had in the
world just because they were tired, when, if they had had a servant along with
them, he could have relieved them of much of their load.

I do wish, Mother, the boys had a servant with them, not only to wait on them
when well, but to attend them if they get sick. There are a great many negroes
with the soldiers, and they all seem pleased and enjoy life very much.

If these suggestions should meet with your favor, send them one of the boys
with some responsible person you may see coming out. Rob would be the best to
send, but rob or Pompey either would do very well. If any soldiers were coming
on, or anyone in charge of supplies for soldiers, it would cost nothing to send one.

I have merely made these suggestions for what they are worth. Do what you
think proper in regard to them. I hope that Langston's health will improve, and
that he will return home with renewed spirits as well as health. I would very much
like to go and see them, but cannot leave here. I still hope that the Texas Regiments
will be sent here, though it is thought that they will go to northwestern Virginia.
I intend writing to them again in a few days.

I was very much surprised to meet a few days since at Fairfax Court House,
Wash Crawford and Mr. Fullerton of Texas. They remained a few days, and came to
the conclusion that there would not be a fight soon, so they returned to Richmond,
making me promise to telegraph them in case a fight was expected.

I can still hear nothing. During the last week Genl Longstreet has had us riding
around making a map of the country. The only excitement we have had was that
caused by the fight at Leesburg several days since, of which you have heard before
this. As pretty full accounts of it have been published, I will not go into the details
of it.[72]

It was a desperate fight, rendered so from the fact that the Yankees had the
Potomac in their rear and could not retreat, but had to face the music. Our whole
force engaged numbered about 12 or 1500. That of the enemy 1500 or 2000. Our
loss was about 130 killed and wounded; that of the enemy will never be known.
We captured over 700 prisoners. Their loss in killed and wounded must have been
three times as great as ours, besides they lost numbers drowned in attempting to
recross the river. The Yankees fought well, but our men fought better. The 8th
Va & 10th Miss Regts. covered themselves with glory. The 17th Miss. was only
brought in toward the close of the fight. It sustained little or no loss. I am glad
the 17th & 18th Mississippi had this opportunity (and profited by it) of redeeming
themselves, for they behaved badly on the 21st of last July.

A day or two after the battle at Leesburg, a report was brought to Genl Evans
that the enemy were crossing the river again in very large numbers. He immediately (without making further inquiries) fell back from Leesburg in this direction
6 or 8 miles, and wrote to Genl Johnston that 20,000 of the enemy had crossed
over. Genl Johnston immediately sent him reinforcements.

The truth of the matter was that only about 2500 of the Yankees had crossed over, when the river suddenly rose to prevent anymore from crossing, and also prevented these from returning, and they were left on this side for 36 hours before they could recross without blankets or provisions.

Genl Evans found this out, and had he done his duty he could have captured the whole lot with little or no trouble. He is very much censured for not attacking them, but the truth of the matter is that he was so elated at his victory at Leesburg that he got a little drunker than usual, and was consequently not in a condition to do anything. Some of the officers under him speak of preferring charges against him. Genl Evans is one of the bravest men I ever saw, and is no doubt a good officer when sober, but he is unfortunately nearly always under the influence of liquor.

We are still expecting an advance on the part of the enemy. I am inclined to the opinion that it would have been made before this, had they not met with the reverse at Leesburg. I do not believe that McClellan will attack here, but he will try to turn one of our flanks. In a very few days our fortifications here will be such that a small force can hold them, and we can then be prepared for any movement that Genl McClellan is disposed to make. Our troops are very impatient at the delay.

There has been a reorganization of this Department of the Army, but it has not yet gone into effect, and will not probably for some time. The Department is called "the Department of Northern Virginia," with Genl Joseph E. Johnston, Commander in Chief. This Department is divided into three Districts, viz. The Valley District, The Potomac District, and The Aquia District.

Maj. Genl T. J. Jackson is to command the Army in the Valley District, Genl Beauregard in the Potomac, and Maj Genl Holmes in the Aquia District.

The army in the Potomac District is subdivided into four divisions, which are to be commanded by Major Genls Van Dorn,[73] G. W. Smith, Longstreet and E. Kirby Smith. I think this arrangement much better than the present one.

I am pretty well acquainted with most of our generals[.] Genl Longstreet gave a dining last week at which were present several distinguished guests, viz: Genls. Johnston and Beauregard, Major Genl G. W. Smith, Brig. Genl. D. R. Jones, Hon. Wm. Porcher Miles of So. Car.,[74] and Hon. Wm. Ballard Preston of Virginia.[75] If my descriptive powers were good, I should some time or other try and give you description of many of our generals, but I do not feel competent to attempt it.

I am sorry to see that a good deal of dissatisfaction is being manifested in the army with President Davis on account of some of his appointments. In consequence of one of his appointments, one of the best generals in the army has resigned and gone home. This is Brig. Genl W. H. T. Walker[76] of Georgia. He was an old army officer, has been in service for more than 20 years, and carries more lead than any man in the army, having been shot in nine different engagements, the most of the times through the body.

The cause of his resignation was this. Mr. Davis appointed his brother-in-law, Dick Taylor (who is nothing of a military man) a Brig. Genl.[77] This was not so very bad, but to gratify Taylor he gives to him Genl Walker's La. Brigade (which was a very fine one) and places Genl Walker in command of a very inferior brigade. Great indignation is felt at it.

One thing is true of Mr. Davis. He is a man of strong likes & dislikes. He has his favorites who he promotes at all hazards, whether competent or not, over many who are really deserving. He is not the great man that I once took him to be, "when distance lent enchantment to the view."

But enough of military affairs. I received a letter a few days since from Mr. Cushing, enclosing me a draft on the P. O. Dept. at Richmond for $46.25, which I suppose will be paid on presentation. I am very thankful indeed for it.

Sis Frank asked in one of her letters if I recd pay for my service, or if I was only fighting for the glory? As Volunteer Aide, I do not receive pay, but I hope soon to obtain a commission which will pay expenses. Genl Waul, who promised to attend to my application when I could make it, has not been at Richmond since I made it. I hope on his return he will succeed in getting it through. I am fighting for patriotism, but if there is any glory connected with it I want to get my share of it.

I have not heard from the boys, Langston & Edwin, for several days. When I last heard they were quite well. I write to them every week. For the last 24 hours I have thought of them all the time, for the reason that there has been a cold, incessant rain for that length of time, and a great many of the soldiers' tents here have been blown down, and everything thoroughly soaked.

I have yet heard nothing from David Scott, although I have written to him through the P. O. several times. I will write again to him, or Captain King, and try and send the letter by hand. His regiment is at Dumfries, some 20 miles from here. Cousin Hattie is still near here and well. She says she will write to Sis Frank when she returns home.

Until I recd Sis Frank's letter making inquiries about Norman's gun, I was under the impression that I had written about it, and I still think that I did from Richmond in the letter sent by Col. Wharton on the evening I left Houston. I started with my gun to the boat, but some of my friends who came with me persuaded me not to be troubled with it, and they would see that I had a gun when I reached here. So I left it with Mr. James T. Cyrus of Houston to send you when he had a chance. Col. Lubbock furnished me with a very nice Sharpes rifle after I reached here. I have written Mr. Cyrus if he has not sent it, to send it immediately to you, care of T. & S. Gibbs at Huntsville, which he will no doubt do.

I have about filled my sheet. So, good night. Write soon and often too.

Yours aff'ly.,
Thos. J. Goree

TO SARAH WILLIAMS KITTRELL GOREE

Headquarters, 2nd Division, A.P.
Near Centreville, Va., Novr 11th, 1861

My Dearest Mother,

I have just finished a letter to Norman,[78] and while my hand is in, will also send you a few lines. I should have done so several days since but for the reason I have suffered so from a boil in my nose, as to render me totally unfit to do anything.

I am now clear of that pest, and am enjoying my wonted health. When I stop and think of the dangers to which I have been exposed for the last five months, and the sickness and suffering around me, I can but feel grateful to a kind and merciful Providence for having taken such care of me, and for having even preserved my health as well as my life.

Since I commenced the practice of my profession, I am aware that I have not led a life consistent with my professions as a Christian, but for some time past I have been led to consider of my course, and I have deliberately come to the conclusion, and have commenced to make my actions conform with my professions. Although I know that I have improved very much since the formation of my resolves, yet I feel and know that there is still room for improvement. I hope that I may be enabled to hold out to the end.

There are many temptations thrown in the way of a young man in the army, but I think I can resist them. When I first came here, I thought that an occasional drink would be beneficial for my health, and would take one sometimes, but I found out that it was all a notion, and that I always felt better without it than with it.

General Stuart, one of the healthiest, stoutest, bravest, and most dashing men in the army, does not touch a drop, neither does he smoke or chew. So it is with Col. Jenkins of the 5th So. Ca., a man who Genl Longstreet pronounces the best colonel in the army.[79]

These two men are each about 28 years old. One is a Brig. Genl of the Cavalry, and the other Colonel of one of the finest, if not the finest, regiments in the army. Col. Jenkins says he is very glad to have met up with me, as I am nearly the only man he had met who would keep him in continuance in his regular habits.

I wish that all the officers of our Army were half so abstemious, but it is not the case. Genls. Johnston & Beauregard, Major General Gustavus W. Smith, Kirby Smith, Van Dorn, Longstreet and Jackson are comparatively temperate men, but Brig. Genls. Elzey, Evans, & Wigfall are always more or less under the influence of liquor, and very often real drunk, and for this reason they are not safe generals, for no man, when under the influence of liquor, can or will act with discretion.

I would not detract from the noble dead, but from all I can learn, both Genls. Bee and Bartow went themselves, and carried their men into places on 21st July, which they could and would have avoided, had they been entirely from under the influence of liquor.

I like Genl Wigfall as a man, but on account of his habits I very much regret that Langston and Edwin are in his brigade. I hope, though, that when he assumes the responsibility of three or four regiments, he will see the necessity of reformation.

I was very gratified to receive a letter from Langston a day or two since, and to know that he and Ed are enjoying such good health. Langston writes in very fine spirits, and I hope that if he can have his health, the life of a soldier will be beneficial in other respects. He says that he and Ed are both very glad that I made the suggestion to you to let them have some one to wait on them. I reckon the poor fellows find it pretty hard.

I expect that the regiment to which they belong, the 5th Texas, will be ordered up here soon. The 4th Texas[80] left Richmond 2 or three [*letter torn*]—If their regiment does come, I think it will be placed near by where we are. And if so I can see the boys often.

I hardly know what opinion to give you about the chances of a battle here soon. I have had a great many in regard to it, but they have not always been correct. We have not yet given up all hopes of an advance of the enemy, but we fear that he will not venture out this Fall. If he does not come before 1st Decr., I think that nothing will be done before Spring here.

However, the latest rumors we have are that the advance will be made about the 15th inst. I sincerely hope that it will, for I do not like much the idea of staying inactive on these bleak hills this winter. And if we have a fight this month, it is possible that we may winter in Washington and Baltimore. Our men are very eager for the fray. They seem to have confidence in themselves to cope successfully with any numbers that McClellan chooses to bring against us.

Genl Longstreet has now a very beautiful command: the 3rd Brig, Genl D. R. Jones, consisting of the 4th, 5th, 6th, and 9th So. Ca. Regiments, the 4th, his old Brigade, now under Genl Ewell, consisting of the 1st, 7th, 11th, and 17th Va. Regts, and the 5th Brigade, Genl Cocke, consisting of the 8th, 18th, 19th, and 28th Va. Regts.

In case of a fight, he can turn out between six and seven thousand strong. I believe that he can take the 5th So. Ca. (Col. Jenkins'), the 17th Va. (Col. Corse)[81] and the 8th Virginia (Col. Hunton),[82] and whip in fair fight any six regiments of Yankees that can be mustered.

We have just heard of the success of the Yankees on the So. Car. Coast, and would feel very low about it did we not think it would encourage McClellan to come out and fight us.[83] What I regret to hear still more is the burning of bridges, etc. in East Tennessee by the traitors there. It will be a warning, however, and cause in the future a sufficient guard to be kept over them.[84]

If there is to be no fight here this Fall, I would like that Genl Longstreet would be ordered South where there will be some fighting. I am tired of this inactivity.

The weather here is becoming quite cold and disagreeable: very heavy frosts every night, but no ice yet. The cold would not be so disagreeable did it not rain every two or three days.

I recd. the draft sent by Mr. Cushing, and feel under many obligations to you for sending it. I have sent it to Richmond, and look for the money every day.

I believe that there is nothing more of interest at present. I have as yet heard nothing from David Scott. Cousin Hattie Bates has returned home. She disliked leaving very much, and I believe would have been willing to remain all the winter. She insists that when I return home I must come through South Carolina, as she intends to marry me off there.

Give my love to Grandma and all my relatives & friends, also to all the negroes. Please write often, and make Bob write occasionally. The letters from home seem now to come very direct and promptly. Direct to Manassas.

Your aff. son,
Thos. J. Goree

TO SARAH WILLIAMS KITTRELL GOREE

My Dearest Mother,   Near Centreville, Va., Decr 8, 1861

It has been some time since I have written to you, but I have in the mean time written to Sis Frank, which I think would answer every purpose. I am now in debt for two letters received within the last few days.

In my last letter to her I told of my visit to Dumfries to see Langston and Edwin, who I found both well and in excellent spirits. I have heard nothing from them since my return, but if there is no fight within a few days I shall go down again to see them. [*several words illegible*] if I do not succeed in getting my commission I will (when it is finally determined to go into winter quarters) go down and winter with the boys as by that plan I will not incur the expense that I am now at. When active operations again commence in the Spring, I can resume my position with Genl Longstreet and render all the service and acquire as much honor as possible.

I have not however despaired of a commission, but am waiting for the return to Richmond of Genl Waul, by whose influence I hope to obtain it. Genl Waul professes to be, and I believe is a good friend of mine. My plan is now to get a commission in the Provisional Army, with orders to report for duty to Genl Johnston, and then get Genl J. to detail me in Genl Longstreet's staff, with whom I am anxious to remain.[85]

I had hoped, Mother, that when I next wrote to you, another battle would have been fought here, and another victory won. But, we have waited long and impatiently for the enemy, but he has not come. For the last two days, however, the indications for his advance have been rather more flattering than heretofore. At least our generals have been more sanguine than usual that a fight would soon take place. I do not know on what information they ground their expectations. I suppose, though, from the fact that recently a great many troops, wagons, & ambulances, etc., have been brought over from the Washington side of the Potomac to this side.

The Northern press and mob are, too, becoming clamorous for a forward movement to Richmond. It is the more general impression here that McClellan will not make his main attack at this place, but that he will attack us at Dumfries and try and turn our right flank. If he does this, I think the 5th Texas Regiment[86] will have the honor of opening the fight, for which honor they all seem very anxious. It is now my impression, though, that he *will* make his main attack here and try and overpower us by numbers. I think so for the reason that at this season of the year the roads are generally very bad, and that he cannot carry much heavy artillery (on that account) toward Dumfries. Whilst by coming to this place he will have two good turnpike roads to advance on. If he should come this winter, I think that he will come with a force of about 120,000 men. We can have about 50,000 men to oppose him with, as we have about that many effective men between Leesburg and Evansport, a distance of about fifty miles. The greater part of these 50,000 men, say 30,000 or 35,000, are in this place, about 3000 at Leesburg, and the balance between here and Evansport.

Genl Hill[87] is now in command at Leesburg in place of Genl Evans, who has been sent to the South Carolina coast. It is an excellent exchange (as Evans, although a very brave man) was too much addicted to liquor, and consequently not suited for a detached command. Genl Hill is equally as brave, is very pious, and does not drink a drop. He is a North Carolinian, and, when the new organization goes into effect, he will have a No. Ca. Brigade in Genl Longstreet's Division.

I am somewhat surprised to find that the troops from the *Old Rip Van Winkle* State are pretty good fighters. The best regiment of cavalry (Ransom's)[88] in the army of the Potomac is from North Carolina. There are several regiments for North Carolina here, and I would not be much surprised if your Cousin Protheus Jones'[89] son is in one of them. Write me in what part of the state, and the name of the town, Col. Jones lives in and will try and find out if his son is here.

I believe that in my last letter to Sis Frank I mentioned the fact that the 4th Ala. Regt is encamped near the 5th Texas, so that the boys and David Scott, when he returns to the Regiment, can often see each other. I suppose Dave is back before this time.

We have had some very cold weather here, some snow and several freezes. The last two days, however, have been very pleasant, almost like Spring. McClellan has no excuse now, as far as weather is concerned, for not coming out and fighting us. We are here in daily expectation of hearing of a big fight in Kentucky.[90] It may be that the fight there and the one here will take place about the same time. The reason why we are so anxious to fight here is that we hope in the event of a battle to winter in Washington or Baltimore.

Mother, give my love to all the family, white and black, also to all enquiring friends. Can't you make Bob write to me. I am anxious to know how the hogs, *and other things,* are getting along in Madison.

Mother, please write often to your son.

Aff'lly.,

Thomas J. Goree

P.S. Perhaps the letters any of you write for Edwin or Langston had better be sent to me (enclosed), and I can send them down to them at once, and by daily courier.

Direct to Manassas.

TO MARY FRANCES GOREE KITTRELL

My Dear Sister Frank,   Near Centreville, Dec'r. 8th 1861

Your long and interesting letters of the 1st & 13th. ultimo were recd within a few days of each other. And although I have just written to Mother, I will also try and write to you, although I am almost at a loss to know what to write that will be interesting.

I am truly thankful, Sis Frank, that you write to me so often, for I know that I would often have the "blues," if I could not hear from you all as often as I do. Mother writes but seldom, but I cannot expect her to write often. I received a long and interesting letter a few days ago from Dr. Campbell,[91] with a postscript by Cousin Lucy, which letter I have answered, and have also written to Cousin Lucy. She said she had written to me before, but I have never received the letter.

In one of your letters you say that "Col. Cleveland has agreed to carry the clothes for Capt. C's[92] Company as far as Red River, and see them started on the way." If he has not left with them before you receive this, I would suggest that he, or some one else, had better come on all the way with them, for if he does not, ten to one the company will not receive them in three months.

Railroad transportation is now so inadequate to the amount of freight to be transported, that it is almost impossible, from all I can hear, to have anything transported through quickly and safely without someone to be with it and attend to it personally. On account of the burning of the RR bridges in East Tennessee all the freight has to be carried around through Georgia and South Carolina.

I was surprised to see the Texas Regiments so well clad as they are, with coats, pants, socks, overcoats, etc., taken in San Antonio last spring.[93] Langston and Edwin said they had a plenty of everything except blankets. Someone had taken one of their best blankets. If blankets are scarce in Texas, or in any event, good comforts will not only be found cheaper to send the soldiers, but I think are warmer, and during the winter will answer a better purpose. I would like to have one or two myself.

I am glad, Sis Frank, that you have made the acquaintances of Mrs. Woodson and her daughters. It is a family that I esteem very highly, and I believe they are very good friends of mine. I know that I stand pretty high in the estimation of Mrs. Woodson's grand-daughter, but with some of her daughters. *Quien sabe?*

Cousin Lucy wrote me that Miss M. was knitting something for a soldier, which soldier she strongly suspected was me. If so, I shall certainly appreciate it very highly. As I will also appreciate the sentinel cap which you said Mrs. Wiley had kindly offered to knit for me. Such a thing will be very comfortable on the high bleak hills of Centreville.

You complain of wanting cold weather. I wish that we could divide with you. If we could, I think there would not be *quite so much anxiety* manifested to go into winter quarters. The ground here has just thawed after nearly a week's freeze.

Some of the soldiers must suffer a good deal, but they are building fireplaces to their tents, and fixing themselves as confortable as circumstances will allow. Some of them have erected very comfortable huts. I suppose that huts will be erected for the whole army, as soon as all prospect for a fight has disappeared.

You seem very anxious to know how I look in uniform, etc. Well, I don't know that it improves my appearance a great deal, particularly now as it is getting rather dingy & dirty. If I get a commission so that I can afford a new suit, I will have my Ambrotype taken and sent you in full Confederate uniform.

If you wish now to know how I look, just imagine or picture me dressed in a plain, neat grey suit, frock or dress coat, and brass buttons. I do not know whether

I have fattened much or not, as I have not weighed. I think though that I have fleshened up a little. I hope though to become quite fleshy before the war is over.

I have had one or two first rate dinners during the last week. About a week since, I had an invitation to dine with Genl D. R. Jones, which, of course, I accepted. He had a large fine ham, a fat turkey, chickens, beef, oysters, salad, pickle, light bread, and a variety of other things.

A day or two afterward we dined with Genl G. W. Smith, who also gave us quite a nice dinner. Genl Van Dorn also gave one, but my horse being lame I did not go down. Genl Longstreet says it was quite a nice affair. At some of the dinners we had speeches from Genls. Johnston, Beauregard, Smith, Van Dorn, Bonham & others, all of whom can fight much better than they speak.

The battle flags I spoke of in my last, have been presented to the army. The troops have been assigned their positions behind the entrenchments. Heavy baggage has been removed to the rear. And we are all now ready and anxious to give Genl McClellan a cordial welcome. If he does not visit us this winter, we will be very much disappointed.

I would not be surprised if the Lincolnites give Galveston a call before the winter is over.[94] If so (I hope for the reputation of Texas) that we will have no Hatteras or Port Royal affair of it. Our troops behaved badly at both those places. They were evidently worse scared than hurt. These big guns are only intended to scare, for it is but seldom they do much execution.

Well, Sis Frank, as I have nothing else to say, I will close with the request that you continue to write as you have done. Give my best love to Uncle Pleas & to Grandma. Tell Grandma, that *"poor little Eddy"* is about one of the tallest men in the company, and is gettting along finely. Kiss all the children for me. Give my love to Aunt Sally and all the other negroes. I enclose your letter in Mother's, and thereby save ten cents.

Your Bro. Aff'ly.,
Thos. J. Goree

TO SARAH WILLIAMS KITTRELL GOREE

My Dearest Mother,   Near Centreville, Virginia, December 14th 1861

I have taken my seat to acknowledge the reception of your truly welcome letter of the 22nd ult., although but a very few days have elapsed since my writing to you. I am somewhat fearful though, that the length and frequency of my epistles will tire you all, especially, as I seldom have anything of much interest to communicate.

The reception and perusal of yours, as well as Sis Frank's & Uncle Pleas letters always afford me the greatest pleasure, for they are not only filled up with interesting items of news, but also with the assurances of your love, and solicitations for my welfare, and also with much good and wholesome advice, which I try to profit by.

Your letter, Mother, I immediately enclosed and sent to Langston & Edwin, and they will, no doubt, receive it today or tomorrow. I have heard nothing from them since I was there, for the reason, I suppose, that there is no mail communication between this place and where they are situated though as I am, I can send a letter to them every day by the regular courier, while they would find it rather difficult to get one to me.

In your letter you express great uneasiness about the boys, which is very natural, for I felt the same uneasiness about them until I visited them and saw how much they had both improved in flesh and health, and saw also how comfortably they seemed to be situated.

I now, of course, feel a solicitude for them, but not that uneasiness about them I once had, and I hope you will not have it either after the reception of my letters. Where they are encamped the cold is not near so severe as here. They have also plenty of timber near them with which to build good, comfortable huts when the order is given to go into winter quarters. When I wrote to you about a servant for them, I did not know then that they messed with Capt. Cleveland, and were so well provided for.

Mother, I am truly thankful to you for the clothes which you write you have provided for me, and I hope you can find some opportunity to send them to me, as I am somewhat in need of them. If you can hear of anything being sent to any of the Texas Companies from our section, say Capt. Cleveland's, Powell's,[95] or Porter's,[96] you could have my things sent to them, and I could get them.

I could not tell from your letter whether you had made us all a suit of the penitentiary goods or just Langston and Ed. If you have made none for me, I would like very much to have a suit, frock coat, double breasted to button all the way up, with seven buttons to a side and stand-up collar to come just under the chin when the head is in the natural position. If you cannot make that coat, just send me a pair of pants, and I will do without the coat.

I told Genl Longstreet what you said about knitting him some socks. He thanked you very kindly, and said "they are just the kind he has been wearing, and that he would like well enough to have a pair." So, you must knit him a very nice fine pair. He said that I must "describe the General to you—in my next." My descriptive powers are not very good, but I will nevertheless try and give you some idea of what kind of a person he is.

Genl Longstreet is forty years of age. He was born in So. Carolina, but emigrated when very young to Alabama. He was appointed to West Point from Ala. At West Point he was in the same class with Major Genl Van Dorn, G. W. Smith, and Mansfield Lovell,[97] all Maj. Genls in our service. There are besides in the North and South some seven or eight others of his class who are now brigadier generals. Genl. D. H. Hill of No. Ca. is one, Genl Rozencrantz was also in his class. Genl Longstreet has been in active service west of the Mississippi (mostly in Texas and New Mexico) since he graduated more than 20 years ago. He was in every battle

that was fought during the Mexican War except Buena Vista, and was twice breveted for gallant conduct. He was severely wounded in the last battle fought there.
When he resigned from the old U.S. Army, he had attained the rank of Major. He
ranked Genl Beauregard in the old army, who was only a Captain. He is a very fine
officer, and is as brave as Julius Caesar. His forte though as an officer consists, I
think, in the seeming ease with which he can handle and arrange large numbers of
troops, as also with the confidence and enthusiasm with which he seems to inspire
them. The latter is, no doubt, caused by the coolness and daring which he exhibited
before them on the 18th & 21st of July, for on both occasions he was in much more
exposed and dangerous positions then any of his troops. Besides, in an action, if he
is ever excited, he has a way of concealing it, and always appears as if he has the utmost confidence in his own ability to command and in that of his troops to execute.

In a fight he is a man of but very few words, and keeps at all time his own
counsels. He very often tells his officers as well as men, whenever they begin to
talk of our retreating or being defeated, that it is nonsensical to have any such idea,
for that in every battle somebody is bound to run, and that if they will only stand
their ground long enough like men, the enemy will certainly run. He is very reserved and distant towards his men, and very strict, but they all like him.

He is the only Major General in the Army that has division drills, and he seems
to manage a division of eight or ten thousand men with as much ease as he would
a company of fifty men.

He is about five feet eleven inches in height, and weighs about 200 pounds, has
light hair, about the color of mine, with blue eyes; has a florid complexion, and a
very amiable, soft expression of countenance. He wears a large, heavy set of whiskers and moustache, which hides the lower part of his face. When on foot, and in
citizens dress, he has rather a sluggish appearance, but he is exceedingly punctual
and industrious. Whatever he has to do, he does well and quickly. When he dresses
up in his uniform and mounts his horse, I think that he presents a better appearance than any other man in the Army. The ladies all say that he is the handsomest.
He is always agreeable with the ladies.

At home with his staff, he is some days very sociable and agreeable, then again
for a few days he will confine himself mostly to his room, or tent, without having
much to say to anyone, and is as grim as you please, though, when this is the case,
he is either not very well or something has not gone to suit him. When anything
has gone wrong, he does not say much, but merely looks grim. We all know now
how to take him, and do not now talk much to him without we find out he is in a
talkative mood. He has a good deal of the roughness of the old soldier about him,
more so, I think, than either Genls. Johnston, Beauregard, Van Dorn, or Smith. He
seems to be a great favorite with the old army officers, who nearly all call him
"Pete." Nearly one half of the old officers have nicknames. Van Dorn is called
"Coon", G. W. Smith, simply "G. W.", Genl D. R. Jones, "Neighbor Jones," etc, etc.

Well, I have tried to give you some idea of Genl Longstreet, of his person, character, etc., and if I had the time and space, I would like to give you also an idea
of some of the others of our leading men here. I probably will do so at some
future time.

I do not believe that there is a better officered army in the whole world than the Army of the Potomac, particularly as far as the Genls and Maj Generals are concerned. Some of our Brigadiers have bad habits, and they might be improved on, but, so long as we have Genls. Jo Johnson & Beauregard, & Major Genls. Van Dorn, G. W. Smith, Longstreet, and E. Kirby Smith, you need have no fears of the results of any battle fought by the Army of the Potomac.

Old Jo Johnston himself is a perfect wheel horse. A few days since some one was telling what impression the different generals had made on him. He said that "when Genl Johnston had difficulties before him, he always put his mind to work to find a solution for them, and if he could not find one, it bothered him terribly. G. W. Smith saw all the difficulties, and appreciated them, but if he could not solve them, he gave himself no further trouble, but generally concluded that at the proper time something would turn up to help him out. But Genl Beauregard," he said, "would always try and counteract any difficulty that he could not get around by digging in the ground, and by throwing up fortifications." But, whatever their methods of surmounting difficulties may be, they are all three great men. McClellan knows who he has to contend with here, they all used to be his most intimate friends, and he dreads them. He and G. W. Smith were bosom friends. Genl Beauregard seems to be the favorite of the army, as he is the dread and terror of the Yankee army.

A few days since, Genl G. W. Smith was here, and someone who had just come from Washington was telling in what awe the Yankees stood of Genl Beauregard. Genl Longstreet remarked: "We could give them Genl Beauregard, and then whip them." Genl Smith shook his head and replied: "Don't say that Pete, for it would be a hard matter for us to do it with him against us." Pete, of course, assented to this. I have merely related this to show you in what estimation Genl Beauregard is held by his brother officers.

Mother, I have just read over what I have written, and I know you are tired of it. I could condense everything I have told you by writing it over, but I have not the time for it. So, you must excuse it. I have written all this in the cold, with my fingers perfectly benumbed. You must give my love to all. Kiss Sudy and Scrap[98] for me. Tell Bob I wish him success in all his undertakings. From all I can hear, I infer that you will have splendid pork this year, as Bob has paid them so much attention.

I am very sorry to hear of the disease amongst your mules, and hope that it has not spread any further. I have had some bad luck with horses, too. My first horse, an ugly one but a very good one, I had to ride so hard over these abominable turnpikes, that I staved him up so that he was constantly getting lame. I got him in pretty good order though, and about a month since swapped him off for a very nice horse. I had not had him more than a week before he got a rope around his legs, and cut them very severely so that I have not been able to ride him much since. He is nearly well though now, and as fat and sleek as a mole. I ride one of the General's horses until mine gets well.

I have not yet received my money. The draft Mr. Cushing first sent me was not fixed up right, and they refused to pay it. He has since sent me a treasury warrant which I have sent to Richmond, and will get the money on it in a day or two.

I now fear that there is to be no battle here this winter. At present there is little or no prospect for one. Mother, you must write to me often. In haste.

Your Son affectionately,
Thos. J. Goree

P.S. The letter before this I intend as a Christmas gift, this one as a New Year's present.

TO ROBERT DANIEL GOREE

My Dear Brother,[99]   Near Centreville, Va., Dec'r. 20th, 1861

Yesterday I had the pleasure of receiving yours of the 26th ult., which seemed to have been an unnecessarily long time on the way. I had thought strange that you had not written me before, and you *must* do better in the future.

I was very glad that you succeeded even as well as you have with your cotton, for from what I had heard of the drought and worms, I was fearful that you would not make half what you have. I suppose that you have corn until you hardly know what to do with it; but you ought nevertheless to be very careful and provident of it, as you may not make so much another year.

If I had written to you a few days ago, I should have advised you to have planted very little cotton next year and a great deal of grain, for the reason that then thought the blockade would have been kept up another year, and another crop accumulating on the one we already have, would have caused neither crop to be worth much. Now, however, I think the early raising of the blockade very probable from the fact that a collision between England and the Federal Govt is highly probable on account of the indignity offered to the British Government in the seizure of the Commissioners Mason & Slidell. You will see news of the state of feeling in England before you receive this.[100]

If England would only open our ports for only a little while so as to supply us with a few more Enfield rifles & Armstrong guns, it would help us out amazingly. But to your farming operations.

I would still advise that when planting time comes, if our ports are still blockaded and no prospect of an early raising of the blockade, I would plant very little cotton and a great deal of grain, so as to raise your own meat and live at home, or on home products. In any event whilst the war lasts you ought to plant much more grain than usual. England is supplied to a very great extent with grain from the North, and if she should get into a war with that govt. we ought to try and supply her with both grain and cotton. I suppose though that Uncle Pleas, Mother and yourself have taken all these things into consideration. I was surprised, Bob, to hear that you would not make meat enough for home use for from what I heard of the very close attention you were giving the hogs in Madison I thought that you would raise an abundant supply. I suppose, though, that if you *do not* have meat enough, you will make it up in forage, as I have also heard that you have also devoted a great deal of attention to the Hay(s) question in that part of the world.[101]

Bob, I have not much news of interest to write you at this time. Everything is very quiet along the lines of the Army of the Potomac. The prospect for a fight this winter has pretty well vanished, and the army is now building huts for winter quarters as fast as possible. The larger part of the army which was here at Centreville has moved back a little ways into the country, and only Genl Longstreet's Division is left here to hold this position. His Division alone can hold it for 48 hours against any force, and that will be more than ample time for the forces which have gone back to come up. I was in hopes that the new organization (by which the Texas troops would be in Genl. Longstreet's Division) would have taken place before going into winter quarters, but for some reason it did not.

For the last ten days we have had beautiful weather, and had McClellan any idea of an advance he would certainly have taken advantage of it. The miserable cowards are afraid to come out, and McClellan knows that if he is defeated, *off goes his head too.*

A telegraphic report received here yesterday says that in a heavy skirmish which the Texas Rangers had with the enemy at Green River, Kentucky, their gallant Colonel Terry was killed.[102] I hope that the report is false, but fear that it is too true. The short time that we were together here attached me very strongly to him. I not only learned to love him as a friend, but I had the utmost confidence in him as a man and admiration for him as a soldier. The news of his death almost stunned me. I slept very little last night thinking of him, and he is uppermost in my mind all the time. In imagination now I can see his tall, manly form, his handsome smiling face, and his brave, determined countenance. I have never seen a braver man, nor one more cool and determined in time of danger. If he has fallen, I know that it was at the head of his men. He used to tell me that Texas Rangers already had a *reputation* as the best fighting men in the world, and that they would have to do some *extraordinary* fighting to sustain it. No doubt but that this idea has caused his death. He wanted always to have the post of danger, knowing that it was the post of honor. He was devoted to the Cause of the South, and willing to lay down his life in its behalf.

He, I think, had but little idea of surviving the struggle, for he knew what the South expected of him and his regiment. No one here except myself, feels more regret at the report of his death than Genl Longstreet. Although he was with the General but a very few days, yet he had the greatest love and admiration for him. He raised his regiment with the expectation of being assigned to duty under Genl Longstreet, and the disappointment of both he and the General was very great when he was sent to Kentucky. Col. Terry was noble, generous and brave, and his place will be hard, I may say, impossible to be filled. He was devoted to his family, and when he was here used to talk daily about his wife and little children. *Peace to his ashes!!!*

I have not heard very recently from Langston & Edwin. I intend visiting them so soon as my horse (which is now quite lame) gets well. You speak of volunteering yourself. I know from my own experience how great your desire must be to engage in the defense of your country, but I hope that you will not yet do so, or if you do, that you will engage in the coast defense, so as to be as near home as possible. I sincerely trust that you will not leave the state, without drafting has to be resorted to. Volunteer before that. Never submit to a draft.[103] You have three brothers in the army out of the state, and public opinion will certainly excuse you. When the enemy lands on the soil of Texas, then go at once to assist in driving them back. Some of us ought if possible to remain at home, and as you are of more use there than I could possibly be, I hope you will remain there.

My loss, if I am killed, I know would be severely felt by our Mother & relatives, but not half so much as yours would be. I have engaged in this struggle as I would in a religious duty, and I am not only willing, but hope that I am prepared if necessary to be sacrificed upon the altar of my country. And I have no doubt but that our brothers Lang & Ed have the same feelings.

I have written, Bob, a much longer letter than I intended. Excuse it. Give my best love to Mother, Scrap, Sudy, Grandma & all. Write soon too.

Your Brother Affly.,
Thos. J. Goree

P. S. Remember me kindly to Eck[104] & Sis Sallie & children.

TO PLEASANT WILLIAMS KITTRELL

My Dear Uncle,   Near Centreville, Va, Decr 21st, 1861

As it has been some time since I wrote you, I will try and write you a few lines today. I wrote Bob on last Friday, and whilst I was writing there was a pretty considerable battle going on at Dranesville, some fifteen miles from here, of which you have doubtless heard.[105] I am sorry to say that we were defeated with a considerable loss, say 50 killed and 150 wounded, etc., notwithstanding our forces fought very gallantly and retreated in good order.

There was a considerable quantity of forage about Dranesville, which Genl Stuart (who has command of the outposts) thought it well enough to secure. So on Friday morning last with four regiments of infantry (two of which—the 6th So. Ca. & 11th Va.—were from Genl Longstreet's Division), a squadron of horse, and Cutt's Battery—4 guns, numbering all together not exceeding 2000 men, and a hundred wagons, he started down after the hay, etc.

When very near Dranesville, a large body of the enemy (who it was supposed had come out for the same purpose) was discovered. Genl Stuart immediately ordered the wagons back and sent forward a company as skirmishers, who drove back the skirmishers of the enemy, killing five or six of them. The enemy were drawn up in the turnpike leading through Dranesville, and the pike formed a kind of breastwork for them. Our troops had to advance on the road leading into the turnpike at a right angle. On each side of this road was a dense pine thicket. Our troops were formed, two regiments on each side of the road, and in the front of the thicket. Our battery, or three pieces of it, was placed in the road about 200 yards from the turnpike. It was a very unfavorable position for it, but there was no other place to put it. The 1st Ky Regt. as it was coming into position unfortunately fired into the 6th So. Ca. Reg. killing 6 and wounding several. The fight was opened by the Kentucky Regt., and in a few minutes became general. The enemy had the advantage in position, as they also, had in guns. They had, too, about 4000 men engaged in the fight, and a reserve of two brigades, say 6000 men.

The battle lasted about two hours, and Genl Stuart only gave the order to retreat when our battery was so disabled as to be in danger of capture. Many of the battery horses were killed, and Genl Stuart himself assisted to carry it off by hand.

The fight was quite a desperate one. A part of the time the left of our line was in 40 or 50 yards of the enemy's right. The firing ceased on both sides about the same time, and some of our troops left the field a half hour after the firing ceased.

I think the Yanks must have been pretty nearly whipped themselves. Some few of our wounded and all the dead were left on the fields. The enemy rifled their pockets and took off their coats and shoes. The So. Ca. Reg. numbered only a little over 300 men, and it sustained about one third the whole loss. Although they had the fire of the enemy in front, and that of their friends for a while in their rear, they did not waver for a moment. Just as the Ala. Regt. got in position, it recd a tremendous fire which killed the Lt. Col. J. B. Martin[106] and shot off the arm of Col. Forney. Although this somewhat scattered the reg., they rallied and fought very well. Maj Woodward[107] of the South Carolina Reg. was wounded.

The Yankees are said to have fought well, but they could not be induced to come to close quarters. Our men could very distinctly hear the orders given by their (the enemy's) officers, and three times was the bugle sounded, and the order to Charge given, but they would not budge an inch. Their officers would rave & swear at them, and call them cowards, but they would not charge.

From all appearances, I fear that we will have to winter here without any general engagement. Much fear is apprehended that unless something is done very soon the next spring will find us here without an army. The large proportion of this army is composed of 12-Mo's. regts, and the terms of enlistment will expire in April & May, the very time they will be most needed. These men will probably most of them re-enlist, but not until they first go home. It is thought by some that McClellan is only waiting for this. If some steps are not taken soon, there will be a deplorable state of affairs here in the spring.

All the So. Ca. regts. are only in for 12 mo's., as also the Va Regts., & many of the Ga., Ala. & Miss Regts. This matter should be looked to, for the defeat of this Army will almost ruin the *Cause*.

Much regret is felt here at the death of Col. Terry. He made a great many friends the short time he was here. He was one of Nature's Noblemen.

I have no other news of much interest to write. I am expecting to start in an

[*The remainder of this letter is missing.*]

1862

"THE FATE OF THE COUNTRY DEPENDS ON OUR SUCCESS"

TO DR. AND MRS. PLEASANT WILLIAMS KITTRELL

My Dear Uncle and Sister,   Near Centreville, Va., Jan'ry 5th 1862

Your letters of the 12th ult. have just a few moments since been at hand, and I take this the only opportunity I may have to reply.

I was very sorry indeed to hear of the death of Henry, and particularly the manner of his death. I little thought that Grandmaw would ever survive all of her servants, but it may be that she will survive many even of her grandchildren.

We are here in daily expectation of a great battle in which it is more than probable four of her grandchildren will be engaged, and if we all survive it, it will only be through the interposition of a kind Providence.

We had almost given up all hopes of an advance on the part of the enemy this winter, but within the last few days our generals have received information which has led them to expect a very early attack. What the information is, I do not know.

Today orders have been issued to the troops to prepare 3 days cooked rations, and have everything ready to take up the line of march at a moment's warning. The surgeons have all been notified to have the ambulances and everything in their line ready. The consequences of which, everything is today (Sunday) bustle and excitement. We are having eggs hard boiled and crackers baked. Genl. Longstreet is firing off and reloading his pistols. The attack is not expected against Centreville, but down on our right at Evansport. Hence all the preparations for a march.[1]

The ground is stiff frozen, and is white with a coat of sleet, which will make it rather bad to march over. In event of a fight, I think we will be equal to the emergency, though I am sorry to say our army is very much crippled up. A great many of our troops are off on sick furlough, many are sick here and not in condition for a fight, besides, many of our horses are very poor, and almost too weak to draw heavy artillery.

But we are more than all crippled by an unfortunate misunderstanding which unhappily exists between Pres. Davis and the leading generals of this army. I do not [know] all the causes of the difficulty, but I am satisfied from what I do know, that the blame is not here.

Van Dorn & E. K. Smith are the only two leading genls. here that Pres. Davis is on very friendly terms with. He does not like Gen. Longstreet, and I believe that he is hardly on speaking terms with Genls. Johnston, Beauregard, & G. W. Smith. Mr. Davis' motto seems to be: "Rule or Ruin." Our generals here are too independent to suit his ideas, and have an unfortunate habit of thinking some for themselves.

Mr. Davis is undoubtedly a great man, but he has his faults, his whims, and his

Pleasant Kittrell Goree, Edwin King Goree, and Robert Daniel Goree, circa 1910. (Editor's collection)

unbounded prejudices. I have nearly lost all the admiration I ever had for him as an honest man and a patriot. If I had time, I would try and give you some reasons for what I have said.

I was already fixed up to go down and see Langston & Edwin on the 1st last, but when I came to ask the General's consent he seemed rather loath to let me leave just now, so I have postponed my trip for a while longer. I, however, heard direct from the boys two days since, and was delighted to learn that they were both in such excellent health. Ran Fisher went down, and I heard from them through him.

Having heard of the great amount of sickness in the Texas Regts., I had become very much distressed about them. They are poor hands to write. I am glad that the health of the two regiments was improving. If the enemy do make the attack at Evansport, the Texas Regts. and 4th Ala will be apt to be in the van.

I have not yet recd a commission, but am daily expecting it. Genl. Longstreet is entitled to two regular aides, and when he was appointed Major General he applied to have me appointed. But, although both of us have written about it, we can hear nothing of it. I wrote last week to Genl. Waul to try and get the applications through if possible. I suspect that there is someone else who is trying very hard to cut me out. But no gentleman would make application for a staff appointment when he found that the General had made application for someone else.

I can think now of nothing else of interest to write. My hand is so benumbed with cold that it is with great difficulty that I write at all. Give my best love to all, and write soon, too.

Yours affectionately,
Thos. J. Goree

TO SARAH WILLIAMS KITTRELL GOREE

Hd. Qrts, 2d Division, 2d Corp, A.P.
My Dearest Mother,   Taylor's House Near Centreville, Va., Jan. 18th/62

I have forgotten how long it has been since I last wrote you, but I am satisfied that it has been since I last received a letter from you. The last letter I recd. was from Uncle Pleas and Sis Frank, bearing date the 12th ult. I replied to that several days since. When I wrote then, we were in daily expectation of a forward movement on the part of the enemy, but since then the "Burnside Expedition"[2] has gone southward, and consequently the excitement here has abated, and all hopes of a battle soon have been dispelled. [*A line is illegible.*]

Indications now are that we are to remain here inactive throughout the winter. Apt as not, though, in a few days something else may turn up to excite our hopes.

When I last wrote I believe that I mentioned that I expected to visit Langston and Edwin soon. Well, I have not yet gone, but still hope to go soon. About the 1st January, I asked Genl. Longstreet to let me go, but he talked as if he was unwilling for me to leave as long as there was a probability of a fight. As soon as that blew over, he went to Richmond and asked me to keep close at home until his return so as to take care of everything. He has been gone a week. I am expecting him back every day, and as soon as he returns I will try again to get leave for a short time.

The object of the Genl's visit to Richmond is to assist in developing some plan to supply the places [of] the 12-months men whose terms of service expire early in the spring. This has become a very serious matter, as this army is composed chiefly of these 12-months men, and no feasible plan has as yet been proposed to induce them to re-enlist, or to supply their places. If something is not done soon, I fear the consequences.

But as to the boys, when I last heard from them they were both very well. I write to them quite often, but they never reply, and it is only by chance I hear from them. Probably paper is scarce with them.[3] I intend, though, to carry some to them when I go down, and hereafter when I write to them I think I shall have to propound regular interrogatives to them (leading ones) and leave a space after every one for them to write "Yes" or "No" as an answer.

In several of my letters home, I have made mention of my endeavors to procure a commission. I intend here to give you a short account of my efforts and the difficulties I had to encounter, & the upshot of the matter, etc.

When we were at Falls Church, and whilst Genl. Longstreet was only Brigadier General, I intimated to him that I would like if possible to obtain a commission.

He told me to make a formal application and he would endorse it and try and have me appointed to some position on his staff, though at the time his staff was complete. I believe that I sent you a copy of his endorsement, which I thought was quite a flattering one.

No notice has ever been taken of this application by the War Department. Well, when the Genl. was appointed Major General, he being entitled to two aide-de-camps (without saying anything to me about it) he made application to the War Dept. to have me appointed his 2nd aide-de-camp. No attention was paid to this application.

Then on the 22nd of Decr he again wrote to them that he was entitled to two aides, and that he wanted me appointed forthwith. He as yet had not told me about it. A day or two after this last letter was written and sent off, Captain Walton, who is also a volunteer aide connected, too, with Genl. Longstreet by marriage, and a very smart man, too, applied to Genl. Longstreet for this vacant position as aide-de-camp.[4]

Genl. Longstreet, thinking that his last letter had been received, and that I had been appointed, told Capt. Walton that he had applied for me, as I had better and stronger claims than anyone else. He told him at the same time that he would recommend him for *any other* position on his staff if there was a vacancy. He gave Capt. Walton leave to go down to Richmond, and reaching there before the General's letter written on the 22nd, was on the strength of this recommendation *nominated* for Genl. L's 2nd aide-de-camp.

On the 29th Decr Genl. Longstreet told me that he had applied to have me appointed, and that it ought to have been received, but as it had not, I had better write to some friend at once to look after it.

I wrote to Genl. Waul (who had promised to assist me in anything of the sort). In a few days I recd an answer from him stating that there was no hope for me, and enclosing a note from Genl. Cooper[5] saying tht Capt. Walton had already been nominated for the position on a recommendation from Genl. Longstreet received before the letter recommending me. I thought there was bad faith somewhere, and that mine was a hopeless case.

I showed the letter from Genl. Waul to Genl. Longstreet. The Genl. was much very vexed. He explained to me everything that had taken place as I have narrated above. He said that we must go to work at once, and that it might not be too late to do something. One chance was left. Walton had been nominated, but the nomination was probably not yet confirmed by Congress.

Genl. Longstreet at once wrote a very strong letter to Genl. Cooper, stating that he had twice recommended & applied for me as his 2nd aide before giving Walton any recommendation at all—that the recommendation given Walton was not intended to interfere with me, for that I had been with him six months and had better claims than anyone else, and that it was not only unjust but contrary to his wishes that those claims should be overlooked, and that he wanted the thing rectified at once.

This letter I enclosed and sent in one to Genl. Waul. Genl. Longstreet also telegraphed Genl. Waul that he had sent two letters supporting my application, but no attention had been given them; that he had just written the third, and that he wanted Genl. Waul to have all further proceedings in the matter stopped until that was received.

Yesterday I received a letter from Genl. Waul in which he says: "My dear Sir— It gives me pleasure to inform you, that you have this day been confirmed as AD Camp to take rank from Decr 31st 1861. Hoping you will reflect credit on our State, & honor on yourself, I am yours, etc.

T. N. Waul"

So, Mother, you see that everything has terminated as well as I would have wished. I have given you a full account of it, thinking it would probably be interesting to you to know the difficulties I had to encounter. I am glad that it all happened just as it did, for it proves the strength of Genl. Longstreet's and Genl. Waul's friendship; for although Walton had married Genl. L's cousin, and Genl. Waul was also connected by marriage with him, yet they both stood up for me manfully and did all they could. I shall always remember such friendship.

Walton is a very clever fellow, and takes his defeat with a very good grace. This will now put me in a position to prevent any of my brothers who are or may be in service from suffering from the want of any little comfort that money can procure. I do not think it right to make money off the country, and so it is my intention (after procuring myself an outfit suitable for my position) to give my brothers in service what they may require to make themselves comfortable.

I do not yet know what my rank, or rather to what rank in the Provisional Army, I have been appointed, but I suppose 1st Lieutenant. If so, my pay will be 90 dollars per month. It will take a month's pay to buy me a uniform, which when I procure I will send you my Ambrotype for which you have several times written me.

My present uniform is rather seedy, and I have been patiently awaiting for the box of clothing you were to send on. I hope that before this you have had an opportunity of sending it. I reckon the boys have not needed it so much as I, as they were very well supplied when I was there.

I expect, Mother, that you are already tired with the perusal of this letter, but before closing, I wish to make some suggestions about your next crop. It will soon be time for planting, and what I could suggest is that you reduce your cotton crop, and plant more grain than usual. You have all, no doubt, thought of the matter, and have come to some conclusions about it. If this course is generally pursued thoughout the South, the small quantity of cotton raised on account of the increase in price would bring almost as much money as a large crop at a reduced price. If the blockade is not raised soon, there will in all probability be on hand next fall two crops, and the more raised this year the less will be the price when it does come into market.

Plant at least half, or more than half your land in grain, the balance in cotton. You can better cultivate the cotton. Make corn enough to raise your meat and some to spare. The women, instead of working in the field as usual, can remain at the house and spin and weave. Nearly everything you may need you can supply yourself, and then you will have but little to buy. I throw out these suggestions merely for what they are worth.

I believe I have nothing else of interest to write at present. When I go to see the boys and return, I will write you again.

> Give my best love to all.
> Your Son Aff'ly,
> Thos. J. Goree

TO SARAH WILLIAMS KITTRELL GOREE

My Dearest Mother,   Centreville, Va., Feb'ry 9th 1862

I am just in recpt. of Uncle Pleas' & Sis Frank's letter of the 17th ult., but as it has been some time since I wrote to you, I will delay writing to them for another week and write to you this week. It does not matter much anyway to whom I direct my letters, as you all see and read them.

I was surprised to hear from Sis Frank's letter that I was expected home on a visit this winter. I cannot imagine how Dr. Bell heard it, for although nothing would afford me more pleasure than to pay you all a visit, still I have had no such intention.

Even if I had had any idea of it, the state of my finances until recently has been such as to have deterred me. And I have so recently obtained a commission that I would not think of applying for a furlough for such a length of time. Had I failed in obtaining a commission, I think that in all probability I should have left here and joined the "Rangers" in Kentucky.

As it is now, if the war should last that long, & we are spared, I will try about the first of next January, 1863, to procure furloughs for Langston, Edwin & myself, and we will all visit home together. But that is a long way off, almost too long to talk about.

In all probability many battles will be fought by this army between now and then, and if we all three survive them, we may look upon it as a kind interposition of Providence in our behalf.

I believe that in my last letter to Sis Frank I wrote pretty fully of Langston & Edwin. From all that I could see and hear they were not only two of the most popular boys in the regiment, but deservedly so. They are kind and obliging to every one. Dr. Breckenridge[6] told me that he had never seen or heard of their being out of humor. They are strictly moral, & ever ready & willing to perform any & every duty imposed upon them. They are fine specimens of *good soldiers*. You may all feel proud of them.

To show you how strictly temperate they are, they would not begin to touch some mild liquor from brandy peaches which I carried down to them, thinking it would be good for them in case of sickness. It was some a friend had sent Genl. Longstreet. I also carried down to them some good warm gloves and a few other articles I thought they might need.

I think now that they are pretty well acclimated, and if they do not expose themselves too much, will not be sick again. At the time they were sick, they would probably have had quite a severe spell had not Drs. Breckenridge & Woodson attended them so closely, and had not Capt. Cleveland prevented their removal to a hospital.

Before leaving them I made both of them promise to write me in case of the serious illness of either of them. I also got Dr. Woodson to promise to write me. I told them also, in case of serious illness, rather than go into a hospital, to find a good private house, and hire a good nurse at any price. You may rest assured that if either of them gets sick this winter or before active operations in the spring, I will go to them. When active operations commence I may not be able to get leave but will always try. We are 20 miles apart and the worst road between you perhaps ever saw.

I wrote Sis Frank that Genl. Longstreet had lost two children with scarlet fever. Since then the third has died with the same disease. Just think of it—three children within one week. The General is very low spirited. He has only one child left.[7]

I, this morning, received a long letter from Cousins James & Mary Goree. They were all well. Don is at Bowling Green, Kentucky. He was in the Arkansas Regiment held in reserve at the battle of Green River when Col. Terry was killed. Cousins Mary & Lucy had been on to see him there.[8]

There is not much news of interest here. A re-organization is now going on. Many of the twelve-months men are re-enlisting, and I think nearly all *will* before their terms expire. The legislature of Va. will probably pass a drafting law soon so as to have her quota in the field by spring. The So. Carolina troops are doing better than I expected.

I do not much expect that anything will be done here before spring. Genl. Beauregard has gone to take command at Columbus, Ky. He expects to return here in April.[9]

I have not yet heard anything from the box you sent me. It may come before the close of the winter. I bought me a pair of coarse pants the other day, worth 3 or 4 dollars, but for which I had to pay $8. When I get my month's pay, I can get such things as I may need.

The weather here has not been so cold as usual, but there has been a great deal of wet weather, several snows & sleets, which makes it very severe on the men. I will write again soon. My best love to all. Write soon to your

Aff. Son,
Thos. J. Goree

Tell Bob I am expecting a letter from him.

TO DR. PLEASANT WILLIAMS KITTRELL

Hd Qutrs 2d Division A. P.

My Dear Uncle,   Near Centreville, Feb'ry 15th 1862

Your kind letter of Jan'ry 17th was rec'd. nearly a week since, & I have twice taken my seat to answer it, but both times felt so low in spirit & despondent from the bad news that has been pouring in upon us that I thought a letter written in such a state of mind would afford you little or no satisfaction. Even now my spirits are not near so buoyant as I would have them, but I can begin to discover a little ray of light amidst the dark storm which has so recently broke upon us.

Since the battle of Manassas an apathy seems to have rested upon our people. We have despised them, & have considered one Southerner as a match for five Yankees. We have thought that the Yankees would always take to their heels after firing a few rounds. The reverses which we have met at Hatteras, Port Royal, Drainsville, Mill Spring, & lastly at Fort Henry & Roanoke have served a good purpose in dispelling these false illusions and causing us to throw off our apathy, and arouse ourselves to renewed assertions & greater than any we have yet made.[10]

But while these reverses have proved to us that our foes are not such cowards as we have heretofore taken them for, it has also disclosed the very disagreeable fact that our forces are not the invincible heroes which we have thought them to be.

It cannot be disguised that the affairs at Hatteras, Port Royal, Fort Henry & Roanoke were absolutely *disgraceful*. Our loss at Roanoke, when the truth be known, will, I think, not be exceeding 50 killed & wounded. It seems that a more gallant resistance was made there than any of the other three points, & I think there was not much gallantry even in that. The noise of the heavy artillery has frightened our men into a surrender. At Mill Spring, our men seem to have fought very well until Genl. Zollicoffer[11] fell, in whom they seemed to have had greater confidence than in Genl. Crittenden.[12] Mr. Davis has made some very bad appointments, & Genl. Crittenden's, I expect, was one. I believe Genl. C. to be a brave and a true man, but he has not the ability such as I think requisite for a Major General. He is an intemperate man, which is his greatest fault. Several years ago he drank very hard, but reformed, and was strictly temperate until after his appointment in our Army. Those who know him say that he can not indulge at all without drinking to excess. I made his acquaintance here, and was very much pleased with him as a gentleman, but thought he was a man of ordinary ability. Genl. Drayton[13] is said to be a very ordinary man. Genl. Wise's was probably a very good appointment, were he in better health. Genl. Tilghman[14] has sufficiently proved that he was not the man for the place.

There certainly has been great mismanagement in Kentucky or the Federals, even after taking Fort Henry, would not have been permitted to have gone up the Tennessee river with their gunboats as high as Florence, Ala. Genl. Beauregard has now gone out there, and it is to be hoped that he will bring about a different state of affairs.

I called on Genl. Beauregard with some others the day he left here, and he then remarked that if he had his own way there, he would try and put things through by April so as to then return to his command here.

I wish, Uncle Pleas, that I could think that the Army of the West was as well officered as the Army of the Potomac. If Genl. Joe Johnston had command there, instead of Genl. Sydney Johnston,[15] I think that we could be *more* sure of success in that quarter. I have never seen a man in whom I had more confidence as a Military Chieftain than Genl. Joseph E. Johnston. I believe him equal to any emergency. Genl. Beauregard, in my estimation, is second to him.

Re-enlisting for the war has commenced in the army. The men are re-enlisting much more readily than I supposed they would. Before spring, I think that the majority of the 12-mo's men will re-enlist. The news of our recent disasters has aroused the men to some extent. It has caused, too, the Virginia Legislature to pass a Military Bill which provides for a draft, and many of the Virginians prefer enlisting under the Confederate to the Virginia Law.

No news here. I now hear very rapid and heavy firing in the direction of Evansport, but do not know the cause of it.[16]

I am expecting to hear from Lang & Ed in a day or two, & when I do, will write to Sis Frank. Hoping, Uncle Pleas, that you will write often, I remain,

Your Nephew Aff'ly.,
Thos. J. Goree

TO MARY FRANCES GOREE KITTRELL

My Dear Sister,   Centreville, Va., February [18,] 1862

I believe that I have recd. two letters, or rather postscripts, from you since last writing to you. I replied to Uncle Pleas' letter of the 17th ult. a few days since, in which one of your postscripts was contained.

I sometimes fear, Sis Frank, that I write to you all such long letters, so often, & so much sameness about them, that they have ceased to be interesting. Whilst I feel that it is my duty to write every week, I confess that I do so, not so often for the sake alone of performing that duty, but also for the purpose of inducing you all to write oftener than you would probably do otherwise.

Any letter from Texas, no matter how short, or on what subject, always affords me much pleasure and satisfaction. I know that some of my letters must be stale & uninteresting, for I often take up my pen to write, having no idea what I shall write about.

I recd. two or three days since your very nice present, the helmet or sentinel cap. It is a very nice present, and I feel under many obligations to you for it. It could not fit better than it does. Your letter to Langston & Edwin recd. at the same time was immediately forwarded to them. I am surprised that you do not receive letters from them regularly, as they assured me that one or the other of them wrote nearly every week. I think it would be better hereafter to direct your letters to them to Richmond. Direct as follows: viz. "Langston J. Goree, care Capt. J. C. Cleveland, Co. H., 5th Regiment Texas Vol., Richmond, Va." Arrangements, I think, have been made to get the mail from Richmond daily.

When I last wrote you I told you how well the boys were, and looked. I am sorry to inform you that when I last heard from them they were both sick.

I recd. a few days since from Dr. Breckenridge (who has been ordered to Manassas on Medical Examining Board) a note stating that when he left camp he "left Ed quite sick, & Lang complaining." He further said, "I am in daily expectation of hearing from a friend there in reference to them both. I will at once forward to you any news I may get of either of them."

As soon as I recd. this note I went over to Manassas to see Dr. Breckenridge. He said that Lang was not much sick, having had two light fevers when he left. He left him in his (Dr. B's) bed, having had him to come over and stay with him on account of his own cabin being crowded. He said that he was more uneasy about Ed, as he thought that he had all the symptoms of camp fever, but he further said that his affection for the boy may have caused him to have thought so. He assured me that he was well situated and attended to, being in a comfortable cabin with Capt. Cleveland. The Dr. thought that without there was a change for the worse in them I need apprehend no danger, and there would be no necessity for my going down.

I have recd. another note from Dr. Breckenridge in which he states that he has just recd. a letter from his young friend, Dr. Roberts,[17] whom he left Lang with, and who, he says, will be very watchful over Ed, altho' he is not attending to him.

Dr. R's letter was written two days after Dr. B. left, and says: "Lang still continues to improve & Ed was a great deal better when I saw him yesterday."

Dr. B. says: "This encourages me very much. If I get at any time any further information about either, I will let you know, of course, at once." Dr. Breckenridge seems to love them both, and has been very kind to them.

I wrote three days since, both to Langston and Capt. Cleveland, begging them to write how they were, and if either Lang or Ed was dangerously sick, to telegraph me at once. I have recd. nothing from them, and am consequently in hopes that their attacks are nothing serious. Both Capt. Cleveland & Dr. Woodson, as also Langston, promised faithfully to inform me at once in case of serious illness. I would go down anyhow, but that the roads are so dreadfully bad, my horse is still quite lame, and it is difficult for an officer to get leave for any length of time on account of the sad reverses to our arms. But I am satisfied that the General will give me leave in case of urgent necessity.

He himself has again gone to Richmond to visit his only surviving child (a lad about 12 years of age) who has taken a relapse and is at the point of death. I do sincerely hope that the little fellow may recover. It will be a very great blow to his parents if he, too, is taken from them.

It seems that our arms have met with many sad reverses this year. Since I have been writing this letter, news has reached us that we have sustained a terrible defeat at Fort Donelson in Tenn, that Genls. Pillow & Buckner, after making a desperate resistance have been captured with 8000 troops, Genl. Floyd making his escape with about 1000 men. We will anxiously await the particulars of this terrible disaster. I hope that it is not so bad as represented. If we are beaten there, our forces will be compelled to fall back from Bowling Green & Columbus.[18]

Affairs look very gloomy indeed in that quarter, but we must trust in Providence, Who, I cannot but believe, is on our side. We must not for one moment despond of our ultimate success, but must arouse ourselves to renewed exertions, determined to conquer or die. I know that I love life & the pleasures of it as well as anyone, but I feel, or pray to feel, willing if necessary to sacrifice it for the good of my country.

There must be more of such spirit among our troops before we can expect to succeed. We must determine to have no more Hatteras, Port Royal, Roanoke & Fort Henry affairs, every one of them an eternal disgrace to our arms. Henceforth, while we depend on Providence, we must also depend on our own strong arm. We must depend on fighting ourselves without waiting for succor from foreign nations. Those who are able and have not yet taken up arms amongst us, must do so at once. Those who are too old for active service must with the women stay at home and pray for our success. If a man cannot get a gun, he should arm himself with a tomahawk, pike or anything with which he can kill the invader. It is better to spend our all in defending our country than to be subjugated and have it taken away from us. *We can* and *we must* succeed. "Better to die free men, than to live slaves."

Tell Bob, that I have hitherto thought it best for him to remain at home, but that I now think it his duty to come to his country's rescue. I know that Mother will surely miss him, but she will have to depend on Uncle Pleas and *"Scrap,"* or probably she may get some one who is not able to stand the hardships of a campaign. I will write to Mother in a few days on the subject. At the same time I advise Bob to enter the service, I would insist that he should remain in Texas, and as near home as possible. Three of us are out of the state; that is enough. It is his duty to remain in the state *if possible.*

There is no news of special interest on our line. Re-enlisting is going on slowly. I have strong hopes that all of this army will re-enlist before their present term of service expires.

I saw Tom Moorman a few days since, the first time for several weeks. He looks well & is in fine health. I learned from him that Howson Kenner has joined a cavalry company, and gone down on the South Carolina coast. His wife is now living with Aunt Lucy. Tom says that Howson has quit drinking, but still refuses to have anything to do with his mother's business. Tom says, too, that if Aunt Lucy was not so patriotic and anxious to have Howson in the Army, she would not begin to submit to the present arrangement of having Howson's wife with her. Tom is waiting to hear from his father before re-enlisting.

I recd., Sis Frank, a "Telegraph," containing Judge Campbell's eulogy over Colonel Terry, also Judge Gray's[19] over Colonel Tom Lubbock. They were both very fine & affecting. If there were two men in no wise related to me, whom I really love, Frank Terry and Tom Lubbock were those men. They were noble, generous & brave. If we are to be subjugated, happy and fortunate are they that they did not live to witness it.

I thought, Sis Frank, when I commenced this, that I would give you some idea of how I am situated, & how we live, etc., but have not room. I will state, however, that I am comfortable and pleasantly situated, & have as yet been exposed to none of the hardships incident to a soldier's life. My position is as desirable as I could, or would, possibly have it. I sometimes think, however, that I would really be happier if in the ranks with Lang and Ed, where I could live as they do, and see & be with them daily, & share the hardships of a private soldier.

But I feel more reconciled after visiting and seeing that they are comfortably situated, & happy & contented. They are general favorites, and being so young, do not have to undergo so many hardships. I shall strive, though, to render their situation as desirable as possible.

I have written you, Sister Frank, a long letter which will probably tire you. Give my best love to Mother, Grandma, & all the others, white and black. Kiss the little children for me, and pray for us daily.

Affectionately your Brother,
Thos. J. Goree

TO SARAH WILLIAMS KITTRELL GOREE

Hd Qurts 2d Division A. P.
Near Centreville, Va., Feb'ry 21st 1862

My Dearest Mother,

It has been only a day or two since I wrote a long letter to Sister Frank, but knowing that you would feel very uneasy after what I wrote about Langston & Edwin, I take this opportunity of enclosing to you a letter that I have just this moment recd. from Langston. It was written some ten days since, but several days after Dr. Breckenridge's letter was written from there.

It is only 20 miles from this to Dumfries, but it takes a letter by mail generally 8 or 10 days to come that distance. You will see from Lang's letter, that he is again well, and that Ed is up and about. It has, I assure you, relieved my mind of a great load of anxiety. I hope, Mother, that you will all write to the boys often, for it will do them a great deal of good. I should like to hear from home every week, but if you cannot write to us both that often, write to them, and neglect me. You will hear from them by Capt. Cleveland before the reception of this.

We all here feel very badly about our defeat at Fort Donelson, and am anxiously awaiting to hear the full particulars in regard to the affair.[20] It is certainly a severe blow to our cause, but we should not be too despondent about it. By exerting ourselves we can yet check the enemy in that quarter, but it is necessary that we should put forth all our energies. Every man who is able to bear arms should now take the field, and, Mother, I think it best that you should no longer keep Bob at home.

I know that it will be hard to do without him, and that you will feel the want of his presence at home very much, but it is a sacrifice that you will have to make, and probably the sooner the better. I do not want him, though, to leave the state, but let him get into service as near home as possible.

Possibly if some new company is being formed in the neighborhood, he might get a lieutenancy in it, if not, he had better join some of the 12-months companies on the coast. I advise this course, so that if at any time an actual necessity should arise for his presence at home, he will be more convenient, etc. I would suggest Capt. Gillespie's[21] as a very good Co.

I wrote Bob several weeks since, and am daily expecting a reply to my letter. When he writes he must tell me what excuse he now makes to visit Madison. I am in hopes, Mother, that you will be blessed with a good crop this year. I regret very much to hear of the long continued drought, for I fear that it may have an injurious effect on the crops.

I hope that a good Providence has ere this sent refreshing showers to you all. The weather here this winter, although not of the coldest, has been very disagreeable. For a day or two it snows, then a day or two of clear cold weather, then a thaw, & then rain, sleet or snow, and so on.

As the courier is waiting to carry this to the P. O., I shall have to close with a promise to write you again soon. Give my love to Bob, Pleasant & Sudy & all the negroes. Also to Grandma, & all Uncle Pleas' family, . . . and his family, and all other friends.

Hoping to hear from you soon, I remain,

Your ever aff. son,
Thos. J. Goree

TO SARAH WILLIAMS KITTRELL GOREE

Headquarters 2nd Division A. P.
My Dearest Mother,   Centreville, Virginia, March 1st 1862

Several days having elapsed since I last wrote you, I have concluded this morning to write you a few lines. We are yet in such a state of inactivity here that I have nothing to do, and no other way to employ & amuse myself than in writing to my relatives and friends. Hence the cause of my writing to you all so very often. I try to make good use of my idle time in this way for when active operations commence again, I will probably not have time to write often.

All the indications now tend to show that the Army of the Potomac will not remain idle much longer, or rather, that the army of the enemy in front of us is about to make some movement that will arouse us from our inactivity.

What this movement is I do not know, but it is reported that Genl. McClellan is about to move a column of forty or fifty thousand men against Genl. Jackson at Winchester in order to turn our left flank, and thereby get in the rear of this army.[22]

In order to be prepared for this, or any other movement on the part of the enemy, Genl. Johnston has ordered all the heavy baggage and all the sick, to be sent to the rear, and has the army in good marching order.

It is not *positively* known whether the large force of the enemy, which has crossed the Potomac above Winchester, is intended to attack Genl. Jackson at Winchester, or whether it is only for the purpose of repairing and reopening the Baltimore & Ohio Railroad.

Should it be to attack Jackson, and the attacking force be a very large one, I am *afraid of the result,* for although Genl. Jackson is one of our best generals, and has an army of veterans, yet his force at best is but a small one, and it has been reduced very much by cold and exposure this winter.

Genl. Jackson has been trying this winter to carry on a winter campaign in which he has succeeded very well but at a tremendous cost of life. Although he has not fought a battle, yet, out of his army of 10 or 12,000 men he is said to have lost more from exposure than we lost in the battle of Manassas. I suppose that now he has a force of not more than 6000 effective men. It is probable that if he be attacked, all the forces that can be spared from here will be sent to reinforce him, for, if he is defeated it will be then absolutely necessary for us to evacuate and give up our present line of defense and form a new line somewhere between this and Richmond.

McClellan knows that he can never attack us sucessfully here, and it is *very* likely that he will attempt a flank movement. But I think that Genl. Joe Johnston will always be ready to thwart his plans in some way. I would feel very much disappointed, as well as mortified and chagrined, if he should suffer himself to be so completely out-generaled as Genl. Sydney Johnston has been in the West.

If, however, he should be, he will certainly be more excusable than Genl. Sydney Johnston, for the latter genl. has had his own way in everything, having authority to make any movement he pleases, as also to call on the different governors for any number of troops that he should want.

With Genl. Joe Johnston it has been just the other way, the President having given him but very little discretion in anything. After the battle of Manassas he and Genl. Beauregard called for only 15,000 more troops so as to commence offensive operations. They were refused.

After we fell back to this point, they proposed a system of furloughs by which our whole army nearly could have been furloughed and back at their posts. *This was overruled.* And now, when more than any other time we need all our men, [many of them] are away, and I doubt whether in the Army of the Potomac there are more than 20 or 25,000 men present for duty. This army should have at least 75,000 effective men to make a successful campaign.

I have almost come to the conclusion that the fate of the Country depends on our success. We shall all feel that it does anyhow, and shall consequently conduct ourselves as becomes the veterans who fought and won the battles of Bull Run & Manassas.

You will never, I hope, hear of any such disgraceful conduct in this army, as has characterized our arms at Hatteras, Port Royal, Somerset, Roanoke, Henry, and Donelson. Great indignation is felt here that 12,000 men at Donelson, with good fortifications, should have surrendered to a force of only 28 or 30,000 men.

We once boasted that one Southerner could whip three Yankees in a fair fight, but the result of that fight does not prove it. If the place *was* untenable, why could not the whole force have made their escape as well as those that *did* get away with Pillow & Floyd? I expect the *truth* of the matter is that Pillow and Floyd ran off and left Buckner. And Buckner, finding his troops completely demoralized on this account, was bound to surrender. All who know Buckner feel satisfied that he can give some reason for his course. He is said to be a brave man, and a splendid officer, a better man than Pillow and Floyd put together.

It's said that Genl. Buckner had proposed a system of fortifications on the Cumberland and Tennessee rivers, which, if Genl. Johnston had adopted, would have saved us our terrible defeats there.

But I expect, Mother, you are tired of military affairs. I recd. a letter from Langston [and Eddy a few days] since. Both he and Ed were quite well. Col. Robertson[23] wrote me at the same time that they were well, and that he had prevented Ed from doing any duty until he had entirely recovered his strength from his late attack.

I wrote not long since to Cousin Protheus Jones in order to find out if his son was anywhere in this army. Cousin Protheus was not at home, but his daughter, Cousin Lucy Jones, answered my letter, extending a very cordial invitation to visit them. I enclose her letter in this. I had intended to apply for a furlough for a few days in order to visit them, but all furloughs are now stopped, and besides I would not leave my post if I could get leave while there is the least chance for any active work. If, however, affairs here should become quiet, I shall try to go down for a short time. I believe that it is only 10 or 12 hours travel from Richmond.

I believe, Mother, that I have given you all the news of interest. I will write every week to some of you, and try and keep you posted, provided communication between this and Texas is not cut off, as it will be if Genl. Sydney Johnston retreats much farther. In the meantime you must all write as often as possible. Give my love to all.

> Your affectionate Son,
> Thos. J. Goree

TO SARAH WILLIAMS KITTRELL GOREE

My Dearest Mother,   Orange CH, Va., March 23rd 1862

Your kind letter of Feb'ry 19th has just been received. The one written at the same time that Bob's was, was received a day or two before we left Centreville. I have this morning mailed your letter to Langston & Edwin, who, I learn, are in the vicinity of Fredericksburg. At least their regiment is near there, and I hope that they are with it.

I am very anxious indeed to hear from them as to how their health is, and how they stood the fatigues & hardships of the march. They, however, had but a short distance to march, say some 30 miles. I think not farther than that.

Our division had about 80 miles to march. We came a very round about way in order to avoid the bad roads. Lang & Ed are about 35 or 40 miles from here. I am very anxious indeed to ride down to see them, but no leaves at all are granted at this time. I shall, however, write to them often, and try and keep you posted as to their health, etc.

We have heard nothing yet from the box of clothing you sent us, and I very much fear that we never shall. Government has almost exclusive control of the railroads, and it is with great difficulty that anything but government stores can be transported over them without it in the personal care of someone coming over. Try and get the express receipt, and if the box is lost the express co. must be held responsible for it. I should like to know how the box was directed, and to what point sent.

I have been quite unfortunate in the way of losing things. After receiving my commission I ordered a nice uniform, coat, pants, hat, etc., and asked a gentleman to bring them up from Richmond for me. But, instead of attending to it himself, he got some one else to attend to it, and the consequence is that the trunk containing the uniform and other things belonging to the gentleman who was to bring it has been lost, and I have very little hopes of ever finding it. If I do not find it, my loss will be about $90.–. I was a good deal put out about it, as the man could have brought it along with him as easily as not, and he had things in the trunk himself.

When I last wrote you I told you that we would probably fall back from Centreville to Gordonsville, & the causes which induced the retrograde movement. You see that I was not far wrong. We have not exactly gone to Gordonsville, but are only 9 or 10 miles from that place. The main body of our army is around this place, our right will be about Fredericksburg, and our left probably at Staunton.

True, that in falling back we have been compelled to give up a very large and rich portion of Virginia, yet, nothwithstanding I think the move was a wise one. McClellan would have never fought us at Centreville or Manassas, but would have tried to flank us at a distance in which, if he had succeeded, he could have gotten in our rear and cut off communication from Richmond, which would have ruined us.

At Centreville our line was so extended, and the roads so bad, that we could not have thrown reinforcements from one point to another with any facility. And more than all, our army was in such a disorganized condition that it would have been impossible to have reorganized it in such close proximity to the enemy. There are doubtless other causes which influenced Genl. Johnston in the movement, but these are the principal ones which have occurred to me.

At this point we can very readily reorganize our forces. We are in a position to reinforce rapidly the right or left as the case may be. We can with little trouble send reinforcements to Genl. Magruder at Yorktown, or Genl. Huger[24] at Norfolk, or in nearly any other direction. We are nearer, too, our supplies at Richmond.

It was a very serious undertaking to move such an army as ours even the very short distance to this place. You can form no idea of the amount of stores, etc. that could not be moved back, and which it was necessary to destroy, not only public but private stores. There was at least one million dollars worth of heavy baggage belonging to the soldiers which it was impossible to get away.

We burned several thousand barrels of flour, a great deal of corn, hay, etc., and at least one million pounds of bacon, and many other things too tedious to mention. Before destroying it, the citizens were allowed to come in and help themselves.

The authorities at Richmond are to blame for permitting such a vast amount of stores to accumulate upon us. Genl. Johnston remonstrated against it time and again, but they paid no attention to him. Just think, if we lost so much when we took our time to move, how much would we have lost had the enemy been pressing upon us? We marched back very leisurely, were some ten days enroute from Centreville to this place, a direct distance of about sixty miles.

I had quite a hard time on the march, as I had to convey orders along our line several times during the day, which was quite a job, as from the head to the rear of our division was 4 or 5 miles. The train of wagons belonging to our division was at least three miles in length.

Although we had a great deal of bad weather on the march, yet we had but very little sickness, not one fifth as much as we usually had at Centreville, and it is a singular fact that troops marching & moving about are not near so apt to be sick as when they remain stationary.

Everything is very quiet now, but I do not know how long they will be so. The impression now is that the enemy will not attack us here, but will more probably move against Fredericksburg. Our division is encamped on the direct road to that place, and can move on very short notice.

Our army is in fine spirits, and do not seem at all discouraged at our late reverses. I have not time to write more now, but will write soon to Sis Frank. Give my best love to all, and write soon to

Your aff. Son,
Thos. J. Goree

Direct letters to me to Orange Court House, care Genl. Longstreet, and letters to Lang & Ed direct to Fredericksburg.

TO SARAH WILLIAMS KITTRELL GOREE

Headquarters, Central Forces, Army of Peninsula
Near Yorktown, Va., April 22nd 1862

My Dearest Mother,

I wrote you about a week since from Richmond enclosing my Ambrotype, but whether you receive it or not is a question, as I see that the enemy have taken possession of the railroad at Huntsville, Alabama, & other places. I will, however, continue to write often hoping that my letters will find their way to you in some way.

We left Richmond on last Wednesday for this place. Came down within ten miles from here on the James River in boats. Genl. G. W. Smith's Division which left Ashland a day or two before we left Richmond, and marched down by land, reached [*several words illegible*] two or three days since. [The Texas Brigade] is encamped only about one and a half miles from our Hd Qutrs.

I have been over twice to see the boys, and was very much pleased to find them both in the enjoyment of good health. The poor boys, though, have recently had quite a rough time of it, having to foot it all the way from Fredericksburg to this place. I find, too, that they were out in all that wet and sleety weather which we had some two weeks since. They had no tents, and were for one night without their blankets. They both, however, seem very cheerful and contented. Notwithstanding the exposure to which the regiment has been subjected, the health of it is much better than it has ever been.

The boys tell me that they found Dr. Breckenridge quite a friend to them on the march, as he would every day take their guns and carry them in his ambulance, which was quite a relief to them. They tell me, too, that he calls around every night to see them, to find out how they are. I told the boys if they needed anything to let me know, and I would get it for them, but they said that they needed nothing but an oilcloth, that they had about $40.00 apiece, and more due them. I will get the oilcloth as soon as I can.

We are now about organized and ready and more than eager for the fray. We have been daily expecting McClellan to make an attack, but he has not done so. Our lines are very close to each other, and the enemy keeps up a pretty constant fire with their artillery & sharpshooters. They are not doing us much damage. Occasionally some of our men are killed by them, who carelessly expose themselves. On account of the scarcity of our ammunition, we very seldom return their fire.

The day that we reached here there was quite a sharp skirmish in which our loss was about 80 killed and wounded; that of the enemy was considerably more. We buried about 40 of their dead, and as a general thing the wounded are about three times the number killed.[25]

I do not know what Genl. Johnston's plans are, but I suppose that if McClellan does not attack soon, we will. I do not much like this country for a battle, there is so little open country. It is generally a thickety, swampy country.

Genl. Johnston is in command of all the forces here. Genl. Magruder commands on the right of our line, Genl. D. H. Hill at Yorktown on the left, Genl. Longstreet the centre, and Genl. G. W. Smith the reserve. The Texas Brigade[26] is in the reserve. I am glad of this, as the boys will not have to perform duty in the trenches, which is very disagreeable. And when the fight takes place, it may be, that it will not be necessary for them to take part in it at all.

Our division has in it now some five or six brigades under Genls. A. P. Hill, R. H. Anderson, Pickett, Colston, Wilcox, and Col. Jno. A. Winston.[27] Some of our troops occupy the same ground, or a portion of that, which Genl. Washington did previous to the surrender of Cornwallis. Our Hd Qurts in 100 yards of Washington's old breastworks. I feel that the fate of Va., if not the Confederacy, depends on the result of this fight. We must win it, or all is lost. I will not say all is lost, but it will be very hard for us to recover from a defeat here.

I fear that McClellan may not fight us here after all. That having drawn our whole army here, he may attempt to leave us and try some other route to Richmond. But Genl. Johnston will be up with him. Our plan evidently is to concentrate and fight McClellan with all our forces, and stake all on one great battle.

It may be that the bad weather which we are now having is preventing McClellan from commencing the attack, for the last three days it has been raining, and it is terrible on our troops; particularly those who have had to be in the trenches in mud and water without fire. If a fire were kindled in the trenches, the enemy would be sure to throw a shell at it.

McClellan has several large gunboats on the York River to cooperate with his land forces. These are, no doubt, intended to be used against the works at Yorktown. I dread them more than all his land forces. While I write, I can hear the roar from their heavy guns as they are endeavouring to throw shells into Yorktown. They threw one a few days since which failed to explode. It was an oblong shell, 19 inches long, 6 inches in diameter, and weighed about 120 pounds.

As there is no other news of interest I will close. Give my best love to all. Langston and Ed also send much love. Write soon. Your letters had better be sent to Richmond. I can get them from there. I will write again soon.

Your aff. Son,
Thos. J. Goree

TO SARAH WILLIAMS KITTRELL GOREE

Headquarters 2d Corps, Camp Near Richmond, May 28th 1862
My dearest Mother,

For two weeks I have had a letter in my pocket ready to send you by the first opportunity but having met with none I have concluded today to write you a few lines more and send with it. I am just in receipt of your letter brought by Capt. Cleveland, received just two months after it was written, but I assure you it was read with as much pleasure as if it had been written two weeks since. The letter enclosed with this was written when we were beyond the Chickahominy. We waited there for a week for an attack from McClelland, but he showed no disposition to meet us. On account of the James River being open to the enemy's gun boats, we had to fall back to the front of Richmond, where we now are in daily expectation of the grand battle. Skirmishes are of daily occurrence, but they do not amount to much. Yesterday there was quite a severe fight above here in which Genl. Branch's command from North Carolina was engaged on our side.[28] What the result of it was I have not yet been able to learn. Genl. Branch was on his way down from the direction of Fredericksburg to join us here and I suppose he was intercepted in his march by the enemy.

We have quite cheering news from the Valley of Virginia. Genl. Jackson it seems has been doing good work there and there is good reason to believe that he may soon cross over into Maryland.[29]

The great fight has soon to come off here and as it has to come, I hope that it will not be much longer delayed. As soon as Genl. J. R. Andersons's[30] & Genl. Branch's commands from the direction of Fredericksburg reach here we will be as well prepared as we can expect to be. These commands will number together 12 or 14,000 men.

Genl. A. P. Hill (whom I mention in my other letter as commanding Genl. Long-street's old brigade at Williamsburg)[31] has just been appointed Major General to take command of this Fredericksburg force. As soon as this force reaches us, I think we will not wait much longer for the enemy to attack us.

I saw Langston & Ed both a few days ago. Ed returned to camp some four or five days since. He is very well with the exception of a bad cold which we all have. Ed was very much distressed that he missed being in the little fight the Texans had on the way up here.[32] He blames Lang for getting sick & causing him to be absent. Ed says he was so well fixed in Richmond that he would not have come away had he not been afraid of missing another fight. Lang is still in Richmond, very comfortably situated indeed. He is looking much better than he was before he was sick. He would have returned before this to camp but having taken fresh cold the Dr. thought it best for him to stay a while longer. I was glad to find him at such a good place. The people with whom he is staying could not be kinder to him than they are. He is with a good Baptist family. The physician who took charge of him when he went to Richmond is boarding at the same place with his wife. They are both very kind to him. Lang & Ed both seem to be pets with them all. They have kindly invited both of them if they get sick again or wounded to come back to their house and they would nurse and take care of them. One of the ladies boarding there told Lang to write you that you deserved a great deal of credit for raising two such boys as himself & Ed. Lang told her that you had been told so before, but she said you had never been told so by a *Virginia* lady.

I was very sorry to hear of the death of poor young Sam Houston.[33] I expect it will almost kill his poor parents. Mart Royston[34] wrote to his brother, Young Roys-ton,[35] that the last time he was seen he had been shot through the thigh and was still shooting at the enemy. *He was a brave boy.* Young Royston is Lt. Col. of Col. Jno. A. Winston's Regiment which is in Genl. Longstreet's Division. Col. Winston & he are both fine officers.

I received the socks by Capt. Cleveland, for which I am very much obliged. The General returns you many thanks for the pair sent him.

If you have an opportunity of sending to Houston, Mother, I *would* like that you would send down and get my things there. They will be much safer at home than there. Please give my best love to all, & write every chance you have.[36]

I Am Your Aff Son
Thos. J. Goree

TO MARY FRANCES GOREE KITTRELL

My Dear Sister,
Headquarters Gen. Longstreet's Corps
Near Richmond, June 17th, 1862

Your truly welcome letter of the 11th has been received, and I am happy to state found us all alive and in the enjoyment of excellent health. Langston has entirely recovered from his attack of pneumonia, and has been with his regt. for about two weeks. I saw both him and Ed a little more than a week since. A day or two after I was over to see them, the division to which they belong was ordered into the Valley to reinforce Genl. Jackson, and had gone off before I even knew that it had been ordered to go. I should have liked very much to have seen the boys before they went off. I gave them your letter, however, when I was *last* over to see them. I hope that they will have a good time in the Valley, and escape all the accidents of battle, and keep in enjoyments of good health. The Texas Brigade has gone to a field where it will have every opportunity to win laurels for itself, and I have no doubt *will* do it.

Well, Sis Frank, I have been in another great battle, and a kind Providence has again protected and brought me out unhurt. The battle of "Seven Pines," fought seven miles from Richmond on 31st May & June 1st, is only second to "Shiloh" in magnitude.[37] It was a victory, but not a complete one, because it was not followed up.

A few days previous to the battle the enemy had crossed over the Chickahominy with a force of about 20,000 men. Genl. Johnston determined to attack these with view of destroying them if possible, and if that failed, then to bring on a general engagement.

The plan was for Genl. Longstreet with two of his divisions (his own old division, & D. H. Hill's) to attack the enemy in front on the Williamsburg road with vigor. This part of the plan was carried out with the greatest success.

Genl. Longstreet's 3rd. Division (Huger's) was to go down the Charles City road and turn the enemy's left flank. For this purpose he was ordered to be in position by sun up. From some inexplicable cause he did not commence to move his troops until 11 or 12 o'clock A.M. and was at least six hours behind time, & the consequence was that the attack, which was intended should be made at 8 o'clock A.M. was not begun until near 2 o'clock P.M., entirely too late for Genl. Huger to attack the enemy's left flank. So, that part of the programme had to be abandoned.

Gen. Whiting with his division was ordered down the 9-mile Road, which is to the left of the Williamsburg Road, and comes into it at the "Seven Pines." The road which Genl. Huger was to have taken also came in about the "Seven Pines."

Genl. Longstreet was placed in command of the whole with the exception of Whiting, who was expected to be under the eyes of Genls. Johnston & Smith, but to act in concert with Genl. Longstreet.

At about 2 o'clock P.M. Genl. Longstreet commenced the attack in front with Major Genl. D. H. Hill's Division. The fighting was the most terrible I ever witnessed. The enemy had felled a great deal of timber over which our men had to advance, and at the farther side of this felled timber they had a fort and breast-works.

Hill's Division soon took them with 6 or 7 pieces of artillery, but about this time the enemy were heavily reinforced, and it seemed very probable that they would retake their works. At this juncture Genl. Longstreet brought up his old division, under Genl. Anderson ("Longstreet's Veterans," as the Yankees called them).

Then the fighting commenced in earnest.

Such a rattle of musketry I never expect to hear again. At every discharge scores of our men were put *hors de combat,* but still our veterans pressed on, whipping fresh reinforcements at every point.

To show how terrible the fire was, here I will mention that the 1st. Virginia Regt. went in with only about 80 men, and of this number it lost about 40. The 11th Virginia also lost nearly half that it carried in.

Dearing's[38] battery, which was sent up near this point, lost 22 out of 36 men, besides some 40 horses.

Our men still pressed on, and long before sundown this part of the field was cleared of living Yankees. Genl. Anderson's S.C. Brigade under Col. Jenkins (Genl. Anderson being temporarily in command of a Division) *immortalized* itself.

Col. Jenkins carried the brigade into action about 3 o'clock P.M., a little further to the left of where Genl. D. H. Hill was engaged. From this time until night he fought unsupported and alone, and advancing all the time. He fought 5 separate & distinct lines of the enemy, whipping each one. He whipped the whole of Genl. Couch's Division,[39] consisting of 12 or 15 regiments, with a little brigade of 1900 men. He passed over several abattis of felled timber, 2 lines of breastworks, cap-tured three pieces of artillery, 250 prisoners, & several stands of colors.

He whipped the fifth line of the enemy at about 3 O'clock P.M. At that time he was near two miles in advance of anyone else. His brigade rested that night in a Massachusetts camp, and had every luxury nearly that you can imagine: a plenty of brandy, lemons, & preserved fruits of all sorts, oil clothes, boots and shoes, opera glasses, etc. etc. etc.

The Yankee prisoners were perfectly surprised when they found he had accom-plished so much with only one little brigade. They told him that every line he met was composed of fresh troops, and that they thought he was receiving reinforce-ments all the time.

Genl. Longstreet was very much surprised, too, when Col. Jenkins came in at night, and reported where his brigade was.

This brigade went into action with 1900 men. It lost 700 killed & wounded, & among this number was more than half of its field officers, and near one third of the line officers. But, it never faltered, nor even stopped. It advanced slowly but steadily for more than two miles, all the time in the face of a galling fire, and nearly all the way over felled timber & the enemy's breastworks.

During all this time when this terrible fighting was progressing in front, we anxiously listened for Genl. Whiting to attack on the left, but we waited a long time without hearing from him. Finally, just before sundown he made the attack with three Brigades (Hatton's,[40] Pettigrew's[41] & Hampton's[42]). He had before sent the Texas Brigade over in the direction we were expecting he would then have the hardest fighting, but Jenkins had gone in ahead of them & cleaned out that part of the field. The battle raged with great fury for a short time on that part of the field. Very few of Whiting's[43] men had been under fire before, the enemy had a good position, [and] the attack was not made so vigorously as ours. The most of Whiting's men behaved badly and were repulsed with a considerable loss of officers & men.

Genl. Johnston was on this part of the field, and although he did not expect to assume command, yet I think that when he saw how things were going there, he took command of that part of the field.

Had our men then gone forward (as they ought to have done), Genl. Johnston would not have been exposed, but as they fell back in the direction he was, he would not retire, & consequently came under fire. He was very severely, though not dangerously wounded. The ball went in about the shoulder

[*Pages 9 and 10 of the letter are missing here.*]

commenced the attack on us with great vigor. Huger's troops, never having been under the fire before, when the order was given to charge, turned and charged back the wrong way. This was another critical moment. However, Genl. Mahone[44] of Huger's Division succeeded in rallying his Brigade, & Genls. Pickett[45] & Wilcox,[46] & Colston[47] or Pryor,[48] commanding brigades of *"Longstreet's Veterans"* coming up, repulsed the enemy, & were driving him before them, when they were ordered to fall [back] a short distance. This order was given when the battle was very closely contested, but was not received by the Brigadiers until after they had the enemy on retreat along the whole line.

The order was given by Genl. D. H. Hill, and it was unfortunate, for it is only on that "fall back" that the enemy make any pretense to a victory. They say that they were badly [*several words illegible*] Saturday.

Their reserve Corps under Sumner[49] came up and snatched away the laurels that the *"rebels"* had won.

We retained possession of the battle field all day Sunday until Monday morning, the enemy keeping very quiet and making no demonstrations of another attack after the repulse they recd on Sunday morning.

Genl. Lee was placed in command of the Army on Sunday evening and ordered the withdrawal of our forces to the positions they occupied before the battle.

It was a very great pity that the fight was not begun 6 hours earlier on Saturday as we would then have finished it that night, and it is also a great pity that Genl. Johnston was wounded as it was his intention to reinforce us and push the attack the next morning. Genl. Lee would have done the same had he been placed in command a few hours sooner.

Our loss in killed, wounded and missing is between 4 and 5000, but that of the enemy much greater. They already acknowledge a loss of 7500, and I believe that it is much more than that.

Our loss in field officers is very heavy. On our part of the field Genl. Rodes[50] was wounded. On Genl. Whiting's part of the field, Genls. Johnston, Hampton &

Pettigrew were wounded, & Genl. Hatton killed. The prisoners taken by the enemy (some 250), were nearly all from this part. Hampton's Legion, SC Troops, in Whiting's Division behaved very gallantly. They lost nearly one half. For the time & the numbers engaged, the battle of "Seven Pines" was the most sanguinary of the war.

Rodes' Brigade, consisting of 3 Ala & 1 Miss Regts., lost over 1000 killed & wounded. Len Abercrombie[51] belonged to the 6th Ala in this Brigade, & was killed. John White, who also belongs to it, was wounded, shot through the thigh.

You know Col. Syd Moore.[52] He is Col. of the 11th Ala in Wilcox's Brigade. He acted very gallantly. He was struck once, just on his watch, which saved his life. Soon afterwards he was shot through the leg, breaking the small bone in the lower part of his leg. He, however, stayed with his Regt. for some time, when his horse was killed from under him.

Col. Jno. A. Winston & Lt. Col. Young Royston of the 8th Ala behaved well; neither hurt. Capt. Tom Phelan, 8th Ala, slightly wounded; Captain Wat Phelan, 3rd Ala, severely wounded; Col. Tennent Lomax,[53] 3rd Ala, killed.

The 4th Ala was under Whiting, though I do not think it suffered much. David Scott & Ed Goree are unhurt.

I tell you, Sis Frank, war is indeed a terrible thing. You have no idea of how one feels when he sees persons cold in death on the field, or being borne away wounded, with whom but a few hours before he was talking & laughing.

I recollect one instance. On Saturday, just before the battle commenced, I was riding along with Capt Weem (Genl. Garland's[54] Adj. Genl.) and was laughing heartily at him for letting his horse throw him. I saw him a few hours afterwards a corpse, shot through the head with a minnie ball.

If I had time or paper, I should like to give you a great many incidents of the battle, but I already tire you. I will, however, give one.

A few days previous to the battle, Genl. Longstreet presented to Col. Jenkins' Regt. ("Palmetto Sharpshooters") a battle flag. A noble, manly fellow was the color bearer. In the fight he was shot down; as Col. Jenkins rode by where he was lying he raised himself on his elbow & exclaimed: "For God's sake, Colonel, take care of my flag."

This flag has 9 bullet holes in it. It had a guard of 12 men, 10 of them were killed & wounded. This flag, at one time, changed hands 4 times in 3 minutes without falling to the ground. It now has inscribed on it "Williamsburg" & "Seven Pines."

As I have mentioned Williamsburg, I will here say that I hear from the authority that I have been promoted from Lt. to Captain, the commission to date back to the 5th May when the battle was fought.

Genl. Stuart has just returned from a successful expedition with his cavalry, accounts of which you will see in the papers.[55] He went all around McClellan's army, capturing many prisoners & horses, destroying 3 transports, over 100 wagons loaded with supplies, railroad telegraph wires, etc. It was the most daring feat of the war.

McClellan, it is thought, has commenced a regular siege, and will attempt to take Richmond by regular approaches. Genl. Longstreet attacked his advance post two days since in hopes of drawing him out & bringing on a general engagement, but he wouldn't take the dare.

But I will say no more of war matters, for I know that you are tired. When I commenced writing I had no idea of writing so much, but I think I could write as much more.

I received a letter a few days since from Cousin Mary Goree & her little girl (Mollie). Don was wounded in the foot at the battle of "Shiloh." She says that they are burning all their cotton on the river to keep it from the enemy. Cousin James is busy all the time visiting the sick, as he is the only Dr. left. All are well there.

I also recd. a letter a day or two since from Cousin Protheus Jones' wife, inquiring about myself, brothers, & David Scott, saying, that if any of us are sick, or are wounded, to come right there, & she & her daughters would take the greatest pleasure in nursing & taking care of us. She said that her husband would have written, but that he had been absent nearly all the time for three months on business for the government.

I have written this letter to you, Sis Frank, but it will answer for all. How or when you will receive it, I do not know. I would have written sooner, had I thought I could have gotten it off.

I hope that you will all write by every opportunity. Write me at Richmond. You had best send letters to the boys to the care of the Texas Depot at Richmond.

You mention that some of your negroes had run away. Which ones are they? I feel anxious & uneasy, Mother, about you and your business since Bob has left. I pray God that He may take care of the widow & the orphans. Write me how everything gets on, and also where Bob is, what regt., and what point the regt. is at.

Give my love to Mother & the children, Grandma, Uncle Pleas, all the children & negroes, & all enquiring friends. Dr. Campbell is in Richmond, but I have not seen him for some time. His brothers, Archy & Doug,[56] are both sick there, and he is waiting on them. Capt. Powell is also quite sick there, & I have just heard that Creed Woodson is, too. I rarely get a chance to go anywhere, but will try and go to see them as soon as possible.

Your Brother Affly.,

Thos. J. Goree

TO SARAH WILLIAMS KITTRELL GOREE

Genl. Longstreet's Corps, Near Richmond, Virginia,

July 21st, 1862

My Dearest Mother,

I should have written you a few lines immediately after the recent battles to have allayed the anxiety and uneasiness that I knew you would naturally feel about us, but Ed told me that, having an opportunity, he had written to you, so I concluded to wait until I had time and opportunity to write you a longer letter. At the time that Ed wrote you we were all some twenty five miles from Richmond, near where we had driven the enemy under cover of their gunboats. It was deemed inexpedient to attack him in his new position, so our whole army was again drawn back to the vicinity of Richmond, where the larger portion of it still is. The short but trying campaign through which we all went, completely used me up, and I was quite sick for a day or two after my return, but a few days' rest brought me up again and I am now in the enjoyment of excellent health. I saw Lang & Ed a day or two since and they are also both very well.

Mother, I cannot feel thankful enough that myself and noble brothers have come out from the recent terrible conflicts unscathed. A kind Providence has undoubtedly interfered in our behalf and preserved us from death. The prayers of a devoted Mother and other loved ones at home have undoubtedly been heard and answered from on High. May the good Lord continue to hearken to those supplications which daily arise is my sincere prayer.

It is very much to be regretted that we were not able in the recent conflict to capture or [*one word illegible*] McClellan's grand army as to have rendered it impossible for it to have recovered from it, but while in this we unfortunately failed. McClellan [*several words illegible*] badly whipped, and his army much demoralized [*several words illegible*] but notwithstanding all this, his retreat was [*word illegible*] and it was well conducted. This was due not to his ability as a general, but rather to the inefficiency of some and shortcomings of others of *our* generals. The inefficiency of Huger & Magruder was no doubt the cause of our failure to render the victory as decisive as could be wished. The whole plan of the campaign as proposed by Genl. Lee was most excellent, and had it been executed, the result would have been glorious. I will not attempt to give a full account of the several battles fought (as the newspapers will be full of these (none of which, however, are correct)) but will only attempt to give you some idea of the plan proposed & the manner in which it was executed. Previous to the battle, our lines & forces were on this side of the Chickahominy. By examining some map you will see the nearest point this river is to Richmond (5 miles), also that from this point it runs gradually forth from Richmond. Well at this nearest point on the river was the left of our lines which consisted of Maj. Genl. A. P. Hill's Division. Our lines from that point extended to the right for 6 or 7 miles; each point of the line about 5 miles from Richmond. Magruder's Division occupied the center of our line & Huger's the right, Longstreet's & D. H. Hill's the reserve. The enemy had three Corps of their army (Summers—Keyes & Heintzleman's) on this side of the river opposite Magruder & Huger while their other two corps (Franklin's & Porter's) lay along the other side fronting A. P. Hill.

The enemy had so fortified themselves in the front & their left flank that but one move was left us & that was to try and turn their right on the other side of the Chickahominy. For this purpose Genl. Jackson with his troops was ordered down from the Valley to cooperate with the divisions of Longstreet, D. H. Hill & A. P. Hill, which were to cross over & their four divisions to constitute the attacking column beyond the river. The plan was for Genl. Jackson to come down from Hanover C. H. in the rear of the enemy's right wing & when he commenced the attack, then for A. P. Hill to cross at the Central R. R. crossing and drive the enemy below the Mechanicsville Turnpike Crossing on the river so that Longstreet and D. H. Hill's Div.'s could cross at that point & join in. I forgot to state that Huger & Magruder were to remain in their positions on this side to watch the movements of the enemy & prevent their coming into Richmond, also to follow them closely in case they attempted to retreat from this side [of the Chickahominy River].

By sunup on the morning of the 26th June, the divisions of Longstreet & the two Hills were in position, ready to perform their part so soon as we could hear Jackson's guns. He was to have commenced the attack at sunup. Hour after hour we impatiently waited for him to open fire. About four o'clock P.M. Genl. Lee (fearing the enemy might suspect what we were up to & prepare) deemed it advisable to wait no longer. So he ordered A. P. Hill to cross & attack, which he did and without much trouble drove the enemy before him to Beaver Dam Creek, about a mile below Mechanicsville.[57] Here they had fortifications & made a stand. This position [*several words illegible*] an attack in front. Hill followed closely and attacked them about sundown in this position. Genl. Longstreet reinforced him with Ripley's[58] Brigade of D. H. Hill's div. The battle raged furiously for near two hours, when we were repulsed with quite a heavy loss. Our heavy loss was occasioned by Gen. Ripley with his brigade attempting to charge the enemy's fortifications over an impassable creek & swamp immediately in front of them. He of course would not have done this had it not been too dark to see the nature of the ground.

During the night Genl. Longstreet's & D. H. Hill's Divisions crossed, & very early in the morning the attack was renewed by Wilcox's, Pryor's and Featherston's Brigades of Longstreet's Division. They were having quite a hot time of it, when luckily Jackson (just 24 hours behind time) came in on the right of the enemy, and they evacuated their position in hot haste. Jackson had been detained by high water & obstructions in the road. The enemy retired from Beaver Dam about three miles down the river, and took a very strong position on Powhite Creek. To this position he crossed over the larger portion of his force from the Richmond side of the river. From here McClellan telegraphed to President Lincoln that he had the rebels in a trap—nearly all of this (the north) side of the Chickahominy, that he (himself) had selected a very strong position in which he had placed 95,000 men and that he had every reason to believe that he could demolish the rebels and be in Richmond the next night.

In this strong position it was determined to attack the enemy. For this purpose Genl. A. P. Hill was ordered to commence the attack in the centre while Jackson & D. H. Hill, who had gone around, were to attack vigorously the enemy's right flank.[59] The enemy's left flank was posted in the strongest position. This (the left part of their line) was posted in the woods on a high hill; on the top & side of this hill they had erected breastworks & barricades of trees, fence rails, etc. Behind these their infantry was posted. In an open field behind these woods was their artillery. At the foot of the hill was a branch or creek, which was about 10 feet wide & 5 or 6 deep, the banks of which were almost perpendicular. On our side of the creek was an open field, some 7 or 800 yards wide. On the Richmond side of the Chickahominy in full view of this field the enemy had a fort in which they had heavy artillery. Troops attacking the enemy's left flank were exposed to three lines of fire from the enemy's infantry on the wooded hillside, and at the same time to showers of grape and canister from the artillery on the hill beyond, as also to shell from the heavy guns on the opposite side of river. Genl. Longstreet placed his division opposite this point, not to attack it but to divert them while Jackson & D. H. Hill turned their right flank. This (Longstreet's) division was intended as reserve.

About 2 or 3 P.M. A. P. Hill commenced the attack in the centre and not being supported in time by Jackson & D. H. Hill who had not attacked the enemy's right as soon as expected, he was pretty nearly whipped, and it was a very critical moment. The only hope was for Genl. Longstreet to move forward & make a successful attack [on] this strong position occupying the enemy's left wing. Genl. Lee gave orders to that effect, and Genl. Longstreet moved forward 4 brigades of his own div. & Whiting's Div., (in which is the Texas Brig) to make the attack. The charge of these troops through the open field was the grandest sight I ever saw. They advanced amid a perfect hail of minie balls, grape, canister & shell. Some of the brigades advanced steadily on, others wavered & fell back, but rallied & came again. The ranks of all were being terribly thinned. Finally the Texas Brigade crossed over. About the same time Pickett's & Wilcox's Brigades & then others [crossed]. The fighting still continued, some regiments of Whiting's Division fell back when Genl. Longstreet ordered forward his old South Carolina Brigade & Genl. Lee says that their advance & charge was the prettiest & grandest sight he ever saw or read of. The Texas Brigade which was on the left of Longstreet's line took several batteries & several hundred prisoners. The So. Ca. Brigade closed the fight on our right by capturing several hundred prisoners. During all this hard fighting by Longstreet's & Whiting's Divisions, Jackson & Hill came in on the left and carried every thing before them. Our loss in this fight was heavy but nothing to compare with that of the enemy.

That night the enemy crossed his forces to the south side of the Chickahominy. He went back minus several thousand killed & wounded, some 4000 prisoners & about 20 pieces of artillery. That night McClellan commenced his grand strategic movement.[60]

On the morning of the 28th we found ourselves in this position, viz. The larger portion of our army on the north side the river, the whole of McClellan's Army on the south side between us and Richmond, Huger & Magruder between them and Richmond. We were between them & the Pamunkey River, their base of operations. What was the next move? Would McClellan make one desperate struggle, & overpower Huger & Magruder, or would he attempt to retreat across to his gunboats on the James River? It had been thought probable that he would attempt to get to his gunboats, and Genl. Lee had ordered Genl. Huger to keep a close watch for such a movement and inform him of the earliest indications of it. In the meantime, Genl. Lee sent down and had the York River R. R. torn up and was making preparations to build bridges for crossing over in the rear of McClellan. The engineers were at work at it. Magruder during the day Saturday (28th) made an attack on the enemy, but finding them in strong force, retired to his position. Thus passed Saturday.

Saturday night Genl. Magruder wrote to Genl. Lee for reinforcements, as he expected to be attacked before morning. The next (Sunday morning) he wrote that the enemy were retreating down the Chickahominy. This was the first positive information Gen. Lee had recd not a word from Huger, although the cavalry officer who was watching the roads had reported that all the indications were that they were retreating. All the answer he recd was "watch them." So soon as Genl. Lee found they were on the retreat, he commenced making dispositions for pursuit. D. H. Hill & Jackson were to build a bridge across the river & press their rear. Magruder, who was already on the same side of the Enemy, was to pursue at once. Huger was ordered to the right down the Charles City road to attack them in flank, while Genl. Longstreet & A. P. Hill were to go still farther to the right on the Darbytown road to make a diversion in front, while Huger attacked the flank.

Magruder started in pursuit and caught up with the rear guard of the enemy about 3 or 4 miles from where he started. He fought them until night, killed wounded captured a great number. That night he was relieved by Jackson & Hill and sent round to report with his div. to Genl. Longstreet. On Monday the (30th) Genl. Longstreet came up with the enemy on the Darbytown road some 15 miles from Richmond. After waiting some time we heard Huger's artillery open quite briskly. Genl. Longstreet thinking that he (Huger) was well engaged with the enemy, sent forward to make the attack in our front. As soon as we fired the first gun, the enemy, who had selected a very strong position, opened on us with 4 batteries of 6 guns each—24 guns. At this time Huger stopped (nor did he do anything more that day) and we found ourselves in a fight with an overwhelming force opposed to us. There was but one way to get out of the scrap and that was to fight out. And here I believe occurred the hardest fight of this war.

As soon as the enemy opened on us so heavily, Genl. Longstreet at once ordered forward his infantry. The So. Ca. Brigade under the gallant Col. Jenkins commenced the attack. Kemper was on the right of Jenkins, Wilcox on the left, & Pickett's, Pryor & Featherston still to the left. One of A. P. Hill's (Branch's Brigade) was ordered as a support to Kemper & Jenkins. Kemper's (which used to be Genl. Longstreet's old brigade) charged & took a battery. The enemy then brought up reinforcements and Branch failing to support Kemper, the battery was retaken and many of the old brigade captured with it. Jenkins in the meantime had taken a battery and still kept forward. His advance at this time was the most desperate I ever knew. A few hundred yards to the left of the battery he took was one that Wilcox was trying to take. Just in Jenkins' front was a very large force of the enemy's infantry which he immediately engaged, when this battery on his left commenced on him with grape and canister. Thus he advanced in the face of a terrible musketry fire at the same time infiladed by artillery. Notwithstanding, he pushed on, charged the enemy and drove them from their position with terrible slaughter. He then brought up Branch's Brigade to hold the position. But as soon as they reached the place and saw how far in advance it was & the number of the enemy a half mile farther on, they turned & fled. Being left so far in advance unsupported,

Jenkins fell back from the position & went to the assistance of Wilcox. The enemy did not return to the position he left. Wilcox during this time had been fighting desperately. He had taken a battery, but it had been retaken, but when Jenkins came in, they made another charge and held it. The fight still raged to the left when three of Genl. Longstreet's & two or three of A. P. Hill's Brigades were engaged. It lasted until after dark when the last battery was taken and the enemy whipped. This could have been accomplished much sooner but Magruder was several hours behind time and did not get up until some time after the battle. We had also expected assistance from Huger, but he said that he had been trying to remove obstructions from the roads so as to get at them. It was also hoped that Jackson & D. H. Hill would assist us, but they had pursued the enemy to White Oak swamp, some 4 or 5 miles from us, and were being held in check by a portion of the enemy's forces.

In this fight as in most of the others, our loss was heavy but not so heavy as that of the enemy. In this fight we took a considerable number of prisoners & 18 pieces of artillery. Nearly all of the brigades of Genl. Longstreet's Division lost one third the number carried into action, killed & wounded. The So. Carolina Brigade (Jenkins') lost more than half & the Ala. Brigade (Wilcox) lost at least one half. The 11th Ala. (Col. Syd Moore's Reg.) out of 10 officers commanding companies lost 8 killed & two wounded. The Palmetto Sharpshooters (Col. Jenkins' Regt.) out of 375 men, lost 44 killed & 210 wounded. His own escape was almost miraculous. His horse was shot twice. A hole was shot through his saddle blanket, his bridle reins cut in two near his hand. An India rubber overcoat tied on behind his saddle has 15 holes through it made by a musket ball & piece of shell. His sword was shot off at the point, & shot half in two near the hilt, & his sword knob was also shot off. Besides all this he was struck on the shoulder with a grape shot (which bruised it severely) and was also struck on the breast & leg with fragments of spent shell.

I met him just as he was coming out of the fight and he was weeping like a child at the destruction of his brave, noble men. He told me that at one time when he saw how fast they were falling around him, he stopped and prayed God to send a bullet through his heart. He says, too, that at times as he would ride up and down the line, his men would turn and give him a look as much as to say, "We can go no further," when he would wave his hand to them and they would again dash forward.

Col. Micah Jenkins is a great friend of mine and he is a favorite with the army. Gen. Longstreet thinks him the best officer he ever saw. He is only 27 years of age & is a perfect model of a Christian hero.

But I must finish my account of the battle which is much longer than I intended and of which I know you must be tired.

The enemy was so hard pushed that he could only retreat at night. Well, on Monday night after the battle he retreated some 3 or 4 miles & took a very strong position known as Malvern Hill near the James River.[61] Early the next day (Tuesday) Magruder's & Huger's Divisions were placed in front of this position & D. H. Hill's & Jackson's to the left & Longstreet's & A. P. Hill's in reserve. Although the troops were placed in position, Genls. Lee & Longstreet deemed it impracticable

Thomas Jewett Goree's commission as first lieutenant and aide-de-camp, dated 31 December 1861 and signed by Confederate secretary of war Judah P. Benjamin. (John W. Thomason Rare Books and Special Collections Room, Newton Gresham Library, Sam Houston State University)

to make the attack from the front. They had gone around to the left to see if they could not find a better position from which to attack. They found a position and had started Longstreet's & Hill's Divisions to it to commence an attack, but concluded it was too late to make the movement. On our return about 6 P.M. we heard a terrible fire in front & thought the enemy had attacked us, but it turned out that Genl. Magruder, contrary to orders had attacked them. The result was that Magruder having engaged his Division, others had to come to his support and very soon the Divisions of Huger, D. H. Hill & Jackson were also engaged. Our men fought desperately, but having to advance through an open field for 1000 yards, they were mowed down by the enemy's artillery. They never got close enough to inflict great damage on the enemy. The battle closed about 10 P.M. when a part of the line was repulsed. In other parts we held our ground.

Our loss was very heavy in killed in this battle, probably as many killed as in all the other fights together. The Army was very badly scattered & disorganized by this fight. The enemy that night continued their retreat, leaving here as elsewhere their dead & wounded. The next morning very early we got ready for pursuit, but a heavy rain coming in, we could not move. We followed on the day after, but found Yankees in such a strong position under protection of their gunboats that it was decided not to attack them. After trying for two or three days to draw them out & failed, our army was moved back to this point, where we are trying to recruit & reorganize as fast as possible. Our army needs this very much. I suppose that it will all have to be fought over again, but although it will cost us many gallant lives, I have no fear for the result.

Jackson's army has again gone up towards the Valley, where he seems to be giving the Yankees much uneasiness.[62] The Yankees have at last agreed to a general exchange of prisoners. Genl. D. H. Hill on our side & Gen. Dix[63] on the Yankee side are the Commissioners appointed to agree upon terms &c.

The Texas Brigade in the recent battles did well. It not only sustained its reputation but gained new laurels. The 4th Texas suffered very severely, the 1st & 5th not near so much. I am glad to be able to give a good account of the conduct of Lang & Ed. On Friday the [27th] the 5th Texas captured a Yankee regiment and Lang had the honor of demanding the surrender & receiving the swords from one of the field officers & a captain, also the sword & flag from the color bearer. I have one of the swords which Maj. Upton[64] gave him for his gallantry. Ed recd. a scratch on the head from a piece of shell in the last day's fight.

When on Saturday morning after the fight on Friday, I went round to see how the boys came out, I could not but shed tears for joy when Capt. Cleveland told me how gallantly Lang had acted. He never faltered during the whole day. In the 4th Texas, Capt. Hutcheson[65] of Grimes was killed, Capt. Porter wounded & since dead, Angus Alston[66] was killed, Syd Spivey[67] wounded. Others whom you probably knew were killed & wounded but I cannot now recall their names. Col. Marshal[68] & Lt. Col. Warwick[69] of the 4th Texas were killed, Col. Rainey[70] of the 1st wounded. In the 8th Ala., Col. Young Royston was slightly wounded in the head, & Capt. Tom Phelan severely wounded. Wat Pheland was severely wounded at Seven Pines. Lt. Col. S. F. Hale[71] of the 11th Ala. was severely wounded in arm, side & leg.

David Scott & Ed Goree in the 4th Ala. were unhurt. Both of them behaved very gallantly. Tom Moorman was not hurt. His regt. was not much engaged. Of our generals, Brig. Genl. Griffith[72] of Miss. was killed & Brig. Genls. Pickett, Featherston,[73] Pender[74] & Elzey were wounded.

Genl. Longstreet was very much exposed & his staff more than he on Friday, Monday & Tuesday. In Friday's (27th) fight I was far more exposed than I have ever been before, but neither myself nor horse was struck.[75]

Thomas Jewett Goree. (John W. Thomason Rare Books and Special Collections Room, Newton Gresham Library, Sam Houston State University)

Genl. Lee has certainly won laurels. The plan of the campaign was certainly well conceived, and it was not Genl. Lee's fault that it was not well executed. Someone the other day congratulated Gen. Lee on his success. He replied that the congratulations were not due to him but to the brave soldiers & officers under him. "Longstreet," he said, "was the staff in my right hand." Genl. Longstreet has undoubtedly acquired as much or more reputation than any other officer in this army. He is now next in command in Virginia to Genl. Lee, Genl. Johnston not yet being fit for duty, Genl. Smith on sick leave, Genl. Huger made inspector of artillery & Genl. Holmes sent to Arkansas. All these rank him, but dispositions were made to remedy it.

It is impossible to form an estimate yet on our losses. Many were killed and wounded but many have run away. The number absent from this army is immense. Some are absent sick, but many absent without leave. Genl. Longstreet's Corps (3 Divisions) number in the aggregate over 50,000 men. Not more than one half are present for duty.

I hope soon that stragglers will return or be brought back, that the sick will recover and that the reduced ranks may be filled with conscripts. Well, Mother, I have written twice as much as I set out to. If you tire before you get [*one line of the letter is illegible*], I thought that probably an account of the battle would be interesting. Dr. Campbell yesterday started for [home and he] went as far as Montgomery with Capt. Powell who has been quite sick & goes off on furlough. The Dr.'s brothers, Archy & Doug, have both been very sick. They, too, have gotten furloughs, also Creed Woodson who has been sick for several weeks. I have a fine Ambrotype of Genl. Longstreet that I will send you by first chance. Would have sent it by Dr. C. but did not have it in Richmond when he left.

Mother, I am very anxious to hear from you all. Please write as often as you can & give all the news. I would like to know if Bob has yet gone and where to. I hope that he may be as fortunate as we have thus far. Mother, give my love to all—white & black. Kiss Sudy, Scrap, and all Sis Frank's children. Give my love to Grandma. I would like so much to see you all. My love to Eck,[76] Sis Sally & children. The boys have better opportunities for sending letters & write oftener than I do. I will, however, write as often as I can. Give my love to all enquiring friends.

Your Aff Son
Thos. J. Goree

TO SARAH WILLIAMS KITTRELL GOREE

My dearest Mother.   Near Winchester, Va., Octr. 10th/62

I delivered your message to Dr. Breckenridge. He says that when he comes to Texas (as he intends doing after the War) you will be the first person he visits, *as he has great curiosity to see the Mother of three such boys.*

I am just in recpt. of two long and interesting letters from yourself and Sis Frank, both written about the middle of August last. Although they were both very old I assure you that they had lost none of their interest on that account, as they were the first and only tidings we had had from home since we left Richmond. I understand that there is now regular mail communication between here and Texas, and I hope that we shall hear from each other more frequently.

Since I wrote you a few days since, nothing of interest has occurred here. Our army is still enjoying the rest and quiet so much needed. Supplies of shoes and clothing are being daily received, and we will soon be in better fighting condition than at any time since the battles around Richmond. I do not know whether there will be any more fighting on this line before spring. There are differences of opinion in regard to it. The Yankees say that McClellan is preparing to advance upon us in this position. I do not believe it, however. I think it more probable that he will endeavour to keep up here while another force operates against Richmond from Fredericksburg or Norfolk. I hope that this campaign is ended for although I am as anxious as any one for the war to be brought to a close, yet I do not want to see any more fighting this fall.

I have just seen an official estimate of the losses in Genl. Longstreet's Corps since we left Richmond. It is a little over 12,000 killed, wounded & missing. I think that this is rather an overestimate. In Genl. Jackson's Corps it will not amount to near so much, as his has not been in so many engagements and has not done near so much hard fighting. The only fighting done in the capture of Harper's Ferry was that done by portions of Genl. Longstreet's Command, which occupied the Maryland Heights.

Genl. Longstreet has in his Corps 21 brigades and over a hundred pieces of artillery, and the above losses occurred in the battles of the Rappahannock, Thoroughfare Gap, Manassas, Boonsboro (or Braddock Gap), Crampton Gap or (Maryland Heights) & Sharpsburg.[77] Hood's Texas Brigade sustained a heavier loss than any other in these engagements, as at the Rappahannock, Thoroughfare Gap, Manassas, Boonsboro & Sharpsburg it was always in front and in the thickest of the fight.[78] It is very probable that Genl. Hood will be promoted to Major Genl. for his gallantry in these various contests.[79] No man deserves it more. He is one of the finest young officers I ever saw, (except my friend Genl. Jenkins) and had we had many more of the like sort at Sharpsburg, we would have whipped the Yankees worse than they were ever whipped before. Genl. Jenkins was quite severely wounded at Manassas which prevented him from participating in the battle in Maryland.[80] South Carolina has four (4) brigadiers here. Jenkins is one of the best in the army. Kershaw is also a very good one, but Evans[81] and Drayton are not worth the powder & lead it would take to kill them.

Congress has passed a bill creating the office of Lt. General, and it is expected that Genls. Longstreet & Jackson will be promoted to that position. If so, I think it very probable that I may get some promotion myself.

Well, Mother, I have written about such things as we talk about and are interested in here, forgetting that they may not be so interesting to you as some others—as for instance *some information in regard to the welfare of your sons & friends.*

Both Ed and myself are in the enjoyment of excellent health. My own has never been better. We heard from Lang a day or two since. He was then in Richmond. I only heard from him through a negro belonging to John Grace,[82] who was with Lang and John Grace at the place I left them when they were wounded.

When I left Lang, I promised to send him a furlough so that he could go at once to our relatives in No. Ca. And I was very much vexed at him when I heard from the negro that he had remained there after receiving his furlough until all of them were captured by the Yankees. I had not only warned him to leave, but Dr. Breckenridge had written him a note at the time the furlough was sent, urging him to leave at once. Why he remained I cannot imagine except probably he was unwilling to leave his comrades (the Grace boys) who [were] probably not well enough to go. They were of course paroled as soon as taken and will no doubt be exchanged before they are ready for service. But I hate the idea of being taken prisoner by such people. The Yankees tried to persuade the negro to go with them, but neither their persuasions nor threats would induce him to go.

The negro says that when he left Richmond they would not allow any soldier to leave the city on furlough, but that he heard they could go in 3 or 4 days. I trust that this may be so and that Lang has gone to No. Ca. before this. He reports Lang's hand as healing very rapidly. It had swelled up a good deal once from eating meat but had gone down when he desisted from it. He also says that Capt. Cleveland was improving and was about to go, or had gone, to Alabama. So soon as I can find out Lang's whereabouts, I will send him some money to buy clothes or anything he may need. I think of writing to Cousin Protheus Jones today, to enquire if he has reached there.

You desire to know, Mother, if we need money, clothing or any thing. I know of nothing, as I have money enough to supply our wants. Lang probably has not much money now, but I will send him some. Ed has 40 or 50 dollars. I do not know how Lang is off for clothes. I find more difficulty in procuring shirts & drawers than anything else, as both they and the material for making them are scarce. I was at a cloth factory in this neighborhood yesterday and bought cloth to make Ed and myself good winter suits. I shall write [*word illegible*] to get his and have it made in No. Ca. [*several words illegible*] is there, if not then in Richmond. The cloth which I purchased for Ed's suit (enough for coat, pants & vest) (4 yds double width) cost me $6 00 per yd. My own cost me $8 00 per yd. In ordinary times the same goods sold at $1.00 & 1.50 per yd. The making of the suits & trimmings &c will no doubt cost me 40 or 50 dollars more.

If the campaign will close so that I will not have to buy more horses, I will have money sufficient

[*The remainder of the body of this letter is missing.*]

Should you have an opportunity please send me some socks. Those you sent me by Capt. C[leveland] I *gave to Lang when I left him.*[83]

1863

"WE FEEL SANGUINE OF OUR SUCCESS"

TO SARAH WILLIAMS KITTRELL GOREE

My dearest Mother,   Near Fredericksburg, Va.—Feby 4, 1863

After looking long and anxiously for some tidings from home, I was delighted about a week since at the reception of your kind letter of the 1st January, brought by Mr. Wood. Having only a day or two previous to its reception written a long letter to Sister Frank, I concluded to postpone answering it for a few days, so as not to tire you all out at once with my long winded, and, I fear, uninteresting epistles.

I was truly rejoiced at the recital in your letter of the good health of the family during the last year, and also at your very successful farming operations. Truly the Lord has blessed and prospered you wonderfully.

I have boasted pretty considerably of the wonders you performed during the last year, and my statements have excited not only surprise but gratification that our people were becoming so independent.

Mr. Wood safely delivered the two packages of socks, etc. I am under many obligations to you for the three very nice pairs you sent me. They came in good time, for I was very much in need of them. I have only worn thin cotton socks during the winter.

I carried Dr. Breckenridge's over to him, and I think he acknowledged the recpt. of them at once in a letter to yourself. He said they were very acceptable indeed. I have Ed's package, which I shall keep until his return, but I suppose he will get so many nice things at home that he will not want these. Acting upon that supposition, I have appropriated to myself a pair of the gloves and am using until his return the sentinel cap.

I wish, Mother, that I could be at home to see the surprise and joy of you all when you hear of Ed's arrival, for I imagine that you are hardly expecting him. I hope that he will have a short trip, so as to give him as much time as possible at home, but there has been [so] much bad weather since he left, that I fear otherwise.

General Robertson says he advised him if he was long on the road, to communicate with Major Sellers[1] at Houston, and get him to give him orders to remain longer than the (60) sixty days granted him. I have but little prospect of obtaining a furlough this winter, and I am disposed to feel very much vexed at General Longstreet that he has not granted me one. I have not had one since I have been a member of his staff, and he has granted, since I made application, two other members of this staff leave, who have not been with him near so long, or performed half the service, that I have.

It is right hard to be refused so, after having performed my duty so long and so faithfully, but General Longstreet says that he is in constant expectation of another attack from the enemy, and in that event cannot spare me.

But I am the more anxious to get off now, as Cousin Bettie Jones[2] is to be married on the 12th of this month, and has extended me a very cordial invitaton to be present.

David Scott was over to see me today. He was quite well. He had received Uncle Pleas' letter by Mr. McDonald,[3] containing the 100.00. In the letter Uncle Pleas mentioned having previously remitted him in a letter to me, sent by Captain Riley,[4] a sum of 100.00. I have never seen or heard anything of said letter. Two or three weeks since, I heard that Riley was in Richmond, and when a day or two since, I saw Dave's letter, I went over to the 5th Texas Regiment & found that he had been up there about two weeks previously, but could hear nothing of any letter for myself. I shall make enquiries to find if he could have possibly left it in Richmond.

Tom Moorman also spent the day with me today. I am very much pleased with Tom. He is a very high-toned, honorable gentleman, is possessed of good manners, fine conversational powers, & is very intelligent.

He was at home not long since. Aunt Lucy[5] was looking better and better contented than he had seen her in a long time. He says that some time since, there was quite a family feud between she and Howson's wife, and that during the time Howson nearly killed himself drinking on account of it, but since the birth of Howson's child, they are again living together in great peace and happiness, the child being a bond of union between them. Howson has quit drinking and is as happy as a lark.

Tom Moorman thinks that an incessant use of opium for some years past has had a very deleterious effect on the constitution, mind and temper of Aunt Lucy. Since the blockade, opium is so scarce that she has not used near so much, & she is becoming herself again. He says that she is very patriotic, & wishes for more sons in the army.

I was very much surprised a few days since to receive a letter from Howson. He was near Williamsburg, Virginia when he wrote. He had a great deal to say about his mother, his wife & his little "soldier" (as he calls his baby) whom he has not yet seen. From the style of his letter, I should judge that he is something like Cousin James Ashford when Cousin J was about twenty one year of age. He inquired very particularly about the family, and especially after Uncle Pleas, who, he says, he was much pleased with.

It will afford me, Mother, much gratification if during the war I can get acquainted with yours & my father's relatives. I know I shall like them all.

Soon after hearing of Colonel Rogers' death I wrote to Mrs. Rogers, but since the reception of your last letter I have written a second letter, fearing she had not rec'd the first.[6]

There is but little news of interest to communicate. I suppose that as soon as the roads become passable for artillery, General Hooker[7] will be fool enough to make an attack on us. If he does, I think he will go the way that McDowell, McClellan, Pope & Burnside have gone. Our generals, I think, have less dread of "Fighting Joe Hooker" than anyone they have yet to contend against.

During the last week or two we have had very bad weather, some rain & a considerable snow. While the snow lasted, the soldiers had a glorious time. They had regular pitched battles with snowballs, two or three thousand men on a side. For the last two days the weather has been terribly cold.

Should this reach you before Ed returns, please send me by him my watch, provided you have no use for it at home.

Please give my best love to all.

Your devoted son,
Thos. J. Goree

TO SARAH WILLIAMS KITTRELL GOREE

My dearest Mother: Petersburg, Virginia, March 13th, 1863

Upon reckoning up today, I was very much surprised to find that a month has passed since I wrote to you, so very rapidly has the time glided by. When I last wrote, we were near Fredericksburg. Since which time Genl. Longstreet has been assigned to the Command of the Dept. of Va. & N. C., with Hd. Qurs. here at Petersburg. He brought with him from the Dept. of Northern Va. two Divisions (Hood's & Pickett's) of his Corps. His other two divisions are still on the Rappahannock under Genl. Lee. This is a separate dept. and extends from Richmond, Va., to Wilmington, N. C., inclusive.[8]

This is considered a very important command, as the enemy are threatening several very important points in it, viz, Wilmington, Goldsboro & Weldon, No. C., & Petersburg, Va. We have forces at all these points, and can concentrate very speedily to any one of them.

For the first time since the war commenced, have we had our Hd. Qurs. in a city, and I am fast becoming very tired of it. I am boarding here in a very pleasant family at $75.00 per month. You no doubt think this an enormous price, but it is less than is generally charged, and we find it cheaper than keeping up our mess with the present enormous prices of provisions.

Soon after reaching here, I concluded to make one more effort to get a furlough, and the General granted me only ten days. So on this I made my long expected visit to Cousin Protheus Jones. I left here at 7 o'clock a.m. and reached his house at 3 P.M. Much to my regret, Cousin Protheus himself was absent from home, nor did he return during my stay. However, I met with a most cordial reception from every member of his family, who all exerted themselves to make my visit as pleasant and agreeable as possible. And right well did they succeed, for I can truly say that never before have ten days seemed to pass so rapidly or delightfully as the ten I spent there. And, as you may imagine, I was *very, very* sorry when the time came for me to leave. I was charmed with every member of the family that I saw, and I saw them all except [*one line illegible*] some two of whom were off at school and the third one with his father. The two married daughters (Cousins Mary Foster & Bettie Harris) were both on a visit to their father's when I reached there and remained for several days.

All of Cousin Protheus' daughters are very elegant and accomplished ladies. I could hardly decide which one I liked best, but I think that I must give the preference to Cousin Jane who is a very lovely woman. She is said to be very much like her Aunt India. She is tall, graceful, has beautiful long black hair, long, dark eyebrows & eye lashes, dark blue eyes and has one of the most amiable dispositions I ever knew. She has a nose, eyes and mouth very much like Uncle Pleas' Willie, and also the same dry, odd humour that Willie has. Cousin Lucy is older than Cousin Jane but she is not so pretty; but I like her almost as well. Cousin Mary Foster is a very nice lady, and has been very pretty though she now looks a little broken. She has two children, one an infant & the other two or three years old. Her husband is a fine, jovial fellow & very much devoted to his wife and children.

Cousin Bettie Harris is the youngest daughter & the prettiest. She has only been married about a month. Although she is well educated and very accomplished, yet she is a perfect child in manner & disposition. Mr. Harris is an elegant young man & quite wealthy. Cousin Bettie thinks there never was another such man, and he thinks she surpasses all other women, though he tells her that it was fortunate that he saw her before Cousin Jane, for then he would have fallen in love with the latter. Cousin Bettie went home a few days before I left and fixed me up a large box of good things to bring back with me, but I unfortunately lost the box in changing cars at Weldon. They would not bring it on the passenger train, and it was stolen from the man I left it with.

Mrs. Jones was as kind to me as if I had been her own son. She insisted in overlooking my clothes and mending them up, and she was very urgent in her invitation for me to come to her house whenever I could get off, and particularly if I was sick or wounded.

I was a great deal with Cousin William, who is in the Quartermasters Dept., but is stationed at home. I liked him very much. He went with me to visit his grandmother's old place, and also your grandfather's place. We also went down and called upon Mr. Geo. Kittrell.[9]

I went one day with Cousins Lucy, Bettie & Jane to spend the day at their grandmother's, Mrs. Hawkins. I was very much pleased with all I met there, and particularly with a cousin of theirs who is living with their grandmother. They all accused me of having lost my heart with their Cousin Bettie [*one line illegible*] it. If, however, I am as well pleased when I see her again as I was the first time, I don't know but that I might lose it. If I had had a longer time to stay I should have gone up to Oxford to see Mrs. Burrel & Mrs. Taylor, but the weather & roads were so bad that I would not go there. Mrs. Jones very kindly offered me her carriage and horses to go if I liked. Mother, you have no idea how I boasted of "my mother" when I was there. I told them all that there never was another such mother as you. All expressed the greatest anxiety to see you, for they had heard their father speak of you so often. I was very much pleased to see one thing. Mrs. Jones & her daughters were all wearing beautiful homespun dresses. I told them that I was bound to let you know that. Well, to wind up, I was delighted with my kinsfolk, and they seemed to be equally pleased with me. They often spoke of Uncle Pleas and the pleasure his visit gave them all. I regretted that my furlough was too short to allow me to visit my relatives in So. Ca. as I had wished to do. However, since I commenced this letter, the General has sent for me and asked me if I did not wish to visit my friends in So. Carolina. Of course I said yes! when he told me that Mrs. Longstreet wished to go down there and would like me to accompany her & at the same time attend to some government business there and in Georgia. I was glad he put in the latter, as I would then be allowed transportation at the cost of the government. I expect to start tomorrow.

I begin to look for Ed back now. I do hope that he had time to remain at home long enough to make his visit pleasant. The weather has been so bad that I fear he has had a wretched time going & coming. Hood's Division is encamped about 12 miles from here. Cousin David Scott is here, and quite well. He is a member of a cavalry co. which is acting as couriers for Genl. Longstreet. The company, however, will be relieved from that duty soon, and will be sent to join a regiment on the peninsula. Tell Uncle Pleas that I found the letter he wrote me by Capt. Riley, with the $100 for Cousin David, in the dead letter office at Richmond.

The regt. to which Dave's Company will be sent is the same to which cousin Howson Kenner belongs. *The prisoners captured at Arkansas Post will [be] leaving here in a few days. Efforts are being made by Genl. Hood and others to keep the Texans all here. I hope that they will succeed.*[10] I wrote to Bob some time since but do not much expect that he will receive the letter. I write this undecided whether [to send] it by mail, or wait an opportunity of sending it by hand. Mother, give my love to all & write soon to your aff. son,

Thos. J. Goree

Direct either to Richmond or Petersburg.

TO MARY FRANCES GOREE KITTRELL

Dear Sis Frank: Near Suffolk, Va., April 21st, 1863

I was very much gratified on my return to Petersburg from South Carolina two days since to find awaiting me your letter of the 8th of February. I should have answered it immediately, but had orders to join Genl. Longstreet here without delay, and consequently did not have time to write so long a letter as I desired. I write this under rather disadvantageous circumstances. Have no pen and ink.[11] Am using the ground as a chair and my valise as a table. It is quite cold, too, and I shall have to run to the fire every few moments to thaw my fingers.

Genl Longstreet commenced active operations about two weeks since. We have driven the enemy into their stronghold & fortifications at Suffolk where we wish to keep them until we can get the corn & bacon from the adjoining counties, of both which there are vast quantities.[12] It is thought that in the three counties in N. Carolina in which we are foraging there can be obtained a sufficiency of bacon to supply our own & Genl. Lee's army for two months. Our army is in line of battle in front of Suffolk, the right of our line resting on the Dismal Swamp & the left on the Nansemond River. So that the enemy, if they wish to attack, must come out in front to do so. It will be very hard for them to turn either flank. On some portions of our line our skirmishers have dug rifle pits within two hundred yards of the enemy's breastworks and they pick off nearly every Yankee who has the impudence to show his head.

Below our left flank on the Nansemond River we have had several batteries fighting gunboats, in which game so far we have been badly worsted. We have disabled two gunboats & had begun to feel very much elated, but night before last, the enemy with gunboats from both above & below, came up and fiercely attacked Stribling's battery (containing five splendid guns)[13] which Genl. French[14] had placed on a point extending into the river in a very isolated position. The battery was in a small fort, and while the gunboats were pouring a terrible fire into it, the enemy (under cover of their fire and the darkness) ran across from the other side a transport laden with a regiment of troops, who silently disembarked, came up in the rear of the fort and captured the battery with two companies of infantry which were in the fort as a support to the battery. It was quite a blow, for the battery was the best we had & the number of men taken was about 140 or 150. But the worst part of it is the encouragement it has given the Yankees. We could hear their whole army cheering so lustily over it, that rendered it more mortifying.

Genl Longstreet is now more anxious than ever that the Yankees will come out of their works and attempt to drive us off. They have a large force, but we feel sanguine of our success. Genl. Longstreet has had Genl. D. H. Hill in North Carolina to make an advance movement for the object of getting supplies. He has succeeded admirably. Everything thus far looks very encouraging in Va. & No. Carolina. There is some prospect that Genl. Lee will very soon make an advance against Hooker. We are all somewhat disappointed that the Yankees were so easily satisfied in their attempt against Charleston.[15] After two years' preparation they were whipped in 2½ hours. I have no doubt that had the other ironclads approached as near as the Keokuk, they would have all shared her fate. But while the ironclads suffered so severely, Fort Sumpter, too, suffered considerable damage. The fight has proved that neither Fort Sumpter nor the ironclads are invulnerable.

I expect, Sis Frank, that you would like to hear something of my visit to South Carolina. I went down as far as Augusta, Georgia, on business for the Government, which I soon attended to, and had two weeks to spend with our relatives in S. C. Half the time I spent with Aunt Lucy & the other half with Cousins Hattie Bates & Frank Caldwell in Columbia. Cousin Frank went up with me to see Aunt Lucy, who appeared perfectly delighted at seeing us both. She was expecting us, as Cousin F. had written to her a day or two before that we were coming. I found Aunt Lucy in excellent health, looking younger & stronger than I expected to see her and altogether different from what I expected. Instead of a feeble, complaining old woman as I expected, I found one who was very active, considering her lameness, and who was as full of life & fun as she could possibly be. She enjoys a laugh and joke as much as any one, and talks about beaus & getting married a good deal.

Several times she commenced telling her troubles & crying, but Cousin Frank was always sure to say something to make her laugh and so turn the conversation as to make her forget what she had commenced. Howson's wife is still living with her and they seem to get along very well together, though it is very evident that Aunt Lucy does not like her *any too* well. I was very well pleased with Cousin Judy. Although she is neither very pretty nor smart, yet I think she is a good, amiable woman and have no doubt but that she makes Howson a very good wife. But Aunt Lucy thinks that she was far beneath Howson, and it is very hard for her to get over it.

Howson & Cousin Judy have a very fine boy about 8 months old, to whom Aunt Lucy is perfectly devoted. His name is Samuel E. Kenner. Sam's eyes at first were very black like his mother's, which distressed Aunt Lucy very much, but now they look as if they were turning to a blue or hazel color, and the old lady is perfectly delighted at it, for she says she would give anything in the world for him to have a Kenner eye. She and Cousin Judy are both very much distressed for fear that something may happen to Howson before he has an opportunity of seeing his boy. Cousin Judy speaks of coming to Va. just to show him to Howson. Although the weather was very bad & disagreeable while I was at Aunt Lucy's, yet I enjoyed myself very much. Aunt Lucy is splendid company, and there is none better than Cousin Frank.

Cousin Dosky Bishop stayed a part of the time with us. I was very much pleased with her. Her great resemblance to yourself made me like her so much the better. We went to see Mr. Bishop & Aunt Patsy. They were both quite well & doing very well. Cousin Frank & myself also spent one day with Cousin Robt. Moorman. I was very much pleased with him & with his old mother, Aunt Minnie Maybin. The only other place we visited was Mr. Bill Lyles,' who married an aunt of Cousin Frank. We had to remain there all night on account of the rain. I was treated everywhere with the greatest kindness and consideration, no doubt caused by the grateful remembrance of our father, for every one I met, white & black, remembered him with respect & love. Every one said I resembled him very much, which of course I was glad to hear, but I thought that the resemblance was more fancied than real. Aunt Lucy said it was a great comfort to see me, for she could see Langston in me. I was much amused at Mrs. Lyles. Mr. Lyles thought I was very much like my father, but Mrs. L. said that I was much more like my mother—(thinking that I was the son of your mother.) In North Carolina Cousin Protheus Jones thought I was *very* much like Mother. His family had never seen Mother but thought I resembled the Normans *very* much.

I found Aunt Lucy, Mr. Moorman, Mr. Bishop & nearly every one else in Newberry, very much in the notion of moving to Texas after the war. Mr. Moorman, I think, will certainly move, & Aunt Lucy says she will if she can sell out. Many inquiries were made after you, both in Newberry & Columbia & many messages were sent to you by me, which I have forgotten. But of one thing you may be assured, that you are kindly remembered by the *many* friends you have in South Carolina. White & black all ask to be kindly remembered to you. All who saw Uncle Pleas while there also send much love to him. Before leaving, Aunt Lucy said she would like to have my likeness so she could look at & see my father. I had some photographs taken in Columbia & sent her one. I send you & Mother one of the same. It would be a very good likeness (so everyone says) if it was not quite so dark.

In Columbia I also had a most delightful time. Cousins Hattie & Frank left nothing undone to render my stay as pleasant as possible. I was delighted with Cousin Hattie in Va. & a better acquaintance has only tended to confirm my good opinion of her. She has a very pretty, interesting little daughter, some 8 or ten months old. Cousin Hattie is a very smart, intelligent woman & a great talker. So is Cousin Frank, who is of a much more lively & cheerful disposition than Cousin Hattie. I was perfectly charmed with Cousin Frank. She is a noble woman, has one of the sweetest and most amiable of dispositions, is full of fun & is a great favorite with every one. I was with her all the time I was in So. Ca. & did not see one single bad trait about her. She visits Aunt Lucy very often & is very attentive and kind to her. I believe that Aunt Lucy enjoys her company more than that of anyone else.

Cousins Hattie & Frank are boarding in Columbia with Mr. James Sims. They are very pleasantly situated. Mr. Bates is in service down on the coast of So. Carolina. Mr. & Mrs. Sims were very kind to me, insisted on my making their house my home while in Columbia, which I did. They have a very interesting family of daughters & some of them very pretty. Mr. Sims was so unfortunate as to lose 60 of his best hands on the Mississippi by the Yankees. Old Uncle Bart & Reuben were very faithful to him & assisted him in saving the remainder. He says but for them he would have lost all.

When he left his plantation, Uncle Bart was very sick, & he left his wife & two other negroes to take care of him, but the old man lived but a short time.

Aunt Lucy was so unfortunate about two years since as to lose two very valuable women with typhoid fever. I think one or both of them were her cooks.

Minnie will no doubt be very sorry to hear of her sister Mary Ann's death. She died some time during last year with consumption. Tell the negroes that I saw several of their friends & relatives who sent them much love. I saw at Mr. Bishop's Massie who was very well & at Aunt Lucy's Uncle Aaron & a sister of old Aunt Sarah, Kizzy, I think her name was. I saw in Columbia a sister of Hannibal and several of Mary Ann's children. All sent many messages of love.

In Columbia I made the acquaintance of a great many pleasant young ladies (I think about 25) & also several very nice married ladies, also two or three widows. Among the widows was one who was evidently very anxious to marry. She is probably an old acquaintance of yours. Her name is Mrs. Wells, formerly Miss Sarah Williamson.

I regretted very much that Cousin Eliza Kenner was sick while I was there. She had an attack of pneumonia & was confined to her bed until a short time before I left. I only saw her one evening. Cousins Hattie & Frank were very anxious that I should see her before I did but they were not on good terms with her mother, so they had her to go to their aunt's, Mrs Blakely's, and we went there to see her & spent a very pleasant evening. I was well pleased with Cousin Eliza. She appears to be a most estimable lady. She is very large & fine looking but not very pretty.

Well, to sum up the whole matter, I deeply regretted when the time came for me to leave S. C. for I was well pleased with nearly every one I met there, and, from what I can hear, every one seemed to have formed a very favorable opinion of me. I had a great many compliments paid me, which would no doubt have made most young men vain, but not so with me. Cousins Hattie & Frank used to tell me every day that my manners & style of conversation reminded them very much of their brother Gus, *which you know was a compliment.* Cousin Hattie used to tell me of many nice things the young ladies said about me. Cousin Frank writes to me, "I was at Aunt Manda's (Mrs. Blakely's) yesterday. She, as well as Aunt Martha & Eliza Kenner, asked particularly about you, & could you have heard the complimentary manner in which they spoke of you, I am almost sure that *you—even you—*as plain, unassuming & as good as you are, would have been compelled to have been a *little* vain." Well, I must stop this or you no doubt will think I am vain.

On my return from South Carolina, I stopped for three days at Cousin Protheus Jones' in N. C. and had a very quiet, nice time. Fortunately Cousin Protheus was at home, and I had the pleasure of seeing him as well as all the members of his family who were absent at the time of my former visit. He had his whole family with him; and he told me to say to Mother that he wished she could see his children, for he thought they were hard to beat. And in way of illustration he told that once his wife's grandfather called his daughters around him when they were all dressed to go to a party & said to them, "Now, girls, you are all going to this party. My advice to you is *to hold your heads high, for there are few sich.*" Cousin Protheus sends much love to Grandma, Mother & Uncle Pleas as also do other members of the family. I wrote Mother an account of my former visit there. Has she received it? I was equally as well pleased with the last.

Well, Sis Frank, I have written you a long letter, and about what I thought would be most interesting to you. I hope you can manage to read it.

I should have written to Mother & yourself oftener, but have had no opportunities for forwarding them. I shall send this to N. C. for Col. Hawkins to carry out. I hope that you will all write by every chance.

I am now anxiously looking for the return of Ed. I had heard nothing of him since he left until a few days since, Willis Darby[16] told me he had heard of his safe arrival at home, & also that he & the Captain would start back about the 1st of April.

I am glad to hear that the prospect for a crop in Texas is so flattering. I hope you will all raise an abundance of every kind of provision.

Everything is still scarce & high here. In Richmond & Petersburg chickens sell for $3.00 apiece & butter at $3.00 per lb. The poor are bound to suffer to some extent. There are many difficulties in our way, but we must struggle on until we attain our independence. We are now in better condition than we ever were with the exception of provisions.

Sis Frank, give my best love to my dear mother & to my brother & sister, also to Grandma, Uncle Pleas & all the children, to Eck, Sis Sally & children, to all my friends & to the servants.

You must all write soon & often. Direct to Richmond, Va. Tell Uncle Pleas that the letter sent by Riley has been safely recd. David is on the other side of James River. I have written to him.

I am, dear Sister, Your aff. brother,

Tom

You have heard of poor Geo Yoakum's[17] death? We also mourn the death of Capt. Turner[18] of Polk Co. who was killed a few days since in the same fort in which the battery was taken that I mentioned in the first part of the letter.

GEORGE E. PICKETT TO THOMAS JEWETT GOREE

Captain,   Hd. Qurs. Pickett's Divn., April 23d. 1863

Your note of this date in reference to the rifled guns taken from Macon's Battery is received. In reply I must state that I am more than surprised at its purport and the apparent censure contained therein.

I had two conversations with the Lt. Genl. Commdg. on the subject of the batteries in this division, in which he not only agreed with me about the necessity of having the rifled guns in the Art'y Battalion consolidated, but feel confident that in the first conversation suggested it.

In our last conversation, which took place the day before we crossed the Blackwater, and while on the subject of the Art'y in the Division, I told him Blunt[19] had two rifled pieces, and Macon two. He said, he thought it would be much more effective to have them all in one battery.

I then said to him: "Genl., I will order those two pieces of Macon's to Blunt's, giving him then a battery of rifled guns." To which he replied: "*Yes.*"

Without his acquiescense and advice, I should have made no changes. If an *order* did not come directly from the Lt. Genl., it was *virtually* one. Had he have had *any objections* to it, a simple word or intimation from him would have been sufficient to have prevented its publication. On the contrary. I thought I was carrying out his wishes distinctly and plainly expressed.

I have ordered Maj Dearing to report to Genl. Longstreet in person, and should be happy if the Lt. Genl. will give him such instructions as he may deem necessary for the efficiency of his Battalion.

The copy of the order referred to is enclosed, and it does not appear that the Lt. Genl.'s name is mentioned.

I am, Captain,
Very resply. your obt. servant,
G. E. Pickett,
Maj. Genl. Comg.

Captain T. J. Goree A.D.C.
Hd. Qrs. Dept. N.C. & Va.

MICAH JENKINS TO THOMAS JEWETT GOREE

My dear Friend,   Hd. Qrs., Petersburg, Va. Aug. 10, 1863

As you have once again gotten within reach, I take advantage of Mr. Reily's going up to your Hd. Qrs. to send a few lines of remembrance.

I have had a very pleasant time indeed, the hospitalities of Richmond & this city having been unsparing. We have made most charming lady friends, and had old comrades here in safety. I could not have been situated more to my pleasure, but I have been longing to be with you all the time, and have made most earnest exertions to that effect. Have you all forgotten us? If not, cannot another effort still bring me to you. My brigade is in the best possible discipline and spirits, and strong in numbers.

I volunteered to go to Charleston and drive the Yankees off Morris Island, submitting a plan of attack through Col. Chesnut[20] to President Davis. The President approved the plan, said my troops were the troops, and I the officer to make it, but that he could not spare me from Richmond.

I am now at Petersburg in command, and have a considerable force under me, but I would rather be back with Hood in the old corps than here.

Present me with warmest regards to the General and my friends on the staff. Try and get leave to visit me for a short time. I want much to see you.

Your sincere friend,\
M. Jenkins

TO SARAH WILLIAMS KITTRELL GOREE

My dearest Mother: Camp Near Chattanooga, Tenn. Oct. 12th, 1863

I have just this moment heard from my friend, Major Sellers,[21] of the opportunity to send a letter across the Mississippi.

I have not written home very often recently from the fact that I thought letters per mail would not reach you, & I had no other way of sending. Since I last wrote you, our Corps has made a change of base from Virginia to Tenn. & the most of them reached here in time to participate in the recent great battle of the Chickamauga.[22] Genl. Longstreet, before leaving Richmond, gave me permission to stop & see our relatives in N. C. I only stayed there two or three days & although after leaving there I made every effort to reach here in time for the fight, I did not succeed. I only reached the field just as the battle closed. Genl. Longstreet was here only 24 hours ahead of me, but in time to take a conspicuous part in the fight.

I found Scrap at Cousin Protheus Jones.' He was very well. I left him there with the expectation of his following me in a few days. Ed, on the way out, got his foot a little mashed in S. C. & stopped at Aunt Lucy Kenner's. I wrote to Scrap to come by there and he & Ed come on together, which I suppose he has done, though they have not reached here. They are both in good health. I expected to have Scrap detailed as courier at Genl. Hood's Hd. Qurs., but the Genl. was unfortunately wounded.[23]

Genl Jenkins, however, who is in command of Hood's Div has promised to have him detailed as soon as he comes & to take good care of him. So has Maj. Sellers. I think I will be able to furnish him with a horse with the money you sent out. We will all three, I trust, get along very well.

I am sorry to have to inform you of the death of Cousin Hattie Bates. She died about a month since with consumption.

There is but little other news of interest. The person who is to carry it is waiting for this & I have had to write in great haste. As soon as you receive it, write me, directing your letter to the care of Mr. W. Dorwin, Shreveport, La. Also direct to care of Genl. Longstreet, Genl. Bragg's Army, Tenn.

My love to all.
Your aff. son
Thomas

1864

"UNTIL OUR INDEPENDENCE IS SECURED"

TO SARAH WILLIAMS KITTRELL GOREE

My dearest Mother,   Morristown, Tennessee, Febry. 8th, 1864

It has been a long-long time since I have written to you, but the other boys have written in the meantime, and I have waited for an opportunity of writing a longer letter than I have had time to do for some months past. The last letter I received from you was written in September last, and was received some time in November before we left Chattanooga.

I was just preparing to write you a long letter in return, when we received orders to make the campaign against Burnside in E[ast] Tennessee.[1] Soon after the commencement of that campaign, our mail communications were interrupted by the Enemy, and we had very little intercourse with the outside world.

At the close of this campaign, I was sent to Virginia on official business, and have just returned here. I was much pleased to find awaiting me on my return a long letter from Sister Frank, dated November 14th. She must read this, and accept it as an answer to her letter, as well as yours.

After the reception of the letters at Chattanooga, I was very uneasy, hearing that you, Mother, had been quite severely bruised by a fall from your horse. As Sis Frank does not mention it in her last letter, I infer that your injuries were not serious, and that you had entirely recovered from them. It is truly gratifying to know that you all at home are in the enjoyment of such good health, and are doing so well in every respect. May such state of affairs continue, is my sincere prayer.

The health of Ed, Scrap and myself is perfect, and has been since you last heard from us. Ed has not been sick since he was at home, nor has Scrap since he joined the Army.[2] As for myself, I have never missed two days' duty from sickness since the commencement of the war.

Scrap (as he has probably written you) is detailed as courier at the Hd. Qurs. of his Division. He is very comfortably situated, and seems perfectly contented. At present his Division is about 20 miles in front of this. I was down to see him yesterday. He told me to say to you that he wrote you a few days since by Capt. Cleveland. Capt. C. has tendered his resignation, which, if accepted, he will return home.[3]

When Scrap came on, Ed put him in as a recruit, which by the rules established entitled him (Ed) to a forty days furlough which he has taken, and is at present spending it with our relatives in North and South Carolina.

When I went to Virginia and had transacted the business I went on, I obtained permission from the Secretary of War to make a short visit to North Carolina, and spent ten days very pleasantly there. While I was there, Ed came on and I left him there when I started back, but he expected to leave in a day or two for South Carolina.

He was very much pleased with our relations there, and they with him. I believe that I wrote you before that Scrap has also visited them after leaving Cousin Sarah G's,[4] and before he joined the army.

He spent several weeks with Cousin Protheus. The whole family seem to have become very much attached to him. All of them say he is the best boy they ever saw, and Cousin Protheus and Cousin Mary say it was almost like giving up one of their own children when he left.

I have desired in some of my visits to North Carolina to go and see Cousin Betty Burrell, but my stays have generally been so limited that no good opportunity has presented; though, when I go again, I shall certainly go to see her.

In my last visit I went to see Cousin Mary Foster and Cousin Bettie Harris, Cousin Protheus' married daughters, and was never treated better in my life. Mr. Foster and Mr. Harris are both nice gentlemen, and well to do in the world. I like them very much.

When in N. C., I have visited very often with Cousins Lucy and Jane Jones, the Hawkins family (Cousin Protheus' mother-in-law's, etc.), and am delighted with them, especially with some of the young ladies in the family, nieces of Cousin Protheus' wife. I think, if spared, I may *probably* visit some of them after the close of the war. I should like to show you some nice socks that some of them presented to me.

I should have liked very much to have gone with Ed to S. C. but, my short leave would not allow me.

Since my return here, I have recd. a letter from Cousin Frank Caldwell in which she says that Aunt Lucy and all are well, except Cousin Eliza Kenner, who is confined to her room nearly all the time. It is thought she has consumption, and will not live long. Poor girl, I saw her last Spring. She was very large and fleshy, and the very picture of health.

I do not think either that Cousin Frank Caldwell will live many years longer, but I hope so, both for her own sake, and for the sake of Cousin Hattie's little girl left to her care. Cousin Frank is a noble woman, and I love her very much. Tom Moorman is not very strong, and it is very probable that Aunt Lucy may outlive them all.

You have doubtless before this, Mother, heard of the death of Uncle William Kittrell. He died about the 1st of October last. Cousin Sallie writes me that he was very sick nine weeks, and suffered very severely during his entire illness. He first had typhoid fever, which turned into galloping consumption. If I can lay my hands on it, I will enclose you Cousin Sallie's letter.

I was very *very* sorry to hear of Uncle William's death. He leaves, no doubt, his family in very limited circumstances. I had hopes that some time during the war it would have been in my power to have made him a visit. The news of his death will be a severe blow to Grandma.

Two or three days ago I received a letter from Cousin Robert Pulliam.[5] He wrote that he had just learned that myself and two of my brothers were in East Tennessee, that he wanted very much to see us at his house and that if he could contribute anything to our comfort, we must inform him and allow him to do so. He lives about 80 miles from here, and I should like very much to make him a visit, but do not know whether I can get off. If I can, I will get Scrap and go up and spend a few days.

The money you sent us in a letter last summer ($100.), and also that by Capt. Hunter[6] ($260.00) all came safely to hand. I used none of it myself, and Ed used very little, as we thought it better to keep it and purchase Scrap a horse. About the time that Scrap came on, I recd. the letter to Cousin Sarah Goree enclosing $200. for Scrap. Scrap has some money besides, and I bought him a very good horse & saddle for $450. About $200. were left after this purchase, which I divided equally between Ed and Scrap.

I managed thus far to get along somehow or other on my pay, but it is hard work, the prices of everything to eat and wear being so enormously high. My pay, $135. per month in Confederate scrip is only about equal to $7.00 in gold. I have my provisions all to buy, and my mess bill for self and servant is about $100. per month.

As to clothes, I have quit buying *them* altogether, and have commenced patching up and turning my old coats. I think I can make out this way for the next year. Cousin Mary Foster gave me enough nice homespun for a coat, which I told Ed *he* might have made up. Cousin Bettie Harris has promised to have woven for me a nice suit of homespun, so, I will be very well fixed up soon.

An overcoat in Richmond costs about $700., a pr of boots $200., and a suit of uniform from $750. to $1000. I had to stay in Richmond one day while I was gone, and my hotel board was $20.00. In Petersburg I stopped at a hotel 5 hours, ate nothing, but only had a bed, and the bill was $5.00.

I would like, Mother, to write you a full account of our recent campaign in East Tennessee, but there is too much danger that my letter may be captured. I will say, however, that had Genl. Longstreet received the proper cooperation from his subordinate commanders, and had his *plans* been promptly and energetically executed by them, he would have made the most successful and brilliant campaign of the war.

Even in spite of the slowness and incapacity of some subordinates, if Genl. Bragg had held his position at Chattanooga for *one* week longer, we would have taken Knoxville together with Burnside and his army. Although the campaign failed in great results, yet, we have many minor successes. Not during the war has a campaign been carried on under such adverse circumstances as was ours. We were cut off from all communication from any direction. Could get no shoes, clothing, or provisions for the men except what we gathered up in the surrounding country. The consequence was that the suffering was *very* great.

The men were all badly clad when we went into winter quarters, and many thousands were barefooted. This was during the months of November and December when the ground was frozen more than half the time. Yet, notwithstandng our condition, we could not get a fair fight out of them—the Yankees. Whenever we advanced on them, they turn and run to Knoxville. Recently they came up near here with all their forces, bragging as they came that they intended driving Long-street out of East Tennessee.

But Longstreet (instead of retreating as they expected) marched down to meet them, and after a very light skirmish he got them on the run, and they did not stop till they got near Knoxville. Had our cavalry pursued vigorously, it is thought they might have captured half the enemy's force. As it was, we captured a few prisoners, a great many stores of different kinds, about 200 wagons, and 1100 beef cattle. The enemy burned and destroyed a great many stores, wagons, artillery, etc. on the retreat.

We have just got RR communication with Virginia, and will soon be well clad and shod, and in a condition to go into Kentucky or anywhere else we may be ordered. Our troops are in good spirits, and generally in very good condition.

The Texas Brigade is not in the condition I would desire to have it. The morale of it is bad. They have got it into their head to go across the Mississippi, and many have gone without leave. I hope, however, soon to see a great improvement.

Genl. Robertson, who has brought the brigade to its present condition, is now under arrest with some very serious charges against him. His trial commences today, and if the charges are sustained, I think it very probable that he will be cashiered and dismissed the service. But, whether acquitted or found guilty, he will hardly take command again of the Brigade again, as Genl. Gregg,[7] a most excellent man, has been assigned to the command of the brigade and will no doubt retain it, whatever be the result of General Robertson's trial.

I think authority will soon be obtained to send to Texas after all the men belonging to this Brigade, and have them brought back here. Justice to the men here who have remained at the post of duty demands that this should be done. Shame upon the men who have gone to Texas for easy service, and have deserted their brave comrades here.

I was very much mortified, as well as surprised, to hear that Willie Darby, who had obtained a furlough to go to Alabama, has signified his intention of trying to get to Texas and remaining there. When officers act this way, what must be expected of the privates!

I would like to visit home as much as anyone—business there demands my attention as much as any one's, but no circumstances could induce me to go under such circumstances. I have always believed, and still believe, that the best place to defend Texas is east of the Mississippi, and here I wish to remain until our independence is secured.

Many people throughout the country are somewhat despondent as to the final result of this struggle, but I feel the greatest confidence in our success. The coming campaign will be a trying one, but I feel that it will be a glorious one for the Southern Arms. We feel very little apprehension here that the enemy will accomplish much in Texas. They cannot make a successful campaign there.

When in Virginia, I saw Judge Gray[8] and Captain Branch.[9] I was very glad to see them, particularly the latter, as he gave me the latest information I had from

Texas. I like Captain B, but I am *very* sorry that he beat Judge Gray, for the judge is the best man Texas has, or can have, in the C[onfederate] S[tates] Congress, except Genl. Wigfall, whom I look upon as the *best man* in Congress.

In some of your letters you asked about Ball Wiley.[10] At one time he was in Anderson's Division which belonged to our Corps, but has since been transferred to Hill's. I met Ball about a year ago in Richmond. He was returning from a furlough. When we went back to General Lee's Army from Suffolk, I enquired for him, and heard that he had resigned and returned to Georgia and was married. Have heard nothing since.

Cousin David Scott is still in Va, but I have not heard from him in some time. Before you get through with this, I fear that you will become very tired, so, I will close. Please give my love to all, and accept much from

Your ever aff. son,
Thomas

Scrap sends his love. He has been in two or three little fights.

TO SARAH WILLIAMS KITTRELL GOREE

My dearest Mother.   Near Gordonsville, Virginia April 26th 1864

Your short but very welcome and interesting letter of the 12th of January last was received more than two weeks ago, but having been almost constantly on the move since then, I have not had the time to write you such a letter as I would wish. Your letter found us all still in the enjoyment of excellent health. I have not seen Ed for some time, but Scrap tells me that he is very well and *looking* very well. Saw Scrap three or four days ago, and I think he is looking better than I ever saw him. While we were in East Tennessee about the 1st of March I sent Scrap to Asheville, North Carolina, to get me a pair of boots—that was a secondary reason. My main reason was for him to visit Cousin Robt. Pulliam and have some vacation. He remained up there some ten days or two weeks, and I have never seen any one as much delighted with a visit, and with the kind treatment received from his relatives, as he was. He says they made a great to do over him & Cousin Robt. & his whole family were as kind as they could possibly be. Cousin R. presented him with a very nice pair of boots. He had a pair made for me and only charged me $60.00 while such boots readily bring $125 00.

Maj. Genl. Field[11] now commands Hood's old division & Scrap is with him as Courier. He is very much pleased—is kindly treated and has five or six very gentlemanly, clever companions. Genl. Field & his staff seem to be very considerate of the comfort of all around them. In my last letter I mentioned that Ed had gone off on a forty days furlough; about the same time I was sent to see Genl. Lee, and got permission to go to North Carolina and spend a few days. I met Ed at Cousin Proth. Jones,' on his way to South Carolina. From there I returned to camp and on the 8th of March I was sent to Charleston to see Genl. Beauregard. Ed returned to camp on the 8th or 9th of March and I missed seeing him then.

I returned from my Southern trip in about a month, just in time to find Genl. Longstreet ready to start for Genl. Lee's Army. I had to come back at once and again had no opportunity to see Ed. His Brigade, however, will be up today, when I will go and see him. From all accounts he had a very delightful time both in North Carolina & South Carolina, especially in the latter state. He is *exceedingly* popular there and has the reputation of being quite a ladies' man. If report is true, he is very much in love with one of the fair ladies in Newberry, and I believe she is very much pleased with him. He found a great many kind friends there who offered him money, clothes, or anything of which he was in need. Aunt Lucy thinks him the greatest boy in the world, almost, & his visit was very cheering to her. Ed stopped again on his return with Cousin Protheus Jones. He was as much charmed with them all there as Scrap & myself had previously been. Cousin Mary Foster presented him with a very nice coat.

Before leaving camp, I expected on my return from Charleston to come by Aunt Lucy's and spend a good long time there, but unfortunately Genl. Beauregard had gone to Florida, and I had to go down near Jacksonville, Fla., to see him.[12] This trip consumed ten days of the time I expected to spend in Newberry, so that on my return I had only time to stay a week there. Although it was raining nearly all the time during this week, yet I had a very agreeable time. I was sorry to find that Aunt Lucy was not looking near so well as she was a year ago. She complains a good deal and seems very low spirited. She is unpleasantly situated, she and Howson's wife not getting along well together. They are no doubt both very much to blame. Her greatest comfort seems to be Sammy (Howson's son) whom she pets & spoils very much. Her next greatest comfort is, I think, the old letters she has rec'd. from you & Sis Frank. Whenever Cousin Frank Caldwell goes to see her, she brings out all of her old letters and has her to read them over to her, especially the one from you, written soon after Pa's death. I did all I could to cheer her up, and told her that after the war she had to come to Texas and live with you. I think it would do her good to get away from where she is. I staid about half my time with Aunt Lucy and the other half with Cousin Frank Caldwell, who boards at Mrs. Chaplin's some three miles off. One night I spent with Cousin Sarah Chick, a daughter of Aunt Betsy Maybin & a sister of Mrs. Pickens of Alabama.

Cousin Frank does not stay with her grandmother for two or three reasons. One is because her sister Hattie died there, another is that it is so very lonely there, and a third is that she has not the greatest admiration for H's wife. Aunt Lucy thinks her first two reasons foolish but readily excuses her on account of the third. She will not stay in Columbia because she sees so many things to remind her of her dead sister. She is boarding at a very nice place. Mrs. Chaplin is a young widow and is the daughter of Mrs. Henderson. Her sister, Miss Jessie Henderson, also lives with her. She, too, is a very amiable, nice lady. I had written Cousin Frank that I was coming and they had made grand preparations to have a picnic for my benefit, but when the day came the ground was too wet to be out on it, and the young people all met at Mrs. Chaplin's house and we had a fine time until 12 o'clock at night. Our old Alabama acquaintance (Mrs. Nance that was now Mrs. Rutherford) learning that I was there, came over and seemed very glad to see me. We went to her house the next day and spent a delightful day. She is looking I believe better than she did in Ala., is a little gray but more fleshy—Is in fine health. She asked me to present her kindest regards to you and to say that she often thinks of your kindness to her Mother. She lives in fine style—has several step children, all grown. One of her stepdaughters, a *beautiful* girl was recently married to Capt. Nance. I think if I had seen her before she was married, I should have fallen in love with her myself.

Cousin Frank has Cousin Hattie's little girl Gussie. She is now nearly two years old and is a very beautiful, sweet and interesting child. Frank is perfectly devoted to her, and she is a great pet with every one, but it does not seem to spoil her in the least. I hope that Cousin Frank will live to raise her. Mr. Bates' health is so bad that he had to quit the army and is now engaged with his hands in getting wood for the RRoads. He lives 20 miles below Columbia, but comes up to see Gussie every two weeks. The more I see of Mr. B., the better I like him. He is a man of *good* common sense, and I think an unselfish *noble hearted* man. He is as kind to Aunt Lucy as if she were his own mother, and seems never to tire of doing her favors. She thinks him one of the greatest men in the world. Cousin Hattie used to have a very high opinion of me, and just before she died, she used to say that next to Frank and Mr. Bates she had rather I should raise Gussie than any one else in the world.

But I started to tell you of all the people I saw in Newberry. I went to Mr. Wm. Lyles,' who has two or three very nice daughters, with one of which Ed is said to be very much smitten. I spent a very pleasant day at Cousin Robt. Moorman's, who is a very nice, interesting man. Cousin Tom was at home [and] contributed much towards making the time agreeable. Wish you knew him. He is quite young, but he is the model of a Christian gentleman. From there we went to Mr. Chick's & spent the night. I was very glad that I went there for I never have seen more clever & kinder hearted people than Mr. & Mrs. Chick. They are quite wealthy, have no children of their own, and seem to desire to do as much good as they can. They were very kind to Ed when he was there, and made him as well as myself promise that if we should ever need *money*, clothes or provisions to send to *them* without any hesitancy, and they would send whatever was needed. Cousin Sarah Chick said they had plenty of money—would always divide with me. She gave me a nice pr. of socks, and a pair of gloves which are the admiration of all who see them. Old Aunt Betsy Maybin lives with them. She is looking in good health but was crippled a few years ago so that she can't walk much. She knits all the time. They all send much love to you & Sis Frank & Eck.

I called to see Aunt Patsy Bishop on our return. She is very well and they are doing very well. Both her daughters, Dorry & Sue, are now at home. Dorry is still very much like Sis Frank, but Sue reminded me much more of poor Sister Ann. She is very much like her. She has two very interesting little children. Cousin Dorry said she intended writing to Sis Frank in a short time. Cousin Frank had just recd

Sis Frank's letter, and was perfectly delighted with it. So was Aunt Lucy and all who had seen it. She has answered before this.

Tell Burt and Jasper that I saw a great many of their relatives & friends who were all well and sent much love to them. Aaron is looking very old.

Cousin Frank & Miss Jessie Henderson came with me as far as Columbia, where I spent a day for the purpose of visiting Cousin Eliza Kenner. She is constantly confined to her bed, and is rapidly declining with the consumption. I would not be surprised any day to hear of her death. She was looking very pretty. Is perfectly resigned and says she would not turn over in the bed to live. Her mother seems very much distressed. Cousin Eliza is universally popular, and she has a great many friends to see her & has every attention that she could possibly have. She & her mother sent much love to Sis Frank. Ed had written her a letter, which gratified her very much.

Thinking that Cousin Lucy and Cousin James would like to hear from Cousin Mary Moore, I went to see her. Dr. Parker very readily admitted me to see her when he knew who I was. The visit made me feel very sad, for she is still very much deranged.[13] As soon as she heard that I was there, she expressed great pleasure and said that she knew I had come to carry her home. She seemed to be very glad to see me when I entered the room & the first question she asked was if I had not come for her. When I told her no, she seemed very much disappointed, but I told her that Columbia was the safest place she could be at these war times, that the Yankees might come to Marion, & besides railroad traveling was now attended with very great danger. She said that she was royalty, and that it was not right that she should be confined in such a place which was only intended for the lower & middle classes, and she then insisted that I should go to Mr. Caldwell's and ask him to let her board there until the war was over. I promised to go by Mr. Caldwell's and told her that if he was willing to board her he could send his carriage for her. She spoke of her children, having recd. a letter from them recently. I tried to get her interested and to talk about Cousins James & Lucy, but she seemed to be interested in nothing but the one idea of getting away from the asylum. She went with me to the door & asked me to be sure & come to see her whenever I came to Columbia, and charged me particularly to use every exertion to get her away. She is looking very old, is quite gray & very much broken. The Dr., though, says she is in much better health than she was several years ago.

I have recently rec'd. a letter from Cousin Lally Nelson accompanying some socks.[14] She insists on our allowing her to assist us in any way she can. All were well at her mother's. Her sister Mary had married a son of old Judge Graham, said to be a very clever, nice young man. On my way from S. C. I stopped two days with Cousin Protheus. Found them all in much distress at the death of little Henry Foster, the eldest son of Cousin Mary Foster.[15] He was quite a promising child & a great pet with the whole family. Her other child came very near dying at the same time. I visit my N. C. relatives & my S. C. relatives and it is very hard to tell which I like best.

I have sent my trunk, with what clothes we do not need this summer, back to

Cousin Protheus' for safe keeping. There is one old lady near them who sews very well and very cheap and and [what se]wing I may have, I send there for her to do. She has made one or two very nice suits for me.

They all there think Scrap the greatest kind of a boy, and were also very much pleased with Ed. Cousin Rob't. Pulliam wrote me by Scrap and said, "Make my kindest regards to your Mother and the rest of the family. Please also express my best & kindest feelings to your dear old Grandmother, your Uncle Pleasant & family." Cousin Robt. is in very bad health. He has suffered and is still suffering very much with rheumatism & neuralgia. He says, "But for my farm I should be in want as many are who a few years since imagined themselves fully indemnified against want. We can't tell what a day may bring forth. The righteous' motto is: 'Do right and commit the issue to the God of infinite love.'" He also says, "If in the providence of God either of you should become destitute, cut off as you are from your plentiful and comfortable home, I am ready to divide with you anything I have. I only desire to be informed of your wants. I have charged Pleasant that in case either of you should be wounded or should become sick, to inform me and make if possible my house your hospital." I assure you that it is very gratifying, situated as we are, to receive such letters. I have recently recd. a very interesting letter from Cousin Sallie Kittrell. All were very well. Also one from Dave Scott. He has been home on furlough. Uncle Pleas, Dave says to please convert any money you may have of his into 4 per cent bonds. He is still in the cavalry stationed near Richmond in the same regiment with Howson Kenner. The money sent by Mr. Bailey to care of Mr. Wm. Brown, Richmond, came safely to hand. It reached there just before the 1st April and they, by paying a small premium, bought interest bearing $100 Notes, which are much better than per cent bonds. After payment of premium and all expenses I had $215.—The $360.00 by Capt. Hunter last year all came safely to hand. I took none of that myself, but divided it between Ed & Scrap. The $215 I kept myself, Ed & Scrap not being in need of any money at the time. I needed it because I had just returned from my Southern trip & my travelling expenses were very large. Government should have paid my necessary travelling expenses but would not because they said there was no law for it. So I have to lose that much. Transportation, of course, was furnished, but other expenses amounted up to a good deal. A meal of victuals costs from $5 to $10.00. Had I not, when I could get them, carried provisions with me, there is no telling what the trip would have cost me. As it was, I am out considerably over $200.00. If everything continues as high as now, you had better send us money when you can to help us out. Dont rush, though, without you have a safe chance.

There is pretty general rejoicing, Mother, that we are back again in the noble old Army of Northern Virginia, but as far as I am concerned, I should have much preferred that we had been allowed to make a Kentucky campaign. I think it would have been better. However, we ag[ain] constitute a part of the greatest of all armies under the leadership of the greatest living chieftan, and if we can succeed in inflicting on Grant a crushing defeat, it will do much towards bringing about a speedy peace. The continued rainy weather has thus far prevented any active operations here, but they can't be delayed much longer. All, however, feel great confidence in the result. The army is in fine spirits and in splendid condition. The enemy's plans are not yet developed, but the impression seems to be that Grant will try & hold Genl. Lee here while Burnside will move against Richmond from some other base.[16] I suppose, of course, a force will be concentrated to meet Burnside. I understand that Genl. Lee expressed the determination to try and wipe the enemy out when he again meets them; he [is] not given to boasting. God has certainly blessed our armies this year. Whenever we have met the enemy—in S. C., Fla., Miss, Tenn., Ky, Va., La., and N C., the victory has been ours, with apparently very little effort on our own part. May these small victories be the harbingers to greater ones, and then may our Noble Country having won its independence be long blessed with peace.

Oh! how I long to be at home more and more [*several words illegible*] and I hope that day will soon come. I can not come home until the fight is fought & the victory won.

I have written you quite a long letter and must close. It is intended for you all. When any of you write, give me all the news. Tell me how Lang is, & how Sudy looks. Everything will be interesting. Direct letters to Army No. Va., Care Genl. Longstreet.

Give my love to *all*, and remember me to any enquiring friends, particularly Mr. & Mrs. Creath & Mr. & Mrs. Davis.

Your ever aff. son,
Thomas

I have recd. a letter from Bob. Am very anxious to hear from him since the fight in La.[17] Write me all about him. Heard Capt. Cleveland reached home. I am sorry not to have [*several words illegible*] before he left.

I have been saying and wishing to a friend that I was at home to get one good dinner. The poor one I had today called it to mind.

Tell Lang I saw Dr. Breckenridge not long ago. He enquired very particularly about him and sent his kind regards to all the family.

Do you ever see or hear anything of my friends the Woodsons? What has [*several words illegible*]. Is Miss Mattie married yet?

Mother, please enquire and find out what you can about Col. Rogers' family, for I feel a great interest in them. Have written once or twice but recd. no reply. Has Dr. Baker returned to Texas?

How is Dr. Hayes' family & Mrs. Pettitt?

How is Mrs. Houston's family?

I suppose Bob could better tell me.

We are to have a grand review in a day or two—Genl. Lee will be here. Genl. Gregg is in command of the Texas Brigade. Genl. Robertson has gone to Texas. I believe that it is expected that Col. Powell[18] will soon be exchanged.

Give my best love to Cousin Lucy Campbell & Cousin James [*several words illegi-*

ble] families. Cousin Lucy, if I mistake not, owes me a letter. I hope she will find it convenient to pay me soon. Sis Frank must write Aunt Lucy a long letter. It will do her a great deal of good.

I expect Ed & Scrap would like to hear all about the horses & dogs.

Do you ever have preaching in the neighborhood? Who preaches? Excuse so many questions, but I am really anxious to know about everything.

TO SARAH WILLIAMS KITTRELL GOREE

[This is the last half of a sixteen-page letter, of which the first eight pages are missing. Its content suggests it was written about 14 July 1864, while Goree was at Lynchburg, Virginia.]

defensive; and invariably repulsed the enemy, with great losses to them, while our own have been comparatively small. Our cavalry have had several severe fights & won glorious victories.[19] Genl. Longstreet's Corps has more than sustained its hard earned reputation. After one of the battles Genl. Lee said that Longstreet's Corps attacked the enemy with greater dash, repulsed them with more steadiness, had fewer stragglers, and kept better in hand than any corps in his army. On another occasion he wrote to Genl. Anderson,[20] who is temporarily commanding the Corps,[21] complimenting him on its splendid conduct & expressing it as his opinion that the corps would take *anything* it was put against. He said he had tried very hard to keep Pickett's Div. from taking some breastworks held by the enemy, but could not. Are not these compliments to be esteemed?

When the Yankees were threatening here, I volunteered my services with Genl. Hays,[22] who was here wounded, but who took active command. After Genl. Early's[23] arrival I volunteered with him and participated in a little fight near here, & one at Liberty 25 miles from here. In the pursuit from here to Liberty I went on ahead with one man, & coming up very near the enemy's rear guard, we captured two Yankees with their horses and equipments. We each took a horse. Mine was a *very* fine large brown mare. She would probably bring $2000 or $2500. I intend to try and trade her for a smaller horse & one better suited to my size.

I wish you had her at home, she would make a splendid carriage or buggy animal. The capture was made in good time, as I fear that Bullet, my old horse, is going blind. I would regret this very much as he has served me so gallantly in nearly all the battles since 2d Manassas. He was stolen from me about the 1st last September, and I never expected to see him again, but much to my surprise & joy, I found him on the 4th day of May last. I had been riding a govt. horse for some time previously.

I have not heard from Dave Scott very recently. I owe him a letter. When I last heard, he was very well—had just returned from home, where he had been & married. He married Miss Wallace, a daughter of Stanhope Wallace. She is said to be a very nice, estimable lady, and has, I think, a considerable property in her own right. Dave is still in the cavalry and seems very well satisfied. I heard from Howson Kenner not a great while since. He had made a narrow escape from capture—lost his horse. I forgot to mention the narrow escape that Genl. Longstreet made from capture just before Hunter[24] reached here. The Genl. & his family had been staying at Campbell C. H. at the house of Col. Alexander,[25] when a raiding party of the enemy numbering about 200, passed through the place and within 100 yards of where the Genl. was. It was early in the morning & he was asleep and did not hear of it until they were gone. They evidently were not aware of his presence there. They were in a great hurry and did not even go to the horse lot. So the Genl's. & Col. Alexander's fine horses escaped. I was riding my horse, and had just left Col. A's about a half hour before they made their appearance, for this place. Had I been there & stirring about a half hour later, not only would I have been taken myself but my capture might have led to that of Genl. Longstreet.

Tom Moorman, who was shot through the chin on the same day Ed was wounded,[26] has recovered & returned to his command. I have recently heard from South Carolina. Cousin Frank writes me that Aunt Lucy's health was improved and she was looking much better than when I was there in the spring. When I last heard from Cousin Sally Kittrell, all were well. She had not recd. your letter.

I heard a few days since from Cousin Lally Nelson. All were well. She has been very kind in writing & sending us socks &c. She begs me to present much love to you all for them. Have not heard recently from Cousin Protheus Jones or Cousin Robt. Pulliam.

Mother, you cannot imagine how very much pleasure the reception of yours and Sis Frank's long letters gave me. It has been so long since I had heard. I believe that I receive all of your letters, but they are a long time coming. I need not assure you of the satisfaction that the accounts of your property, of the kind solicitude of all our friends, of their welfare, affords me, nor of my distress at the notices of the death of friends, servants and relatives. I had not before heard of the death of Cousin John Ashford. It is deeply to be deplored. He was a devoted husband & father, a good citizen and a noble man. It must be a severe blow not only to his wife, but to Aunt Polly.[27] I am sorry to hear that Cousin James Goree is still in bad health. Please present my kindest regards to him & family, also to Cousin Lucy & family. Tell Cousin Lucy that when I was at Liberty a few weeks since, I saw Dr. & Mrs. Frierdon of Danville. They were quite well and sent much love to all. Liberty had been in possession of the Yankees for several days previously, and Mrs F. was much delighted at our appearance. She stood in the porch and witnessed the skirmish we had there with the enemy's rear guard, altho the bullets were flying in every direction. Tell her to tell Mrs. Woodson that I recd. a letter from Dr. Phil a short time since. He was well & doing well.

Tell Lang that Ed says he intends to get hold of him for having his dogs shot. I did not know until the reception of your letter Sis Frank, that Bob was in the cavalry. I thought he belonged to some infantry command. When did he make the change? Write me all about him, his address & c. Was sorry to learn that he had lost his horse & more so at his misfortune in being captured. He was lucky in being exchanged so soon. It is gratifying to hear such good reports of the children, and also of the servants.

Tell Sue that she must so improve herself that when we return home, we may find an elegant & accomplished young lady. She must not begin to think too much of beaux, or think of marrying before she is 18 or 20.

I am glad that she is childish, if it will keep such notions from her head. Lang is old enough and ought to marry if he can find a nice person to suit him. Miss Celeste Slaughter says that you must not let all of Ed's sweethearts marry before his return home.

When Ed gets well enough to travel, he will have such a long furlough before his leg will be strait enough to return to duty that he will no doubt fall in love with some of the many pretty North or South Carolina girls. He will go to one or the other of those places as soon as he can. He will certainly not be able for duty before next spring, and I hope by then the war will be over. Had I not had to have been with Ed, I should have gone South with Genl. Longstreet and spent the summer in South Carolina or Alabama.[28] My time here, though, has been as pleasant as I could expect under the circumstances. I feel very anxious that Genl. Longstreet should get back to the army. I hear from every one that his services are *very much* needed there. Genl. Lee needs him not only to advise with, but Genl. Longstreet has a very suggestive mind and none of the other Lt. Genls. have this.

I hope that after you wrote you continued to have good seasons in Texas. I have been very apprehensive that you would have a drought there. The crops here have not been very good. The wheat crops are short, and the corn is suffering very much for rain. So is the grass. There is a prospect now for seasonable weather, which, if we have soon, will be in time to save the corn. The patients in hospitals are suffering on account of scarcity of vegetables occasioned by dry weather.

I have acknowledged in previous letters the recp't. of the $200 sent to care of Cousin Sarah Goree for Scrap, also the $225 to us sent to Mr. Brown of Richmond. The govt. has not paid us for some time and we are consequently somewhat short of funds now, though we manage to get along.

You must remember us kindly to all our friends & relatives, and to the children and servants. Give my best love to Grandma, Uncle Pleas, Sis Frank & all. This letter is intended for Sis Frank as well as Mother. Ed sends his best love to all. I will write again soon.

Be sure some of you & write by every opportunity. Rest assured that if you do not hear from me every month or six weeks it is not because I neglect to write. I know the uneasiness that you *must* feel and I desire always to relieve it.

Your ever aff. son,
Thomas

TO SARAH WILLIAMS KITTRELL GOREE

My dearest Mother,   Lynchburg, Virginia, July 22d, 1864

I wrote you quite a long letter a few days ago which I sent to Richmond to be forwarded to you, and have just recd a note that it was started off immediately by Mr. H. D. Robertson of Washington County who is going straight on.

In that letter I gave you a pretty full description of Ed's wound, his condition, etc. It was then improving slowly, but four or five days ago he had another relapse, and is not now doing so well. I feel quite uneasy about him.

Since I last wrote, quite a large abscess has formed from his knee to about six inches above. That was opened yesterday, and discharged a large quantity of matter, which has very much relieved the acute pain in the knee.

This morning he seems quite bright and cheerful, though still suffering some pain. I do not know what course the Drs. will pursue next. If the opening of the abscess does not succeed, I think it probable that they will resort to amputation.

I mentioned this probability to Ed yesterday, and he seemed to receive it very calmly and resignedly: says if necessary, he is very willing for it and will bear up under it the best he can. It is unnecessary, my Dear Mother, to conceal from you the fact that Ed is in a very critical condition. While there are chances that he will recover, there are some against. Let us hope for the best, but at the same time be prepared for the worst.

Since I last wrote, his appetite has improved, which is very favorable. The ladies on the hill continue to send him whatever they may have that is nice. Whether it should please God to take him away, or to spare him, it will be a great consolation to know that during his illness he has had every comfort and recd every attention that he possibly could away from home.

I shall write again in a few days, and let you know further of his condition, for I know the anxiety you must have felt since you heard he was wounded, and will continue to feel about him. I have recently heard from Scrap. He was *very* well and writes in good spirits. I have not heard from General Longstreet, and do not know how soon he will return to his command.

We all feel perfectly safe here in Virginia, but feel very uneasy about our affairs in Georgia, particularly since General Johnston has been relieved. I am fearful that it will prove to be a very unfortunate change.[29]

I have not time to write more news, but will do so very soon. Give my best love to all.

Your aff. son,
Thomas

TO PLEASANT WILLIAMS KITTRELL

My dear Uncle: Lynchburg, Va., July 22nd, 1864

Enclosed please find a letter for Mother. I have written to her that Ed was worse since I last wrote more than a week since, but thought it best not to communicate to her my worst fears. I will leave that for you to do, in whatever manner you may think most prudent. I have tried to *prepare* her for the worst.

If you have recd. my former letters you will know the character of his wound. He was shot just below the knee in the fleshy part of the leg, the ball striking the bone, and ranging downwards. It remained in the leg several weeks before it could be found & cut out. The bone was not thought to be injured. In the meantime, from some cause, there was produced an inflammation of the knee joint, from which he has suffered terribly for five or six weeks. At times the inflammation would somewhat abate, but the least motion or jar would produce a recurrence of it. There seems to be very little recuperative power about him, for the wound instead of granulating & filling up & discharging healthy matter as it should do, has discharged rather thin pus, of a greenish color & mixed with blood, until nearly all the muscles of the calf of the leg seem to be destroyed. The Drs. now think it probable that the bone was injured. I have been *very uneasy* about him ever since the inflammation of the knee joint, but the Drs. said that only time and patience were required to work a cure.

During all this time he has not had much appetite, but with the use of whiskey & iron it has been somewhat improved. For some time Dr. Terrell[30] has been painting the leg above the knee with iodine for the purpose, I believe, of preventing the inflammation from extending above, but yesterday morning it was discovered that a large abscess had formed above from the knee for probably six inches. Dr. Terrell called together a board of consultation consisting of Drs. Owen, Minor & himself, all three surgeons of high standing.[31] Their conclusions were about these. 1st, that if the leg was suffered to remain as it was, that he would certainly die in the course of a week or ten days. 2d, if the abscess above the knee was opened it might relieve the knee to some extent, but the discharges from it would be *so great* that his system could not long stand it, particularly as he seemed to have so little recuperative power. 3d, the only thing which offered the *least* encouragement was amputation, but his condition is such as to render it extremely probable that he would either sink under the operation or survive it only a few hours. Drs. Owen & Terrell were of the opinion that the probabilities of shortening his life more than counterbalanced any benefits to be hoped for from amputation. They think that while there *may* be a chance, that it is not at all probable he would survive it more than 36 hours. Dr. Minor thinks that if amputation is had he will have not exceeding 2 chances in a hundred to recover, but he thinks even this would justify the risk of shortening his life.

It was, however, determined yesterday to open the abscess and have another consultation today to determine on the amputation. I shall have Dr. Houston, for whose judgement every one has the greatest respect, to attend. The matter will no doubt be left to me, and while I want every thing done that can be, I shall be very loath to consent to an amputation, when it is almost certain that life will be shortened by it.

Though I cannot refuse, if the others should agree with Dr. Minor today. The abscess was opened yesterday and discharged, I think, more than a quart of pus. Ed is not fully aware of his critical condition, but I shall inform him when the Drs. come to a final determination. He knows that he is in much danger, but still has strong hopes of recovering. It will be a *hard, hard* task, my dear Uncle, for me to tell him the truth. For some time I have had the ministers to visit him, and have talked to him myself about dying. He feels very deeply on the subject, and seems to put his trust in Christ, though his mind is not yet clear on the subject. God grant that it may be, and that he may die (if die he must) a triumphant & happy death. How often have I wished in the last few days that he was at home. It would be not only such a comfort to him, but also to our dear mother to have him there. I hope that you will break the sad news to Mother as gently as possible. God in His kind providence may yet spare him, but there is hardly room for hope.

Scrap is quite well, or was a week ago. I have not heard from Dave S[cott] since he wrote me informing me of his marriage. Give my love to Grandma, Sis Frank & all the children & servants. Write soon and often to

Your aff. nephew,
Tom

Direct as usual to Richmond or Army Northern Virginia—

TO SARAH WILLIAMS KITTRELL GOREE

My dearest Mother,   Lynchburg, Va.—Aug. 4th, 1864

Having an opportunity to send a letter across the Miss[issippi], I hasten to avail myself of writing you a few lines.

I wrote both to yourself and Uncle Pleas a few days ago informing you of Ed's condition, which letter, if you have recd. it, will render you extremely anxious to hear again as soon as possible.

I forwarded those letters to Richmond to be sent to you, and it may be that this will reach you as soon or before those do. I mentioned in Uncle Pleas' letter, if not in yours, that the Drs. thought the *chances* were *against* Ed's recovery and that you should be prepared for the worst.

Since then, there seems to have been some improvement, but I do not know whether it is permanent or not. His appetite has somewhat improved, and he seems more cheerful, but I regret to say that there is no improvement in the inflamed knee, which is the cause of all the trouble. The Dr. thinks that as long as the knee does not improve that there is but little hope for him.

There is little or no improvement in the terrible bedsore on the back, and I worry very much and fear that another sore is coming on his right hip. Although we do everything to prevent them, yet these sores seem to be unavoidable. It has been about three months since Ed was wounded, and two months of that time he has been constantly confined to his bed. He has to lie altogether on his back. We use a pad to keep the sore off the bed.

I wish, my dear Mother, that I could write you a more favorable account, but I think it better that you should know his exact condition. I told Dr. Terrell this evening that I wished to write home, and would like for him to tell me what he thought of the case.

He said that he did not think he would recover, that the inflamed knee with this abscess of the leg, and the bed sores in his emaciated condition would cause him gradually to decline. But he said that having a good appetite he might build up and struggle through it.

Although I have given you this unfavorable opinion of the Dr., yet I can but believe sometimes that he will get well. Should it please God to take him away, I think we particularly want to believe that he has experienced the Christian's hope. He is often visited by several ministers, all of whom think that "he has passed from Death unto Life." He has suffered in a noble cause, and should he die, he will have been one more to sacrifice his life on the altar of his country.

He had the pleasure of a visit from Scrap a few days since. He got a furlough for six days for the purpose of visiting his sick brother. His visit seemed to cheer Ed very much. Scrap is very well, and has grown considerably even since I saw him three months ago.

The ladies here continue as kind as they can to Ed. Several of them visit him [*fragment missing*]. How often do we wish that you and Sister Frank could be here.

I cannot write more now, as the gentleman is waiting for the letter. Will write again in a few days. My love to all. Ed sends his best love. Write soon.

Your aff. son,
T. J. Goree

Excuse pencil. My pen won't write on this coarse paper.

TO MRS. GIDEON (LAURA G.) NELSON

Dear Cousin Lally,   Lynchburg, Va., August 20th, 1864

A day or two since, I wrote you that Scrap was probably needing some things. You had better not send him anything at present, and it is possible that he may get a furlough soon and come on to Alabama.[32]

Even if he does not go there, he will probably get one to some of our other friends. He wrote me yesterday that he was unfortunately wounded in a recent fight near Richmond.[33] The wound is quite a severe one, and will probably keep him from duty for some time, and I doubt whether the Drs. will give him a furlough with it.

They may transfer him from Richmond to some hospital not far off. I have written him if he could not get a furlough, to get a transfer to the hospital at Kittrell Springs, North Carolina, near which some of our relations live, with whom he is a great favorite.

He was wounded in the left arm, the ball entering just below the elbow, and breaking one of the bones. His horse was killed, which he seems to regret I think more than his own wound.

He says that one of Genl. Field's staff is supposed to be killed, and another one of the couriers seriously wounded.[34] Nearly all the horses belonging to the staff and couriers were killed or wounded. No other news of interest.

Ed continues to improve slowly, and I now feel very hopeful of his recovery. Enclosed I send you a photograph (not a very good one) of Genl. Longstreet, which please present to one of your little boys for me. When you write me, tell me all about your children.

My best love to all.

Very affly. your cousin,
T. J. Goree

[Written on the back of this letter.]

Aunt Sarah:

I find since writing my letter that my last letter from Cousin Thomas is in Marion, I sent it to Ma to read. I send you two anyway—the last one but one—knowing you will love to read them.

TO SARAH WILLIAMS KITTRELL GOREE

My dearest Mother,   Lynchburg, Virginia, Aug. 20th, 1864

I wrote you about a week since by Captain Harding,[35] who expected to start in a few days for Texas. I will write again this morning, and will send my letter to Richmond, hoping it may be promptly forwarded from there.

I have heretofore written you such unfavourable accounts of Ed that I know you will feel an intense deal of distress and uneasiness. Do not suppose for an instant that I intended, when I wrote those letters, to alarm you unnecessarily. I merely performed what I conceived to be a sad but necessary duty, for at the time, judging from Ed's appearance, and from the expressed opinion of the best surgeons in the city, I thought there was no earthly chance of his recovery.

Now I am happy to assure you, thanks to a kind Providence, that there has been a very perceptible improvement in his condition, and that the surgeons have become very hopeful of his final recovery. His appetite still continues good, and his face looks fuller. The improvement in his spirits is equally as much, or more, decided.

The inflammation in the knee joint has very much abated, and I think the abscess and wound are also better. The bedsore on his back seems somewhat improved, and the one on his hip is no worse. I feel almost sure that with good, careful nursing, which he will certainly have, he will struggle through.

I do not wish you to understand that he is entirely out of danger, but that the chances are in favor of his recovery.

I received a letter from Scrap three days ago, telling me of a narrow escape he had made, which was that the enemy threw a shell at Genl. Field's staff and couriers (9 in all), which fell in a few feet from them, and exploding, wounded five horses. Nobody hurt.

Yesterday I received another letter, stating that the next day in the fight a shell had struck and torn one of the legs of his horse to pieces, and that nearly every horse on General Field's staff was killed or wounded. The object of his letter was for me to assist him in making arrangements to get another horse.

In the course of the letter he mentioned the fact, which he seemed to consider of minor importance compared with the horse question, that he himself had received quite a severe wound in the left arm, just below the elbow, one of the bones being broken.

He said that it was giving him some pain, but that he intended going before the board in a day or two and endeavour to get a furlough and go to North Carolina. I wrote him that he had better get a transfer from Richmond to the hospital at Kittrell Springs, nine miles from Cousin Protheus, and from there he could get permission to stay at Cousin Protheus', and report to the hospital every few days for surgical treatment.

I think it better that he should have regular surgeons to watch his arm. He wishes, if he can, to go to Asheville to Cousin Robert Pulliam. Wounded as he is, he will hardly be able to return to duty before November or December, probably January. I am very thankful that his wound is no worse. I do not yet know how I will manage to replace his horse, but will make some arrangement before his return to duty.

I might spare one of mine, but unfortunately, one of them (my best horse which I have had for two years) is about to go blind. The Govt. will pay Scrap $600. for his horse, but that will only be a drop in the bucket at the present prices of horses, and the present value of Confederate money.

I recd. a very kind letter a few days ago from Cousin Lally Nelson which I enclose for you to see. She has been excedingly kind to me. I recd. a letter a day or two since from South Carolina [*fragment missing*] were well. Aunt Lucy's health is somewhat improved. Mr. Bates, Cousin Hattie's husband, and one of the kindest, best men in the world, insists that he shall be informed as soon as Ed is able to travel, and he will take great pleasure in coming on here for him. Ed is very popular in S. C., and they all feel much interest in him.

Away from the army, as I am, I have but little news of general interest to write, more than you will see in the papers. Scrap was wounded in the battle of Fussel's Mill or "White's Tavern,"[36] about 10 miles from Richmond on north side of James

River. Ed sends much love. Present my best love to all, and accept much for yourself from your ever

Aff. son,
Thomas

TO SARAH WILLIAMS KITTRELL GOREE

My dearest Mother: Lynchburg Virginia, August 26th, 1864

I believe that about one week has elapsed since I last wrote to you. I try to write
regularly once a week now and I hope that you have recd. my letters regularly. I
fear that you may have recd. the letters written when we had but little hopes of
Ed's recovery, and may not have recd. those of more recent date, announcing his
convalescence; if so, your anxiety must be intense.

Ed continues to improve, so slowly, though, as to be almost imperceptible from
day to day, but at the end of the week it is very evident that he is much better than
at the commencement. Dr. Hamner, one of the surgeons here, has invented a splint
for his leg which obviates the necessity of taking it out when it is necessary to
apply fresh bandages. Hence, the knee joint is all the time at rest and has improved
very much in consequence. The wound and abscess are both doing well, but the
most decided improvement within the last week has been with the bed sores on the
back & hip. Both seem to be improving rapidly. By the exercise of a little ingenuity, I
have managed to fix the bed so that he has to press very little or none upon them.
The ladies in the neighborhood and the surgeons are still very kind and attentive
to him. He is doing now just as well as can be expected, and you can abate considerable of the uneasiness which I know you feel about him.

In my letter last week I wrote you that Scrap had been wounded. I mention it
again in case you should not get that letter. I have only received the one letter from
him since he was wounded. In that, he neglected to tell me at what place he was
in Richmond. I wrote to him at Genl. Field's Hd. Qurs. and requested that my
letter be forwarded to him, which no doubt has been done or will be done. I wrote
to him for fuller particulars about himself. Will write you again as soon as I hear
from him. His wound, he wrote me, was just below the elbow of the left arm—
one of the bones was broken. He seemed to regret more that his horse was killed
than that himself was wounded. He no doubt thinks that his wound will heal up &
get well but that it is a hard matter these hard times to get another horse. I will
endeavor to manage some way to get him one before he returns to duty. Scrap
wrote that he intended going to Cousin Protheus Jones', but since then the enemy
have occupied the railroad between Petersburg & Weldon and he can't get there
without going round by Danville, Va., & Greensborough & Raleigh, N. C. I think
it probable that on this account he may get a furlough to S. C. or to Alabama. He
prefers, if he can get there, to go to Cousin Robt. Pulliam's. I have never seen any

one as much carried away as he is with Cousin Robt. and his family. I believe that he keeps up a correspondence with both Cousins Ella and Nora.

I have been much pleased to hear such good reports of the condition of affairs in the Trans-Miss Dept. and especially to hear of the good crops. I trust that your crop is not an exception. Virginia has not been so fortunate. A drought has prevailed in many portions of the state which has cut very short the corn crop. I very much fear that there will be much suffering here if the war continues another year. Only think that now flour sells at $300 per barrel, Corn meal at $10.00 per bushel & bacon at $8.00 per lb. & other things in proportion. I do not see how the poor manage to get along.

I suppose it is almost useless to say anything [about] military operations, as you no doubt will see all that I know in the *newspapers*. The chief points of interest now are Petersburg, Atlanta, Mobile and the valley of Virginia. In the valley, the Yankees have again retreated to the Potomac. Our force there is sufficient to contend successfully with that of the enemy wherever they may choose to give us battle. The situation at Petersburg is not so favorable as a few days ago. Grant, continuing his movement by the left flank, has occupied in strong force a position on the Weldon railroad. In trying to dislodge him from this position, we have been repulsed but with what loss I have not been able to learn. We captured, though, in the different engagements about 4000 prisoners. Grant, in occupying this position, is no nearer the capture of Petersburg and Richmond than before. I hope, too, that it will prove a disadvantage to him. He will be more exposed to a flank movement from our side, and his lines will be so much extended that it may be in our power to break through them and possibly cut off a large portion of [*letter torn*] from their base on the James River. The advantages, though, which he gains if he retains the position, are considerable. He cuts one of our lines of communication with the South and is in a position where he can send out his raiding parties and annoy us very much on the south side and Danville Railroads. He, however, can do nothing more than annoy us. The gallant Hampton has generally brought his raiding parties to grief and will no doubt do it again.

I do not feel the same confidence about Atlanta that I do about Richmond & Petersburg. Our policy ought to be to risk no general engagement without it is necessary to hold a position of *vital* importance to us. Richmond and Petersburg *are places* of *vital* importance. *Atlanta is not;* but the President thinks differently. Johnston was removed because his policy was to give it up rather than run too great a risk in holding it. Hood was appointed because his policy was to hold it at all hazards. Johnston's army was far inferior to that of the enemy and he was *right* in wishing to keep his army intact even at the sacrifice of Atlanta so as to inflict a blow on the enemy at a more fitting time & place. He had retreated over 100 miles & had successively occupied strong positions in which the enemy had attacked and been repulsed with heavy loss while our own was trifling. By this means he was wearing away Sherman's army without a corresponding loss on his own part. An advance of another hundred miles on Sherman's part would have so wasted away his army that Johnston without the least difficulty could have retained the balance. Johnston in his several engagements on his retreat—with a loss of say

10,000 men—had inflicted upon their [army] a loss of at least 40,000. Well, Hood takes command and attacks the enemy in his entrenchments. He loses 8 or 10,000 men and inflicts a loss upon them of about 5,000. He captures a few stands of colors & pieces of artillery. He whips on one part of the field and is whipped on another. What is gained? Nothing, but ground is lost. So much for a change of policy & commanders.

Should our army be whipped at Atlanta, the blow will come nearer prostrating the Confederacy than any she has yet recd. We hear but little from Mobile, and hardly know what to think of the situation there.[37] I suppose the result depends on whether we have a sufficiency of troops there to man the defenses. The fall of Forts Morgan & Gaines are not necesarily fatal to our success at Mobile. Confidence is generally felt in our ability to hold the place.

In my last letter to you, I sent Sue the photographs of some of our distinguished Generals—Lee, Johnston, Hood & Jackson. Hope she recd. them safely. Have just recd. a letter from the Agt. of the Texas Dept. in Richmond who writes me that he sent the letter by Capt. Farmer[38] of Houston. I wrote you by Capt. Harding of Polk Co. [*letter torn and several words illegible*] that he will not start for several days yet. He also writes: "Scrap is at the Howards Grove Hospital[39] in Richmond—was over to see me yesterday—is doing very well." So you see he is able to be about. You no doubt have the feeling that I once had about hospitals, and think Scrap would be better off at a private house. There has been a great improvement in hospitals generally and my mind has undergone a great change in regard to them. Probably with a wound like Scrap's he would do as well in private quarters, but where a wound is severe like Ed's it is *best* that the patient be in a hospital, for there he has the benefit of careful and experienced nurses, and, better still, he has the careful and constant attention of the surgeons which it is impossible to obtain in private quarters. I feel satisfied that Ed [will be] better off in a good hospital. I have heard nothing from Cousin David recently. Wrote to him several days since but recd. no answer. No other news of interest.

Give my best love to all. Ed sends his love. Write soon and often to

Your aff. son,
Thomas

TO MARY FRANCES GOREE KITTRELL

My dear Sister: Near Richmond, Va.—Octr. 21st/64

Your most welcome and interesting letter of the 6th of August was received only a day or two since. I had almost despaired of hearing from home again, the letters written in May by Lt. Shotwell[40] being the last I had recd. I, too, have been remiss in writing for the last month, occasioned not so much from want of inclination to write, as for lack of opportunity. Previous to this I have written very frequently, and as my letters were all sent by responsible persons, I have every hope that they have been duly received.

You will perceive that since last I wrote I have changed my base from Lynchburg to near Richmond. I left Lynchburg on the 1st of this month to join Genl. L[ong-street], regretting very much to have to leave there before Ed was sufficiently recovered to be about and to do well without me. Our lady friends there begged me not to feel the slightest uneasiness about leaving him as they would see that he was well taken care of. I have recd. two letters from him—he writes very cheerfully, and says that he still continues to improve slowly. The bedsore on his back is healing slowly—those on the hip and side of the knee have healed up—the abscesses on the leg are also improving. He now sits up in a chair from 2½ to 3 hours per day, when he only sat up less than an hour before I left. So you see there *is an* improvement. The *very kind friend* (Mr. Slaughter)[41] at whose house he has been staying in Lynchburg, has recently had to break up housekeeping for the purpose of joining the army. Consequently, Ed has removed over to Burton's hospital—next door. He will be almost as comfortable there as in a private house—and as they have experienced nurses there, will no doubt receive *better* nursing there.

Dr. Terrell (a brother of Judge Terrell of Austin)[42] is in charge of the hospital. He has been Ed's attendant physician—is a fine surgeon—and has always manifested the greatest interest in Ed. I know that he will continue to bestow on him every possible care and attention. The ladies, too, will continue their kindness and send him delicacies that are not furnished in the hospital. In his last letter he mentioned that Mrs. Cobbs had sent him two splendid dinners and Miss Sallie Cobbs had sent a very nice breakfast, a part of which was a nicely broiled squirrel—which he says he enjoyed very much. I shall have to make this an excuse to write a letter of thanks to Miss Sallie (who, by the way, is one of the sweetest girls I ever saw.) I hope that it will not be many weeks now before Ed is well enough to go to some of his relatives. He has recd. urgent solicitations from Cousin Protheus to come to his house—also from Cousin Robt. Pulliam, Aunt Lucy Kenner and Cousin Lally Nelson. I think he is now disposed to go to Aunt Lucy's. I do not much think that he will be fit for service in a long time again, and I shall get him to use every endeavour to get on the retired list—do not know whether he can succeed in doing so.

I recd. a letter from Scrap written on the 26th of September, which I intended to have sent home, but have mislaid it. He was at Cousin Robert Pulliam's and had been there several days when he wrote. His furlough lacked only a few days being out, but as his wound had not entirely healed, he intended going before a medical examining board to get an extension of it. I have since heard that he got an extension of thirty (30) days. He ought to be back in about ten days now. Scrap writes as if he were perfectly delighted—says that you all at home could *not* have given him a *warmer* reception than he met with from Cousin Robert and his family. They are as kind to him as they can possibly be. Cousin Robert says if Ed will come to his house, he will send his carriage to meet him at Morganton the terminus of the railroad, a distance I expect of about 60 miles. He would no doubt be as pleasantly & comfortably situated there as anywhere.

Well, as I have told you about all I know of Ed & Scrap, I suppose I can with propriety say something of myself. My health, as it has been since the commencement of the war, is excellent. Sometimes I have a little cold which makes me feel badly for a few days, but I do not recollect ever to have missed a day's duty on account of sickness. In this respect I have been particularly blessed. When I left Lynchburg to join Genl. L[ongstreet] here, he expected to report for duty at once, but afterward concluded to wait a few days longer, to see if his arm would not improve some. His right arm is paralyzed from the effects of his wound, and is entirely useless to him. The Drs. think it will be a year or longer before he will recover the use of it. He only reported for duty two or three days since and was assigned by Genl. Lee to his old command, but he is hardly able for active service.[43] He says, however, that his services are more needed than ever before, and that he feels it his duty to render all the assistance he can. Genl. Lee seems delighted to have him back again, but he can not possibly be more pleased than the old 1st Corps is at his return to their command. We rode along the lines one day last week, and it was very gratifying to the Genl. to see the wild enthusiasm manifested by the veterans of his command on his appearance amongst them after such a long absence. When the men saw him coming, they mounted the breastworks and while he rode down the lines made the welkin ring with cheers for the *"old bull of the woods,"* as they love to designate him. It is gratifying to Genl. L. to know that though he is no favorite with the President & Bragg, yet he has what is much better, the unbounded confidence of Genl. Lee and the officers and troops of his command.

I hardly know what to say of the military situation. Everything around here gives evidence that Richmond is safe. Two or three weeks ago much uneasiness was felt, but now everyone seems to feel perfect confidence. Our troops are good and our fortifications are strong, and Grant will find it an exceedingly difficult matter to overcome them. The ranks of our army are being rapidly filled by the reserves and detailed more from different states. It is hoped and expected to get 10,000 men from Virginia alone. We must have *more* men, and the places of detailed men will have to be supplied by negroes—and, if needs be, I say put the negroes in the ranks and make soldiers of them—fight negro with negro.[44] I believe they will fight as well or better for us than for the Yankees, and we had better even free the negroes to gain our own independence than be subjugated and lose slaves, liberty and all that makes life dear.

We have just heard the sad news that the enemy have inflicted another severe defeat on old Early in the valley.[45] The report is that Early attacked two corps of the enemy and drove them 12 or 15 miles, capturing 18 pieces of artillery—that he then encountered a 3d corps and drove it 6 miles, capturing many prisoners, but that the enemy then rallied, attacked Early, routed him, recaptured the 18 pieces of artillery and captured 30 of Early's pieces besides. This is a serious blow to us and it is impossible yet to tell what bearing it will have on our affairs in Virginia. Should Sheridan now be able to carry out the original plan of taking Lynchburg, it will very much imperil Richmond. I hope, though, that we may yet be able to retrieve the disaster. We used to love to call Banks,[46] when he was in the Valley,

Jackson's commissary; equally as appropriately the Yankee's could call Early Sheridan's ordnance officer. He has lost in his campaign in the Valley near 70 pieces of artillery. Some time ago up there Early sent out Maj. Genl. Ramseur[47] on a little expedition. He came back pretty badly whipped. Early, in his fine falsetto voice, accosted him on his return with, "Well, Ramseur, you have gone and played hell." I think that if Genl. Lee were in the habit of using such language he might make use of the same expression to Early when he returns. Early has one of our best divisions (Kershaw's) with him, and I regret the more that he should waste the troops of our corps as well as his own. It is to be hoped that Genl. Lee will put some one in his place that *can* take care of troops and artillery.

We all look with much anxiety and interest to the result of the campaign in Ga. Hood has placed himself in a critical position, and he will either

[*The remainder of the body of the letter of 21 October 1864 is missing.*]

                        Tell Lang to go at once & follow Bob's example.[48] I would myself but am now too far from home, and when the war is over I will be too old. But he must not wait.

I have not recd. nor heard anything of the $250 which Mother sent by the young man you mention. What is his name?

Did Sue receive the photographs of Genls. Lee, Johnston, Jackson & Hood which I sent her? If so, tell her to acknowledge the recpt. of them at once. I will write to Mother in a few days. It makes no difference *who* I write to, my letters are *intended* for all—like Mr. Stanton's dispatches to Genl. Dix—except my letters are *truthful* and his dispatches are not.[49]

I am much obliged to you for writing to Mrs. Rogers. I was afraid that she had never recd. my letters, and would come to the conclusion that I was indifferent to her affliction. I wrote again not long ago.

You must make the boys write to me. I shall answer their letters with a great deal of pleasure. Any and everything that they may write will be interesting. Although I have been away from home nearly 3½ years, I have lost none of my interest in it.

I should like so much to visit home, if but for a few days, but cannot indulge myself in that pleasure until after the close of the war, unless they should take a notion to send my chief to the Trans-Mississippi.

TO ROBERT DANIEL GOREE

My dear Brother,   Near Richmond, Virginia, Decr. 18th, 1864

Some time since, I recd. from you *two* letters written in August from your camp near Harrisonburg, but very soon after they came to hand, I heard that your division had left that point to go, probably, to Missouri, so I did not write, not knowing to what point to direct a letter; but about a week since, I recd. your letter dated in October, and I now take this, the first opportunity, to reply to it. I am very much delighted that you have written to me so frequently of late, and hope that you will keep it up. I don't know to what cause to attribute your improvement in that respect; but I suppose to your *wife* at any rate *she* shall have the credit of it. Even at this late day, Bob, you must accept my congratulations on your marriage. They should have been offered you long since, had I known your post-office. You have shown your *good sense* in marrying *when* you did, as much almost as your *good taste* in marrying *whom* you did. You long knew before you were married the very high appreciation that I entertained for Melissa. I wish you both all the happiness imaginable. I have intended for a long time writing to her, but have neglected it; think I shall do so today.

I received a letter from Ed on the same day that I recd. your last. He is still in hospital in Lynchburg, Va., and of late has improved quite rapidly. He had a great many abscesses on his leg, all of which he says have healed. A place on the calf of the leg, from which the ball was cut out, still continues to run & probably will for some time to come. He is able to get up and down stairs and to walk about some with his crutches. His leg on account of having been drawn up so long is crooked at the knee, and it will be a *long, long* time before it will become straight again. The examining board of Surgeons at Lynchburg have recently recommended him for unconditional retirement. Should he succeed in getting on the retired list (of which there is hardly a doubt) he will try to get home next Spring. Ed, poor fellow, has had a hard time of it, and at one time the surgeons all thought there was no possible chance for his recovery, but close, careful attention and good nursing saved him.

Scrap returned some time since from his wounded furlough. He has entirely recovered from the effects of his wound, and his elbow is not stiff, as was feared it would be at one time. During the first part of his furlough he staid at Henderson, N. C., with Cousin Protheus Jones; he then went to Asheville, N. C., and remained with Cousin Robt. Pulliam. He went to Asheville weighing 120 lbs. and came away weighing 150 lbs. You would not recognize him if you were to meet him in the road—he is as fat as a guinea pig. Scrap is a gallant and faithful soldier. He is still a courier for Genl. Field, and is well pleased with his place. His horse was killed the day that he was wounded, but on his return I gave him one of mine.

David Scott belongs to Gary's Brigade of Cavalry, which is temporarily under Genl. Longstreet's Command, and camped four or five miles distant from our Hd. Qurs. Dave, however, went home on a horse furlough about a month since and has not yet returned. I suppose you have heard that he was married again. He married last spring a daughter of Stanhope Wallace, who is said to be a very interesting woman. She is quite pretty as well as quite wealthy. Howson Kenner belongs to the same regiment as Dave. I see him occasionally—he appears to be a good hearted, clever young man, but I think not very smart.

We are quietly settled down here, I suppose for the winter, or until Genl. Grant arrives at the conclusion that it is useless for him to longer expend his energies & resources in a vain endeavour to take Richmond. But he holds on in our front because I believe he does not know what else to do. He knows that to storm our works would destroy his army. And, whatever way he turns, he can't go far before he encounters Confederate bayonets. He can only move at present to the rear, for front and flanks are well guarded. Genl. Longstreet is in command of all the troops between Petersburg & Richmond, and on the north side of the James in front of Richmond. This line is near 20 miles long, but it is so strongly fortified that we would like the best in the world for Grant to *try* to break it with 100,000 men. Genl. Lee is at Petersburg with the troops around there. You all in the Trans-Miss. Dep't. need have no fears about Richmond unless Grant can get a *much* larger army than he has at present. Our troops have erected comfortable cabins, and are well fixed for the winter. They are in splendid spirits and ready, if not anxious, for a fight.

The situation in Georgia is not at all encouraging. Sherman has succeeded in marching through from Atlanta to the Atlantic coast near Savannah, and I feel in constant dread of hearing of the fall of that city, which I suppose has a comparatively small force for its defense. Sherman made this long march without much difficulty because we had but a small force to resist his advance. It was truly a great misfortune, the removal of Genl. Johnston from the Army of Tenn. Let his enemies say what they may, but next to Genl. Lee, he is the greatest *chieftan* in the Confederacy; in truth, he is superior to Genl. Lee in many respects. If he has not gained great victories, it is because he has never had the force at his control, nor ever been properly supported by the President who dislikes him. Had he been left in command, Atlanta would never have been given up, for he could & would have held it. He was blamed for retreating from Dalton to Atlanta, yet the odds against him were *greater* than those against Genl. Lee. Yet Genl. Lee was forced back with far greater rapidity from the Rapidan to Richmond, than was Genl. Johnston from Dalton to Atlanta. And never a word of reproach was uttered against Genl. Lee. But when Genl. Johnston was removed, why was not Genl. Beauregard, or some other officer of character and distinction appointed to the place? But Hood, a *tolerable* division Commander and *very poor Corps* Commander, was appointed. He issued a *flaming, fighting, boastful*, braggart address, casting a slur upon the glorious old Johnston, by saying that the day for being flanked out of position was passed. He fought three battles around Atlanta and was worse *whipped & easier*, and worse *outflanked* than has ever been anybody during this war, not even excepting his prototypes (the *braggarts*, Pope & Hooker).[50] He then starts on a wild-goose chase into Tennessee. After piddling about for a long time, he fights the battle of Franklin.[51] He is again whipped, and in one hour & forty minutes sustains a loss of 4000 men & 13 general officers, some of the best he had. He was whipped by a part of two corps of the enemy—the same two corps which Genl. Longstreet about a year since *routed* at Dandridge, East Tenn., with the skirmishers of Hood's old Div.

It makes me angry to even think on this subject, and I feel that somebody should be *hung* for a change which has resulted so disastrously to our cause. President Davis is to blame for having suffered his *prejudices* to influence him in a matter of such *vital* importance. Hood is to blame because he wireworked to get Johnston out and himself in. He inflamed the President's prejudices, but the grand scamp and the man who ought to be hanged is General Braxton Bragg.[52] *His* misrepresentations, *his lies*, induced the removal of Genl. Johnston. You probably do not feel so warmly on this subject as myself, hence I will say no more about it; have probably already written too much, as well as imprudently, about it.

I do not see any present prospects of an early peace. The enemy seem to be more determined than ever to subjugate us. We can only get peace by continuing to fight for it. It is better to die than be subjugated, and I for one am ready and willing to fight to the bitter end.

You say that things are getting on well in the Trans-Miss. Dept. What do you mean by well? Price has been run out of Missouri.[53] Is that *well?* Steele still holds Little Rock.[54] The 19th Corps was supposed to come in from there and help whip Early in the valley of Va. A. J. Smith's Corps crosses & recrosses the Miss[issippi] at pleasure.[55] It fought you at Pleasant Hill; it recrossed the river after Forrest; it then went back & ran Price from Missouri. Now it has come back to help whip Hood. Do you call all this *well?* If your officers can't & won't send troops to this side of the Miss. where they have been and are so much needed, they ought to have made such an *active* campaign as to have kept the enemy from reinforcing this side at pleasure. You all must do *better* over there.[56]

You have spoken in your letters, Bob, of endeavoring to get a detail. I should like to see you have one, *if you can keep it;* but you might keep it three or six or even twelve months, and then have it revoked. Men will be so much needed in the army that all details of that kind will be certain to be revoked sooner or later. Now the question is, whether you had better retain your present *comfortable* position, or run the risk of having your detail revoked and going into the ranks? I believe you are now Q[uarter] M[aster] Sergeant. It is comparatively a soft place—had you not best hold on to it while you have it? I merely suggest this to you.

I have recd. two or three letters from home recently and am much gratified to know that all are well, and that everything is getting on so smoothly. Mother seems to be much pleased with Lang's management, and I have no doubt that he is very efficient. In writing home, I have advised Lang to marry. I think that he ought to do so; but Sis Frank writes that he does not seem to have the least notion of it. As you have tried it yourself and know the advantages of it, maybe your advice will have more influence with him.

I should like very much to be at home this winter, but the expense and difficulties of travel are so great that I have long since despaired of getting there until after the war. I have many good friends on this side of the Miss., some of whom I visit when I can get a leave of absence.

Do you ever see Mart Royston? He is on Genl. Wharton's staff. Should you see him, please present my kind regards to him, as also to any other of my old friends with whom you may chance to meet up.

You have never explained to me how it was that you were taken prisoner at Pleasant Hill. You belong to the Q. M. Dept and I did not know that *it* was ever in danger except from raiding parties who go round to the rear. You must explain how it was when you write again.

Since writing the above, the news has come that Hood has again been badly whipped near Nashville. I have only hoped that we might get his *army* back again from Tenn. Now I very much fear that it will be entirely destroyed. *It is too bad!* Well, we must look the thing boldly in the face and try and use every effort to rectify it.

Bob, you must write to me often. I am always delighted to hear from you. I hope that we may all meet again around the fireside at home. When you write again, write me all about yourself. Scrap and Ed would send messages if they were here.

Your aff. brother,
Tom

R. G. Goree
Gould's Batt.[57]
Macley's Brig.[58]
Forney's Div., etc.
Marshall, Texas

"THE PRESERVATION OF THE HISTORY OF
WHICH WE ARE ALL SO PROUD"

TRAVEL DIARY OF THOMAS JEWETT GOREE
26 JUNE–6 AUGUST 1865

Campbell C. H., Va., June 26, 1865

At the time of Genl. Lee's surrender I was quite unwell and so could not start for Texas with Pleasant and others who were going home. I thought that by the time I was well enough to travel it would be difficult to find company going south and to travel alone in the unsettled state of the country would be too dangerous. So decided to send my horse on to Texas and go to Lynchburg and remain a while and then try and get home via N. York, N. Orleans, Galveston &c. I was encouraged to this, too, by Genl. Longstreet who had decided to go to Texas and proposed this route for himself. The only difficulty in my way was the want of funds, but I thought by some means to overcome this. Col. Powell proposed to me to find his wife who he supposed was in Richmond and take charge of her to Texas. She would furnish fund[s] &c. Afterwards upon enquiry found that previous to surrender she had gone South. I started my horse home by Mr. Duncan[1] who promised to take good care of him and to use every exertion to get him there. I hope he will succeed. I did not sell my horse because he was in thin order, because he was too thin in order to bring his worth. Besides he was a fine thoroughbred and I was anxious to get him home because of his fine blood.

Genl. Longstreet and myself came here from Appomattox C. H. where he expected to hear of Maurice[2] & two of his horses, sent off night before surrender, under charge of Lt. Alexander. Heard they had passed through Lynchburg the day after the surrender.

We remained here at Campbell C. H. one night, then went to Lynchburg, Genl. L. to see his family and I to see my brother Edwin, who was in hospital there, and other friends. I became the guest of my good friend, Jno. F. Slaughter, Esq. Spent my time in visiting Ed and friends in the city. After being there a few days, the Genl. concluded we had better not go through the North, but by private conveyance through the country. We had an ambulance and two good mules besides two horses of the Genl's. We had arrived at Lynchburg on the 14th of April and remained until the 29th, when we made a start for Texas. Came as far as this place, when Lt. Alexander, who had just returned home, informed the Genl. that he had not seen nor heard of his horses since he left Lynchburg on the 10th of April. The Genl. after hearing this thought it best to delay our departure until he received some tidings of them. I remained here about a week and then returned to Lynchburg.

In about a month, Genl. L. heard that his horses were at his brother's in Georgia.

About this time, the Genl. found that it would probably be necessary for him to visit Washington previous to going to Texas on some private business. He made application, but there was a delay of several days before the permission was granted. In the meantime he received a letter from his brother-in-law, Mr. Garland, advising him not to come North, but to remain in Lynchburg until he came on. He only came on last week, & today I expect the Genl. down. In this long delay my patience had been completely exhausted, and I have several times been tempted to start by myself, but the Genl. depended on me to go with him, and my obligations to him are such that I felt it my duty to do so.

Ed started from Lynchburg southward on the 3d of June. He had no money and I then had none to give him, but Yankees give transportation and furnish rations, and he can get along without it until he gets to some of our friends. I should have liked to have gone with him, but felt under obligations to go with the Genl. If there is railroad connection, Ed proposed to go on to Alabama; if not, he probably stopped with our relations in S. C.

I remained in Lynchburg until the 12th when my friends, Mr. & Mrs. Slaughter, started for New Jersey to see her relatives. During my stay of several weeks at their house, I recd. every possible kindness and attention, by which they have placed me under everlasting obligations to them. I hope that some day I may both have the means and opportunity to return some of their kindness. A day or two before I left, Mr. S., unsolicited, handed me $30.00 in specie, telling me not to return it until perfectly convenient to do so. This was certainly very considerate and a great favor when money is almost unobtainable. Mrs. Slaughter, altho a Northern woman, has a good warm heart. I became very much attached to both her & Mr. S. I recd. many little tokens of friendship from them. Ed was an inmate of Mr. S.'s house for seven months last year when wounded. I was there with him for six months. Mrs. S. during that time was in the North, but Mr. S. made us welcome, and to the kind attention to Mr. S.'s sisters, and other ladies in Lynchburg, he is no doubt indebted for his life. *God bless* them all.

I came back here from Lynchburg to spend the balance of my time with Col. Jno. D. Alexander, another friend whose family have shown me much kindness. I am sure that I have no cause to complain of the lack of Virginia hospitality.

I have chafed very much at the long delay to which I have been subjected. My anxiety to see once more the loved ones at home is very great, besides I feel that I ought to be there, but three long months must pass before I can have the pleasure of sitting at the family board.

Mother no doubt thinks that I show very little anxiety to reach home after an absence of more than four years. Wrote today to Mother, sent letter to care of E. H. Cushing,[3] Houston. Also wrote to Cousin Lucy Jones.

June 28th.

Off at Last.

Genl. L. came down day before yesterday. Yesterday we had the ambulance fixed. I wrote yesterday to my friends, Mr. & Mrs. Slaughter.

Left Campbell C. H. this morning at 9 o'clock. Our party consists of Genl. Long-street, his son (Garland Longstreet), Jim (a servant), and myself. The Genl. & Jim go in the ambulance, & Garland and myself on horseback. I constitute the advance guard. Jim is a negro belonging to Mr. Frierson near Shreveport, La., who takes this opportunity to get home.

Travelled today 30 miles, and have stopped for the night at Mr. Wm. Pannel's at Chalk Level, a very clever and hospitable gentleman. Roads quite rough. Mules jaded. Ambulance too heavily loaded. Crossed today Staunton River.

Thursday, June 29th.

We were *very* hospitably entertained at Mr. Pannel's. Very kind, nice people, several very pretty and agreeable daughters. Left there at 8 o'clock, passing through Pittsylvania C. H. Stopped for lunch about 2 miles this side. Came on in the evening near a little place called Whitmell and staid for the night with Mr. Phillip Thomas, a plain but clever man. He was a schoolmate of my old friend, Charlie Breedlove who was raised in this neighborhood. Roads today better. Country poor.

Friday, June 30th.

Started this morning at 7 o'clock. Came on 15 miles to Mr. Saml. Hairston's, a very wealthy old gentleman with whom we dined. The old man brot out his Porter which the Genl. & I enjoyed. Had a splendid dinner. Roasting ears for dinner. The old gentleman, very anxious for us to stay all night. Mr. H. is now very wealthy, owning 8000 acres of land and several hundred negroes. He has four children, each one wealthier than he is. At one time he owned more than 2000 slaves. After leaving Mr. H.'s this evening, passed thro a beautiful country, the valley of the Dan River. Crossed this evening the Smith River. Passed thro a little place called Leaksville. Had some difficulty in getting a place to stop. Finally taken in by Mr. Marlin, residing 1½ miles this side of Leaksville. Caught in a very heavy rain. Traveled today 29 miles. Crossed into North Carolina.

Saturday, July 1st

Accommodations last night very indifferent. No corn for horses. Stopped at noon near Madison. Fed horses with corn & fodder. Roads today very hilly and rough. Crossed Mayo River near Madison and Dan River at Hairston's Ford or Sawra Town. Stopped for the night at Mr. Lash's, 6 miles east of Germantown.

Sunday, July 2d

Very hospitably entertained at Mr. Lash's. Asked the amt. of our bill. Reply was, "No charge against men who have fought the battles of my country." Passed thro Germantown, a small, dilapidated-looking place. Stopped at midday near Hoovertown. Dr. Jones very kindly gave us oats for our stock. Yankee flag displayed at this place. Strong Union. Met with a young Mr. Conrad who invited us to go with

him to his father's and spend the night. We travelled this evening 10 miles. Crossed
the Yadkin River near Mr. Conrad's house at Conrad's Ferry. Mr. C. lives six miles
from Huntsville.

July 3d, Monday.

We were very hospitably entertained at Mr. Conrad's last night. Left there after
breakfast this morning. He gave us corn to feed our horses on at noon. Travelled
this morning 15 miles. Expect to go 8 or 9 miles further to Mr. Dalton's. Advised to
go there by Mr. Conrad. Roads today very good. Country poor & thinly populated.
General handed me today $30.00 in greenbacks. He had given me previously $9.45
U.S. cur[rency]. Reached Mr. Dalton's early in the evening, having travelled today
23 miles. Mr. D.'s is one of the nicest looking places I have seen in N. C.

July 4th., Tuesday

We were very hospitably entertained at Mr. Dalton's last night. His wife was
sick but his daughter (an only child) did the honors with much grace. If the Yankees
had not freed all the negroes, this would be the place for a young man in search of
a wealthy wife. The young lady is not pretty, but very well educated and has been
raised to business.

No bill to pay at Mr. D.'s. Left there between 7 & 8 o'clock this morning. Travelled 16 miles, when we stopped to get some forage at a Maj. Allison's. He insisted
that we should take dinner with him & have our horses fed, to which we consented. This gentleman is a rich old bachelor, but he has a nice establishment. He
has living with him Capt. Davis & wife, the latter his niece. She is a charming
woman, a daughter of Judge Pearson, Ch. Justice of N. C. Miss Boyle, a refugee
from Washington City, is also here. These kind people insisted very strongly upon
our spending the night, but the Genl wd. not consent. Mrs. Davis knew Capt.
Burns[4] of Houston. Sent her kind regards. Miss Boyle asked me to make some
enquiry about Lt. Ford of the 4th Texas.[5]

Left here a little after 3 P.M. to go to Lewis Ferry on the Catawba River. Passed
thro Statesville. Took the wrong road and went two miles out of the way. Reached
Mr. Lewis' in the night, having travelled 32 miles today and that, too, to find that
the boat was sunk and no chance to cross here. Put up for the night with Mr. Lewis.

Wednesday, July 5.

Treated very kindly last night by Mr. Lewis. No charge. Quite a nice young lady
there, Miss Calloway, refugee from Wilkesboro, N. C. By coming to Lewis Ferry
we had come 5 or 6 miles out of the way. Started early this morning. Crossed the
river (Catawba) at Island Ford. Had some difficulty in finding the ford. Stopped at
noon & bought some oats from a regular Union man. Genl. gave me 50 cts. green-
backs to pay for them. He did not like to take that kind of money. We left at 3
o'clock. Travelled about 10 miles but not finding a place to stop, bought some oats
and camped out. Travelled today 26 miles. *Roads very rough* & country poor. We

are 3½ miles from Lincolnton. The Genl.'s roll of bedding dropped out of ambulance today. Sent back when we missed it but could not find it.

Thursday, July 6th.

Took a cup of strong coffee which Jim made. After which I lay down on the grass and slept very comfortably all night. Horses fared well: plenty of corn, oats and nice pasture to run in. We started about 7 o'clock this morning and came to Lincolnton. We stopped here to see Genl Hoke[6] and he insisted so strongly that Genl. consented to remain with him until after dinner. In meantime had some repairs done to ambulance, also mules' shoes fixed. Had a very nice dinner at Genl Hoke's. Several gentlemen dined there with Genl Longstreet and others called on him during the day. Started from there 4½ o'clock P.M. Genl Hoke rode a mile or two with us. Came ten miles; could get no place to stay and so have to lie out again. Disliked it because we have no forage for horses.

Have turned them in an old wheat field where they will get a little picking. Garland Longstreet took wrong road this evening and did not get up until late.

Friday, July 7th.

Started at daylight. Had no supper last night nor breakfast this morning. Horses seemed fresh & travelled well. We expected to go to Dr. Miller's, five miles west of Shelby for dinner. Genl. Hoke recommended this place. Much to our disappointment, though, found out in Shelby that Dr. Miller did not live on our road. Yankee regiment stationed in Shelby. After leaving Shelby, travelled 8½ miles before we could get dinner for ourselves & forage for our horses. All hands hungry and so did full justice to our frugal repast. Horses feasted on oats. Rested here four hours. Started at 3 P.M. Crossed Broad River; came ten miles. Stopped tonight at Mr. Kemp's. The old woman a curiosity. Very much delighted to have the honor of entertaining Genl. Longstreet. Hope we will have no bill to pay. Nice pears. A good supper. Our horses have nothing but oats. Travelled today 31 miles. Crossed state line this morning. One week to the hour in N. C.

Saturday, July 8th

To my surprise, Mr. Kemp had a bill. Charged us six dollars. Very kindly invited us to call whenever we passed. Came today to within 1½ miles of Spartanburg & stopped for noon. Bought corn for our horses, $1.00 per bushel. Wrote a note to Howson Kenner to send from Spartanburg. *Very* sorry that I cannot go by to see relatives in Newberry. Principal object in writing was about brother Ed. Hope he is with Aunt Lucy.

It was nearly 4 P.M. when we left our nooning place. Passed through Spartanburg. A very pretty village. Saw there two of our army friends (Col. Walker & Captain Foster). Col. Walker[7] promised to carry my letter to Maybinton. Came on 8 miles from Spartanburg and stopped for the night with Mr. Bivings. Recommended to go there by Col. Walker. Crossed today a branch of Broad River & two branches of Tiger.

Sunday, July 9th.

Found the Bivings *very nice, clean* people.

Eldest son was in Jenkin's Brigade. Anxious for us to spend the day. No charge of course. Put us up a snack. Found my horse's back quite sore. Nearly 8 o'clock when we started. Came 18 miles before we stopped to noon. Roads good. Started again at 4 P.M. Passed through Greenville, the prettiest place I have seen since we left Va. Got directions there and came 7 miles this side to house of Mr. King, where we spent the night. Crossed today branches of Tiger River, the Enoree River, & Saluda River. Traveled today 30 miles.

Monday, July 10th

Bill last night $4 00. Started this morning to take the route by Pickens C H., but missed the road and came to Pickensville. Then concluded to come on by Old Pendleton C. H. After having come 14 miles, stopped to noon at the house of Mr. Walker, 8 miles from Old Pendleton. Got a very good dinner. Bot oats for horses. Paid 37 cts. Came on to Pendleton where we stopped to have our mule's shoes fixed. Then [in] about an hour several of the citizens came and paid their respects to Genl. L. Mr. Sitton invited us to remain all night. Young Mr. Sitton of the P.S.S.[8] gave the Genl. a bottle of old peach. Came on 4 miles further and have stopped for the night at Fort Hill, the residence of Mrs. A. P. Calhoun, once that of the great Jno. C. Calhoun.[9] The people are exceedingly kind and hospitable. They insist that Genl. L. will rest a day with them. Do not know that he will do so, but hope he will.

Travelled today 26 miles. Roads generally very good. General handed me today $20.00

Tuesday, July 11th

The Genl. would not consent to spend the day with the good people at Fort Hill. I was very much pleased with all whom I met here. Mrs. C., Miss C. & two grown sons, Capts. I went out to the library of the great ancestor, Jno. C. Calhoun, which is arranged just as it was at his death. I could but think while here how fortunate this great man was not to live to see the disgrace and ruin of his country which he strove so hard to prevent.

We left here at 10½ A.M. Mrs. Calhoun filled our *provision box* with nice bread, ham, pickles, butter, peaches, cantaloupes, besides putting in the ambulance two fine watermelons. Stopped to noon after travelling 10 or 12 miles. Enjoyed Mrs. C.'s nice lunch and one of the watermelons for which I paid 60 cts.

Started at 4 o'clock. Traveled till some time after dark.

Bought oats.

Could get no house to stay at, so have camped out. It makes no difference, as we have provisions for ourselves and forage for horses. We have travelled today 25 miles. Crossed at Ft. Hill bridge the Seneca River and later in the day several other streams whose names I did not learn.

When I went to start from Mrs. Calhoun's this morning, much to my surprise and regret found Beauregard (the horse I ride) very lame. Find that he is foundered. Had to ride in ambulance & let Garland lead him. Travels tolerably well after going a little way.

Wednesday, July 12.

I was up before day this morning & stirred up Jim and had horses fed. I made a fire and boiled pot of coffee & fried some ham. Breakfast consisted of cold rolls, ham & coffee, and 2d course of peaches & cantaloupes.

We got off quite early. Beauregard still very lame. After coming three miles, crossed the Tugaloo River at Jarrett's Bridge. After crossing the river, stopped for some time at Jarrett's shop to have a bolt made for ambulance. Charged $10.00. Left the shop 8½ o'clock. Travelled 10 miles over the worst road I ever saw. It was *almost* impassable. Stopped about 1 P.M., bought oats for which the Genl. gave me 50 cts. in change. We had for lunch today crackers, sardines, ham, watermelons & cantaoupes. Started again about 3 P.M. The roads much better. Reached Clarksville before sundown. Came to the house of a relative of Genl. L's. No one at home. Took possession. Genl. invited to stay at Mr. Kelsturm's, Garland and myself at Mr. Bean's. Had a splendid supper at Mr. B.'s. After supper some very nice music. Came back to stay all night with our baggage. Promised to return in the morning to Mr. B.'s. to breakfast. Travelled today 23 miles. We start in the morning for Mr. Wm. Longstreet's, brother to the Genl., 16 miles distant, where it is proposed to rest several days. Passed thro mountainous country today. We were very anxious to come by Tuccoa Falls today but heard that the road that way was impassable.

Thursday, July 13th

Garland & myself slept in Mr. Campbell's house where our baggage was deposited. Took breakfast at Mr. Bean's. Very nice people. A Miss Walton there. Nice young lady. Started from Clarksville about 10 A.M. Travelled over an exceedingly rough road, but not quite so bad as part of the road yesterday. Reached Mr. Wm. Longstreet's, who lives 1½ miles from Cleveland about 4 P.M. Mr. Longstreet not at home, gone to Athens. Expected back Sunday. I am very much pleased with Mrs. Longstreet and her sister, Miss Davis. They are acquaintances of my cousin, Miss Nelson.[10]

We found Maurice here with the horses. He was delighted to see us. Has been *perfectly faithful* to his trust. His horses looking well.

July 30th.

We have been here at Mr. Wm. Longstreet's since the 13th inst. Have had a very quiet, pleasant time. Mr. L. and family are *very* nice & agreeable people. On the 21st inst. we made an excursion to the top of Mount Yonah, which is said to be the highest mountain in Georgia. We had a fine, extensive view of the surrounding country, but the ascent was so tiresome & difficult that we were so exhausted when we reached the summit as not to be able to enjoy it to the fullest extent. On the

26th we went down to Clarksville and in company with Mr. Bean's family made an excursion on the next day to Tellula Falls.[11] The scenery at the falls is grandly beautiful, though I was somewhat disappointed with the falls themselves. The volume of water was not so great as I had anticipated. We did not have time, however, to see all the views. Returned to Mr. L.'s from Clarksville on the 28th.

We leave here on our journey southward tomorrow. Have remained a week longer than we anticipated on account of Genl. Longstreet having recd. a message from his friends, Genl. Tombs[12] and [blank in manuscript] that they wished to see him. The excursion to Tellula was made to meet these gentlemen, but they became afraid to venture out, and we did not see them. Our party will be increased by Maurice with the Genl's two horses, and Mr. Wm. Longstreet, who is going to Miss. We carry 4 days' rations for ourselves & horses & propose camping out.

July 31st.

Started at 7 o'clock this morning. Travelled 15 miles and stopped to noon. In the evening crossed the Chattahoochee River to east side at Clark's Bridge. Passed through Gainesville, Ga., & have camped for the night 2 miles west of Gainesville. Toll over Clark's Bridge $1.25. Travelled today 28 miles.

Aug. 1st.

It rained during the night. The mosquitoes, too, were troublesome so that I spent rather a bad night. Got off at six o'clock. Crossed to west side of Chattahoochee at Brown's Ford. When we stopped for dinner today, found two bolts in ambulance broken. Maurice went to shop and had two new ones made, price 50 cts. Passed through Cumming, Forsyth Co. Poor looking place. Have camped tonight 7 miles west of Cumming. Roads today rough. Maurice complains of being indisposed. Rained on us today.

Aug. 2d.

Had a very comfortable night's rest last night. Our horses had a very good pasture to run in. When we had come two miles, found that Garland had left his father's oilcloth coat at camp. Refused to go back for it. I went back, but someone had passed & picked it up. Followed on. Found the man & recovered the coat. Caught up with the party when we stopped to noon. Genl. L. presented me with overcoat. I gave my old cape to Maurice.

We came on this evening to Marietta where we stopped an hour or two to replenish our stock of provisions. This place has a garrison of Yankees and I purchased from Yankee commissary 2 hams, a box of hardbread and some sugar & coffee. Saw two colored ladies riding out in a fine carriage. We camped for the night three miles west of Marietta.

August 3d.

Left camp early this morning.

Travelled today 31 miles. Roads tolerably good.

Stopped to noon 2 miles east of Dallas. Passed this morning within 2 miles of the New Hope battleground.[13] The country for several miles east of Marietta to Dallas has been made almost a complete waste—the fencing all destroyed and all the best houses burned. It will take many, many years for the country to recover its former prosperity. Travelled this evening through the town of Dallas towards Van Wert; travelled over a rough mountainous country. Fell in during the evening with Major Byrd,[14] formerly Quartermaster of Wofford's Brigade.[15] At his invitation I rode in his ambulance and had my horse led. We camped a little more then three miles from Van Wert.

The Maj. had along a very large nice watermelon which we enjoyed very much. We were joined tonight by a Mr. Thompson of California, an acquaintance of Mr. Wm. Longstreet's, who proposes travelling with the party to Mississippi.

August 4th.

Passed this morning through Van Wert, a small dilapidated looking place. Stopped here with Maurice to have horse's shoes fixed. Others went on. Maj. Byrd left us here. Caught up with the party about 11 o'clock. Stopped to noon near the house of Mr. Goring [?]. Bought oats from him for horses. The Genl., Mr. L. and myself took dinner with him. He had a son there who resides in Rusk Co., Texas.

After leaving Mr. G.'s travelled 8 miles and camped near Judge Hutchings'. Horses had corn & good pasture. Mrs. H. sent us down some nice milk. Mr. Thompson has something the matter with his eye and is suffering very much with it.

Aug. 5th.

Got a very early start this morning. Travelled 16 miles before stopping to noon. Stopped near a house & had a ham boiled and bought 5 chickens which we had fried. We travelled this evening to within 2½ miles of White Plains. 2 or 3 miles before reaching Camp, Genl. Longstreet, who was behind in the ambulance, was accosted by a drunken man who wished him to drink with him and wanted also to trade his horse for a mule. On Genl. L.'s refusal, he rode off but before a great while he overtook the ambulance again and with a cocked pistol in his hand ordered the driver of the ambulance to stop. He then put his pistol inside as if endeavoring to shoot the Genl., when the Genl. seized the pistol & wrenched it from him. Where upon the man put spurs to his horse and made away as fast as possible. The Genl. will report the circumstance to the Yankees and try & have them arrest him.

Aug. 6th.

The Genl. & his brother slept in the house near which we camped. It rained quite a shower during the night but we managed to keep dry. Passed this morning thro White Plains. Road today splendid. Purchased corn this morning. Stopped to noon near the place of Dr. Snow near Oxford. The Dr. came down and invited us up to dinner but we did not go. He sent us oats for our horses and some corn to carry and sent us also some nice melons, peaches & grapes, besides having our jar filled with butter. The Dr. is a very nice gentleman. Lived at the commencement of the war in Tyler, Texas. Came out with 1st Tex. Reg. Was wounded & discharged.[16] Passed this evening in Oxford. The Genl. stopped and reported the man who assaulted him yesterday. The Yankee officers promised to send and have him arrested.

Travelled little further yet before we could find a camping place; finally camped on a large creek short [distance] from Talladega where I had the [several words illegible] & change of [one word illegible]. Especially fine night's sleep.

[The rest of the final page is illegible.]

JAMES LONGSTREET TO THOMAS JEWETT GOREE

My dear Captain,   New Orleans, La., Feb. 25th, 1866

I have wished to write you often since we parted but have not been able to satisfy myself that my letter in these uncertain times would ever reach you. I have determined, however, to make the effort.

The immediate object of this letter is to get you to send me your photograph. I am anxious to have one of each of the members of my staff, and am writing to them for those. Will you have yours taken and sent me as soon as you can? In the mean time write me, and let me know where you are, and I will send you mine if you haven't it.

I don't know whether you have heard from any of the members of the Staff or not. I have heard from Sorrel,[17] Cullen[18] & Latrobe,[19] and saw Manny[20] & Fairfax[21] in Washington last fall. All are well, and seem well content.

I hope that you are doing well, and in a fair way to recover the severe losses, etc. of the last four years. Dr. Barksdale was here a few days ago, and has just gone back to Va.

Mrs. Longstreet joins me in expressions of warmest regards for yourself and your mother's family. I hope that your brother is with you before this, and that he may yet recover from his severe wound.

I may possibly make a trip to Texas next month, and am particularly anxious to know where you are that I may, if possible, see you.

I remain, very truly yours,
J. Longstreet

Capt. T. J. Goree
near Cold Spring Polk Cty Texas

JAMES LONGSTREET TO THOMAS JEWETT GOREE

My dear Captain,   New Orleans, La., March 15th, 1866

Your kind letter of the 4th is just received. In despair of hearing from you or of you I sat down and wrote you at a venture near Cold Spring. I hope that you will get the letter. The chief object of it is to get your likeness or carte de visite. I am writing for one of each of my staff officers.

They are all at their homes except Latrobe in Europe. We are doing pretty well here for new beginners but our trade is almost entirely in Western produce.[22] If this will keep up so as to feed us for a time, I hope that we may get some cotton when the next crop comes in. I would enjoy a trip through Texas very much but am too poor to indulge in that luxury. I shall make a trip through that part of it which is tributary to N. O., however, on business, and can in that way combine pleasure with interest. And, when I am able, you may rest assured that I shall make you a visit of pleasure. If there was a chance of my getting enough of trade to warrant me in making the trip, I should do so this summer and fall. But the present indications would not warrant it. If you can send us any cotton, we will share with you the commissions. That is, let you in for one fourth commissions on all that you can influence to our house. As there are three of us that will be giving you a share equal to each of the rest of us. If you make any effort at this, keep a memorandum of all who promise you, and the number of bales so as to send us and we shall in that way be able to render your account. The commission now is about four dollars to a good large bale, so that your share would be a dollar per bale—at present rates. If you can control a few thousand bales for us, it would be a right handsome outside operation for you.

Maurice is with my horses at Macon, Miss. Jim left me for his home last Septr. I have heard nothing of him since.

Dr. Barksdale has been here on a visit which he seemed to enjoy very much. He has returned to his home in Richmond.

The Owens[23] are well and join in kind salutations. Mrs. Longstreet also sends her kindest remembrance for you and regards to your mother and family. I [hea]rd of your brother after he had gone through. Tell him that [he] ought not to have passed without giving us a call.

I remain Very Truly Yours,
J. Longstreet

Capt. T. J. Goree
Huntsville Texas

JAMES LONGSTREET TO THOMAS JEWETT GOREE

Office of Longstreet, Owen & Co.
Genl. James Longstreet, Wm. M. Owen, Edward Owen
Cotton Factors Commission Merchants
No. 37 Union Street New Orleans

My Dear Captain,   March 9 1867

Your much esteemed favor of the 5th Feby. was duly received. When it reached me I was confined to my room by a badly sprained ankle, and your letter was handed to Col. Owen for attention. He tells me that he knows so little about machinery and its application to cultivation that he is loath to give an opinion about the articles that you want and that he has therefore hesitated about writing you until I could get out and examine the articles. I am getting about again and will look at the various articles of improved machinery in a few days and write you what I think of them.

As to sending your cotton to this market, you should consult your own judgment. I believe that you will realize more by selling here than you can at Galveston. You can see the quotations, however, and determine for yourself. My judgment is based upon the fact that persons often buy in Galveston and sell in this market. As long as this can be done, it seems to me quite evident that those who make the cotton can do better with it by sending to this market. This is unquestionably the cotton market of the country, and when people start to send their cotton to market they ought to send it all the way to market instead of stopping on the way to sell.

I remain Very Truly Yours,
J. Longstreet

Capt. T. J. Goree
Texas

JAMES LONGSTREET TO THOMAS JEWETT GOREE

James Longstreet, Pres't. C. Williams, Sec'y.
Office of the Great Southern and Western
Fire, Marine & Accident Ins. Co.
No. 21 Carondelet Street
New Orleans

My dear Captain,   [March] 28th 1867

I think, from the imperfect affairs in the way of machinery for agriculture, that it will be better for you to wait till the next season before making purchases. There are changes and improvements being made every day almost. So that if you buy now you will find that you will like others better next year. I think that they will be listed this year and you will do better to wait till next season.

As for differences of market between this and Galveston, I don't know that I am any better posted than you. I know, though, that cotton is frequently bought in Galveston and sold here on speculation. I conclude then that if speculators can make money in that way, planters could.

I dont know when I shall be able to visit you. My time is much cut up and I fear that I may not get to Texas this year.

I remain very truly yours,
James Longstreet

Capt. T. J. Goree
Near Huntsville Texas

THOMAS JEWETT GOREE TO ROBERT E. LEE

Near Huntsville, Texas Octr 22d 1867
Genl R. E. Lee
Lexington, Va.[24]

Dear Sir:

I had the honor a few weeks ago to address you a letter in reference to admitting my brother & young Kittrell & Hayes to matriculate for five months.[25] I intimated in that, that circumstances might compel us to withdraw them even sooner than the end of the short term.

I very much regret now to have to inform you that those circumstances have arisen. We find it impossible to make pecuniary arrangements to continue my brother & nephew longer at school. Dr. Kittrell is one of the victims to the terrible scourge which has visited so many portions of our state (yellow fever). His family were dependent on his practice, and his death has left them without means.

Dr. K. was the guardian of young Hayes, and it will be necessary for him to come to look after his interests.

I wish very much that the young men could remain with you, not only for the present session, but even until the completion of their course. My nephew has a fine mind, is very ambitious, and could he remain until he graduated, would reflect credit upon the Institution.

The yellow fever is gradually disappearing from our little villages, after having afflicted us terribly, taking off probably 8 or 10 percent of the population. I am up today for the first time, after a severe struggle with it.

Hoping Genl. you will appreciate the necessity for the course we have taken, I am with much respect

Yr friend & obt. servt.
Thos Goree

EDWARD PORTER ALEXANDER TO THOMAS JEWETT GOREE

Dear Goree: Columbia, So. Ca., Apr. 24th 1868

Your most welcome letter of the 8th was forwarded to me[26] here & reached me yesterday. You can't imagine the pleasure it gave me to hear from you & especially that you are both willing & able to give me some help in the task I fear I have foolishly undertaken. Gen. Longstreet begged me to do it & I thought I could finish it in a three-month vacation (I have been Professor of Math. & Engineering in the University here for over two years) & I consented.

I have worked at it now two vacations & all the leisure I could possibly steal from my duties day by day for nearly two years & I have hardly made a beginning.

What I want is not the general facts that everybody knows but the details & they only exist in the memories of survivors & I have to elicit them by correspondence & you cannot imagine how utterly hopeless a task this seems. For every one hundred letters and circulars I send, I get about ten replies, & of these ten, about six simply say that they have lost all records & can't remember anything they think important enough to write. About three promised to write something they remember "as soon as they get time" & about one sends me what I want to get or ought to get from him.

Even Sorrel & Gen. Longstreet are as unsatisfactory as the rest. I have never been able to get your address before. The only address I have received for Walton was incorrect & of the staff & regimental officers of Hood's old Brigade I haven't been able to get a single address but one and he sent a letter with only promises as yet unfulfilled.

You may be sure, therefore, that I appreciate your kind offer. I will proceed at once to tell you how you may not only do me a great favor but contribute, materially I have no doubt, to the preservation of the history of which we are all so proud & which our children will value as much as ourselves.

I particularly need help on the following parts of the history and, as I will work at them in order, you may take a little time to them and send me just everything you remember about them. Even the most trifling things often assist me in reconciling conflicting or clearing up of doubtful points.

First I have very insufficient data about Williamsburg & I would like to have all you can send by June 1st.

Second Tell me all you know about Seven Pines. D. H. Hill claims the battle for himself & his division—at least in great part & perhaps truthfully. I have no desire to dispute it but want to know what you think of it. Also all you know about Huger's delay. I was on Johnston's staff then and from what I saw then & documents I have since seen, I have been more disposed to attribute Huger's delay to Gen. Johnston's indefinite orders than to Gen. H. Please tell me all you know about it & what troops of Huger's fought at all—if any—also which of Longstreet's & especially tell me about the affair on the second day at Seven Pines (June 1st). The Yankees represent a glorious victory, our people say there was no fight. I heard heavy firing & one of my correspondents says that on that day his brigade "retreated slowly" "because Mahone gave way on his flank." Do you know anything about it? Of course I don't want to cover up anything, but to tell the honest truth—in which there is all the glory we need wish. I can give you to the middle of June to tell about that as fully as you can.

Third I want not only Jenkin's letter about the Blackwater but I want a connected & detailed account of the whole Suffolk campaign—including all Longstreet did while in command at Petersburg. I remained at Fredericksburg & I have not been able to get from Longstreet or Sorrel or anybody else one word about that campaign. So do please write me a connected account of its object & movements in full.

[*The remainder of the letter is missing.*]

JAMES LONGSTREET TO THOMAS JEWETT GOREE

My Dear Captain,   Hot Springs, Ark., May 12th, 1875

I am collecting all of the information that I can get of the battle of Gettysburg, and must ask you during your leisure hours [to] jot your recollections of everything connected with the battle down, and send them to me. I want every item that you can give me from the day that we marched from Chambersburg until we returned to Culpepper Court House. All that you positively know and remember, all that General Lee said in your hearing as well as all that I said, are particularly important.

My reason for asking so much trouble on your part is an address published in the December (1874) number of the Southern Magazine by Parson Pendleton,[27] in which he attributes the loss of Gettysburg to treachery on my part.

If I can collect sufficient data, I shall write and publish a complete account of Gettysburg, which will put the matter at rest. Mr. Pendleton delivered this address in Mississippi and through Southern States in 1873, and my friends then asked me to answer his assertions and I determined to do so, but about that time General McLaws and General Humphreys[28] published accounts completely vindicating the First Corps and myself which I thought sufficient and preferred to let the matter rest there, as an account by me would necessarily be more complete and might bring up old matters that were better left, when they can, to be forgotten. His recent publication or republication has started many friends again in their petitions that I shall fight the old battle over again.

I am here on a visit to try the effect of these waters on my crippled arm and shoulder. I have worked myself completely down since I went to New Orleans, and now have been laid up for the last six or eight months. As I am not fit for anything else, I have concluded that I must go over Gettysburg this summer, if ever. I expect to return to New Orleans about the first of June, and after a week or two then I hope to go to the mountains of Ga. for the summer. Letters sent to New Orleans will be properly forwarded if I am not there.

                                        I remain
                                Very Sincerely Yours,
                                    James Longstreet

THOMAS JEWETT GOREE TO JAMES LONGSTREET

Genl. James Longstreet
Hot Springs, Ark.   Law Office of Abercrombie & Goree
My dear Genl.,   Huntsville, Texas, May 17th, 1875[29]

Your favor of the 12th inst. has just been received and contents noted—It is needless to assure you how glad I am to hear once more directly from you, but I am truly sorry to learn of the bad state of your health, and hope that during the summer you may recuperate and be as stout and well as formerly. It has been a long time, General, since we have corresponded, but my failure to write you occasionally has been from no lack of the warmest feelings of friendship for you. Not a year has passed but that I have promised myself time and again to write to you. With my heart full of gratitude, I often think of you and of many acts of kindness shown me, and the innumerable marks of esteem and confidence bestowed upon me by you during the four long and trying years that we were together. Although we may differ in our *political opinions,* yet I have always given you credit for honesty and sincerity of purpose, and it has made no difference in my kindly feelings towards you personally, and I trust that it never will.

In regard to the business portion of your letter, I will take great pleasure in complying with your request, at as early a day as practicable. Just now in preparing for our courts I have not the time to do the work. At this late period there are many things which it might be important to note that have escaped my memory.

I was present, however, just after Pickett's repulse, when Genl. Wilcox came up and when Genl. Lee so magnanimously took all the blame of the disaster on himself. Another important circumstance which I distinctly remember was in the winter of 1864 when you sent me from E. Tennessee to Orange C. H. with some dispatches to Genl. Lee. Upon my arrival there, Genl. Lee asked me into his tent where he was alone with two or three Northern papers on his table. He remarked that he had just been reading the Northern official reports of the Battle of Gettysburg, that he had become satisfied from reading those reports that if he had permitted you to carry out your plans on the 3d day, instead of making the attack on Cemetery Hill, we would have been successful. He said that the enemy seemed to have anticipated the attack on their centre, in consequence of which they had withdrawn the larger part of their force from their left flank, and from Round Top Mountain, and that if you had made your flank movement early on the morning of the 3d day as you desired that you would have met with but little opposition. To this conversation I am willing, if necessary, to make affidavit.

On the 2d and 3d days of the battle before the fighting commenced, I know that Genl. Lee was constantly with you, and that any movement that you made, as well as all delays, was with his advice or concurrence

When Pendleton delivered his lecture in Galveston in 1873 in which he made his charges against you, a report was made of his lecture in the city papers—and at the time I fully made up my mind to reply through the papers, but being in Galveston soon afterwards, and finding that his charges had rather created a feeling of indignation against him, and especially among soldiers who had fought and bled with you, I deemed it unnecessary to say anything.

Pendleton has presumed upon your present unpopularity to make charges which he otherwise would not have dared to utter, or which if he had, would have created such a storm of indignation as would have completely and forever overwhelmed him

It does seem preposterous and absurd to me, and must to every soldier of the Army of Virginia, the idea of such an old *granny* as Pendleton presuming to give a lecture or *knowing anything about* the battle of Gettysburg—Although nominally *Chief of Artillery,* yet he was in the actual capacity of Ordnance Officer, and, as I believe, miles in the rear. I know that I did not see him on the *field* during battle

It was a notorious fact and general[ly] remarked that he was almost entirely ignored by Genl. Lee, as Chief of Artillery, and the management of it given to the Corps Chiefs of Artillery.

I think that I once prepared an account giving my recollections of the Gettysburg Campaign, either for Genl. E. P. Alexander, or for Jno. B. Sener of Va. It was written when everything was fresh in my mind, and if I could get it might be of some service to me in preparing my a/c for you. Do you know the present address of the above named parties? If you can conveniently do so, I would like that you furnish me a copy of the Southern Magazine (Decr. no.)—Where is it published?

I will send this to Hot Springs as it can reach there before the 1st of June. When you write again, tell me more of yourself, your wife, and family. As you are probably aware, I am married. Have a splendid wife and two interesting children living, a girl & boy. Have lost two boys.

With my kindest regards I remain Truly & Sincerely your friend,

Thos. J. Goree

JAMES LONGSTREET TO THOMAS JEWETT GOREE

My Dear Captain,   Hot Springs, Ark., May 21st, 1875[30]

I have your valued favor of the 17th and thank you, not only for your kind attention, but especially for the tender feeling of friendship that you express and cherish, and assure you that my high appreciation of your moral and mental worth is unabated. 'Twould be strange indeed if the bonds of four years of severe service in a common cause through four years of trials that do not come upon men once in a century, could be severed by time or trials. I feel the same deep interest in you and yours to-day as ever. I seldom think of the war or of Texas that you do not come into my mind—and often comes to my mind the meeting with your brother at the

Wilderness, just after he was hurt, and my effort to conceal all feelings, and to hide tears, unbidden, that forced themselves upon me.

I knew that you were married but had not heard so much of your affairs as your letter contains. Am glad to know that you are happy, as I always knew that you must be whenever you made your mind up to marry. Have you taught your wife to make the nice dish of Welsh-rabbit that you used to treat us with occasionally in camp?

I presume that the difference in our politics is not so great as appears, if sifted to the bottom. The end that we seek, I know, is the same, the restoration of the Southern people to their natural and proper influence. The best and speediest means of arriving at this end has been [the] only difference. And in Louisiana, particularly in New Orleans, the most violent Democrats now admit that mine would have been the best policy for that state. It is too late though now, and affairs will have to drag along in that state.

Your letter covers the especial point that I wanted your evidence upon, which is the remarks made by General Lee upon the occasion of your visit to his head-quarters in the winter of 1863 & '64. In what month was your trip to Orange C. H. made? Gen. Lee told me the same thing in reference to my plan for Gettysburg. A writer for Blackwoods' Magazine, March, 1872, quotes Gen. Lee on the same subject as follows. "If," said he on many occasions, "I had taken General Longstreet's advice on the eve of the second day of the battle of Gettysburg and had filed off the left corps of my army behind the right corps in the direction of Baltimore and Washington along the Emmettsburg Road, the Confederates to-day would be a free people." It had often been reported to me just before Gen. Lee's death that he often, and in the most poignant distress, referred to that occasion as the one on which the cause was lost, and with a full sense of his own responsibility in the matter, but he was mistaken in his conclusion, I think. That is, in his conclusion as to the result of the war. I have not a doubt about the result of the battle if he could have permitted me to operate as I wished, but I am now inclined to think that an overruling Providence had ordained that slavery in these states should cease forever in the year 1865, and it is hardly possible that it should have ceased if we had been made an independent nation. And I shall always regret that I did not see Gen. Lee before he died, that I might endeavor to relieve his mind of this awful burden of his responsibility.

I shall look with interest for your minute details of Gettysburg and should like you to include the Wilderness battle. Where we were when the order to march for Wilderness was recd., the hour of its receipt, time of march, road &c. &c? Southern Magazine is published in Baltimore. I have but one copy or would send it [to] you. That was sent by a friend who insists that I reply to Pendleton's address.

I leave for N. O. next week—say 26th. With feelings of kindest interest in your good wife and yourself and little ones, I remain Most Sincerely Yours,

James Longstreet

JAMES LONGSTREET TO THOMAS JEWETT GOREE

My Dear Captain,   New Orleans, La., June 2d, 1875

I have just received letters from Colonels Taylor, Venable and Marshall,[31] assuring me that they had not heard of Pendleton's "sunrise" attack until they saw [?] his address when I got Parson Jones' book.[32] (Had to send to New York for it). He and Gen. Early now put the hour of attack at "daylight," which in that climate makes a difference of one or two hours. But the singular part of the book is that it clearly indicates that Gen. Lee, after failing to pursue the Federals with the four divisions that he had on the field on the first, ordered me, after the enemy had an entire night to rally his demoralized force, throw up temporary works, and draw up his other troops, to attack at daylight with two divisions, unaided by even a demonstration from either of two other corps, and drive the enemy from his stronghold. And Gen. Early says that if I had attacked at daylight, "it must have resulted in brilliant and decisive victory."[33] If his opinion as to military affairs was of much value, I should consider it a high compliment to our two divisions to claim for them such results, but I think him better authority as to the readiest and quickest means of turning his army over to his adversary than any other branch of the "Art of War."

Do you remember the occasion when Gen. Lee sent to Magruder and asked him not to make a certain attack upon the supposed position of the enemy, as no one was there except our young friend, Capt. Meade.[34] Jones puts this just after Malvern Hill. It was just after Gaines Mill, I think. I wish, whilst I am at it, to correct all of Jones' & Early's irregularities connected with me and mine. Meade, I believe, was under my orders at the time.

I remain
Very Sincerely Yours,
James Longstreet

Capt. T. J. Goree
Huntsville
Texas

JAMES LONGSTREET TO THOMAS JEWETT GOREE

My Dear Capt. Goree,   Atlanta, Ga., 22d Augt., 1881

Yours of the 16th instant was duly received, and it gave Mrs. Longstreet and myself great pleasure to hear from you and of yours. I am much pleased to know that the authorities of Texas know how to appreciate you, and I hope that you may always retain their confidence which I know you so well merit.

Occasionally I see Fairfax and Erasmus Taylor,[35] who are as kind as ever. Sorrel

I hear from occasionally, and hear of Latrobe once in a while. The latter has returned to his home in Baltimore. He and Sorrel are married since the war. Fairfax is not doing so well of late years, but I hope that fortune's wheel may again turn in his favor ere long. Walton and Manning are, as you say, dead. The latter many years ago, the former, during the yellow fever some three or four years ago. We have two children more than when you last saw us: a son and a daughter. All are well and stopping at Gainesville till the weather is cool enough for them to come down for the winter.

Tom's wish that I held the position in Texas of Marshal instead of Ga. reminds me of the thought that has often occurred to my mind since I came to Ga. I have some fine lands in Texas that I should have gone to instead of coming here and investing my means in the poor lands of this state.

Wife joins me in kindest expressions for your good wife and the little ones.

I remain Very Sincerely Yours,
James Longstreet

JAMES LONGSTREET TO THOMAS JEWETT GOREE

U. S. Marshall's Office Northern District of Georgia
Atlanta, Ga., 27th Dec., 1881

My Dear Captain Goree,

Yours of the 19th instant introducing Lt. Gov. Story[36] was left at the office, and duly received. I was absent when Gov. Story called, and when I went to look him up, he had gone. I regret that I failed to see him during his visit.

When your nephew was here, I was much engaged with court business. As soon as I could get out, I went to the Exposition grounds to look him up, but learned here that he had gone back to Texas. It will always be a great pleasure to see any of your friends, as well as yourself. For I do not know that [I] can mention any one to whom I feel stronger attachment.

Very Truly Yours,
James Longstreet

Capt. T. J. Goree
Austin, Texas

JAMES LONGSTREET TO THOMAS JEWETT GOREE

My Dear Captain,   Gainesville, Ga., 18th Feby., 1885

I will ask as a great favor that you will occupy your spare time in putting down your recollections of our campaigns during the late civil struggle for me.

I expect to write all of my experience of the war, and your retentive and accurate memory will be of great service to me if you can let me have your assistance.

I shall be glad to get all that you can send me of facts of your own knowledge and of reports, or hearsay points, as all may assist my memory in weaving the actual facts into narration. My mind was so occupied in active operations, that as soon as one thing was accomplished or passed, I dismissed it from my mind, and in that way shall overlook many interesting and minor details if I can get no assistance from you. Give me any incident connected with Gen. Lee and myself, as these will particularly aid me in recalling events. I will say that you cannot give me more than I need if you give the daily and hourly occurrences of every part of the four years.

Very Truly Yours,
James Longstreet

Send me the matter as you put it down without waiting to complete the whole.

JAMES LONGSTREET TO THOMAS JEWETT GOREE

My Dear Captain,   Gainesville, Ga., 22d Feby., 1885

Your kind letter of the 17th instant is received.

I shall with pleasure write Mr. Burgess as you have kindly suggested. I hope you will study over the Sharpsburg campaign for two or three weeks or more if you prefer, and send me the benefit of your reflections in the minutest details. The points not written up are now those that I want most, and thus often go further towards giving light of operations than official reports, i.e., such light as the historian most needs.

Before reaching Frederick, Gen. Lee proposed to me to make the surround and capture of Harper's Ferry.

I objected that the move would be imprudent, as we were in the enemy's country where he would receive information of any and all such movements within ten or twelve hours of our starting; that his army though badly beaten, was not so demoralized, but he must move out against us in any event. But when he found we had dispersed our forces, he would not only move, but rapidly, and attack. This fact I think I have frequently mentioned to members of the staff. Do you recall that I had done so?

Wife and all well, and hope this may find you and yours the same.

J. Longstreet

Captain T. J. Goree
Huntsville
Texas

JAMES LONGSTREET TO THOMAS JEWETT GOREE

Gainesville, Ga. 8th March, 1885
Captain T. J. Goree
Austin, Texas

Dear Captain,

Yours of the 24th ult recd. & noted.

I will be pleased to give any assistance to Goggin[37] in my power. I can give him a letter of introduction to my kinsman Lamar and have him introduce him to the P[ost] M[aster] General favorably. This may put Goggin in a fair way to the place he seeks. If you see him again, please ask him to jot down and send me every item he can of the Maryland campaign as well as Chickamauga and Knoxville.

I am now at work on the Maryland campaign including the return to Virginia after Sharpsburg and hope to have your aid as well as Goggin's. I don't want things that have been published, but every item of conversation, official acts, &c &c that you can recall that has not been published.

Very Truly Yours,
James Longstreet

Mrs. Longstreet bids me add her kind messages.

JAMES LONGSTREET TO THOMAS JEWETT GOREE

My Dear Captain,   Gainesville, Ga. 24th July, 1885

I am trying to get up items for a narration of adventures, especially of the Confederate War.

My purpose in the present writing is to ask you whenever anything of marches, orders, battles, or anecdotes connected with the war occur to you, to put them down in writing and send them to me.

Anecdotes of battles are usually of interest, as giving the readers better ideas of what war is.

If any of the old Texas Brigade are with you, or if you meet with any, I hope you will ask them to send me anything that occurs to them of interest that I may put down their little contributions and large ones if they will be so kind as to send them.

Wife joins me in kindest remembrances.

Always yours,
James Longstreet

JAMES LONGSTREET TO THOMAS JEWETT GOREE

Piedmont Hotel
James Longstreet, Prop'r

Gainesville, Ga.
30th Jay. 1887

My Dear Captain,

I think you were present when Custer came in on the day of surrender and called on me for surrender. If you were, won't you give me your recollections of the interview?

Very truly yours,
James Longstreet

E. PORTER ALEXANDER TO THOMAS JEWETT GOREE

New York Hotel

Dear Goree,

New York, Nov. 29, 1887

I am writing for Century a brief a/c of the surrender.[38]

Please give me your recollection of the interview between Longstreet & Custer at the time.

To be of service I must have it in a fortnight. Address me at *Savannah*, Georgia, & greatly oblige.

(In haste) Sincerely yours,
E. P. Alexander

THOMAS JEWETT GOREE TO EDWARD PORTER ALEXANDER

Decr. 6th, [1887]
Genl E. P. Alexander
Savannah, Ga.

My dear Genl.:

I have just received your favor of Nov. 29th from New York, and sent to Austin.

I was with Genl. Longstreet on the road near Appomattox when the interview was had with Genl. Custer. My recollections from what I heard myself, and what I heard from others at this time, is about as follows:

Genl Gordon & Genl. Fitz Lee, with the remnants of their commands, were in front, near the town of Appomattox, and were fighting severely, and being hard pushed by the enemy in our front. Genl. Longstreet was commanding the rear of our army consisting of Fields' & Mahone's Divisions but they were not engaged. Genl. Lee had gone through the lines to try and meet Genl. Grant. Genl. Gordon being heavily pressed, sent to Genl. Longstreet for reinforcements, which the Genl. was unable to furnish him. I think it was the third time that he sent that Genl. Longstreet sent Maj. Thos Sims[39] of his staff to Genl. Gordon with directions that he send a flag of truce to the enemy in his front, and obtain a cessation of hostilities. Genl. Gordon asked Maj. Sims to be the bearer of such flag—to which he consented and rode forward. He was soon met by Maj. Sims, who delivered to Genl. Custer the message from Genl. Gordon requesting cessation of hostilities. Custer demanded of Sims that there must be an unconditional surrender of the army to Genl. Sheridan. Sims mentioned the fact that he was only a staff officer on Genl. Longstreet's staff, when Custer requested that he be conducted to Genl. Longstreet.

Orders were given in meantime for cessation of hostilities, and Sims escorted Genl. Custer to the top of the hill across the branch to Genl. Longstreet, where was present Genl. L[ongstreet], nearly all his staff and I think yourself and some of your staff. A brief colloquy was held between Genl. Longstreet and Genl. Custer— a part of which I heard—and a part of which Genl. Longstreet repeated afterwards. Genl. Custer renewed his demand for an unconditional surrender to Genl. Sheridan, who was in command of the Federal troops in front. Genl. Longstreet told him that Genl. Lee was in command of the army, and he alone had authority to surrender it—that he, Genl. Lee, had gone back to find Genl. Grant with a view of negotiating a surrender—and that he [Longstreet] could not comply with his demands.

Genl. Custer persisted in his demand, but Genl. Longstreet firmly and courteously refused. Finally Genl. Longstreet seemed to lose his patience, and in substance told Genl. Custer that he could not and would not surrender the army, that he (Longstreet) was not half whipped yet, and if he (Custer) was not satisfied to await the result of the conference between Genl. Lee and Genl. Grant, he could return to his command, and commence hostilities again as soon as he pleased, and he would see that he met with a warm reception. This seemed to settle Genl. Custer's demand for the surrender to Genl. Sheridan, and he agreed to await the conference between Genls. Lee and Grant. This terminated the interview.

I do not pretend to give the exact language, but simply the substance, having heard a part myself, and heard Maj. Sim's statement—of the flag of truce—and being with Genl. Longstreet constantly until August, 1865, I heard him tell it very often—and I think the above version is substantially correct.

After the surrender was made in the McLean House, I recollect very distinctly the return from there of Genl. Lee and Col. Marshal. As they rode up the road, on both sides of which our troops were bivouacked, they commenced cheering him, and rushed en masse to the road, and so surrounding them that it was with difficulty they could make their way through the crowd. They finally made their way to Genl. Longstreet's headquarters on the side of the hill and dismounted—the troops having followed on, and still surrounding. They [the troops] mounted on the top of the wagons, and even on the backs of the horses, when Genl. Lee made the brief talk, telling about the surrender, the terms &c. When he ceased talking there were no dry eyes in that crowd. Many of the old ragged veterans rushed up and shook Genl. Lee's hand. I was standing very near him, and heard a ragged soldier, as he shook the General's hand—his voice choked with emotion, say, "General I hope we may soon be exchanged, and fight them again." The Genl. replied, "Yes, my friend, I hope so." Immediately after this one came another, more ragged if possible than the first, and he was crying as if his heart would break—and between his sobs, he said, "Genl., I wish every damned Yankee was in the bottom of hell. Don't you?" To this the Genl. maintained a dignified silence.

Another circumstance I will recount. After the surrender, Genl. Longstreet determined to come to Texas, and I think had mentioned the fact to Genl. Lee. When Genl. Lee was about to take his departure for Richmond, a great many of his old officers called at his headquarters to bid him "Good-bye." As Genl. Lee passed around, he had some pleasant remark to make to each one whom he bade good-bye. I was standing next Genl. Longstreet, and he warmly embraced the Genl., and then turning to me, and shaking my hand said—"Captain, I am going to put my old War Horse [Longstreet] under your charge. I want you to take good care of him."

At the time, I have mentioned when Genl. Lee came by our headquarters and made his talk, Genl. Gregg,[40] a federal officer, who had been captured near Farmville, was present (being on parole at our hd. qurs.) and saw the demonstration.

I believe you are the only writer who has mentioned the fact that the surrender took place in McLean's house, and that McLean's place near Manassas was near the scene of almost the first battle of the war. I knew McLean when he lived near Blackburn's Ford, and met him at his house in Appomattox on the day of the surrender.

On the 30th of January last, Genl. Longstreet asked me for my recollections in regard to the Custer interview, which I gave him, and which he afterwards wrote me were substantially correct.

I have written you, Genl., very hurriedly, and probably more than you wanted, but I hope that you may cull out something that may be of service to you.

I always think of my intercourse with you with the greatest of pleasure, and nothing would give me more pleasure than to meet with you.

Your friend truly,
Thos. J. Goree

THOMAS J. GOREE TO HOUSTON *DAILY POST*
31 January 1888

Longstreet and A. P. Hill

To the Editor of The Post:

The statements contained in a publication in your paper a few days since in regard to a misunderstanding between Generals Longstreet and A. P. Hill during the war are not altogether correct, and especially is that statement incorrect in regard to a challenge having been sent by General Hill and declined by General Longstreet. During a part, if not all the time, of what is known as the seven days' fighting around Richmond, General Hill's light division was a part of General Longstreet's command, and fully performed its part in that wonderful campaign which reflected so much credit on the Confederate arms. Immediately after the campaign the Richmond papers contained reports of several battles, and especially the battle of Frazier's farm, in which nearly all the credit of the fight and victory was given to General Hill's division, doing an injustice to other divisions of Longstreet's command that contributed as much as the light division to the victory. Colonel G. M. Sorrel, Longstreet's adjutant general, felt called upon in behalf of the other portions of the command to correct the reports as published. This led to a considerable correspondence and feeling between General Hill and Colonel Sorrel, General Hill finally refusing to have any official or personal relations with Sorrel, and for a short time it was feared that a duel would result. When General Hill refused to have any communication with headquarters through the official channel of General Longstreet's adjutant general, then General Longstreet sustained his adjutant general, and the matter was settled by Hill's division being transferred from Longstreet's to Jackson's command. The relations between Longstreet and Hill were strained for a short time only, and they were warm friends until the day of General Hill's death. General Hill's feeling was against Sorrel, and for a long time they did not speak to each other, but they were both gallant soldiers and noble men. As an evidence of General A. P. Hill's nobility of character, in the fall of 1864 he made application to have Colonel Sorrel, who was still chief of staff of General Longstreet, promoted to be brigadier general and assigned to the command of a brigade in his division. It was done, and General Sorrel in his new position maintained the enviable reputation which he had acquired on Longstreet's staff. General Hill recognized his merits, and magnanimously laid aside his personal feelings for his country's good. General Sorrel was very severely wounded just before the surrender at Appomattox. He is now a prominent business man in Savannah, Ga. Longstreet and Hill were both noble soldiers of the Confederacy, and it is to prevent an injustice being done either of them that this statement is made.

Confederate

GILBERT MOXLEY SORREL TO THOMAS JEWETT GOREE

Dear Goree: Savannah, Ga., March 5, 1888

It is a long time since we have exchanged a word but I have heard of you from time to time, and always with pleasure, that you were well and in positions of importance and responsibility. For myself, you may know that for some years I have been in the transportation business—connected with the Georgia Central Rail Road first as the agent here of its marine service and connections to Northern ports and now as the manager of these steamship lines. It has brought no wealth or much ease but has maintained me in responsible position with enough to go through with. So much for myself, thinking you might like to know where I am, and I would like in return to hear of yourself.

Everybody has been busy with affairs and no time has been at my command for much correspondence, but I have an ever continuing & growing feeling of affection for those with whom I was so long associated like yourself in the "great days" now settling so long in the past. Let me have a line from you.

I have some suspicion that you have been writing a little about those past events, and as to myself very kindly and considerately. The Houston Daily Post of Jany. 31st, 1888, reached me with a marked contribution—entitled "Longstreet & A. P. Hill" and signed "Confederate" which I guess must be from my friend Goree. I know of no one of our corps so well acquainted with the incident therein recited as yourself and I owe you my thanks for the correction so fully and accurately given.

Accurate in all except that reference to a duel between Hill & myself—It had gone beyond my rank and was between the Major Generals until healed by Genl. Lee.

I so well recollect the whole affair terminating as to myself with Longstreet's order to go to Genl. Hill's camp and place him in arrest—the care with which the young officer arrayed himself for this duty and the somewhat natural trepidation of presenting himself to a Major General to place him in arrest. The occasion however was smooth, formal, and courteous—Afterwards I had nothing but kindness from poor Hill. It was to him I owed the vacant Georgia Brigade and to him I was indebted for much help and encouragement in reorganizing it while under his command.

Is our old friend Goggin in Texas? Genl. McLaws is here but out of position at present. I shall be very glad to hear from you, dear Goree, and renew my thanks for your timely and partial contribution in the Post.

Yrs. ever sincerely,
G. M. Sorrel

Capt. Thos. Goree

GILBERT MOXLEY SORREL TO THOMAS JEWETT GOREE

My dear Goree: Savannah, Ga., Apl. 2, 1888

While in New York recently your letter of Mch. 17th was forwarded to me and I was sincerely glad to hear from you, of your doings and of your good family. To think how lean we were in those days; you with only 125 lbs., myself about the same and now to hear of your "heft" of 175! I come myself ten pounds short of you, but I have been blessed with continued good health. I send you a photo which I must confess, however, was taken as far back as 1876. Have had none done since. I may say it is still a fair likeness although I am of course much whiter. My hair and beard quite silver. Nothing stops for old Time.

I had written you Mch. 5th and for some reason addressed it to San Antonio. It was returned to me "unclaimed" yesterday and I cannot do better than let it go now to proper address just as it is.

You got the Hill-Longstreet matter very nearly straight and there is little to add to it. I think it began soon after our return from Westover. Hill, you will recollect, had a good writer in his Division, Jno. W. Daniell,[41] I think, and the really splendid performances of that division were fully set forth in the Examiner. But some injustices, probably quite undesigned, were done to our own stout division whose work was second to none, and you may recall that we were all fighting mad. While this feeling prevailed, Longstreeet came to me one day with sketch of a short letter and asked if I objected to send it to the Whig (I think it was the Whig) and sign it as A. A. G.—Only too willing, and off it went. I don't recall more of its substance except that it was a decidedly flat contradiction of many of the statements of the Examiner writer. Nothing more was heard of it until some days after when the two divisions found themselves near the river turnpike and Hill temporarily under Longstreet's Command. Some note in usual form of courtesy was sent to Hill (routine business of Adjutant General's office) to which answer came back that Genl. Hill declined to communicate with Maj Sorrel. This, of course, took me to Longstreet and my chief at once wrote to Hill requiring him to obey the order. A refusal still followed and perhaps there was still another note between the two generals but, Hill still disobeying, result was I was sent to put the Maj. Genl. in arrest as I have already sketched. Then it seems the serious matter began between the two Major Generals. I did not see the correspondence but understood it was of decidedly hostile character, and very grave results were impending when they were happily healed by the intervention of General Lee. The divisions never after, as you will recall, served together. This is how I recall the incident after lapse of 25 years: long, long ago, is it not, Goree.

You are quite right in saying the difference left no sores; I believe Hill was always friendly afterwards with Longstreet. He certainly was with me. Very unexpectedly I found myself called to command one of his Georgia Brigades and I now have in my possession a copy of his letter in which he asked for me and the endorsement of Lee, Cooper, Seddon and the final "make the appointment" of "J[efferson] D[avis]." The original would have great autographic value for me. I have failed in getting anything but an official copy.

If you come across any of our old friends, please give them my love and best wishes—Goggin, Lindsay Walker[42] or any others. I have met Latrobe but once—Alexander is now the chief of our RR System being both President of the Georgia Central System and their Steamship Lines of which I am the manager.

Do, Goree, send me a photo of yourself. I want to see how you look. When you go North again, try to take in Savannah.

Yrs. ever sincerely,
G. M. Sorrel, Savanah

Major Goree
I have been long married with no children.

GILBERT MOXLEY SORREL TO THOMAS JEWETT GOREE

My dear Goree,   Savannah, Georgia, Aug. 17, 1890

You must write to Cullen and make him send you a copy of the group recently photographed at Richmond. We dined with him after the unveiling of the Lee statue, a "First Army Corps dinner." There were Longstreet, Kershaw, Field, Alexander, Latrobe, Barksdale, some Washington artillery men, and some Virginians. A very enjoyable occasion on which you were not forgotten.

Longstreet looks old, feeble, indeed badly broken up, but in the procession he received a splendid and well deserved ovation from the old soldiers.

When we rose from dinner, it was proposed that a group should be photographed next day, and it has been handsomely done. The men in it are Longstreet, Field, Kershaw, Alexander, Latrobe, Cullen and Barksdale. I much prize my copy, although very sorry I am not in it. They waited for me some time, but I was staying with the Stewarts at Brook Hill, about four miles out of town, and they had planned for me to visit the spot where Jeb Stuart fell, to put some flowers on the little shaft that his soldiers have raised where that fine cavalry leader perished. I could not get into town for the picture, much to my misfortune.

I am sure Cullen has some copies, and will be glad to send you one. Address: Dr. J. S. D. Cullen, Richmond, Va.

The day in Richmond was a great and memorable one, never to be forgotten. The statue is an imposing artistic success. A sufficiently good portrait it is, horse and rider, the figure of The Commander; of a great dignity, yet full of force and fire. It is worth stopping as you pass through, to study it well, especially familiar as we were with the form of our great General.

I shall always, dear Goree, be glad to hear from you, and am

Yours ever sincerely,
G. M. Sorrel

JAMES LONGSTREET TO THOMAS JEWETT GOREE

J. S. Thornton
Thornton, Wright & Co.
Bankers
My Dear Captain,   San Antonio, Tex., W. B. Wright, 22 Jany, 1891

Your good note recd.

I am now out for an hour and will at the end of this time stop to see you at the Menger.[43]

Yours truly,
J. Longstreet

THOMAS JEWETT GOREE TO ELIZA THOMAS NOLLEY GOREE

Menger Hotel
San Antonio, Texas
H. D. Kampmann, Prop. H. W. Browder, Chief Clerk

My dear Tommie,   San Antonio, Texas, Jany. 23rd, 1891

You will see I am in San Antonio. Came yesterday morning. General Longstreet was delighted to see [me], and seems to appreciate my visit very much. He seems very feeble, and is so deaf that it is hard to converse with him. He is the guest of Capt. J. J. Stevens, who has insisted on my coming and staying with him while here. Will go back to Austin in the morning. I am trying to get a promise from Genl. L[ongstreet] to make us a visit. Can't say yet whether or not he will come.

You will see from papers about my chances. I have none, but no change will be made at once. I think Capt. Smither will be retained. I am doing what I can to have Capt. Douglass appointed in my stead.[44]

Hogg assured me that I need not give myself one moment's uneasiness about Gillaspie's getting anything.

I will go back to Austin tomorrow, and may come on home tomorrow night, or remain there two or three days. Am going to see Mrs. Cunningham today.

Love to all.
Affly.,
Thos. J. Goree

JAMES LONGSTREET TO THOMAS JEWETT GOREE

My Dear Colonel Goree,   Gainesville, Ga. March 20th, 1892

Your favor of the 16th instant is received, and gave me much pleasure. If left to my own feelings, it would give me sufficient pleasure to pack up and go on my visit to you and yours at once but I feel more and more the importance of putting my record on paper at the earliest moment. I have just learned that I will soon be able to get the last of the war records, now publishing by the War Department, and for them I have been waiting to be sure that my narrative should be sustained by the records of the period to which it relates. The records will not be complete, as many have been lost, but most points can be made manifest by parts of the correspondence and reports.

I think you will be a little surprised in some regards. Affectionate salutations for Mrs. Goree as well as your noble self.

Yours sincerely,
James Longstreet

Can you get for me the words of the "Bonnie Blue Flag"[45] originally sung in Texas dring the war?

JAMES LONGSTREET TO THOMAS JEWETT GOREE

My Dear Colonel Goree,   Home, 5th—27th—92

I am looking up some Confederate war songs, and want especially "The Bonnie Blue Flag." Can you put me in the way of getting it? I hear of a book of ten songs in which words are given for "The Bonnie Blue Flag," but ladies here tell me that they are not the words of the song as sung in the war.

> Always yours,
> J. Longstreet

JAMES LONGSTREET TO THOMAS JEWETT GOREE

My Dear Colonel Goree,   Home, June 9th, 1892

Your interesting letter of the 6th instant is recd. and noted. I hope that you may be able to get the words of the song, for I can't be satisfied without it—unless I may find it in Georgia. Several ladies are on the search for me and have been for some months.

Referring to the resolution you write about, I beg to say that between the lines of all of these efforts are to be read mental reservations not suited to the occasion. The reason, I suppose, is that they are usually written by someone who is in politics who wishes to leave a hole through which to escape if occasion should require.

I started to write, as you suggested, a response, but the thing stands out so clear that it seemed to me it would have been better not to call up any names. Under this conviction it would be difficult to write in the spirit I wish to feel and express for my comrades.

> Sincerely yours,
> J. Longstreet

JAMES LONGSTREET TO THOMAS JEWETT GOREE

My Dear Colonel Goree,   Home, June 17th, 1892

Your kind letter and inclosures came duly to hand. I regret putting you to all the pains you have taken in the matter of the song. I thought that I mentioned that

I had the book of songs but that they were of recent addition. Ten song[s] of the war is the one I wanted. The recently made songs would not fit in a matter of war record. The homespun dress and the palmetto hats[46] I remember particularly in the old words as the girls were wont to sing and glorify in them. I made a trip through parts of Texas in 1866, and remember how the Texas girls would jump at the sound of Dixie and the Bonnie Blue Flag—and it is the words as sung in those days that I am seeking. That you should have gone to such trouble in copying, gives me trouble.

I am going now to hope to make you a visit next winter, if I succeed in putting my work off of my hands. I will make an unusual effort to do so. And am pleased to say that my health is so improved that I want to go back to San Antonio to show Mr. and Mrs. Stevens that I am not naturally the cross one that I appeared when suffering from the grippe. It is only the last two or three months that I have felt entirely relieved of it.

Affectionate salutations for your good wife as well as yourself.

Sincerely yours,
J. Longstreet

I hope you can excuse this penciling. It comes so much easier to my stiff arm.

JAMES LONGSTREET TO THOMAS JEWETT GOREE

My Dear Colonel Goree,   Home, Augt. 26th, 1892

I am just now closing out the East Tennessee campaign and to give an accurate account of affairs it is necessary to mention the case of General Robertson so far as to account for his leaving us, and the appointment of his successor. As my memory may be a little out, I will ask you if he (Robertson) was brought before a court or was the case passed over and his successor appointed, and give me the full name of his successor, Gregg, who, by the by, figures or will figure at the opening of the Wilderness.

Then I want your photograph with your official signature on the face so that it can be facsimiled.

With affectionate salutations for yourself and family.

Yours Truly,
J. Longstreet

If anything occurs to you of interest in the Tennessee campaign, please note it for me in case I may have omitted it.

I have found the words of the song that I was looking for, "The Homespun Dress."

JAMES LONGSTREET TO THOMAS JEWETT GOREE

My Dear Colonel Goree,   Home, Sept. 4th, 1892

Your favor covering the photos duly received; the letter as well. You did not sign officially. Please send on slip of paper official signature, that I may try and have it facsimiled—and attached to the picture.

As I have some apprehension about the return of the picture once it gets into other hands, the war time photo is returned for Mrs. Goree. She has the original and can have a picture of the present replaced at anytime and as I hope for your success in the election, it will be better to have one of the State Treasurer to replace the one that I must send to the publishers. I mail with this the returned photograph.

I am glad at times to feel that I am not in politics. In 1867, when the Reconstruction Acts passed, I was anxious to keep the South out of the troubles that she has passed through since, and that was about the extent of my interest in affairs of state. For my pains I had nothing of good from them, or even appreciative expressions of sentiment.

> With respectful salutations for your good wife I remain
> Yours very Truly,
> J. Longstreet

I have no thought of going to Dallas or any other place till my papers are in the hands of publishers. Then, my health permitting, I hope my first visit will be to New Birmingham if you are not moved before that to the state capital.

Can't you write off and send me an account of our ride on the night of the 1st of April, 1865, from Richmond to General Lee's headquarters, at Petersburg.

JAMES LONGSTREET TO THOMAS JEWETT GOREE

My Dear Colonel Goree,   Gainesville, Ga. Nov. 4th, 1892

Can you give the particulars of the interview between General Custer and myself when he rode down to call the surrender of the Army? I am anxious to give an accurate account of it, and of the words that passed between us, and think your recollections may be clear if you were near enough to hear. If you were not, do you know anyone who was? Dr. Cullen has published an account of it, but I think, in fact I know, that it is not accurately drawn. He is a little inclined to the sensational.

I know very well what passed in my mind, but am not sure that I spoke it all.

> Yours truly,
> J. Longstreet

JAMES LONGSTREET TO THOMAS JEWETT GOREE

My Dear Colonel Goree,   Home 11. 12. 1892

Your kind letter received.

We have news of the Texas vote for president, but none of the local elections, so I am hoping for you.

My mind is clear of the meeting between Custer and I. He said, "In the name of General Sheridan I demand the unconditional surrender of this army." I said, "I am not the Commander of this army and if I were would not surrender it to General Sheridan"—but how the after remarks came in, I do not so clearly remember. The substance of this was about as you have stated, but I am anxious to have the precise words if possible.

Alexander writes me that he only heard part of the interview. He also writes me that after General Lee rode to the rear, I ordered Mahone and Wilcox' division to reinforce Gordon, that a report was made to me of a place at which we could break through, that I sent Col. Haskell[47] on his blooded mare to recall General Lee from the meeting proposed by his aide to our rear; that I sent him with part of his artillery to post the division of Mahone and Wilcox with his artillery, and that that was the last line of battle formed by any part of the Army of Northern Virginia. I remember ordering the troops forward and seeing some of them pass while Custer was yet with me. Cullen has published an account of the interview, but as you know is a little inclined to be sensational. So I can't well accept his account.

Sincerely yours,
J. Longstreet

Colo. T. J. Goree
New Birmingham Texas

JAMES LONGSTREET TO THOMAS JEWETT GOREE

My Dear Colonel Goree,   Home, 7th 7th, 1894

Your esteemed favor of the 29th ultimo is received and was read with pleasant recollections of allusions to the past.

I am glad to hear that you are nearer to me than when at Birmingham, and am trying to find it in myself to resolve to visit you next winter, but fear to venture a positive promise. My daughter is now grown and is the only member of the family with me, so my movements must depend in a measure upon her. As long as there is room for hope, I shall think of visiting you when the weather gets colder.

Of your reference to the reunion at Houston next year, I must suggest that I am not of the United Confederate Veterans Association. It costs something to join that organization and our little county association is poor and has not been able to get in. Besides, the grand organization was started for political purposes, which is not altogether agreeable to our organization—and it is especially unpleasant to those who manage the United Confederate Veterans to have me amongst them. I had no notice of the reunion at Birmingham, Alabama, this year and have no idea that I can have notice of the one to be at Houston next year. It is especially unpleasant to General Gordon for me to be of the reunion, even as a guest. The old soldiers, when they see me, forget their new leader in peace, and it tries his patience. He remembers the talk given when he fled the Battle of Seven Pines, the disreputable break of his division under Early at Cedar Run that led that panic, the worse case at Stedman, where he put ten thousand men into the Union forts to be killed, his run of fourteen miles as rear guard on the day of Sailor's Creek, and quitting his duty as such, taking with him the artillery on that route, and leaving Ewell and Anderson without a gun, to take his duties as rear guard. This is an epitome of his military career and he knows that I know it and will tell it. He has made a grand newspaper record since the war, and has now the benefit of it, but is fast losing the place in the minds of the people that come from claims trumpped since the war. Contemptible as was the career of Early, it was better as a soldier than that of Gordon. Or I could more appropriately say, it was not so bad, for better don't suit the career of either.

I was invited to the New Orleans reunion because the Washington Artillery insisted that I should be. That is how came I there. I was called to the night meeting of that reunion by the soldiers, much to the disgust of the managers. When I entered the building, the soldiers and officers rose and cheered and cheered till I reached the stand and bowed acknowledgment of their good feeling. Right soon, the business was interrupted by calls for opportunity to come up and shake my hand, and ended by hurrying Gordon and others of the managers from the stand in order to make room for the soldiers to come up and meet me. So you may know that I cannot be called to another reunion.

My invitation to the unveiling of the Lee statue was brought about in a similar manner. I had been left out of the arrangment intentionally or otherwise. The Washington Artillery when they voted to go, wrote to go as my escort, assuming that I was expected. Finding that I was left out, they thought that they should not go as an organisation, and so intimated to the Richmond managers when they concluded to invite me, under the impression, I suppose, that I would decline. When there, I was assigned position in the general procession intended to be with the Washington Artillery as I had requested, but my carriage attracted more attention, I suppose, than was expected and we were sidetracked, but that only made it more unpleasant for the managers. Generals Fitz Hugh Lee, Gordon, and other grandees rode along, but little noticed by the troops in line, but as they passed our carriage they broke and crowded about us and hurried around in such crowds as to block the street, which threatened to break up the procession, and, when urged on, tried to take the horses from the carriage and pull it along with them, and it was all that Latrobe and Cullen could do to urge them on and preserve their line of order. These items are mentioned to show how unpleasant it would be for the United Confederate Veterans to have me with them. Then a political organization of that kind is not a proper one. Everywhere except in the South, soldiers are accepted as comrades upon equal terms without regard to their political affiliations. So I have come to regard it a high compliment to be excluded from the U. C. V., as my absence becomes more conspicuous than would be my presence.

With affectionate salutations for yourself and wife and children and grandchildren, I remain

Sincerely Your Friend,
J. Longstreet

You see that I am not yet cured of the old soldier habit, once we are started on war times we find it difficult to reach a stopping point.

JAMES LONGSTREET TO THOMAS JEWETT GOREE

Home, Sept. 11th, 1894
Colo. T. J. Goree, Texas

My Dear Colonel Goree,

It seems that I failed to express myself clearly about the U. C. V. reunions. It is the marked attentions that they are generous enough to show that troubles me, in that it displeases the leaders of the U. C. V. and causes them to put out a new supply of their scandalous rumors that start afresh the newspapers.

I can't say anything now definite yet about the proposed visit to Texas. With salutations for your family I remain Yours Always,

J. Longstreet

GILBERT MOXLEY SORREL TO THOMAS JEWETT GOREE

Ocean Steamship Company of Savannah

G. M. Sorrel, Manager
N. York, June 19, 1896

Dear Goree,

The enclosed letter (newspaper clipping) from Longstreet will be very familiar to you. A copy was most kindly sent me from Lynchburg by you and from it one of my friends in Savannah unexpectedly put it in print for the first time.

I hope you are well and happy. I am doing a steady grind of work here—steamships—and sometimes meet Latrobe, and he hears often from the Old General. I hear the book sells well.

Always Yrs. Sincerely,
G. M. Sorrel

LONGSTREET TO LEE
Savannah *Morning News,*
June 1896

A Bit of Confederate History,
The Recommendation That Brought Gen. Sorrel Promotion

Gen. Longstreet's book has caused to be brought forth quite a number of incidents of the late war, which that distinguished Confederate necessarily passed over very briefly in his narrative. In the Battle of the Wilderness, May 6, 1864, Longstreet's corps moved to the support of A. P. Hill's corps early in the morning, and checked the onward movement of the enemy. In this attack Gen. G. M. Sorrel, (then Lieutenant Colonel and Chief of Staff of Gen. Longstreet), under the orders of his chief took Mahone's, Wofford's and (G. T.) Anderson's brigades, and swinging around to the right, the Confederates carried everything before them. For his gallantry on that occasion, Col. Sorrel was made a brigadier general on the recommendation of Gen. Longstreet, in the subjoined letter:

Lynchburg, Va., May 19, 1864.—
Sir—   Gen. R. E. Lee. Commanding, etc.:

The peculiar character of the position occupied by the enemy in my front on the 6th inst. was such as to render a direct assault impracticable. After a brief consultation with the commanding generals, a move was agreed upon, turning and attacking the enemy's left flank. Lieut. Col. Sorrel, my Chief of Staff, was assigned to represent me in that movement, with instructions as to the execution of it. The flank attack made by three brigades was to be followed by a corresponding movement of the other brigades of the command. This attack, made under the supervision of Lieut. Col. Sorrel, was executed with much skill, promptness and address, and the enemy was driven from his position in haste and some confusion.

It occurs to me that this is one of the instances of skill, ability and gallantry on the battlefield which should commend itself to the high approval of the executive.

I therefore take great pleasure in recommending Lieut. Col. Sorrel's promotion to brigadier general, for distinguished conduct on this occasion. I should have reported this case much earlier and asked for promotion upon the spot, but that I was struck down by a painful wound a few moments after the execution of the movement. I am still unable to write, and hence must ask the privilege of signing this by my aide-de-camp.

I am, General, very respectfully, your most obedient servant.

(Signed.) J. Longstreet,
Lieutenant General,
(Signed.) by T. J. Goree,
Aide-de-Camp

NOTES
INDEX

NOTES

SHORT TITLES

Annals of the War. *Annals of the War, Written by Leading Participants, North and South.* Philadelphia, 1878; rept. Dayton, Ohio, 1988.

Blackburn, "Terry Rangers." J[ames] K[nox] P[olk] Blackburn. "Reminiscences of the Terry Rangers." *SWHQ* 22 (1918): 38–77, 143–79.

Blessington, *Walker's Texas Division.* [John P. Blessington.] *The Campaigns of Walker's Texas Division.* New York, 1875.

Boatner, *Dictionary of the Civil War.* Mark M. Boatner III. *Dictionary of the Civil War.* New York, 1959.

Chilton, *Unveiling and Dedication of Monument to Hood's Texas Brigade.* F. B. Chilton, comp., *Unveiling and Dedication of Monument to Hood's Texas Brigade on the Capitol Grounds at Austin.* Houston, Tex., 1911.

Cooling, *Forts Donelson and Henry.* Benjamin Franklin Cooling. *Forts Donelson and Henry: The Key to the Confederate Heartland.* Knoxville, Tenn., 1987.

Crute, *Confederate Staff Officers.* Joseph H. Crute, Jr. *Confederate State Officers.* Powhatan, Va., 1982.

Crute, *Units.* Joseph H. Crute, Jr. *Units of the Confederate States Army.* Midlothian, Va., 1987.

Cullen, *Peninsula Campaign.* Joseph P. Cullen. *The Peninsula Campaign, 1862.* Harrisburg, Pa., 1973.

Cunningham, *Doctors.* H. H. Cunningham. *Doctors in Gray: The Confederate Medical Service.* Baton Rouge, La., 1958.

Current, *Encyclopedia of the Confederacy.* Richard N. Current, ed. *Encyclopedia of the Confederacy.* 4 volumes. New York, 1994.

Cutrer, "John Wesley Rabb." Thomas W. Cutrer, ed. "'We are Stern and Resolved': The Civil War Letters of John Wesley Rabb, Terry's Texas Rangers," *SWHO* 91 (1987): 185–226.

Davis, *Jeb Stuart.* Burke Davis. *Jeb Stuart: The Last Cavalier.* New York, 1957.

Davis, *Bull Run.* William C. Davis. *Battle at Bull Run: A History of the First Major Campaign of the Civil War.* Garden City, N.Y., 1977.

Dawson, *Reminiscences.* Francis W. Dawson. *Reminiscences of Confederate Service, 1861–1865.* Charleston, S.C., 1882: rept. Baton Rouge, 1980.

Dowdey, *Seven Days.* Clifford Dowdey. *The Seven Days: The Emergence of Robert E. Lee.* Boston, 1964.

Dyer, *Gallant Hood.* John P. Dyer. *The Gallant Hood.* Indianapolis, 1950.

Faust, *Encyclopedia of the Civil War.* Patricia L. Faust, ed. *Historical Times Illustrated Encyclopedia of the Civil War.* New York, 1986.

Fletcher, *Rebel Private.* William Andrew Fletcher. *Rebel Private, Front and Rear.* Beaumont, Tex., 1908; rept. Austin, Tex., 1954.

Foote, *Civil War.*   Shelby Foote. *The Civil War: A Narrative.* 3 vols. New York, 1958–74.

Freeman, *Lee's Lieutenants.*   Douglas Southall Freeman. *Lee's Lieutenants: A Study in Command.* 3 vols. New York, 1942–44.

Fremantle, *Fremantle Diary.*   James Arthur Lyon Fremantle. *The Fremantle Diary.* Boston, Mass., 1954.

Gallagher, *Struggle for the Shenandoah.*   Gary W. Gallagher, ed., *Struggle for the Shenandoah: Essays on the 1864 Valley Campaign.* Kent, Ohio, 1991.

Giles, *Terry's Texas Rangers.*   L[eonidas] B. Giles. *Terry's Texas Rangers.* Austin, Tex., 1911; rept. Austin, Tex., 1967.

Govan and Livingood, *A Different Valor.*   Gilbert E. Govan and James W. Livingood. *A Different Valor: The Story of General Joseph E. Johnston.* Indianapolis, 1956.

Graber, *Terry Texas Ranger.*   [Henry W. Graber.] *The Life Record of H. W. Graber, a Terry Texas Ranger, 1861–1865.* Dallas, Tex., 1916; rept., with introduction by Thomas W. Cutrer, Austin, Tex., 1987.

Hassler, *Commanders.*   Warren W. Hassler, Jr. *Commanders of the Army of the Potomac.* Baton Rouge, La., 1962.

Heaps and Heaps, *The Singing Sixties.*   Willard A. Heaps and E. Porter Heaps. *The Singing Sixties: The Spirit of Civil War Days Drawn from the Music of the Times.* Norman, Okla., 1960.

Heitman, *Register and Dictionary.*   Francis Bernard Heitman. *Historical Register and Dictionary of the United States Army, from Its Organization, September 29, 1789, to March 2, 1903.* Washington, D.C., 1903; rept., Urbana, Ill, 1965.

Hood, *Advance and Retreat.*   John Bell Hood. *Advance and Retreat.* New Orleans, 1880; rept., ed. and introduction by Richard N. Current, Bloomington, Ind., 1959.

Johnson, *Texas and Texans.*   Frank W. Johnson. *A History of Texas and Texans.* Ed. Eugene C. Barker and Ernest William Winkler. New York, 1914.

Johnston, *Narrative of Military Operations.*   Joseph E. Johnston. *Narrative of Military Operations, Directed, during the Late War Between the States by Joseph E. Johnston, General, C.S.A.* New York, 1874; rept., with introduction by Frank Vandiver, Bloomington, Ind., 1959.

Krick, *Lee's Colonels.*   Robert K. Krick. *Lee's Colonels: A Biographical Register of the Field Officers of the Army of Northern Virginia.* Dayton, Ohio, 1979.

Long, *Civil War Day by Day.*   E. B. Long. *The Civil War Day by Day: An Almanac, 1861–1865.* New York, 1971.

Longstreet, *Manassas to Appomattox.*   James Longstreet. *From Manassas to Appomattox.* Philadelphia, 1896; rept., ed. with introduction and notes by James I. Robertson, Jr., Bloomington, Ind., 1960.

McPherson, *Battle Cry of Freedom.*   James M. McPherson. *Battle Cry of Freedom: The Civil War Era.* New York, 1987.

Marvel, *Burnside.*   William Marvel. *Burnside.* Chapel Hill, N.C., 1991.

OR.   *War of the Rebellion . . . Official Records of the Union and Confederate Armies.* 128 vols. Washington, D.C., 1880–1901.

Owen, *Washington Artillery.*   William Miller Owen. *In Camp and Battle with the Washington Artillery.* Boston, 1885; rept. Gaithersburg, Md., n.d.

Paddock, *North and West Texas.*   B. B. Paddock. *A Twentieth Century History and Biographical Record of North and West Texas.* 2 vols. Chicago, 1906.

Parrish, *Richard Taylor.*   T. Michael Parrish. *Richard Taylor: Soldier Prince of Dixie.* Chapel Hill, N.C., 1992.

Piston, *Lee's Tarnished Lieutenant.*   William Garrett Piston. *Lee's Tarnished Lieutenant: James Longstreet and His Place in Southern History.* Athens, Ga., 1987.

Roberts, *Texas.*   Oran M. Roberts. *Texas.* Vol. 15 of Clement A. Evans, ed. *Confederate Military History.* Extended ed. Atlanta, 1899; rept. Wilmington, N.C., 1989.

Robertson, *A. P. Hill.*   James I. Robertson, Jr. *A. P. Hill: The Story of a Confederate Warrior.* New York, 1987.

Roman, *General Beauregard.*   Alfred Roman. *The Military Operations of General Beauregard in the War Between the States.* 2 vols. New York, 1884; rept., with introduction by T. Michael Parrish, New York, 1994.

Sanger and Hay, *James Longstreet.*   D. B. Sanger and Thomas Robson Hay. *James Longstreet, Soldier, Politician, Officerholder, and Writer.* Baton Route, La., 1952.

Sears, *To the Gates of Richmond.*   Stephen W. Sears. *To the Gates of Richmond: The Peninsula Campaign.* New York, 1992.

Sherman, *Memoirs.*   William T. Sherman. *The Memoirs of General William T. Sherman by Himself.* New York, 1875; rept., with introduction by B. H. Liddell Hart, Bloomington, Ind., 1957.

SHSP.   *Southern Historical Society Papers.*

Simpson, *Compendium.*   Harold B. Simpson. *Hood's Texas Brigade: A Compendium.* Hillsboro, Tex., 1977.

Simpson, *Hood's Texas Brigade.*   Harold B. Simpson. *Hood's Texas Brigade: Lee's Grenadier Guard.* Waco, Tex., 1970.

Sorrel, *Recollections.*   G. Moxley Sorrel. *Recollections of a Confederate Staff Officer.* New York, 1905, 1917; rept., with introduction by Bell I. Wiley, Jackson, Tenn., 1958.

Swanberg, *First Blood.*   W. A. Swanberg. *First Blood: The Story of Fort Sumter.* New York, 1957.

SWHQ.   *Southwestern Historical Quarterly.*

Tanner, *Stonewall in the Valley.*   Robert G. Tanner. *Stonewall in the Valley: Thomas J. "Stonewall" Jackson's Shenandoah Valley Campaign, Spring 1862.* New York, 1976.

Taylor, *Destruction and Reconstruction.*   Richard Taylor. *Destruction and Reconstruction.* New York, 1878.

Thomas, *Bold Dragoon.*   Emory M. Thomas. *Bold Dragoon: The Life of J. E. B. Stuart.* New York, 1986.

Thomason, *Jeb Stuart.*   John W. Thomason, Jr. *Jeb Stuart.* New York, 1948.

Trudeau, *Last Citadel.*   Noah Andre Trudeau. *The Last Citadel: Petersburg, Virginia, June 1864—April 1865.* New York, 1992.

Wakelyn, *Biographical Dictionary of the Confederacy.*   Jon L. Wakelyn. *Biographical Dictionary of the Confederacy.* Westport, Conn., 1977.

Walker, *Penology for Profit.*   Donald R. Walker. *Penology for Profit: A History of the Texas Prison System.* College Station, Tex., 1988.

Warner, *Generals in Blue.*   Ezra J. Warner. *Generals in Blue: Lives of the Union Commanders.* Baton Rouge, La., 1964.

Warner, *Generals in Gray.*   Ezra J. Warner. *Generals in Gray: Lives of the Confederate Commanders.* Baton Rouge, La., 1959.

Warner and Yearns, *Confederate Congress.*   Ezra J. Warner and W. Buck Yearns. *Biographical Register of the Confederate Congress.* Baton Rouge, La., 1975.

Webb, *Handbook of Texas.*   Walter Prescott Webb et al., eds. *The Handbook of Texas.* 3 vols. Austin, Tex., 1952, 1976.

Wellman, *Giant in Gray.*   Manly Wade Wellman. *Giant in Gray: A Biography of Wade Hampton of South Carolina.* New York, 1949; rept. Dayton, Ohio, 1980.

Wert, *Longstreet.*   Jeffry D. Wert. *General James Longstreet: The Confederacy's Most Controversial Soldier.* New York, 1993.

Wiley, *Life of Johnny Reb.*   Bell I. Wiley. *The Life of Johnny Reb.* New York, 1943.

Williams, *Napoleon in Gray.*   T. Harry Williams. *Beauregard: Napoleon in Gray.* Baton Rouge, La., 1955.

Wise, *Long Arm of Lee.*   Jennings Cropper Wise. *The Long Arm of Lee: The History of the Artillery of the Army of Northern Virginia.* New York, 1959.

Wright, *Staff Officers.*   [Marcus J. Wright, comp.] *List of Staff Officers of the Confederate States Army.* Washington, D.C., 1891.

Wright and Simpson, *Texas in the War.*   Marcus J. Wright, comp., and Harold B. Simpson, ed. *Texas in the War, 1861–1865.* Hillsboro, Tex., 1965.

Yeary, *Boys in Gray.*   Mamie Yeary. *Reminiscences of the Boys in Gray, 1861–1865.* Dallas, 1912; rept. Dayton, Ohio, 1986.

ABBREVIATIONS

TJG   Thomas J. Goree   SWKG   Sarah Williams Kittrell Goree

INTRODUCTION

1. Charles Reagan Wilson, *Baptized in Blood: The Religion of the Lost Cause, 1865–1920* (Athens, Ga., 1980).

2. For the Longstreet controversy, see Longstreet, *Manassas to Appomattox;* Helen D. Longstreet, *Lee and Longstreet at High Tide* (Gainesville, Ga., 1904; rept. Wilmington, N.C., 1981); H. J. Eckenrode and Bryan Conrad, *James Longstreet: Lee's War Horse* (Chapel Hill, N.C., 1936; rept. 1986); Sanger and Hay, *James Longstreet;* Thomas L. Connelly and Barbara L. Bellows, *God and General Longstreet* (Baton Rouge,

La., 1982); Piston, *Lee's Tarnished Lieutenant;* and Wert, *Longstreet.*

3. Longstreet, *Manassas to Appomattox,* 400; James Longstreet, "Lee in Pennsylvania," *Annals of the War,* 434.

Douglas Southall Freeman and Grady McWhiney rebut TJG's defense of Longstreet's behavior at Gettysburg with the retort that "it would be easy to criticize these statements and to dispute the authority upon which they rest. But General Lee's own words seem a sufficient contradiction of Longstreet's remarkable claim."

Lee, they point out, certainly had confidence in the probable success of Pickett's attack, else he would not have ordered it. Had "all things worked together," he wrote on 31 July, the charge would not have failed. Only in retrospect, with more information than was at hand on 3 July 1863, "was he prepared to admit that he would have followed a different course." Douglas Southall Freeman and Grady McWhiney, eds., *Lee's Dispatches: Unpublished Letters of General Robert E. Lee, C.S.A., to Jefferson Davis and the War Department of the Confederate States Army, 1862–1865* (New York, 1957), 114n.

4. Paddock, *North and West Texas* 2:455–56; Johnson, *Texas and Texans* 2:2000–2001.

5. TJG to SWKG, 20 Nov. 1854.

6. TJG to SWKG, 26 May 1857.

7. TJG to SWKG, 3 July 1857.

8. Royall T. Wheeler to SWKG, 5 Oct. 1858.

9. *Biographical Souvenir of the State of Texas* (Chicago, 1889), 333; Webb, *Handbook of Texas* 2:918; Royall T. Wheeler to TJG, 27 Feb. 1859.

10. TJG to SWKG, May 26, 1857.

11. Dallas *Weekly Herald*, 21 Sept. 1859, 1:3. The other members of the committee were Jonathan M. Wade, L. G. Culpepper, Charles E. Jones, and Procter P. Porter. Wade, a veteran of the battle of San Jacinto, was the former publisher of the Montgomery *Patriot* and at the time was deputy surveyor for Montgomery County. Porter was to become the captain and Jones the first sergeant of Company H, Fourth Texas Infantry, organized at Huntsville on 7 May 1861. Webb, *Handbook of Texas* 2:849; Wright and Simpson, *Texas in the War*, 211.

12. TJG to SWKG, 13 Dec. 1860, 22 Jan. 1861.

13. TJG to SWKG, 2 Feb. 1861.

14. Roberts, *Texas*, 262; Sorrel, *Recollections*, 117; Wright, *Staff Officers*, 63.

15. Sherman, *Memoirs* 2:402; Paddy Griffith, *Battle Tactics of the Civil War* (New Haven, 1989), 55. For additional insights into the life and duties of a Confederate staff officer, see Sorrel, *Recollections;* William Gleason Bean, *Stonewall's Man: Sandie Pendleton* (Chapel Hill, N.C., 1959); Henry Kyd Douglas, *I Rode with Stonewall: The War Experiences of the Youngest Member of Jackson's Staff*

(Chapel Hill, N.C., 1940); John Esten Cooke, *The Wearing of the Gray: Being Personal Portraits, Scenes, and Adventures of the War* (New York, 1867; rept., with introduction by Philip Van Dorn Stern, Bloomington, Ind., 1959); W. W. Blackford, *War Years with Jeb Stuart* (New York, 1945); and Theodore Stanford Garnett, *Riding with Stuart: Reminiscences of an Aide-de-Camp,* ed. Robert J. Trout (Shippensburg, Pa., 1994).

16. William Howard Russell, *My Diary North and South* (New York, 1954), 208–9.

17. *OR*, I, 12, pt. 2:567, 21:571–72; Sorrel, *Recollections*, 117.

18. TJG to Col. Edward Dromgoole Nolley, 14 Nov. 1867; Sorrel, *Recollections*, 219; Longstreet, "Lee in Pennsylvania," 434.

19. Dawson, *Reminiscences*, 87, 128, 192.

20. Sorrel, *Recollections*, 5, 105–6.

21. Fremantle, *Fremantle Diary*, 213; Longstreet, *Manassas to Appomattox*, 400; *OR*, I, 27, pt. 2:363.

22. FitzGerald Ross, *Cities and Camps of the Confederate States,* ed. Richard B. Harwell (Urbana, Ill., 1958), 128; Frank Vizetelly, *Illustrated London News* 43 (5 Dec. 1863): 557, 574.

23. Sorrel, *Recollections*, 218.

24. *OR*, I, 32, pt. 2:566; Sanger and Hay, *James Longstreet*, 278.

25. *OR*, I, 42, pt. 3:1142–43.

26. Eliza Thomas Nolley was born 11 Nov. 1845 at Montgomery Hill, Baldwin County, Ala., the daughter of Edward D. and Mary Frances Nicholas Nolley. At the time of her marriage she was principal of the Andrew Female College in Huntsville. She died at Huntsville on 5 Sept. 1929.

27. Webb, *Handbook of Texas* 1:1.

28. Walker, *Penology for Profit*, 147–48; Dallas *Morning News*, 3 Oct. 1929.

29. Walker, *Penology for Profit*, 147–49.

30. Ibid.; Austin *Statesman*, 22 Jan. 1891; "Major Thomas J. Goree Pays General Longstreet a Visit," San Antonio *Express*, 23 Jan. 1891.

31. For a discussion of the Southern boom

town of the 1880s, based on the model of Birmingham, Ala., see Edward L. Ayers, *The Promise of the New South: Life after Reconstruction* (New
York, 1992), 59–62.

32. Robert Crawford Cotner, *James Stephen
Hogg: A Biography* (Austin, Tex., 1959), 295–313;
Fred Gannt, Jr., *The Chief Executive in Texas: A
Study in Gubernatorial Leadership* (Austin, Tex.,
1964), 260–61; Sorrel, *Recollections*, 219; Roberts,
Texas, 422–23; Texas, Senate Journal, 29th Legislature, 1st sess., 10 March 1905; L. E. Daniell, *Personnel of the Texas State Government with Sketches
of Distinguished Texans* (Austin, Tex., 1887), 38–39.

33. Sanger and Hay, *James Longstreet*, 405–6,
408; San Antonio *Express*, 23 Jan. 1891; Savannah
Morning News, 19 June 1896.

34. "Major Thomas J. Goree," *Confederate Veteran*, May 1905, 238; Clarence R. Wharton, *Texas
under Many Flags* (Chicago, 1930), 5:277.

35. *Legislative Record*, 7 March 1905; Dallas
Weekly Herald, 21 Sept. 1905, 1:3; Johnson, *Texas
and Texans* 2:2000–2001; Helen Dortch Longstreet to Eliza Thomas Nolley Goree, 16 May
1905.

36. An older and less reliable transcription of
the TJG letters is located in the Department of
Archives at Louisiana State University. Bell I.
Wiley, who in 1948 was a member of the LSU
history faculty, first called the library's attention
to the importance of these letters, having himself been introduced to them by Ben Ames Williams, a Longstreet descendant. The LSU
transcription was prepared from the original letters, lent to the Department of Archives by a
son of TJG, Robert Edwin Goree of Hickory
Hill Plantation, Aberdeen, Miss. Langston James
Goree V was generous in sharing family pic-
tures as well as biographical data gleaned from
his many years of research into the Goree family genealogy. In addition, T. Michael Parrish of
the Lyndon B. Johnson Library and Museum,
Austin, Tex., and Paul Culp of the John W.
Thomason Rare Books and Special Collections
Room of the Newton Gresham Library, Sam
Houston State University, Huntsville, Tex.,
have been especially bountiful in their assistance to and cordial encouragement of this
project.

1861. "I HAVE MADE UP MY MIND TO DO MY DUTY"

1. Pleasant Williams Kittrell, a physician and
planter, was the brother of SWKG. In 1848, after
the death of his first wife, Kittrell married Mary
Frances Goree, the daughter of Langston James
Goree and his first wife, Susan Kenner Goree.
Kittrell thus became both TJG's uncle and his
brother-in-law. Kittrell moved to Texas with Gorees in 1850 and purchased a plantation called
Prairie View a few miles north of Madisonville.
Kittrell was Sam Houston's personal physician
and was in attendance when the hero of San Jacinto died on 26 July 1863. Thereafter the Kit-
trells purchased the Steamboat House, the
Houston residence in Huntsville, Tex. Webb,
Handbook of Texas 1:967.

2. On the night of 26 Dec. 1860, six days
after South Carolina passed its ordinance of secession, a 128-man garrison under Maj. Robert
Anderson occupied Fort Sumter in Charleston
Harbor. Secessionists under Brig. Gen. P. G. T.
Beauregard ringed the fort with batteries and demanded its surrender. On 29 March, President

Lincoln ordered a naval expedition to relieve the
beleaguered garrison, and on 3 April, Confederate gunners turned back the U.S. schooner
Rhoda H. Shannon. Anderson refused Beauregard's surrender ultimatum, and at 4:30 A.M., 12
April, the shelling began. The garrison returned
fire, and for thirty-six hours the bombardment
continued until fires within the fort threatened
the powder magazine. Anderson surrendered in
the early afternoon on 13 April. Richard N. Current, *Lincoln and the First Shot* (Philadelphia,
1963); Swanberg, *First Blood;* Roy Meridith, *Storm
over Sumter: The Opening Engagement of the Civil
War* (New York, 1957); John Shipley Tilley, *Lincoln Takes Command* (Chapel Hill, N.C., 1941.

3. Robert Anderson (1805–1871), a native of
Kentucky and an 1825 West Point graduate, was
appointed commandant of the garrison at
Charleston, S.C., in November 1860. Although a
Southerner by ancestry, birth, and marriage and
sympathetic with the institution of slavery, Major Anderson remained loyal to the Union and

refused to surrender Fort Sumter until it was reduced to submission by Confederate bombardment.

4. Pierre Gustave Toutant Beauregard (1818–
1893), a Louisiana Creole, graduated second in
the West Point class of 1838 and was serving as
the academy's superintendent when his state seceded. On 20 Feb. 1861 he was appointed a brigadier general in the Confederate States Army.
Assigned to Charleston, S.C., he took command
of the volunteers investing Fort Sumter and ordered the bombardment that sparked the Civil
War. Returning to Richmond in triumph, Beauregard was given command of the Confederate
forces at Manassas Junction, Va. With Joseph E.
Johnston, Beauregard won the first battle of
Manassas on 21 July. Although promoted to the
rank of full general on 31 Aug., Beauregard was
unable to work harmoniously with President
Davis and so was transferred early in 1862 to the
western theater of operations. In April 1864 he
returned to Virginia to command the defenses
of Richmond. Roman, *General Beauregard;* Hamilton Basso, *Beauregard: The Great Creole* (New
York, 1933); Williams, *Napoleon in Gray.*

5. Commodore Silas Horton Stringham
(1797–1876), James Buchanan's naval consultant,
advised the president to reinforce Fort Sumter,
believing that the navy's light, speedy ships
could run the South Carolina batteries quickly
under the cover of darkness. His suggestion,
however, came to nothing. Swanberg, *First
Blood,* 233.

6. Fort Pickens, in Pensacola Harbor, was no
less than Fort Sumter a potential flash point in
April 1861. When Florida seceded on 10 Jan.
1861, the Federal garrison in Pensacola withdrew
to Fort Pickens on Santa Rosa Island, outside
the range of Rebel guns. Secessionist leaders,
backed by 5,000 Confederate volunteers under
Brig. Gen. Braxton Bragg, demanded the fort's
surrender, but its commandant, Lt. Adam J.
Slemmer, refused. President Buchanan ordered
the warship *Brooklyn,* with 200 soldiers on
board, to Pensacola, but these reinforcements
were neither to land nor to commence hostilities. This standoff continued until 5 March, the
date of Lincoln's inauguration, when the new
president ordered the troops aboard the *Brooklyn*
ashore. Because the secretary of the navy had
not signed the order, however, the commander
of the warship refused to land the troops. Not
until 12 April, the day that they received word of
the bombardment of Fort Sumter, did Union reinforcements enter Fort Pickens. Bragg evacuated the city on 9 May 1862.

7. Brasher City, La., was renamed Morgan
City in 1876.

8. Sarah Williams Kittrell Goree, the daughter of Rowland Bryant and Mary Norman Kittrell, was born in 26 April 1807 in Granville
County, N.C. She was educated at Chapel Hill
where she spent most of her youth. At the time
of her marriage to Langston James Goree on 27
Nov. 1834 she was living with her parents in
Greensboro, Ala. She served as matron of the
Judson College in Marion, Ala., and later was a
regular contributor to the Dallas *News* until her
death on 17 June 1903 at the age of ninety-seven.
SWKG was said to be "in many ways a very remarkable woman," possessing "rare development and harmony of powers of heart and
mind," and was one of the era's few college-
educated women. Paddock, *North and West
Texas* 2:455–56; Johnson, *Texas and Texans*
2:2000–2001.

9. James Longstreet, on his way to Richmond to offer his services to the Confederate
army, was also aboard this schooner. "At Gales-
ton we took a small inland sailing-craft," he
wrote in his military memoir, "but were a little
apprehensive, as United States ships were reported cruising outside in search of all vessels
flying the Stars and Stripes. Our vessel, however,
was only boarded once, and that by a large Spanish mackerel that made a misleap, fell amidships, and served our company with a pleasant
dinner." On this voyage Longstreet first met
TJG, "an intelligent, clever Texan, who afterward joined me at Richmond, and served in
faithful duty as my aide-de-camp from Bull Run
to Appomattox Court House." Longstreet, *Manassas to Appomattox,* 32.

10. Creed and Mary Woodson, natives of
Georgia, moved to Montgomery, Tex., before
the war. There Dr. Woodson practiced medicine
and became TJG's friend and neighbor. The
Woodsons' sons Creed Taylor Woodson and
Philip T. Woodson, a physician, served in the
Army of Northern Virginia. Simpson, *Compen-
dium,* 203.

11. Thomas Saltus Lubbock (1817–1861), a South Carolina native, immigrated to Texas as a volunteer soldier during the Texas Revolution. With the outbreak of the Civil War, Lubbock sailed from Galveston to Richmond where he and Benjamin Franklin Terry petitioned Jefferson Davis for "authority to raise a company or battalion of guerrillas." With Terry, Lubbock raised the Eighty Texas Cavalry. Terry served as the regiment's colonel and Lubbock as its lieutenant colonel. In poor health, Lubbock left the regiment at Nashville and never returned to it. With the death of Colonel Terry on 17 Dec. 1861, Lubbock, then sick in a Bowling Green hospital, was advanced to command of the regiment but died within a few days. Francis R. Lubbock, *Six Decades in Texas: or Memoirs of Francis Richard Lubbock* (Austin, Tex., 1900); Giles, *Terry's Texas Rangers*, 18.

12. Benjamin Franklin Terry (1821–1861) was a native of Kentucky who moved to Texas in the early 1830s. A wealthy planter, Terry was elected a delegate to Texas's secession convention, as were his friends Thomas S. Lubbock and John A. Wharton. The three ventured together first to the Confederate capital at Montgomery, Ala., and then to Richmond in order to procure a commission to raise a regiment of cavalry for Confederate service. Their conduct as volunteer aides at the battle of Manassas was rewarded with the government's sanction to raise and command the Eighth Texas Cavalry. In his first battle, on 17 Dec. at Woodsonville, Ky., only a few miles from his birthplace, Terry was killed leading a charge. Giles, *Terry's Texas Rangers*; Blackburn, "Terry Rangers"; H[elen] J. H. Rugeley, ed., *Batchelor-Turner Letters, 1861–1864* (Austin, Tex., 1961); Graber, *Terry Texas Ranger*; Cutrer, "John Wesley Rabb," 185–226.

13. On the night of 10 June 1861 seven Federal regiments under Col. Ebenezer W. Pierce marched out of Fortress Monroe to attack Col. John B. Magruder's works at Big Bethel, Va. After an hour of uncoordinated and unsuccessful assaults, Pierce retired from the field. The tiny engagement gave the South a considerable morale boost, and trophies from the battle were displayed in Richmond shop windows.

On 17 June, at Vienna, Va., some fifteen miles below Alexandria, Col. Maxey Gregg and the First South Carolina Infantry captured a train bearing a detachment of Ohio troops sent into the area to repair and protect the Loudoun and Hampshire railroad. Although a minor engagement, it was of considerable embarrassment to the Federals.

TJG is in error, however, in his assessment of the result of the engagement at Philippi in what is now West Virginia. There, on the night of 3 June, a column of Federal soldiers under Brig. Gen. Thomas Armstrong Morris surprised and overwhelmed the sleeping Confederate garrison. The resulting Rebel route was known derisively as "the Philippi races" and was influential in the decision of the western counties of Virginia to break away from their state.

14. John Austin Wharton (1828–1865) was born in Tennessee but was brought to Galveston as an infant. There he became a lawyer and was elected to the state's secession convention. Wharton was elected captain of Company B, Eighty Texas Cavalry, and after the deaths of Benjamin F. Terry and Thomas S. Lubbock, he took command of the regiment. He was advanced to the rank of brigadier general on 18 Nov. 1862. On 6 April 1865 Col. George W. Baylor assassinated Wharton at John B. Magruder's headquarters in Houston during a quarrel over "military matters." Giles, *Terry's Texas Rangers*, 25.

15. Louis Trezevant Wigfall (1816–1874) was born in South Carolina but immigrated to Texas in 1848. Elected to the U.S. Senate in 1859, he became one of the most outspoken advocates of secession. Wigfall served as a volunteer aide to P. G. T. Beauregard during the Fort Sumter crisis, and although elected as a delegate to the Provisional Confederate Congress, he chose to accept a commission as colonel of the First Texas Infantry and was promoted to brigadier general and commander of the Texas Brigade. Wigfall remained with the army until elected to the First Confederate Senate in November 1861. Wigfall's attachment to Davis eroded, and by 1864 their rupture was complete. Thereafter he became Joseph E. Johnston's staunchest supporter in the Senate. Alvy L. King, *Louis T. Wigfall: Southern Fire-eater* (Baton Rouge, La., 1970).

16. Thomas Neville Waul (1813–1903) was born in South Carolina but moved to Texas in 1836. He was appointed to the Provisional Congress of the Confederate States, but after his defeat in a run for the seat in November 1861, he recruited Waul's Texas Legion and was commissioned as its colonel on 17 May 1862. He and his

command were captured at Vicksburg, and after his exchange he was promoted to brigadier general and served in the trans-Mississippi theater for the remainder of the war. Robert A. Hasskarl, *Waul's Texas Legion, 1862–1865* (Ada, Okla., 1976).

17. A W. H. Denson served in Capt. W. B. Hart's company, McIntosh's Battery, Alabama Artillery. "Paroles of the Army of Northern Virginia," *SHSP* 15(1887): 60.

18. William Hume was born in Mississippi in 1838 and was brought to Huntsville by his family at age twelve. John White, born in Alabama in 1840, moved to Huntsville sometime before 1860. He is perhaps the John White who served in Company B, Sixth Alabama Infantry. Walker County, Texas, Census, 1850 and 1860; "Paroles," *SHSP* 15(1887): 242.

19. Milledge Luke Bonham (1813–1890) was a native of South Carolina. In 1857 he was elected to the U.S. House of Representatives but resigned with his state's secession. He was appointed a brigadier general in Confederate service and commanded the center brigade of Beauregard's forces at the first battle of Manassas. Bonham resigned from the army in January 1862 to take a seat in the Confederate Congress. In January 1863 he was elected governor of South Carolina and with the expiration of his term was recommissioned as a brigadier general under Joseph E. Johnston.

20. Joseph Brevard Kershaw (1822–1894) was a native of South Carolina. He attended his state's secession convention in 1860 and was elected colonel of the Second South Carolina Infantry in 1861. After seeing action at Fort Sumter and First Manassas, Kershaw was promoted to brigadier general, 13 Feb. 1862, and to major general, 18 May 1864. After taking a distinguished role on all of the operations of I Corps until after the fall of Richmond, he was captured at Sayler's Creek on 6 April 1865.

21. Joseph Eggleston Johnson (1807–1891), a native of Virginia, resigned from the U.S. Army to accept a brigadier general's commission in the regular Confederate States Army. Placed in command of Harpers Ferry, Johnston successfully eluded Union general Robert Patterson and joined P. G. T. Beauregard's army on the field of Manassas in time to turn the tide of that battle in favor of the South. Rewarded with promotion to full general and command of the South's principal field army, Johnston conducted the affairs of the Confederate Army of the Potomac until he was severely wounded at the battle of Seven Pines in June 1862. Upon his recovery Johnston was assigned to the command of Department of the West. His tenure there was characterized by a chronic bitter quarrel with Jefferson Davis. Johnston, *Narrative of Military Operations*; Gilbert E. Govan and James W. Livingood, *A Different Valor: The Story of General Joseph E. Johnston* (Indianapolis, 1956); Craig L. Symonds, *Joseph E. Johnston: A Civil War Biography* (New York, 1992).

22. Philip S. George Cocke (1809–1861) was born in Virginia and with his state's secession was appointed colonel of the Nineteenth Virginia Infantry. During the first battle of Manassas, he commanded the brigade that held Blackburn's Ford and was commended by P. G. T. Beauregard for his successful defense of the vital crossing. On 21 Oct. 1861 he was promoted to brigadier general, but after only eight months of Confederate service, "shattered in health and mind," Cocke took his own life.

23. David Rumph ("Neighbor") Jones (1825–1863) of South Carolina resigned from the U.S. Army in 1861 and was appointed chief of staff to P. G. T. Beauregard at Charleston, where he is said to have removed the U.S. flag from Fort Sumter. Related by marriage to Jefferson Davis, Jones was appointed brigadier general in the Confederate States Army on 17 June 1861. He admirably managed a brigade at First Manassas and was subsequently promoted to major general from 10 March 1862. Shortly after the Sharpsburg campaign, Jones developed serious heart trouble and died at Richmond.

24. Thomas Jonathan ("Stonewall") Jackson (1824–1863), Robert E. Lee's most celebrated lieutenant, was commandant of cadets at the Virginia Military Institute at the outbreak of the war. His brigade distinguished itself at the first battle of Manassas where Jackson won his famous sobriquet, "Stonewall," for his tenacious defense of Henry House Hill. As a reward for his success, Jackson was promoted to major general on 7 Oct. 1861. From there his rise to fame was meteoric until his death on 10 May 1863, from wounds sustained from friendly fire at the

battle of Chancellorsville. Frank Vandiver, *Mighty Stonewall* (New York, 1957).

25. Richard Stoddert Ewell (1817–1872), a native of the District of Columbia, resigned from the old army on 7 May 1861 and accepted a commission in the Confederate States Army. Ewell was promoted to brigadier general on 17 June 1861 and fought with distinction at the first battle of Manassas. Promotion to major general followed on 24 Jan. 1862. Ewell performed admirably as Stonewall Jackson's second-in-command during the Shenandoah Valley campaign, and following Jackson's death at Chancellorsville, he was appointed to command of II Corps and promoted to lieutenant general. The demands of corps command seem to have exceeded Ewell's talents or emotional strength, and his subsequent performance has been severely censured. Percy G. Hamlin, *"Old Bald Head:" Richard Stoddert Ewell, Portrait of a Soldier and Making of a Soldier* (originally published in two parts: Strasburg, Va., 1940, and Richmond, 1935; rept. Gaithersburg, Md., 1988).

26. At noon on 18 July, Brig. Gen. Irvin McDowell's Army of Virginia cautiously approached Centreville. Contemplating a move against the Confederate right flank, the Federal commander detached Col. Israel B. Richardson's brigade on a reconnaissance in force to Blackburn's Ford on Bull Run. Heavy skirmishing with Longstreet's brigade resulted in the loss of fifteen Confederates killed and fifty-three wounded and nineteen Federals killed with thirty-eight wounded and nineteen missing. Upon learning that Blackburn's and Mitchell's fords were strongly held, McDowell altered his battle plan, deciding instead to turn the Confederate left flank. David, *Bull Run*, 112–31.

27. At First Manassas, Longstreet's staff officers were Lt. Frank S. Armistead, assistant adjutant general; Lt. Peyton T. Manning of Mississippi, ordnance officer; Capt. Thomas Walton of Mississippi, aide; TJG, aide; "and some quartermasters and commissaries detailed from the regiments." Sorrel, *Recollections*, 18.

28. In his report on the battle at Bull Run, 28 July 1861, Longstreet wrote of his volunteer staff: "Cols. B. F. Terry and T. Lubbock were very active and energetic. When unoccupied, they repeatedly volunteered their services to make reconnaissances. They were very gallantly

seconded by Captains T. Goree and [John H.] Chichester, who were also very useful in conveying orders." Beauregard, in his report to Adj. Gen. Samuel Cooper, seconded Longstreet's praise, adding that on the day following the battle, the Texans accompanied the troops who took possession of Fairfax Courthouse. There Terry, "with his unerring rifle, severed the haliard, and thus lowered the Federal flag found still floating from the cupola of the courthouse there. He also secured a large Federal garrison flag, designed, it is said, to be unfurled over our intrenchments at Manassas." *OR*, I, 2:502, 544.

29. TJG's maternal cousin David B. Scott was born in Greensboro, Ala., on 9 Oct. 1838, the son of Samuel M. and Mary B. Scott. He attended Oglethorpe College in Georgia, taught school for a short period, and served as a private in Capt. Porter King's Company G, Fourth Alabama Infantry. The regiment, commanded by Evander M. Law, was attached to Bernard E. Bee's brigade. Later in the war Scott was transferred to Company H, Seventh South Carolina Cavalry. In June 1864 Scott married Mary Maria Wallace. Before the war he had purchased a plantation near Huntsville, Tex., but after the war he returned to Scott's Station, his plantation near Marion, Ala., where he died on 7 June 1890. Obituary by Rev. John Knox Spence in unidentified newspaper cutting, copy in possession of editor.

30. Thomas Moorman of Maybinton, Newberry County, S.C., is TJG's cousin, the grandson of his father's sister, Lucy Goree Kenner (Mrs. Samuel E. Kenner).

31. Repulsed by Longstreet's brigade at Blackburn's Ford on 18 July, Irvin McDowell opted to sweep around the Confederate left and turn Beauregard's army out of its defensive position behind Bull Run. With 12,000 men McDowell crossed the creek above Beauregard's line. The brunt of the Federal attack was borne by the brigade of Nathan G. Evans. As Evans's troops slowly gave ground, they were reinforced piecemeal by elements of Barnard E. Bee's and Francis S. Bartow's brigades, but by early afternoon the weight of Federal numbers pushed the Southerners beyond the Warrenton Turnpike, the road to Richmond. By this time, however, units from Johnston's army began to arrive on the field, and Thomas J. Jackson's regiments hurried to the front to make a tenacious stand on

Henry House Hill, checking the Federal advance and providing a rallying point for the disorganized Confederates. With the line stabilized the fighting continued for two hours of attack and counterattack until, about 4:00 P.M. the last of Johnston's brigades turned the Union right and rolled up McDowell's line. What had been a remarkably close fight quickly degenerated into a rout as panicked Federal soldiers rushed for the safety of the rear. Nearly as thoroughly shattered by victory as their enemies were by defeat, the Confederates were unable to capitalize on their victory with an effective pursuit. Davis, *Bull Run.*

32. Daniel Tyler (1799–1882), a native of Connecticut and a West Point graduate, was commissioned a brigadier general and commanded one of McDowell's divisions at the first battle of Manassas. There his disregard for orders and mishandling of troops contributed to the Federal disaster. Tyler was mustered out of the army on 11 Aug. 1861 but was reinstated the following March.

33. Delaware Kemper (1833–1899), a native of Virginia, was elected captain of the Alexandria Light Artillery company in April 1861. He was promoted to major on 25 June 1862 and to lieutenant colonel on 2 March 1863. He was severely wounded at the second battle of Manassas. On 7 April 1963 he was ordered to the Department of South Carolina, Georgia, and Florida. Crute, *Units,* 393–94.

34. Longstreet reported for duty at Manassas Junction on 2 July 1861 and was assigned to command of three regiments that he was to organize into a brigade. The First Virginia was commanded by Col. Patrick T. Moore, the Eleventh Virginia by Col. Samuel Garland, Jr., and the Seventeenth Virginia by Col. Montgomery D. Corse. The colonels, Longstreet later wrote, were "all active, energetic, and intelligent officers, anxious to acquire skill in the new service in which they found themselves." All three of these regiments served in I Corps for the duration of the war. Ibid., 350, 358–59, 362–63, 368; Longstreet, *Manassas to Appomattox,* 33.

35. Robert Patterson (1792–1881) distinguished himself in the War of 1812, and during the Mexican War he served as a major general under Winfield Scott. In 1861, at age sixty-nine, Patterson was appointed commander of the Department of Pennsylvania. Ordered to seize Harpers Ferry, Patterson responded timidly, allowing Joseph E. Johnston to elude his superior force and march to the aid of Beauregard's embattled Confederates at Manassas Junction. Scott removed Patterson from command. Robert Patterson, *A Narrative of the Campaign in the Valley of the Shenandoah in 1861* (Philadelphia, 1865).

36. Edmund Kirby Smith (1824–1893) accepted a commission as brigadier general in the Confederate army and contributed materially to the Southern success at the first battle of Manassas where he was wounded. Following his recovery, he was assigned to duty in the West. In October 1862 he was promoted to lieutenant general and given command of the Trans-Mississippi Department. Joseph Howard Parks, *General Edmund Kirby Smith, C.S.A.* (Baton Rouge, La., 1954).

37. Organized and trained by Ephraim Elmer Ellsworth, Ellsworth's Zouaves, also known as the First New York Fire Zouaves and officially as the Eleventh New York Infantry, was among the most colorful of Union military units. Even after discarding its flashy blue and scarlet uniforms, the regiment maintained its place in the public's attention with its rowdy behavior. The regiment achieved early notoriety when Ellsworth was killed on 24 May 1861 while removing a Confederate flag from the Marshall House Hotel in Alexandria, Va. He was the North's first officer casualty and became a national hero.

38. The Hampton Legion was recruited among the wealthiest young men of South Carolina and armed and equipped in the spring of 1861 by its commander, planter Wade Hampton. Although originally organized as mixed command of infantry, cavalry, and artillery, early in the summer of 1862 the legion was broken into its component parts with the artillery assigned to Maj. James F. Hart as Hart's South Carolina Battery; the mounted companies attached to a regular cavalry regiment; and the infantry companies, commanded by Lt. Col. Martin W. Gary, attached to Hood's Texas Brigade. Wellman, *Giant in Gray.*

39. Francis Stebbins Bartow (1816–1861) was elected to the secession convention of his native

Thomas Jewett Goree in
1899. (Editor's collection)

Georgia and then to the Confederate Congress,
but after Fort Sumter he joined the army as colonel of the Eighth Georgia Infantry and was assigned to command of one of Joseph E.
Johnston's brigades. At the first battle of Manassas, his command was in the thickest of the
fighting on Henry House Hill, and Bartow
proved himself an able commander before receiving a mortal wound. His last words were
reported as, "They have killed me boys, but
never give up the field."

40. This "regiment" was Maj. Chatham R.
Wheat's First Special Battalion, popularly
known as the "Louisiana Tigers." After organization at Camp Walker in New Orleans and Camp
Moore in Tangipahoa Parish, the five companies
were sent to Virginia where they became the
first Louisiana troops to see battle. At First Manassas the battalion played a decisive role in holding the Union attack on the Confederate left
until reinforcements arrived. The unit served
well under Brig. Gen. Richard Taylor in Jackson's Valley campaign and during the Seven
Days battles, but after the death of Major
Wheat at the battle of Gaines' Mill the colorful

but often uncontrollable Tigers were disbanded
and scattered among other units of the Louisiana Brigade. Charles L. Dufour, *Gentle Tiger: The
Gallant Life of Roberdeau Wheat* (Baton Rouge,
La., 1957); Arthur W. Bergeron, Jr., *Guide to Louisiana Confederate Military Units, 1861–1865* (Baton
Rouge, La., 1989), 149–51; Terry L. Jones, *Lee's Tigers: The Louisiana Infantry in the Army of Northern
Virginia* (Baton Rouge, La., 1987).

41. Porter King (1824–1890) served as a member of the Alabama state legislature and as a circuit court judge. He was elected captain of
Company G of the Fourth Alabama Infantry
and was promoted to lieutenant colonel of the
Forty-first Alabama Infantry on 16 May 1862. He
was dropped from the regiment's roll soon thereafter. Brown was a kinsman of TJG by marriage.

42. This intrepid holy warrior was James Sin-
clair, who was appointed chaplain of the Fifth
North Carolina Infantry on 15 May 1861. He re-
signed on 8 Nov. 1861 to take command of the
Thirty-fifth North Carolina. Weymouth T. Jor-
dan, Jr., comp., *North Carolina Troops, 1861–1865*
(Raleigh, N.C., 1973), 4:128.
   An excellent discussion of the duties of the

army chaplain and his often ambiguous relationship with combat may be found in James I. Robertson, Jr., *Soldiers Blue and Gray* (Columbia, S.C., 1988), 173–85.

43. Lafayette Sabine Foster (1806–1880), a native of Connecticut, was elected to the U.S. Senate in 1854, serving until 1866 when he failed to received the Republican nomination, probably because of his opposition to the Radicals.

44. Owen Lovejoy (1811–1864) was minister of the Congregational church at Princeton, Ill., and a dedicated abolitionist. In 1856 he was elected to the U.S. House of Representatives as a Republican. In Congress, Lovejoy was a disciple of Abraham Lincoln and an early Radical, attacking the South with the same vigor and venom as Thaddeus Stevens and Charles Sumner.

45. TJG is uncharacteristically well off the mark here. The actual totals of the two armies amounted to approximately 35,000 for the North and 34,000 for the South.

46. As historian Michael Adams has pointed out, the Yankee notion of "masked batteries" at Bull Run amounted almost to an obsession. The term seems to have first appeared in Brig. Gen. Robert C. Schenck's account of his ambush by Confederate forces near Vienna, Va., on 17 July 1861. In his report Schenck excuses his blundering into two Rebel fieldpieces supported by some infantry by creating fictitious "raking masked batteries." These spurious camouflaged emplacements apparently had the effect of imbuing Irvin McDowell with an exaggerated fear of offensive operations in Virginia, thus demonstrating how, in Adams's words, "the rebel was becoming a larger-than-life figure" and "mastering the imagination" of his Northern foremen. Michael C. C. Adams, *Our Masters the Rebels: A Speculation on Union Military Failure in the East, 1861–1865* (Cambridge, Mass., 1978), 63–64; Davis, *Bull Run,* 70–72.

47. TJG's maternal grandmother was Mary Norman Kittrell, the wife of Rowland Bryant Kittrell. She died of yellow fever in 1867.

48. Jacob Thompson (1810–1885) was born in North Carolina but moved to Mississippi, where in 1839 he was elected to the U.S. House of Representatives. In 1857 he was appointed secretary of the interior by James Buchanan. With the secession of Mississippi, Thompson resigned to join the army and was appointed a lieutenant colonel and an aide to P. G. T. Beauregard. In 1862 he became inspector general of John L. Pemberton's Army of Mississippi and was captured with the fall of Vicksburg in July 1863. Exchanged, Thompson left the army to serve in the Mississippi legislature.

49. This is Sarah Elizabeth King Goree, the wife of John Rabb Goree of Perry County, Ala.

50. George Doherty Johnston (1832–1910) was elected mayor of Marion, Ala., in 1856 and to the state legislature in 1857. With Alabama's secession he became a second lieutenant in Company G, Fourth Alabama Infantry, serving with distinction at First Manassas. In January 1862 he was promoted to major and transferred to the Twenty-fifth Alabama Infantry with which he served at Shiloh. For the remainder of the war he served with the Army of the Tennessee, rising to the rank of brigadier general.

51. Bernard Elliott Bee (1824–1861) was born in South Carolina, but his family moved to the Republic of Texas in 1836. A West Point graduate and Mexican War veteran, Bee was appointed brigadier general in the Confederate army and assigned to the command of a brigade in Beauregard's Army of Virginia at Manassas Junction. His men sustained the brunt of the Federal assault in the first battle of Manassas, and Bee is said to have ordered his men to "Rally behind the Virginians! There stands Jackson like a stonewall!" thus giving Thomas J. Jackson his famous sobriquet. Bee fell mortally wounded just as the enemy assault began to recede.

52. Henry Alexander Wise (1806–1876) of Virginia served in the House of Representatives, as the U.S. minister to Brazil, and as the state's governor. An outspoken advocate of states' rights and slavery, Wise quit politics when Virginia seceded and was appointed a brigadier general in the Confederate army. His lack of military skill, however, contributed to his defeats at the hands of Federal forces in the Kanawha Valley of present West Virginia in 1861 and on Roanoke Island, N.C., in 1862.

53. On June 11 1861 the mountainous counties of western Virginia seceded from their state,

forming the new state of West Virginia. George B. McClellan moved 20,000 Federal troops into the region to support the Unionists there and on 11 July drove Confederate general Robert S. Garnett from Rich Mountain. This victory was followed on 13 July by the rout of the remainder of Garnett's tiny army at Carrick's Ford. McClellan was called to Washington to take command of the Army of the Potomac, and one week after the first battle of Manassas, Robert E. Lee was called to the field for the first time to oversee four small Confederate "armies" whose task was to repel the Federal invasion of western Virginia and abolish the Unionist government at Wheeling. With demoralized troops, feuding subordinates, and an impossible logistical situation, Lee learned the meaning of frustration in a fruitless three-month campaign in the Kanawha Valley. In early November, when he was recalled to Richmond for reassignment on the South Carolina coast, Lee's star was at its dimmest. Foote, *Civil War* 1:127-31.

54. "Sis Frank" is Mary Frances Goree Kittrell, TJG's half sister. TJG's letters to her are addressed to Huntsville, Tex.

55. "Sudy" is TJG's only full sister, Susan Margaret Goree, who was born in 1848 and died in 1931. In 1868 she married Hugh Lawson Hayes and became the mother of eleven children. In 1863 Hayes's sister Melissa married TJG's brother Robert Daniel Goree. After his death she married Dr. John W. Thomason and became the mother of John W. Thomason, Jr., the famed Marine Corps officer, illustrator, and author.

56. Leonard Anderson Abercrombie was born in Montgomery County, Ala., in December 1832, read law in Tuskegee, and was admitted to the bar in 1854. Later that year he immigrated to Madison County, Tex., but moved in 1856 to Huntsville where in 1860 he was elected district attorney. Abercrombie was a member of the state's secession convention and after serving as a private in the Ninth Texas Infantry was elected lieutenant colonel of the Twentieth Texas Infantry in 1862. After the war he and TJG established the firm of Abercrombie and Goree in Huntsville. In November 1886 he was elected to the Texas Senate and served three terms. He died in Philadelphia on 23 Dec. 1891. Norman G. Kittrell, *Governors Who Have*

Been, and Other Public Men of Texas (Houston, Tex., 1921), 143; John Henry Brown, ed., *The Encyclopedia of the New West* (Marshall, Tex., 1881), 129-30.

57. John Horace Forney (1829-1902), a native of North Carolina, entered Confederate service as colonel of the Tenth Alabama Infantry and saw action at First Manassas. Wounded at Dranesville, Va., in December 1861, he was promoted to brigadier general on 10 March 1862 and to major general on 27 Oct., a rise in rank which probably outstripped his abilities. After brief service as commander of the departments of Alabama and Florida, he was given a division of Lt. Gen. John C. Pemberton's army and was captured when Vicksburg fell. After being exchanged Forney was sent to the trans-Mississippi where he superseded John G. Walker as commander of the Texas Division.

58. Foraging by Civil War armies came in two varieties. One was the authorized requisition of civilian goods by military personnel; the other was merely unsanctioned plundering. So inefficient did the Southern supply system become that many times soldiers were forced to rely on foraging to subsist themselves. In whichever form, Texas troops seemed especially adept. James Longstreet is reputed to have remarked that "the Texas boys are great fighters . . . none better. But they are purely hell on chickens and shoats." Even Robert E. Lee once chided the commander of his Texas brigade, "Ah, General Hood, when you Texans come about the chickens have to roost mighty high." Early in the war unauthorized foraging was viewed as a serious offense. When, in December 1861, Pvt. Oscar Nash of the Seventeenth Texas Infantry shot a hog, he was placed under arrest and made to pay for the animal before he was released from the guardhouse, and on 8 January 1863 three soldiers were drummed out of Walker's Texas Division for "hog-stealing." If every unauthorized forager in the division had been so punished, however, its general soon would have found himself commanding scarcely a corporal's guard, for, as Pvt. John Blessington rhetorically inquired, "Boys, ask yourselves if you were ever guilty of 'hog-stealing' during the late unpleasantness?" Norman D. Brown, ed., *Journey to Pleasant Hill: The Civil War Letters of Capt. Elijah Petty, Walker's Texas Division, C.S.A.* (San Antonio, 1982), 22; Blessington, *Walker's Texas Division*, 68;

Harold B. Simpson, "Foraging with Hood's Brigade from Texas to Pennsylvania," *Texana* 1 (1963): 258–76.

59. John Bankhead Magruder (1807–1871), a native of Virginia, was commissioned as major general in Confederate service and commanded the Rebel forces at Yorktown. He deceived George B. McClellan as to his strength and caused the Union commander weeks of needless delay. Lack of aggressiveness during the Seven Days battles cost him the favor of General Lee, however, and he was reassigned to the command of the District of Texas, New Mexico, and Arizona.

60. Arnold Elzey Jones (1816–1871) was a native of Maryland and a West Point graduate. A veteran of the Seminole War and the Mexican War, Elzey was elected colonel of the First Maryland Infantry, which he commanded at the first battle of Manassas. Promoted to brigadier general, he distinguished himself during Jackson's Valley campaign but was severely wounded at the battle of Gaines' Mill and did not return to the army until 4 Dec. 1862.

61. James Ewell Brown Stuart (1833–1864) was "the eyes and ears" of the Army of Northern Virginia. With the secession of his native Virginia, Stuart was appointed colonel of the First Virginia Cavalry. He was instrumental in screening Joseph E. Johnston's army from observation by Robert Patterson in the Shenandoah Valley, thus allowing Johnston to join Beauregard at Manassas. Promotion to brigadier general followed on 24 Sept. For his daring "ride around McClellan" during the Peninsula campaign, he was promoted to major general. At Chancellorsville, Stuart temporarily assumed command of the II Corps following the wounding of Stonewall Jackson and A. P. Hill. During the Gettysburg campaign Stuart was conducting a raid deep into eastern Pennsylvania that deprived Lee of his valuable intelligence services. Despite a relative decline in the quality of Southern cavalry after 1863, Stuart continued to perform brilliantly until his death at the battle of Yellow Tavern. TJG's great-nephew, John W. Thomason, Jr., was the author of one of the standard Stuart biographies. Thomason, *Jeb Stuart;* Davis, *Jeb Stuart;* Thomas, *Bold Dragoon.*

62. Langston James Goree II, known to his family as "Toby," was the third surviving son of Langston James Goree and SWKG. He was born in 1841 at Marion, Ala. After his father's death Goree moved first to Walker County and then to Waco, Tex., where he enlisted as a private in Company H, Fifth Texas Infantry. In May 1862 he was promoted to fourth corporal. Goree was wounded at Second Manassas and again at Sharpsburg where he lost two fingers of his left hand and was discharged on a surgeon's certificate of disability on 20 Dec. 1862. After the war Goree went to Baltimore to study medicine. He returned to Huntsville where he established a dental practice, but moved first to Waco and then, in 1867, to Navasota in Grimes County where he practiced dentistry until his death in November 1887. Goree was married at New Waverly, Tex., to Martha Francis ("Fannie") Wood, who was born in 1850 in Walker County. They were the parents of seven children. Goree was active in the United Confederate Veterans, the Hood's Texas Brigade Association, and the Knights of Honor. Goree was a Democrat, and although he belonged to no church, he was regarded as one of the most ardent prohibitionists in the state. Simpson, *Compendium,* 229; Johnson, *Texas and Texans* 2:2000–2001.

63. Edwin King Goree, the fourth surviving son of Langston James Goree and SWKG, was born in 1842. With his brother Langston J. Goree he enlisted in John C. Cleveland's Company H, Fifth Texas Infantry on 20 Aug. 1861. He was detailed as a surgeon's orderly in July 1862 and on 21 Jan. 1863 received a sixty days' furlough to Texas, but he was present for duty at every major battle fought by Longstreet's I Corps until receiving a near-mortal wound on 6 May 1864 at the battle of the Wilderness. He was paroled at Lynchburg on 15 April 1865 while still on convalescent leave. After the war he was associated with the Sam Houston State Normal School (now Sam Houston State University) and with the state penitentiary at Huntsville. Edwin King Goree died in 1914. He never married. Simpson, *Compendium,* 229, 526, 557; Yeary, *Boys in Gray,* 274; Chilton, *Unveiling and Dedication of Monument to Hood's Texas Brigade.*

64. This attitude was unusual for a Texan of the time. Corp. John Wesley Rabb of the Eighth Texas Cavalry wrote to his mother on 29 June 1862 that although his younger brother Virgil Sullivan Rabb had received a commission, "he

has to walk. I would rather be a corporal in Company F of the Texas Rangers than to be first Lieu in a flat foot company." Since the earliest days of the republic, Texas soldiers had shown a marked preference for mounted service. At the outbreak of the Mexican War, Governor James Pinckney Henderson observed that "our people will not volunteer to serve on foot to the extent required." Although he believed that "there would be no difficulty in raising forty Companies provided they were mounted," he informed Maj. Gen. Zachary Taylor that "Texians are generally good horsemen and prefer to be employed in that way."

Likewise, William Andrew Fletcher, who had the distinction of seeing service in both Hood's Texas Brigade and Terry's Texas Rangers, remembered that infantry troops held their mounted comrades in vast contempt. Such remarks as "Mister, here's your mule!" "There goes the buttermilk cavalry!" "All those fellows do is find Yankees for us infantry to kill!" and "A hundred-dollar reward for just one dead cavalryman!" were met with such equally contemptuous retorts as "wagon dogs," "web feet," and "mud sloggers." Richard Taylor placed the feud in perspective. "Living on horseback, fearless and dashing, the men of the South afforded the best possible material for cavalry. They had every quality but discipline." Cutrer, "John Wesley Rabb," 202; James Pinckney Henderson to Zachary Taylor, 3 May 1846, Governors' Letters, 1846–60, Texas State Archives, Austin; Fletcher, *Rebel Private*, 82; Taylor, *Destruction and Reconstruction*, 60.

65. "No military event deserving notice occurred on our part of the frontier during the remainder of the summer," Joseph E. Johnston wrote of August 1861. He did, however, note that "at the beginning of September the army was encamped about Fairfax Court-House, with strong outposts at Munson's and Mason's Hills, with the cavalry on their flanks." The Confederates evacuated Munson's Hill on 20 Sept. Johnson, *Narrative of Military Operations*, 69, 74.

66. William S. Rosecrans (1819–1902), a native of Ohio, quickly rose to the command of the Army of the Mississippi. Rosecrans performed competently at the battles of Iuka, Corinth, and Murfreesboro. In 1863 he maneuvered Bragg out of Chattanooga before being struck a heavy counterblow at Chickamauga. Rosecrans was relieved of command and replaced by U. S.

Grant. William M. Lamers, *The Edge of Glory: A Biography of General William S. Rosecrans, U.S.A.* (New York, 1961).

67. From 20 Aug.—the day that western Virginia Unionists at Wheeling declared the state of Kanawha—until 26 Aug., heavy skirmishing took place at Hawk's Nest, Laurel Fork Creek, Springfield, Piggot's Mill, Cross Lanes, Wayne Courthouse, and Blue's House in the Kanawha Valley between the forces of William S. Rosecrans and Robert E. Lee. The fighting was indecisive, and the campaign sputtered to an end with the coming of winter.

68. TJG's first cousin Jonathan R. Kittrell was the first attorney general of Nevada and later practiced law in Fresno, Calif.

69. Howson C. Kenner of Newberry, S.C., was TJG's first cousin. At the time of the surrender at Appomattox, Kenner was a sergeant in Company C, Seventh South Carolina Cavalry. "Paroles," *SHSP* 15 (1887): 480.

70. On 1 Feb. 1862 Creed Taylor Woodson, the son of Dr. Creed and Mary Woodson of Montgomery, Tex., was appointed fourth corporal of Company D, Fifth Texas Infantry. He was promoted to third corporal on 23 Aug. 1862 and to second corporal in March 1863. In October 1862 he was detailed as a nurse in Richmond's Winder Hospital and on 10 July 1863 was transferred to the cavalry. Simpson, *Compendium*, 203.

71. John Buchanan Floyd (1806–1863), a former governor of Virginia and secretary of war in the Buchanan administration, was appointed a brigadier general in Confederate service. His record in western Virginia was not distinguished, and in December 1861 he was transferred to command of Fort Donelson, Tenn. The garrison surrendered to U. S. Grant on 16 Feb. 1862, but only after Floyd had turned the command over to Brig. Gen. Simon Bolivar Buckner and fled with his brigade. Jefferson Davis removed Floyd from command.

72. On Monday, 21 Oct. 1861, a Confederate force commanded by Nathan G. Evans repulsed a Federal reconnaissance-in-force across the Potomac River at Ball's Bluff, or Leesburg, Va. The 1,700 Southerners drove the roughly equal number of Union troops back into the river, killing their commanding officer and 48 others, wounding 158, and leaving 714 unaccounted for,

many of whom drowned. Coming as it did early in the war, this small and strategically inconsequential battle was hailed as a great victory in the South and mourned as a demoralizing defeat in the North.

73. Earl Van Dorn (1820–1863), a favorite of his fellow Mississippian Jefferson Davis, was promoted to brigadier general on 5 June and to major general on 19 Sept. 1861 and assigned to command of the Trans-Mississippi Department. Defeated at the battle of Elkhorn Tavern, he and his army were ordered to cross the Mississippi River but arrived too late to participate in the battle of Shiloh. He was removed from command for mishandling his army at the battle of Corinth but was then given command of the cavalry of John C. Pemberton's Army of Mississippi. He executed a daring raid on Holly Springs, Miss., on 20 Dec. 1862 which succeeded in destroying Grant's supply base. After showing promise as a cavalry commander, Van Dorn was assassinated by the husband of a woman with whom he was having an affair. Robert G. Hartje, *Van Dorn: The Life and Times of a Confederate General* (Nashville, 1967).

74. William Porcher Miles (1822–1899) resigned from the U.S. House of Representatives to become a delegate to South Carolina's secession convention. Miles served as an aide to P. G. T. Beauregard at the first battle of Manassas and after his election to the Confederate Congress remained one of the general's most vocal advocates.

75. William Ballard Preston (1805–1862) served in the U.S. House of Representatives from Virginia as an antislavery Whig and as secretary of the navy in the Zachary Taylor administration. Although Preston opposed secession, he was elected to the Provisional Confederate Congress where he was a staunch supporter of Beauregard and the so-called western bloc.

76. William Henry Talbot Walker (1816–1864) of Georgia was a veteran of the Seminole and Mexican wars and commandant of cadets at West Point. Walker was appointed a brigadier general in the Confederate States Army, but in protest against Jefferson Davis's policies, he resigned his commission. Later he was reinstated and assigned to the Army of Tennessee where he was promoted to major general. Russell K. Brown, *To The Manner Born: The Life of General William H. T. Walker* (Athens, Ga., 1994).

77. Richard Taylor (1826–1875), the son of President Zachary Taylor and brother-in-law of President Jefferson Davis, began the war as commander of the Ninth Louisiana Infantry and earned promotion to brigadier general on 21 Oct. 1861 and to major general on 28 July 1862. Transferred to the Department of West Louisiana, Taylor defended his adopted state for two years, achieving his greatest victory in the repulse of N. P. Banks's Red River expedition in April 1864. His autobiography, *Destruction and Reconstruction,* is among the finest of Confederate memoirs. Taylor, *Destruction and Reconstruction;* Parrish, *Richard Taylor.*

78. Norman Goree Kittrell, the son of Dr. Pleasant Williams and Frances Goree Kittrell, was born on 28 July 1849 in Greensboro, Ala. His parents brought him to Texas in 1850. Kittrell attended Washington and Lee University and was admitted to the bar in 1870. He became district attorney for the twelfth judicial district in 1884, serving until 1886 when he became judge. He resigned in 1892 to return to private practice in Houston, but in 1888 he returned to public life when he was elected to the Texas legislature. From 1903 until 1908 he was judge of the sixty-first judicial district. He also published five books of Texas history and folklore and was a frequent contributor to the Houston *Chronicle.* Kittrell died on 23 Jan. 1927. Webb, *Handbook of Texas* 1:967.

79. Micah Jenkins (1835–1864) was elected colonel of the Fifth South Carolina Infantry and fought with distinction at the first battle of Manassas. After recovering from a severe wound sustained at Second Manassas, Jenkins assumed command of John Bell Hood's old division, which he led a Chickamauga and during the Knoxville campaign. He was mortally wounded by his own men at the battle of the Wilderness, felled by the same volley that struck down James Longstreet.

80. The Fourth Texas Infantry was one of the three Texas regiments to serve in Hood's Texas Brigade of the Army of Northern Virginia. The Fourth Texas was recruited in Travis, Bexar, McLennan, and other central Texas counties and was commanded by four colonels including John Bell Hood and John Marshall. The regiment participated in all of the campaigns of I Corps from Seven Pines to Appomattox where

it surrendered 15 officers and 145 men. Simpson, *Hood's Texas Brigade.*

81. Montgomery Dent Corse (1816–1895), a native of Virginia, commanded the Seventeenth Virginia Infantry at the first battle of Manassas. He was promoted to brigadier general on 1 Nov. 1862 and assigned to George E. Pickett's division. His brigade was on detached duty when Pickett made his ill-starred charge at Gettysburg but fought in all of the other engagements of the I Corps until captured at Sayler's Creek on 6 April 1865.

82. Eppa Hunton (1822–1908) served in Virginia's secession convention and was elected colonel of the Eighth Virginia Infantry. After distinguishing himself in the defense of Henry House Hill at First Manassas, he was promoted to brigadier general. Eppa Hunton, *Autobiography of Eppa Hunton* (Richmond, 1933).

83. On 7 Nov. 1861 Federal forces seized control of Port Royal, S.C., only two days after Robert E. Lee was appointed to the command of the Confederate Department of South Carolina and Georgia. Although Lee, according to Secretary of War Judah P. Benjamin, should have been able to "concentrate all our forces at any point that might be attacked," Federal forces moved ashore from Hilton Head Island on 6 Dec. and operated in the area of Beaufort and Port Royal Ferry, S.C.

84. Tennessee was sharply divided by secession, with most of central and west Tennessee favoring the Confederacy and most of the citizens of east Tennessee remaining loyal to the Union. These loyalists contributed 30,000 volunteers to the Northern cause and engaged in guerilla warfare against the Confederacy until their region came under Federal control in September 1863. Especially notable was the campaign of sabotage launched in November 1861 in anticipation of an invasion of the state by Union troops under George H. Thomas. Tennessee Unionists burned five railroad bridges and ambushed a number of Confederate outposts, but the expected Federal incursion was called off by William T. Sherman. Confederate authorities declared martial law, arrested hundreds of Unionists, and executed five guerillas for the burnings. McPherson, *Battle Cry of Freedom,* 304–6.

85. As of 31 Dec. 1861 TJG was listed as a captain and volunteer aid-de-camp to Brig. Gen. James Longstreet. Wright, *Staff Officers,* 63.

86. The Fifth Texas Infantry, one of the regimens of John Bell Hood's famed Texas Brigade, was recruited from Harris, Colorado, Leon, Walker, Montgomery, Washington, Jefferson, Milam, Polk, Trinity, and Liberty counties and organized at Richmond in October 1861. More than half of its officers and men were killed, wounded, or captured at Gettysburg, and it surrendered only 12 officers and 149 enlisted men at Appomattox. James Jay Archer was the regiment's first colonel. Simpson, *Hood's Texas Brigade.*

87. Daniel Harvey Hill (1821–1889), a South Carolina native and a Mexican War veteran, was commissioned as colonel of the First North Carolina Infantry and was promoted to brigadier general on 10 July 1861. After the battle of Sharpsburg, he was appointed commander of the Department of North Carolina. Hill commanded a corps of the Army of Tennessee at the battle of Chickamauga and in the Chattanooga campaign. His outspoken criticism of Bragg's handling of the army resulted in his removal from command and in Jefferson Davis's refusal to sponsor his confirmation as lieutenant general. Leonard Hal Bridges, *Lee's Maverick General: Daniel Harvey Hill* (New York, 1961).

88. Robert Ransom, Jr. (1828–1892), resigned from the old army to accept a commission as colonel of the First North Carolina Cavalry. Promoted to brigadier general, he commanded a brigade of Longstreet's division during the Seven Days battles.

89. Protheus Jones of Henderson, N.C., was SWKG's first cousin.

90. On 20 May 1861 the Kentucky legislature formally resolved to keep that state neutral in the war between its Northern and Southern neighbors. This neutrality was broken on 3 Sept. when Confederate major general Leonidas Polk seized the Mississippi River towns of Hickman and Columbus. U. S. Grant responded by moving his army across the Ohio River into Paducah. Kentucky volunteers flocked to both armies, and a pro-Southern convention passed an ordinance of secession at Russellville in November. Kentucky was integral to Albert Sidney Johnston's defense of the western Confederacy, but with the loss of forts Donelson and Henry in February 1862, the line evaporated and the state was lost to the South. J. Stoddard Johnston,

Kentucky, vol. 9, *Confederate Military History*, ed. Clement A. Evans (Atlanta, 1899), 3–56; Cooling, *Forts Donelson and Henry*.

91. Clarke Calhoun Campbell, a Texas physician, was related to the Gorees by his marriage to TJG's first cousin Lucy Caroline Goree of Perry County, Ala. His youngest sister, Frances Rebecca Campbell, became the second wife of TJG's brother Robert Daniel Goree in 1869.

92. John C. Cleveland recruited Company H (locally known as the "Texas Polk Rifles") of the Fifth Texas Infantry in Liberty, Trinity, and Walker counties and was elected captain at the Polk County community of Cold Springs in July 1861. The company was mustered into Confederate service, "for the war," on 29 Aug. Cleveland was detailed to recruiting services in Texas from February until April 1862 but returned to his company in time to receive a wound at the second battle of Manassas. He briefly commanded the Fifth Texas on 19 and 20 Sept. 1863 before receiving a second wound at the battle of Chickamauga. He was granted convalescent leave to Texas in February 1864, and there he retired for disability on 16 March 1865. Simpson, *Compendium*, 227.

93. On 1 Feb. 1861 the Texas Secession Convention adopted an ordinance of secession. At San Antonio on 16 Feb., Bvt. Maj. Gen. David Emanuel Twiggs, commander of the Department of Texas, yielded U.S. arms, stores, and munitions to a force of Texas volunteers. Thomas W. Cutrer, *Ben McCulloch and the Frontier Military Tradition* (Chapel Hill, N.C., 1993), 177–87.

94. Although the Federal blockade of Galveston began in July 1861, another fifteen months passed before a naval force succeeded in taking the city. On 1 Jan. 1863 John Bankhead Magruder launched a combined land and sea assault on the occupying Federals, recapturing the vital port. Galveston was the only major port remaining in Confederate hands at the end of the war. Charles C. Cumberland, "The Confederate Loss and Recapture of Galveston, 1862–1863," *SWHQ* 51 (1947): 109–18, 121–30; Alwyn Barr, "Texas Coastal Defense, 1861–1865," *SWHQ* 65 (1961); 4, 13–18.

95. Robert M. Powell was captain of Company D of the Fifth Texas Infantry, locally designated as the "Waverly Confederates." Powell

was promoted to major on 22 Aug. 1862, to lieutenant colonel on 30 Aug. 1862, and to colonel commanding the Fifth Texas Infantry on 1 Nov. 1862. He was wounded and taken prisoner at Gettysburg and confined at Johnson's Island, Ohio. He was paroled at Fortress Monroe on 6 Feb. 1865 and thereafter assumed command of Hood's Texas Brigade, which he led through the Appomattox campaign. Wright and Simpson, *Texas in the War*, 213; Simpson, *Compendium*, 4.

96. At Huntsville on 7 May 1861, Procter P. Porter was elected captain of Company H—the "Porter Guards"—of the Fourth Texas Infantry. He was wounded at Gaines' Mill and died of typhoid fever on 20 July 1862 while recovering from his wound. Wright and Simpson, *Texas in the War*, 211; Simpson, *Compendium*, 146.

97. Mansfield Lovell (1822–1884), a native of the District of Columbia, accepted a Confederate commission as major general in October 1861 and was assigned to command of the defenses of New Orleans. When the city fell in April 1862, Lovell was assigned to the command of a division under his West Point classmate Earl Van Dorn but was relieved for a lack of aggressiveness at the battle of Corinth. Charles L. Dufour, *The Night the War Was Lost* (New York, 1960).

98. Pleasant Kittrell Goree, known to his friends and family as "Scrap," was born on 22 May 1845 at the Judson Female Institute in Marion, Ala., the youngest of the five Goree brothers. He was described as having gray eyes and a fair complexion and standing five feet, six inches tall. Goree attended school in Huntsville, but when Langston J. Goree was wounded and returned home, Pleasant Kittrell Goree joined Company H, Fifth Texas Infantry, at age sixteen, enlisting in Polk County on 11 Aug. 1863. Because of his diminutive stature, his brother TJG exercised his influence to have Scrap detailed as a courier to division headquarters, reporting to Brig. Gen. Charles William Field, commander of Hood's old division, on 1 Dec. 1863. He was shot through the collarbone at the battle of Fussell's Mill, or White Oak Swamp, some nine miles below Richmond, on 16 Aug. 1864. He recovered to see action at Cold Harbor and the siege of Petersburg, however, and was paroled at Appomattox on 12 April 1865. In 1867 Scrap Goree entered Washington College, now Washington and Lee University, where Robert E. Lee referred to him

as "my messenger in gray." Goree was unable to finish his degree, however, due to economic reversals on the Goree plantation. He married twice, first to Fannie Mangum who died soon thereafter, and then to Melissa Young, a daughter of W. F. and Mary Hayes Young. For twenty years he served the community of Midway, Tex., as a commissioner and for forty as a justice of the peace. In 1884 he published *Agricultural Report of Madison County, Texas,* at Loughridge. In 1927 he applied for a Confederate veteran's pension. Pleasant Kittrell Goree died in Midway on 22 April 1933. Simpson, *Compendium,* 229, 526; Yeary, *Boys in Gray,* 274; S. W. Geiser, "Men of Science in Texas," *Field and Laboratory* 27 (1959): 23; "Pleasant Kittrell Goree," Confederate Service Record, General Services Administration, National Archives and Records Service, Washington, D.C.; TJG to Robert E. Lee, 22 Oct. 1867, Washington and Lee University Library, Lexington, Va.

99. Robert Daniel Goree was born in Perry County, Ala., in 1840. He was educated at Baylor College, then at Independence, Tex., and upon graduating became a planter in Polk County. On 25 March 1862 he enlisted at Madisonville as a private in Capt. George B. Forrest's Company B of Col. Robert Gould's Sixth Texas Cavalry Battalion, Horace Randal's brigade, John G. Walker's Texas Division. On 9 Aug. he was appointed quartermaster sergeant of his battalion, and later he was promoted to captain. He saw service in the Red River campaign in 1864 and was captured at Pleasant Hill on 9 April. On 6 April 1865 he was detailed from the army for twelve months as a "second class agriculturalist" and was mustered out of service at the war's end at Hempstead, Tex. After the war Robert Daniel Goree resided first in Madison and then in Houston County until 1882 when he moved to the northwest Texas county of Knox to enter the cattle business and real estate development. The town of Goree in Knox County is named in his honor. In 1897 he moved to the Baylor County community of Seymour. Robert D. Goree was married twice, first to Frances Campbell and, in 1863, to Melissa Hayes. He became the father of six children. Simpson, *Compendium,* 526; Paddock, *North and West Texas* 2:455–56; "Robert D. Goree," Confederate Service Records, General Services Administration, National Archives and Records Service.

100. On 8 Nov. 1861 James M. Mason and John Slidell, Confederate diplomats, were en route from Havana to their posts in London and Paris aboard the British mail steamer *Trent* when the ship was forcibly stopped and boarded by officers and men of the USS *San Jacinto.* Despite the protests of the British captain, Mason and Slidell were removed from the ship and taken prisoner by Capt. Charles Wilkes. Wilkes had acted without the knowledge or consent of his government, and his action brought cries of outrage from the British. Only after Queen Victoria's government issued an ultimatum threatening war if the diplomats were not released, however, did the Lincoln administration relent and set Mason and Slidell at liberty to continue their mission. The *Trent* affair was the United States' closest brush with war with England and the Confederacy's best hope of involving a major foreign power on its behalf.

101. The "Hay(s) question" is an allusion to Robert D. Goree's courtship of Melissa Hayes, whom he married in 1864.

102. Officially the Eighth Texas Cavalry, the Terry Texas Rangers was perhaps the most effective cavalry regiment, North or South, in the Civil War. Raised and commanded by Benjamin Franklin Terry until his death at Woodsonville, Ky., the regiment served with distinction in virtually every battle and campaign of the Army of Tennessee. Blackburn, *Reminiscences of the Terry Rangers;* Cutrer, "John Wesley Rabb"; Fletcher, *Rebel Private;* Giles, *Terry's Texas Rangers;* Graber, *Terry Texas Ranger.*

103. With the waning of martial enthusiasm by the end of 1861 and the consequent decline in the number of volunteers, the Confederate government was forced to resort to conscription to keep its armies manned. In April 1862 the Confederate Congress enacted the First Conscription Act, which declared all able-bodied, unmarried white males between the ages of eighteen and thirty-five liable for the draft. The Second Conscription Act, passed in September 1862, and the Third Conscription Act, passed in February 1864, extended the ages of liability from seventeen to fifty. Many forms of legal evasion were available to exempt the potential draftee, however, including purchase of a substitute, payment of a $300 commutation fee, or employment in such occupations as medicine, mining, railroading, and telegraphy. The exemption of any individual overseeing as many as twenty slaves involved in agricultural pursuits

caused much bitterness in the South, giving credence to the accusation that the struggle was "a rich man's war and a poor man's fight." Albert Burton Moore, *Conscription and Conflict in the Confederacy* (New York, 1924).

104. Samuel Escridge ("Eck") Goree was TJG's half brother by their father's first marriage. He was born in 1823, married Sarah Elizabeth Wiley ("Sis Sally"), and became the father of six children. At the outbreak of the Civil War, Eck Goree was elected sergeant of Company K of the Eighth Texas Cavalry. After seeing action with the Army of Tennessee, Goree returned to Texas where he served for six months during 1863 and 1864 as a private in the Fourth Regiment of Texas state troops.

105. A sharp fight took place at Dranesville, Va., on 20 Dec. 1861 when a Confederate foraging party, escorted by J. E. B. Stuart with four regiments of infantry, 150 cavalrymen, and a battery of artillery, happened upon Federal foragers under the protection of E. O. C. Ord and five regiments of infantry, a squadron of cavalry, and a battery of artillery. Stuart attempted an assault against the well-placed Federals but was repulsed with 194 casualties. Once his wagons were safely on the road, Stuart disengaged and followed them back toward Centreville. Ord's losses amounted to 68.

106. James Benson Martin (1825–1861) was born in Habersham County, Ala., practiced law in Talladega and Jacksonville, and was elected first as a judge and later as a member of the Alabama legislature. Elected lieutenant colonel of the Tenth Alabama Infantry on 4 June 1861, he was killed in action at Dranesville, Va.

107. Thomas William Woodward (1833–1902) was born in South Carolina and on 19 Feb. 1861 was elected major of the Sixth South Carolina Infantry. After receiving a severe thigh wound at Dranesville, he was dropped from the regiment's muster role but was later reassigned as quartermaster of the Twentieth South Carolina Infantry and assistant quartermaster of Kershaw's Brigade. Thomas W. Woodward, *Address of Major Thomas W. Woodward, Delivered before the Survivors' Association of the Sixth Regiment, South Carolina Volunteers* (Columbia, S.C., 1883).

1862. "THE FATE OF THE COUNTY DEPENDS ON OUR SUCCESS"

1. Despite all of the rumors of war, the Army of the Potomac was not advancing. Not until 31 Jan. 1862, when Lincoln issued the peremptory President's Special War Order No. 1 commanding McClellan to seize the railroad between Manassas Junction and the Shenandoah Valley by 22 Feb., was the Federal general-in-chief stirred to action. Stephen W. Sears, *George B. McClellan: The Young Napoleon* (New York, 1988), 149–51.

2. On 7 Jan. 1862 Ambrose Burnside was named commander of the Union Department of North Carolina, and four days later he sailed from Hampton Roads, Va., with 15,000 troops. In response, Confederate authorities named Henry A. Wise to the command of Roanoke Island, but when on 25 Jan. the Federals put ashore, their landing was not resisted. Against virtually no opposition Burnside captured Roanoke Island in February and New Bern, N.C., on 14 March. William Marvel, *Burnside* (Chapel Hill, N.C., 1991), 41–96.

3. Bell I. Wiley has observed that "the declining fortunes of the Southern Confederacy may be strikingly traced in the degeneration of the stationery used by ordinary soldiers." Soldiers and their families commonly used old wrapping paper, fly pages from books, and even the reverse side of wallpaper. The scarcity of paper, combined with the South's dizzying rate of inflation, sent the cost of a single quire of paper to five dollars and "a bunch of envelopes" to three dollars at a time when a Rebel private earned but eleven dollars a month. Wiley, *Life of Johnny Reb*, 196.

4. Nicholas Dawson observed that Thomas Walton, another of Longstreet's aides-de-camp, was a kinsman of the general's, "through whose influence he had received an appointment in the Commissary Department. He really did general staff duty." Dawson found Walton thoroughly unpleasant and "always supercilious" and before Knoxville nearly fought a duel with him. Walton had made the comment that "when the Confederate States enjoyed their own government, they did not intend to have any 'd—d foreigners' in the country." Dawson, an Englishman, inquired what was to become of such men as

himself who had fought for the cause, to which Walton "made a flippant reply." Dawson reacted "rather warmly," and Walton answered him with a swing of his fist. The Englishman blocked the blow, slapped Walton, and on the next morning sent him a challenge by Capt. Fitz-Gerald Ross, a Scot in Austrian Service who was then observing the operations of the Confederate army. Walton, who was not inclined to fight, offered to make "an ample apology in writing." After a day or two passed and no apology was forthcoming, Dawson again sent Ross to Walton. Walton "took the position that he had been hasty in his action and that if he had not promised to do it he would not make an apology at all." Ross, as Dawson's second, then took up the quarrel, and Walton at last rendered his apology.

Walton's reputation as a poker player was prodigious, but his standing as a gentleman was further tarnished when he sent to Thomas F. Maury, one of the corps' surgeons, for the $2,000 that he had lost on the previous night "before that gentleman was out of bed in the morning." Dawson, *Reminiscences*, 102–3, 128.

5. Samuel Cooper (1798–1876), a native of New Jersey, was appointed adjutant general of the U.S. Army in 1852, and in 1861—due to his close friendship with Jefferson Davis and the influence of his Virginia-born wife—accepted the position of adjutant general of the Confederate States Army. His tenure, which lasted until the end of the war, has been characterized as adequate if not outstanding. His service to future historians, however, was of inestimable value as he preserved all of his records after the fall of Richmond and turned them over intact to Union officials.

6. R. J. Breckenridge was appointed surgeon of the Fifth Texas Infantry on 8 Nov. 1861. In March 1862 he received a temporary assignment to the army medical board in Richmond and was appointed chief medical inspector of the Army of Northern Virginia in the fall of 1862. Simpson, *Compendium*, 168.

7. Longstreet's family life was one of many sorrows. His infant son William Dent Longstreet died in Washington on 19 July 1854. A daughter, Harriet Margaret, was born and died in 1856. His sons Augustus Baldwin Longstreet, who was born in 1850, and James, who was born in 1857, and a daughter, Mary Anne, who was born in 1860, all died of scarlet fever in January

and February 1862. Thus, only one of his six children born before the war survived it. Four more Longstreet children were born after the war. Wert, *James Longstreet*, 96–97; Piston, *Lee's Tarnished Lieutenant*, 120.

8. James and Mary are TJG's first cousin James Langston Goree, a physician, and his wife, Mary Dixon Goree. Don was their son, Donald Dixon Goree, who was wounded at Shiloh, and Lucy is their daughter, Lucy Campbell Goree, who after the war married Col. Edward Pearsall Gregg, former commander of the Sixteenth Texas Cavalry. Shortly after this writing the couple left their Jefferson County, Ark., home to take refuge with the Gorees in Texas.

9. In January 1862, due largely to the insistence of a delegation of representatives of the Mississippi Valley states, Beauregard was ordered west to take command of the left wing of Albert Sidney Johnston's army, headquartered at Columbus, Ky. Pleased to be out from under the meddlesome influence of Jefferson Davis, Beauregard accepted his new assignment with alacrity, but to many observers this transfer seemed but an administration ploy to remove a troublesome general from the principal theater of operations. Beauregard did not return to the East until the final days of the war. Williams, *Napoleon in Gray*, 113–17.

10. The events alluded to are Confederate defeats of greater or lesser significance, all of which helped to erode Southern morale. On 7 Nov. 1861 Flag Officer Samuel Francis du Pont led a powerful Union naval squadron into Port Royal Sound, S.C., and quickly pounded the outgunned Rebel forts into silence. With beachheads thus established Thomas West Sherman landed 12,000 troops to occupy Port Royal and Hilton Head. Although the Federals failed to exploit their victory as a base for offensive operations, Port Royal became an important coaling station for the Union navy and a refuge for fugitive slaves from the South Carolina hinterland.

11. Felix Kirk Zollicoffer (1812–1862), a veteran of the Second Seminole War and a powerful Whig politician, was appointed a brigadier general in the Confederate army on 9 July 1861 and was given command of the Department of East Tennessee. In November 1861 he unwisely marched his small army into Kentucky where he was joined by his immediate superior,

George Bibb Crittenden. At Mill Springs on 19 Jan. 1862, Zollicoffer and Crittenden were attacked by Union forces under George H. Thomas, and Zollicoffer was killed while riding between the lines.

12. George Bibb Crittenden (1812–1880), the son of Senator John Jordan Crittenden and a veteran of the Mexican War, was commissioned a major general in the Confederate army and given command of the Southern effort to liberate Kentucky. In January 1862 he was ingloriously defeated at Mill Springs. Crittenden was said to have been drunk on the field, and an outraged public demanded his removal from command. He was subsequently discovered drunk at his post at Iuka, Miss., with his troops "in a wretched state of discipline." He was court-martialed and resigned from the army in 1862.

13. Thomas Fenwick Drayton (1808–1891) was a member of South Carolina's antebellum legislature. Commissioned as a brigadier general in Confederate service by his West Point classmate and lifelong friend Jefferson Davis, Drayton was assigned to command of the military district of Port Royal, which he defended unsuccessfully against a Union naval force in October 1861. In June 1862 he was reassigned to command of a brigade of Longstreet's division. Drayton proved an incompetent field commander, and at Sharpsburg his command, in the words of Robert E. Lee, "broke to pieces." Drayton was subsequently transferred to the Trans-Mississippi Department.

14. Lloyd Tilghman (1816–1863), a Marylander by birth, was commissioned a brigadier general and assigned to command of Fort Henry on the Tennessee River. Although he believed its location to be inappropriate, he conducted as spirited defense against U.S. Grant's attack and was able to extricate most of the garrison before surrendering on 6 Feb. 1862. After being exchanged Tilghman was assigned to command of a brigade in Mississippi and was killed in action at the battle of Champion's Hill.

15. Albert Sidney Johnston (1803–1862) was born in Kentucky but emigrated to Texas in 1836. Within a year he had risen to brigadier general and commander of the army, and from 1838 to 1840 he served as secretary of war for the Republic of Texas. After the Mexican War he was appointed commander of the Second United States Cavalry. Johnson accepted appointment as a full general in the Confederate army with command of all Southern forces west of the Allegheny Mountains. Unable to hold Kentucky and Tennessee against Union invasion, he delivered a counterstroke at Shiloh where he was mortally wounded. William Preston Johnston, *The Life of Gen. Albert Sidney Johnston* (New York, 1878); Charles P. Roland, *Albert Sidney Johnston: Soldier of Three Republics* (Austin, Tex., 1964).

16. From Evansport, Va., a detachment of Joseph E. Johnston's army covered one of the approaches to Manassas Junction. When George B. McClellan made the first step of his long-awaited drive into Virginia, Johnston ordered the evacuation of Evansport on 7 March 1862, and the detachment there marched south to rejoin the remainder of the Confederate army at Fredericksburg.

17. John J. Roberts, a physician, enlisted as a private in Company E, Fifth Texas Infantry, but was appointed assistant regimental surgeon on 15 Nov. 1861. He was wounded at the battle of the Wilderness and advanced to regimental surgeon on 10 Aug. 1864. He was paroled at Appomattox. Simpson, *Compendium*, 169.

18. On 16 Feb. 1862, after a four-day battle and siege, Confederate generals John B. Floyd, Gideon J. Pillow, and Simon B. Buckner surrendered Fort Donelson to the forces of U. S. Grant. The fall of this strategically vital fortress on the Cumberland River made inevitable the loss of all of Kentucky as well as Nashville and western Tennessee to the South. Cooling, *Forts Henry and Donelson;* Nathaniel Cheairs Hughes, Jr., and Roy P. Stonesifer, *The Life and Wars of Gideon J. Pillow* (Chapel Hill, N.C., 1993).

19. George H. Gray (1828–1891) was born in Virginia but moved to Mississippi and then, after service in the Mexican War, to Texas where he was elected chief justice of Travis County. During the latter half of the Civil War, he lived in occupied New Orleans but returned to Texas in 1865 with his brother-in-law, A. J. Hamilton, who, as governor, appointed him clerk of the Texas Supreme Court. Gray was removed from office as "an impediment to Reconstruction." Webb, *Handbook of Texas* 1:723.

20. In his attempt to carry out Richmond's directive that all Confederate territory be held against Union incursion, Albert Sidney Johnston

detached elements of his army across the length of Tennessee and Kentucky, trying to defend an untenable line, perforated by navigable rivers, against a numerically superior Union army supported with a strong riverine navy. Taking advantage of the attenuated Southern line, Ulysses S. Grant penetrated Johnston's position by way of the Tennessee and Cumberland rivers, capturing forts Henry and Donelson on 6 and 16 Feb. 1862, respectively. The strategic importance of these capitulations was considerable. Not only were the Confederates forced to abandon their foothold in Kentucky and to give up a large portion of Tennessee, but the stage was set for the splitting of the entire Confederacy by a drive down the line of the Mississippi River to Vicksburg. Stanley F. Horn, *The Army of Tennessee: A Military History* (New York, 1941), 80–121; Thomas Lawrence Connelly, *Army of the Heartland: The Army of Tennessee, 1861–1862* (Baton Rouge, La., 1967), 46–142.

21. This is James Gillaspie (1805–1867) of Huntsville who had commanded a company under Sam Houston at San Jacinto and another under Texas Ranger colonel John C. Hays in the Mexican War. During the Civil War this veteran volunteer soldier raised and led a company in the Fifth Texas militia regiment, stationed at Galveston. In 1867 Gillaspie was appointed superintendent of the state penitentiary at Huntsville. Webb, *Handbook of Texas*, 1:689.

22. This report was false. Instead, on 8–9 March 1862 Stonewall Jackson, commander of the small Confederate army in the Shenandoah Valley, left his winter quarters at Winchester to attack the forces of James Shields at Kernstown, initiating the famed Shenandoah Valley campaign. Tanner, *Stonewall in the Valley*, 103–9.

23. Jerome Bonaparte Robertson (1815–1891) was born in Kentucky but emigrated to Texas in 1836. He was elected to the state senate and was a delegate to the state's secession convention. Robertson was elected captain of Company I of the Fifth Texas Infantry, was promoted to lieutenant colonel in November 1861, and on 1 June 1862 assumed command of his regiment with the rank of colonel. On 1 Nov. 1862 Robertson was promoted to brigadier general, taking command of Hood's Texas Brigade, which he led from Fredericksburg to Chickamauga. During the Knoxville campaign Robertson incurred Longstreet's displeasure for "delinquency and

pessimism" and was court-martialed and relieved of his command. Longstreet, *Manassas to Appomattox*, 517–18; Wright and Simpson, *Texas in the War*, 90–91; Webb, *Handbook of Texas* 2:487.

24. Benjamin Huger (1805–1877) served as Winfield Scott's chief of ordnance during the Mexican War. With his native South Carolina's secession, he was appointed a brigadier general and given command of the department of eastern Virginia. Promoted to major general on 7 Oct., Huger was given command of a division during the Peninsula campaign but was harshly and unfairly censured by Longstreet for its mishandling during the Seven Days battles. Relieved of field command, Huger was assigned as inspector of artillery and ordnance and, in 1863, was transferred to duty as chief of the ordnance bureau of the Trans-Mississippi Department.

25. This was presumably the skirmish at Howard's Mills on the Warwick River near Cockletown on the Peninsula. This fight was a preliminary to the siege of Yorktown, which formally began on 5 April.

26. The Texas Brigade of the Army of Northern Virginia was perhaps the most aggressive of all Confederate brigades and was reportedly Robert E. Lee's favorite. The brigade won its first glory under John Bell Hood at the battle of Gaines' Mill when it broke the seemingly impregnable Union line with the force of its impetuous assault. Such recklessness cost the unit the heaviest casualties of any brigade, North or South, in the Civil War, losing two-thirds of its strength at Sharpsburg and surrendering only 617 of its aggregate strength of 5,300 at Appomattox. Simpson, *Hood's Texas Brigade*.

27. John Anthony Winston (1812–1871), a former governor of Alabama, was elected colonel of the Eighth Alabama Infantry on 11 June 1861 but resigned on 16 June due to chronic rheumatism.

28. Lawrence O'Bryan Branch (1828–1862) was an officer in the Seminole War and a member of the North Carolina House of Representatives. After commanding the Thirty-third North Carolina Infantry, he was promoted to brigadier general and assumed command of the Confederate forces at New Bern, N.C., but was able to offer only limited resistance to Ambrose Burnside's amphibious operations against the area. Transferred to the Army of Northern Virginia,

Branch was killed in action at the battle of Sharpsburg.

29. To relieve the pressure on Confederate forces on the Peninsula, Thomas J. Jackson was ordered to the Shenandoah Valley in March 1862. There he was to create a diversion by threatening Washington and thus pinning potential reinforcements to McClellan's army to the defense of the capital. Although commanding an army of only 4,500 men, Jackson seized the initiative on 23 March by boldly attacking the Kernstown garrison. Reinforced to 17,000 men, Jackson then attacked and defeated John C. Frémont's army at McDowell on 8 May and then turned on Nathaniel P. Banks, driving him from the Valley in a series of running battles from Front Royal on 23 May to Winchester on 25 May. Deeply concerned by Jackson's successes, the Lincoln administration ordered Irvin McDowell and his 20,000-man army at Fredericksburg into the Valley, thus depriving McClellan of expected reinforcements, and instructed Frémont and Banks to trap the Confederates in the lower Valley. Circled by three converging armies, Jackson raced south, narrowly evading the Union trap and earning his men the sobriquet "Jackson's Foot Cavalry." The campaign closed with Jackson's successful attack on Frémont's army at Cross Keys on 8 June and on McDowell's troops at Port Republic on 9 June. Having neatly extricated his command, he rejoined Joseph E. Johnston's army east of Richmond in time to take part in the Seven Days battles. Tanner, *Stonewall in the Valley.*

30. Joseph Reid Anderson (1813–1892), as head of the Tredegar Iron Company of Richmond, was one of the South's most important industrialists. Despite his position as chief executive officer of the South's most crucial factory, Anderson was commissioned a brigadier general in the Confederate States Army and proved a credible field commander until wounded at the battle of White Oak Swamp. Anderson resigned from the army on 19 July 1862 and returned to Richmond where he spent the remainder of the war supervising the casting of Rebel ordnance.

31. Ambrose Powell Hill (1825–1865), a veteran of the Mexican War and the Third Seminole War, was elected colonel of the Thirteenth Virginia Infantry and promoted to brigadier general on 26 Feb. 1862 and to major general on 26

May. With the reorganization of the army after Jackson's death, Hill was promoted to lieutenant general and given command of the newly constituted III Corps. Hill's performance as a corps commander never measured up to his promise as a division commander; he seems to have been the victim of various psychosomatic illnesses when faced with great responsibility. Hill was killed during the final days of the siege of Petersburg. William Woods Hassler, *A. P. Hill: Lee's Forgotten General* (Chapel Hill, N.C., 1962); Robertson, *A. P. Hill.*

32. This is presumably the fight at Eltham's Landing, Va., 7 May 1862, a rearguard action in Joseph E. Johnston's retreat up the Peninsula in which Hood's Texas Brigade received its baptism of fire. In a six-hour action the brigade, spearheaded by the First Texas Infantry, drove William Buell Franklin's division back a mile and a half to the safety of the Federal gunboats on the York River, thus allowing the Confederate wagon train to retreat unmolested toward Richmond. Simpson, *Hood's Texas Brigade,* 97–99.

33. Sam Houston, Jr., the eldest son of the first president of the Republic of Texas, was born in Washington-on-the-Brazos, Tex., on 25 May 1843. Despite his father's Unionism, he left the Bastrop Military Academy in 1861 to become the second lieutenant of Capt. M. V. McMahan's Texas Horse Artillery. Wounded and captured at the battle of Shiloh, he was interned at Camp Douglas near Chicago. Exchanged in the fall of 1862, he was appointed second lieutenant of Company E of Col. Joseph J. Cook's First Texas Heavy Artillery and saw duty in Louisiana. After a desultory postbellum career in medicine and writing, he died in Independence, Tex., on 20 May 1894. Sidney Smith Johnson, *Texans Who Wore the Gray* (Tyler, Tex., 1907), 174–75; Webb, *Handbook of Texas* 1:847; Wright and Simpson, *Texas in the War,* 135.

34. Mart H. Royston (ca. 1835–1890) was born in Alabama but emigrated to Texas sometime before 1861. With the outbreak of the Civil War, he was appointed adjutant of the Eighth Texas Cavalry. He was promoted to major on 10 Nov. 1863 and was appointed assistant adjutant general to John A. Wharton. After the war Royston was elected Texas state treasurer but was removed as "an impediment to Reconstruction." Webb, *Handbook of Texas* 2:551; Giles, *Terry's*

Texas Rangers, 17, 37; Blackburn, "Terry Rangers," 11; Wright, *Staff Officers,* 143, 206.

35. Young Lea Royston (1819–1884) was born in Perry County, Ala., where he practiced law until 2 May 1861 when he was elected captain of Company A of the Eighth Alabama Infantry. He was promoted to major on 20 March 1862, to lieutenant colonel on 5 May 1862, and to colonel on 16 June 1862. He was wounded at the battle of Frayser's Farm on 30 June 1862 and again, severely, at the battle of Salem Church on 3 May 1863. Thereafter he was transferred to post duty at Selma, Ala., until the end of the war.

36. Longstreet, in his report on the engagement at Williamsburg on 5 May 1862, commended TJG and the other members of his staff. "All of these officers," he wrote to Joseph E. Johnston, "so conducted themselves on the field as to give me great pleasure, satisfaction, and assurance." *OR,* I, 11, pt. 1:568.

37. The battle of Fair Oaks, or Seven Pines, 31 May–1 June 1862, was the first in a bloody series of battles in which the Confederate army seized the initiative from the Army of the Potomac and began to drive it back down the Peninsula. Within sight of the city of Richmond, George B. McClellan divided his command, moving two of his corps across the Chickahominy River to link with an army presumed to be marching south from Fredericksburg under Irvin McDowell. When McDowell was diverted to counter Jackson's threat to Washington and spring rains sent the Chickahominy out of its banks, however, Joseph E. Johnston sensed the opportunity to destroy McClellan's isolated detachment. Longstreet's divisions were directed to envelop and attack the Federal right wing under Erasmus D. Keyes at Seven Pines on the morning of 31 May while troops under D. H. Hill and Benjamin Huger attacked along the enemy front. Poor staff work and lack of coordination caused massive delays, however, and at last, at about 1:00 P.M., Hill attacked alone. Although costly, Hill's charges crushed the Federal right and drove back the enemy line. Not until 4:00 P.M. did William C. Whiting's division, temporarily under Longstreet's command, move forward. Near Fair Oaks it collided with elements of Edwin V. Sumner's corps, which had been ordered across the Chickahominy to reinforce Heintzelman and Keyes. Whiting's charge was repulsed,

and Johnston, riding close to the front, was severely wounded. At the end of the day only one of Longstreet's own brigades had been in action. The following morning, with Gustavus W. Smith in command of the Confederate army, Longstreet was again ordered forward but again proved dilatory. He attacked with only two of his brigades and was easily repulsed. Later in the day Robert E. Lee arrived from Richmond to take command of the Southern army and at 2:00 P.M. ordered his troops to disengage. Although a tactical victory for the North, Fair Oaks so unnerved McClellan that he yielded the initiative to the Confederate army and began his painful withdrawal down the Peninsula.

For their role in the battle, Longstreet thanked his staff "for their activity, zeal, and intelligence in carrying orders and the proper discharge of their duties." Longstreet himself, however, certainly emerged from the battle with his reputation tarnished. By altering Johnston's instructions to attack along the Nine Mile Road and actually marching down the Williamsburg Road, Longstreet hopelessly entangled and delayed his troops, and by attempting to cast the blame onto one of his subordinates, Benjamin Huger, he further disgraced himself in the eyes of the army. Cullen, *Peninsula Campaign,* 54–57; Dowdey, *Seven Days,* 84–128; Sears, *To the Gates of Richmond,* 117–45; *OR,* I, 11, pt. 1:941.

38. James Dearing (1840–1865) was commissioned second lieutenant of Company C in the famed Washington Artillery Battalion of New Orleans. In 1862 he was promoted to captain and given command of the Lynchburg Battery attached to George E. Pickett's brigade. In 1863 he became a major in command of an artillery battalion in Longstreet's corps. After Gettysburg he was transferred to cavalry service and early in April 1864 was promoted to colonel and given command of the horse artillery of the Army of Northern Virginia. On 29 April 1864 Dearing was commissioned a brigadier general and assigned to the command of a brigade in William Henry Fitzhugh Lee's cavalry division. In a rear-guard action covering the army's retreat toward Appomattox, Dearing engaged in a pistol duel with Federal lieutenant colonel Theodore Read. Read was killed in the encounter, and Dearing was mortally wounded, becoming the last Confederate general to die of wounds received in action. Owen, *Washington Artillery,* 448; Wise, *Long Arm of Lee,* 184.

39. Darius Nash Couch (1822–1897), a native of New York, was appointed colonel of the Seventh Massachusetts Infantry and was advanced to brigadier general in 1861. He served with the Army of the Potomac through the battle of Chancellorsville and was promoted to major general, but his outspoken mistrust of Joseph Hooker and his continued close ties with the discredited McClellan caused him to request transfer. Thereafter Couch commanded the Pennsylvania militia during the Gettysburg campaign and fought at Nashville and in Sherman's campaign in North Carolina.

40. Robert Hopkins Hatton (1826–1862), a native of Ohio, was elected to the U.S. House of Representatives from Tennessee in 1859. On 26 May 1861 he was commissioned colonel of the Seventh Tennessee Infantry. He was promoted to brigadier general for his performance at the battle of Savage's Station, but only eight days later, at the battle of Fair Oaks, he was killed at the head of his brigade.

41. James Johnston Pettigrew (1828–1863), a North Carolina native, served as a professor at the Naval Observatory at Washington, D.C., and as a member of the South Carolina state legislature before the Civil War. After taking part in the capture of Fort Sumter, Pettigrew was elected colonel of the Twelfth South Carolina Infantry, promoted to brigadier general in 1862, and wounded and captured at Fair Oaks. Exchanged, he rejoined the Army of Northern Virginia for the Gettysburg campaign and, in Pickett's charge, was wounded in the hand. Pettigrew was mortally wounded on 14 July in the rearguard action at Falling Waters, Md., and died three days later. Clyde N. Wilson, *Carolina Cavalier: The Life and Mind of James Johnson Pettigrew* (Athens, Ga., 1991).

42. Wade Hampton (1818–1902) raised and was elected colonel of South Carolina's Hampton Legion. After promotions to brigadier general and major general, he was made commander of the cavalry corps of the Army of Northern Virginia after Jeb Stuart's death at Yellow Tavern. Promoted to lieutenant general on 15 Feb. 1865, Hampton was transferred to South Carolina. Wellman, *Giant in Gray*.

43. William Henry Chase Whiting (1824–1865) of Mississippi resigned from the U.S. Army to accept a commission as a major and an appointment as chief engineer in Joseph E. Johnston's Army of the Shenandoah. He was promoted to brigadier general on 21 July 1861 and commanded a division during the Valley and the Peninsula campaigns. Whiting was transferred to North Carolina where he designed and constructed Fort Fisher. Promoted to major general in 1864, he was ordered back to the defense of Petersburg, but his failure on that field drew heavy criticism, and at his own request he was returned to Wilmington. On 5 Jan. 1865 Whiting was mortally wounded leading a counterattack at Fort Fisher. Rod Gragg, *Confederate Goliath: The Battle of Fort Fisher* (New York, 1991), 53–61, 252–53.

44. William Mahone (1826–1895), president of the Norfolk and Petersburg railroad at the time of the outbreak of the Civil War, was appointed colonel of the Sixth Virginia Infantry, commanded a brigade of Huger's division during the battle of Fair Oaks and the Seven Days battles, and was promoted to brigadier general on 16 Nov. 1861. Except for a period of recovery from a severe wound sustained at the second battle of Manassas, Mahone remained with the Army of Northern Virginia until Appomattox, especially distinguishing himself and winning promotion to major general for his ferocious counterattack at the Crater.

45. George Edward Pickett (1825–1875) was commissioned a colonel in the Confederate army and promoted to brigadier general in 1862, leading a brigade of Longstreet's division. Promoted to major general for his service in the Sharpsburg campaign, Pickett was given command of a division of I Corps. On 3 July 1863, the third day of the battle of Gettysburg, he led his command against Cemetery Hill in an attempt to break the center of Meade's army but was repulsed with heavy losses. On 1 April 1865 Philip H. Sheridan attacked Pickett's division at Five Forks and drove it from the field, thus virtually completing the encirclement of the Confederate army. Lee thereupon removed Picket from command.

46. Cadmus Marcellus Wilcox (1824–1890), a North Carolina native, fought in the Mexican War and served as an instructor at West Point where he wrote the influential text *Rifles and Rifle Practice*. With secession Wilcox was elected colonel of the Ninth Alabama Infantry. In 1861

he was promoted to brigadier general and assigned to command of a brigade in Longstreet's
division. He believed Longstreet culpable for the
heavy losses suffered by I Corps at Gettysburg,
and when the two quarreled Wilcox was transferred to A. P. Hill's corps with a promotion to
major general.

47. Raleigh Edward Colston (1825–1896) was
appointed colonel of the Sixteenth Virginia Infantry and late in 1861 was promoted to brigadier general. Colston failed to distinguish
himself under Longstreet and left the army on
sick leave until December 1862. In spring 1863
Stonewall Jackson, formerly his colleague at
VMI, gave Colston a command in II Corps, but
he performed poorly at Chancellorsville and
was relieved. Thereafter he served in the defense of Petersburg and at the end of the war
was commander of the Lynchburg garrison.

48. Roger Adkinson Pryor (1828–1919) was
editor of the Richmond *Enquirer* and a member
of the House of Representatives from Virginia.
He was in Charleston during the Fort Sumter
crisis and is said to have declined the offer to
fire the first shot at the Federal fort. After a
term in the Provisional Confederate Congress,
Pryor took command of the Third Virginia Infantry. Promoted to brigadier general in 1862,
Pryor commanded a brigade through the
Sharpsburg campaign when, ostensibly because
of the unit's heavy casualties, but certainly at the
insistence of Lee and Longstreet, the brigade
was broken up, and Pryor resigned from the
army. Mrs. Roger A. Pryor, *Reminiscences of Peace
and War* (New York, 1904).

49. Edwin Vose Sumner (1797–1863) was a native of Massachusetts and a veteran of the Mexican War. He commanded II Corps of the Army
of the Potomac during the Peninsula campaign.
Although he was the object of mild criticism for
his behavior at Sharpsburg, Sumner commanded Ambrose Burnside's Right Grand Division at Fredericksburg but requested that he be
relieved when Joseph Hooker ascended to command of the Army of the Potomac. Transferred
to the Department of Missouri, Sumner died in
route to his new duty station.

50. Robert Emmet Rodes (1829–1864) led the
Fifth Alabama Infantry at First Manassas and
was soon thereafter promoted to brigadier general and assigned to the command of a brigade

in D. H. Hill's division. In the spring of 1863 he
assumed command of Hill's division. Promoted
to major general after the battle of Spotsylvania,
Rodes accompanied Jubal A. Early to the Shenandoah Valley in 1864, where he was killed in action while commanding the Confederate rear
guard after the disastrous third battle of Winchester. Jeffry E. Wert, *From Winchester to Cedar
Creek: The Shenandoah Campaign of 1864* (Carlisle,
Pa., 1987).

51. Leonard B. Abercrombie, a Texas resident, was a graduate of the University of Virginia. *SHSP* 33 (1905): 43.

52. Sydenham Moore was born in Rutherford County, Tenn., on 25 May 1815. After graduating from the University of Alabama in 1836, he
began the practice of law in Greensboro, Ala.
He served in the Mexican War and in campaigns
against the Cherokee Indians before being
elected to the U.S. House of Representatives in
1857. Moore resigned from Congress to become
colonel of the Eleventh Alabama Infantry on 11
June 1861. On 20 Aug. 1862 he died of wounds
sustained at the battle of Seven Pines.

53. Tennent Lomax (1820–1862) was born in
Abbeville, S.C., graduated from Randolph-
Macon College, and served as an officer in the
Mexican War. Elected lieutenant colonel of the
Third Alabama Infantry on 28 April 1861, he was
promoted to colonel on 31 July. Lomax was
killed in action at the battle of Seven Pines.

54. Samuel Garland, Jr. (1830–1862), entered
the war as captain of Company C, Eleventh Virginia Infantry, and was soon elected colonel of
the regiment. For his performance in the defense of Williamsburg, Garland was promoted
to brigadier general and assigned to command
of a brigade of D. H. Hill's division. He was
killed during the defense of South Mountain,
Md.

55. On 12 June 1862 Jeb Stuart and 1,200 of
his cavalrymen set out from Richmond on their
famed "Ride around McClellan." Dispatched by
Robert E. Lee to learn whether the right flank
of the Federal army was anchored on the Pamunkey River or vulnerable to a flanking attack, Stuart and his troopers slipped around the
right wing of the Army of the Potomac, auda-
ciously turned south and crossed the Chickahominy River on McClellan's rear, evaded
pursuit to the James River, and then turned back

toward Richmond where they reported to Lee on 15 June. They had ridden a one-hundred-mile circuit around the enemy army with the loss of but a single man. Stuart quickly became a national hero, and McClellan's natural trepidation was increased by the feat of Rebel horsemanship. Thomason, *Jeb Stuart*, 134–55; Davis, *Jeb Stuart*, 107–30; Thomas, *Bold Dragoon*, 111–29.

56. Archibald Rowland G. Campbell moved from Alabama to Galveston, Tex., before the Civil War and enlisted in Company B of the Fourth Texas Infantry on 4 April 1862. He was wounded at the second battle of Manassas and was discharged due to a lung disease on 25 Nov. 1862. After the war he became a prominent attorney in Houston and Galveston. Douglas McQueen Campbell, a private in Company D, Fifth Texas Infantry, was discharged for "inability" on 28 June 1862. He later became a physician. Simpson, *Compendium*, 105, 198; Sam B. Graham, ed., *Galveston Community Book: A Historical and Biographical Record of Galveston and Galveston County* (Galveston, Tex., 1945), 195–96.

57. Goree is mistaken here, for Lee did not order A. P. Hill's assault at Mechanicsville. Hill undertook this action on his own initiative at 3:00 P.M., 26 June, after Stonewall Jackson failed to attack McClellan's vulnerable right flank by 8:00 A.M. as Lee had instructed. The Confederate offensive, although ultimately successful, was both costly and decidedly against Lee's wishes to avoid a frontal assault on the entrenched Union forces before Jackson should turn their right flank. Nevertheless, Lee never censured Hill for his aggressive behavior, presumably because he appreciated a general who fought. Robertson, *A. P. Hill*, 66–75.

58. Roswell Sabine Ripley (1823–1887) served in the Mexican War, and his history of that war, *The War with Mexico* (1849), remains a standard. Although a native of Ohio, he was a lieutenant colonel of Confederate artillery during the bombardment of Fort Sumter. On 15 Aug. 1861 he was promoted to brigadier general and named to the command of the Department of South Carolina. He was transferred to the Army of Northern Virginia in 1862, but his performance left much to be desired, and after he was severely wounded during the battle of Sharpsburg, he was retuned to South Carolina where his future assignments carried less responsibility.

59. Here TJG is again mistaken. Expecting

Jackson to arrive at any moment, Hill delivered his attack of 26 June without instructions from Lee and, according to one source, in disregard of Lee's orders. Although correct in his belief that the Confederate forces should maintain the initiative against McClellan's outnumbered and isolated right wing, Hill failed properly to assess the strength of Fitz John Porter's entrenched corps behind Beaver Dam Creek and so watched as his division was mauled without reaching its objective. Robertson, *A. P. Hill*, 71–77.

60. As a result of the Confederate breakthrough at Gaines' Mill, McClellan thought himself outnumbered and determined to "save his army." Thus on the night of 27 June he ordered a retreat to the James River. Lee's army pursued and, despite its bloody repulse at Malvern Hill on 1 July, drove the Army of the Potomac to its transports at Harrison's Landing. Dowdey, *Seven Days*, 211–81; Sears, *To the Gates of Richmond*, 210–355.

61. The battle of Malvern Hill, fought on 1 July 1862, was the last of the Seven Days battles. After the Confederate army had driven the Army of the Potomac from the gates of Richmond and forced it back down the Peninsula in a series of running battles, Robert E. Lee was convinced that McClellan and his embattled army were sufficiently demoralized and disorganized to be destroyed by a final assault. The Federals, however, had retreated in good order and were superbly entrenched on Malvern Hill where they were supported by 250 cannon. Poor Confederate staff work caused Lee's attacks to be delivered piecemeal, and each was shot to pieces before reaching the Union lines. More than 5,300 Southerners fell on the slopes of Malvern Hill, over half to artillery fire. Although McClellan lost only 3,214 men and maintained a prodigious numerical superiority, on 2 July he continued his retreat to the James River. Dowdey, *Seven Days*, 282–346; Sears, *To the Gates of Richmond*, 309–39.

62. On 13 July 1862 Robert E. Lee dispatched Jackson and his three divisions to Gordonsville, Va., to "restrain, as far as possible, the atrocities" that Federal major general John Pope, who had taken up a position on Lee's left and rear, "threatened to perpetrate upon our defenseless citizens." Jackson reached Gordonsville on 19 July, but for two weeks no action occurred.

Then, on 9 Aug., Jackson's command clashed with Nathaniel P. Banks's corps of Pope's Army of Virginia. In a day of heavy fighting, Jackson repulsed Banks's assault and counterattacked, driving the Federals from the field. The battle of Cedar Mountain was a prelude to the second battle of Manassas. Robert K. Krick, *Stonewall Jackson at Cedar Mountain* (Chapel Hill, N.C., 1990), 7.

63. John Adams Dix (1798–1879), a native of New Hampshire, served in the War of 1812 and as a U.S. senator and as secretary of the treasury during the Buchanan administration. On 16 May 1861 Dix received Abraham Lincoln's first commission as a major general of volunteers, making him the ranking volunteer officer in the U.S. Army. He saw no field duty but held various department commands in the East. Foremost among his services was the suppression of the New York draft riots in July 1863.

64. John Cunningham Upton (1828–1862) entered Confederate service as captain of Company B, Fifth Texas Infantry, and quickly moved up the ranks, first to major on 1 June and then to lieutenant colonel on 18 July 1862. When Jerome B. Robertson was wounded at the second battle of Manassas, Upton was named regimental commander but later the same day was shot in the head, dying instantly.

The regiment that the Fifth Texas overran was the Fourth New Jersey Infantry. Its silk battle flag was sent to Texas as a trophy but was returned to New Jersey after the war. Simpson, *Hood's Texas Brigade*, 60n, 125, 151; Webb, *Handbook of Texas*, 2:824.

65. John W. Hutcheson, captain of Company G, Fourth Texas Infantry, was mortally wounded at the battle of Gaines' Mill on 27 June 1862, dying on 29 June. Simpson, *Compendium*, 137.

66. Angus D. Alston, a private in Company D, Fifth Texas Infantry, was killed in action at Gaines' Mill, 27 June 1862. Simpson, *Compendium*, 197.

67. J. Syd Spivey enlisted as a private in Company H, Fourth Texas Infantry, and was wounded at Gaines' Mill. On 15 Dec. 1862 he was appointed fourth sergeant, and on 7 march 1863 he was elected third lieutenant of his company. He was again wounded on 2 July 1863 at Gettysburg and sometime later was elected first

lieutenant. He was paroled at Appomattox. Simpson, *Compendium*, 147, 152.

68. John Marshall (1812–1862), owner and publisher of the Austin *State Gazette*, was a leading figure in the Texas Democratic party and an ardent secessionist. Marshall journeyed to Richmond where he received authorization from his old friend Jefferson Davis to raise the Fourth Texas Infantry for Confederate service. In September 1861 he was elected the regiment's lieutenant colonel. When its colonel, John Bell Hood, was promoted to brigadier general on 3 March 1862, Marshall was promoted to colonel and advanced to command. He was killed in action at Gaines' Mill. Wright and Simpson, *Texas in the War*, 101–2.

69. Bradfute Warwick (1839–1862) was born in Richmond, graduated from the Medical College of New York, and served for a time in Garibaldi's Army of Liberation and Unification. Returning to Virginia in 1861, he was appointed a captain on Henry Alexander Wise's staff but sought and received an appointment as major of the Fourth Texas Infantry on 2 Oct. 1861. He was soon promoted to lieutenant colonel. At Gaines' Mill he was shot down at the head of his regiment, carrying the regimental colors. Warwick was promoted to colonel on the same day but died of his wounds on 6 July. Simpson, *Compendium*, 90, 545; Wright and Simpson, *Texas in the War*, 102.

70. Alexis Theodore Rainey (1822–1891) was elected captain of Company H, First Texas Infantry, on 24 June 1861, promoted to major on 1 Oct. 1861, and to lieutenant colonel only three weeks later on 21 Oct. He was made regimental commander with the rank of colonel on 3 Jan. 1862 but was severely wounded at the battle of Gaines' Mill and was subsequently transferred to duty in Texas.

71. Stephen Fowler Hale (1816–1862) was born in Kentucky, served as a lieutenant in the Mexican War, and was elected to the Alabama legislature and to the Confederate States Congress. On 11 June 1861 he was elected lieutenant colonel of the Eleventh Alabama Infantry but temporarily commanded the Ninth Alabama during the spring of 1862. He was mortally wounded at Gaines' Mill, dying at Richmond on 18 July.

72. Richard Griffith (1814–1862) served as a

first lieutenant in Jefferson Davis's First Mississippi Rifles during the Mexican War. He was elected colonel of the Twelfth Mississippi Infantry and on 12 Nov. 1861 was promoted to brigadier general and assigned to command of the Mississippi brigade of the Army of Northern Virginia. Griffin was mortally wounded at the battle of Savage's Station.

73. Winfield Scott Featherston (1820–1891), a native of Tennessee, served in the Creek War and as a member of the House of Representatives from Mississippi. He was elected colonel of the Seventeenth Mississippi Infantry and posted to the Army of Northern Virginia in 1861. On 4 March 1862 he was promoted to brigadier general, and in 1863, at his own request, Featherston was transferred to the Army of Mississippi.

74. William Dorsey Pender (1834–1863) resigned from the U.S. Army to accept a commission as colonel of the Third (later the Thirteenth) North Carolina Infantry. He was promoted to brigadier general after the battle of Fair Oaks and to major general on 27 May 1863. Pender was mortally wounded at Gettysburg.

75. After the fighting of 26 June–2 July 1862, including the battles of Mechanicsville, Gaines' Mill, Glendale, and Malvern Hill, Longstreet reported to Col. Robert H. Chilton, Gen. Robert E. Lee's chief of staff, that TJG and his fellow staff officers had "displayed great gallantry, intelligence and activity. They have my warmest thanks and deserve much credit from the Government." *OR*, I, 11, pt. 2:798.

76. Samuel Escridge ("Eck") Goree was elected sergeant of Company K of Terry's Texas Rangers. After seeing action with the Army of Tennessee, Goree returned to Texas where he served for six months during 1863 and 1864 as a private in the Fourth Regiment of Texas state troops.

77. Engagements were fought at Rappahannock Station on 23 Aug. and at Thoroughfare Gap on 26 Aug. 1862, preliminary to the second battle of Manassas. The battle of Boonsborough, or as it is more often called, South Mountain, and the battle of Crampton's Gap, or Maryland Heights, were fought on 14 Sept. 1862 during the Sharpsburg campaign.

78. As an example, the First Texas Infantry suffered 82 percent casualties of its 226 men engaged at the battle of Sharpsburg, the highest percentage loss of any regiment on either side in the entire war. Although the Texas Brigade was to have been held in reserve, Hood reported that his men had "slipped the bridle and straggled to the front." When it had been shot to pieces in the infamous cornfield near the west end of Lee's line, Hood reported his division "dead on the field." Stephen W. Sears, *Landscape Turned Red: The Battle of Antietam* (New York, 1983), 197–202; Crute, *Units*, 321–22.

79. John Bell Hood was promoted to major general on 6 Nov. 1862. In his letter of recommendation, Jackson noted that Hood had "rendered distinguished service" during the Seven Days battles and that during the Sharpsburg campaign "his duties were discharged with such ability and skill as to command my admiration. I regard him as one of the most promising officers in the army." Dyer, *Gallant Hood*, 144.

80. Five of the thirty-five general grade officers of the Army of Northern Virginia were wounded at Second Manassas, Micah Jenkins, Charles W. Field, and William Mahone severely. Freeman, *Lee's Lieutenants* 2:142; *OR*, XII, 2:567 and XIX, 1:842.

81. Nathan George ("Shanks") Evans (1824–1868) of South Carolina commanded a brigade at First Manassas. He was promoted to brigadier general and continued with the Army of Northern Virginia through the Sharpsburg campaign. Transferred to Joseph E. Johnston's army during the Vicksburg campaign, Evans was court-martialed first on a charge of intoxication and later on a charge of disobedience. Although acquitted on both accounts, Beauregard removed him from command for general incompetence.

82. John W. Grace, second corporal of Company H, Fifth Texas Infantry, was reportedly discharged from service on 2 Feb. 1862 when he provided a substitute, one M. B. Grace. Simpson, *Compendium*, 227.

83. In his 20 Dec. 1862 report on the battle of Fredericksburg, Longstreet wrote that his staff officers, TJG and the others, "gave me their usual intelligent, willing aid." *OR*, I, 21:571–72.

1863. "WE FEEL SANGUINE OF OUR SUCCESS"

1. This is William H. Sellers, then adjutant of the Fifth Texas Infantry. Sellers was originally elected first lieutenant of Company A, Fifth Texas Infantry, but was appointed regimental adjutant on 6 Oct. 1861 and adjutant of Hood's brigade in February 1862. On 1 March 1864 he became Robert E. Lee's assistant adjutant general with the rank of lieutenant colonel. Wright and Simpson, *Texas in the War*, 212; Simpson, *Compendium*, 5, 168, 173; Wright, *Staff Officers*, 147.

2. Bettie Jones is the daughter of Protheus Jones of Henderson, N.C.

3. Daniel McDonald was a private in Company G (the Milam County Greys) of the Fifth Texas Infantry. He was wounded and captured at Gettysburg and, after his exchange at Fort Monroe on 18 May 1863, was again wounded at Petersburg in July 1864 and at White Oak Swamp on 16 Aug. 1864. He was paroled at Appomattox on 12 April 1865. Simpson, *Compendium*, 223.

4. Capt. John W. Riely (which TJG most often spells "Riley") was G. W. Smith's adjutant during the Peninsula campaign and Longstreet's adjutant during the Gettysburg campaign. Crute, *Confederate Staff Officers*, 124, 179.

5. Aunt Lucy is Lucy Goree Kenner, the wife of Samuel E. Kenner of Newberry, S.C., a member of the South Carolina House of Representatives. She was the mother of Howson Kenner and the grandmother of Thomas Moorman.

6. William Peleg Rogers, TJG's prewar law partner, was born in Georgia on 27 Dec. 1819. In 1840 he married Martha Halbert of Tuscaloosa, Ala., and in 1842 he was admitted to the Mississippi bar. In 1846 he raised and was elected captain of Company K of Jefferson Davis's First Mississippi Regiment and fought with distinction at the battles of Monterrey and Buena Vista. In 1849 President Zachary Taylor appointed Rogers as U.S. consul at Vera Cruz, and when he resigned the position in 1851, he moved to Texas where he soon became a prominent attorney at Washington-on-the-Brazos and, in 1857, one of three members of the law faculty at Baylor University. Rogers moved his family to Houston in 1859 and there entered politics as a pro-Union supporter of Sam Houston's campaign for governor. With Lincoln's election to the presidency the following year, however, Rogers became a secessionist and as a delegate to the state's secession convention.

Rogers then accepted a commission as lieutenant colonel of the Second Texas Infantry under Col. John C. Moore and in March 1862 was ordered with his regiment to join Albert Sidney Johnston's Army of Tennessee. He arrived just in time to distinguish himself at the battle of Shiloh. With Moore's promotion to brigadier general on the second day of the battle, Rogers was promoted to colonel and to the command of the Second Texas. At Corinth, Miss., on 4 Oct. 1862, Rogers led his Texans in a gallant but doomed assault on the Federal entrenchments. After placing his regiment's colors atop the breastwork of powerful Battery Robinett, Rogers fell, his body riddled with bullets. The Federal commander, William S. Rosecrans, reported, "He was on of the bravest men that ever led a charge," and ordered that he be buried with full military honors. Webb, *Handbook of Texas* 2:499.

7. Joseph Hooker (1814–1879) served in the Second Seminole War and the Mexican War and as adjutant at West Point. With the coming of the Civil War, Hooker was appointed a brigadier general and led a division during the Peninsula campaign. There he won the sobriquet "Fighting Joe" as well as a promotion to major general and command of I Corps of the Army of the Potomac. Advanced to the command of the army on 26 Jan. 1863, Hooker forfeited an initial tactical advantage at Chancellorsville to Lee's bold and aggressive counterattack. During the opening week of the Gettysburg campaign, Hooker was returned to the command of I Corps. After Gettysburg he was assigned to command of XI and XII corps and sent to the relief of Chattanooga. When Sherman passed him by for command of the Army of Tennessee, Hooker once again asked to be relieved. Hassler, *Commanders*, 126–58.

8. At Petersburg on 26 Feb. 1863, Longstreet took command of the Department of Virginia and North Carolina. From there he launched his fruitless Suffolk campaign. In formally informing the War Department of his action,

Longstreet listed TJG among his general staff, to be "obeyed and respected accordingly." Longstreet, *Manassas to Appomattox*, 324–25, 329; Freeman, *Lee's Lieutenants* 2:467–94; OR, I, 18:896.

9. William and George Kittrell were SWKG's cousins.

10. Fort Hindman at Arkansas Post, Ark., sitting high on a hill overlooking a bend in the Arkansas River, was one of the strongest bastions in the Confederacy. Hoping to clear this obstruction to Federal navigation of the Mississippi River, John A. McClernand, commander of the Union Army of the Mississippi, and David Dixon Porter, commander of the naval forces in the area, landed below the fort on 10 Jan. 1863 with an army of 32,000 men and a flotilla of three ironclads and six gunboats. The fort was defended by three Confederate brigades, including James Deshler's Texas brigade. After two days of shelling by the Federal ironclads, all but one of the Rebel cannon were silenced. Although Confederate infantry had been successful in repulsing Federal attacks on the fort's entrenchments, by about 4:00 P.M., 11 Jan., a fierce bombardment by the Union fleet caused white flags to begin appearing along the Confederate line. Five thousand Confederates were taken prisoner as well as large stores of weapons and commissary and quartermaster supplies. Coming as it did on the heels of several Confederate victories, the battle was significant as a boost to Northern morale. Because they had been party to the surrender, the exchanged Texas Confederates were not considered worthy to join Hood's Texas Brigade but were accepted by Patrick Cleburne's division of the Army of Tennessee where they performed heroically for the duration of the war. Norman D. Brown, ed., *One of Cleburne's Command: The Civil War Reminiscences and Diary of Capt. Samuel T. Foster, Granbury's Texas Brigade* (Austin, Tex., 1980), 3–41.

11. Ink was, indeed, a "scarce, pale and expensive" commodity. Like many other items in the blockaded Confederacy, it was often manufactured at home from inferior materials. Pokeberries and oak galls were common ingredients of ersatz Rebel ink. Pen points and staffs, too, were increasingly hard to come by as the war progressed, with Southern letter writers making use of quills made of goose and turkey feathers or pieces of cane. One enterprising Texas soldier learned to write home with a cornstalk pen.

"When it wont write on one Side I turn over on the other. Pen points are worth a dollar a peace," he commented, and "Scarce at that." Wiley, *Life of Johnny Reb*, 197, 198.

12. On 18 Feb. 1863 Robert E. Lee agreed to a plan to detach George E. Pickett's and John Bell Hood's divisions of Longstreet's corps from the Army of Northern Virginia and send them on a campaign against the Federal works at Suffolk in southeast Virginia. This was Longstreet's first experience with an independent command, and he handled it poorly, failing to take the initiative against the enemy while depriving Lee of badly needed troops along the Rappahanock front. At Lee's insistent urging Longstreet finally advanced on Suffolk on 11 April but failed to take the works and returned to the army too late to take part in the battle of Chancellorsville. Longstreet, *Manassas to Appomattox*, 324–26; Freeman, *Lee's Lieutenants* 2:467–94.

13. Robert Mackey Stribling (1833–1914) was elected captain of the Fauquier Light Artillery in July 1861. Stribling's battery accompanied Longstreet's two divisions on the Suffolk campaign where it was captured after, in Longstreet's words, it was "inadvertently posted by the officer in charge of the artillery on a neck running out into a bend of the Nansemond River." Thus exposed, it was cut off by Federal gunboats and forced to surrender. Longstreet, *Manassas to Appomattox*, 325; Wise, *Long Arm of Lee*, 720–721; Freeman, *Lee's Lieutenants* 2:485–87.

14. Samuel Gibbs French (1818–1910) was a native of New Jersey and a veteran of the Mexican War. He was appointed a brigadier general in 1861 and promoted to major general in 1862. After accompanying Longstreet on the Suffolk campaign, French was transferred to Joseph E. Johnston's army in Mississippi. Samuel Gibbs French, *Two Wars: An Autobiography of General Samuel G. French* (Nashville, 1901).

15. At noon on 7 April 1863, Rear Adm. Samuel F. du Pont led seven monitors and two ironclad battleships, the *Keokuk* and *New Ironsides*, into Charleston Harbor in an attempt to close this vital Confederate port. Rebel mines and obstructions slowed Du Pont's flotilla, and seventy-seven pieces of heavy artillery mounted in Fort Sumter and Fort Moultrie shot it to pieces, scoring 400 hits, sinking the *Keokuk* and heavily damaging all of the monitors. Although Du Pont

was relieved of command for his failure, the Confederate success came largely as a result of the skill of the Confederate commander, P. G. T. Beauregard, as a military engineer and the accuracy of his artillerymen. Williams, *Napoleon in Gray*, 175–79; Warren Ripley, ed., *Siege Train: The Journal of a Confederate Artilleryman in the Defense of Charleston* (Columbia, S.C., 1986).

16. Willis B. Darby enlisted as a private in Company H, Fifth Texas Infantry, but was promoted to second sergeant in November 1862 and to third lieutenant on 1 Jan. 1863. Despite being listed as absent without leave in Texas in February 1864, he was elected second lieutenant that July before being dropped from the rolls by order of the War Department on 27 Aug. He reenlisted as a private and was present for the surrender at Appomattox. Simpson, *Compendium*, 227, 229.

17. George Yoakum, a private in Company D, Fifth Texas Infantry, died of typhoid fever at Richmond on 6 April 1863. Simpson, *Compendium*, 203.

18. Isaac ("Ike") N. M. Turner was the youngest captain in Hood's Texas Brigade. At age twenty-two he was elected to command Company K, Fifth Texas Infantry, and during the winter of 1862–63 he served as an acting major in command of a special battalion of Texas sharpshooters. He was killed in action at Suffolk on 14 April 1963. Simpson, *Compendium*, 243, 549.

19. Joseph Gray Blount (1837–1875) of Georgia became captain and commander of James Dearing's Lynchburg Battery on 23 Jan. 1863. On 27 Oct. 1864 he was promoted to major and transferred to Robert Mackey Stribling's battalion, the Thirty-eighth Virginia Artillery Battalion.

20. James Chesnut, Jr. (1815–1885), resigned from the U.S. Senate and was elected to the Confederate House of Representatives. Commissioned a colonel in the Confederate army, Chesnut served on Beauregard's staff during the Fort Sumter crisis and at First Manassas. Thereafter he became aide-de-camp to Jefferson Davis until receiving an appointment as brigadier general on 23 April 1864 and an assignment as commander of South Carolina's reserve forces. Chesnut was the husband of the diarist Mary Boykin Miller Chesnut. C. Vann Woodward, ed., *Mary Chesnut's Civil War* (New Haven, 1981); C.

Vann Woodward and Elisabeth Muhlenfeld, eds., *The Private Mary Chesnut: The Unpublished Civil War Papers* (New York, 1984).

21. W. H. Sellers was assistant adjutant general of John Bell Hood's division during the period that I Corps served in Tennessee. Crute, *Confederate Staff Officers*, 91.

22. Following the failure of the Gettysburg campaign, Robert E. Lee dispatched Longstreet and his corps, one-third of Lee's army in Virginia, to aid the Confederate effort in Tennessee. After the battle of Murfreesboro in December 1862–January 1863, William S. Rosecrans's Federal Army of the Cumberland had moved into southeast Tennessee, occupying Chattanooga and threatening Georgia and the lower South. Longstreet's divisions, Richmond believed, could turn the tide of battle in the West and restore Tennessee to the Confederacy. Longstreet arrived in northern Georgia in time to contribute decisively to the Confederate victory at Chickamauga, 19–20 Sept. 1863. After the battle, the last great Confederate victory in the West, Braxton Bragg besieged Rosecrans's army in Chattanooga, hoping to starve it into surrender before it could be reinforced. U. S. Grant, however, with elements of other armies brought together to relieve Rosecrans, broke the Confederate siege in a fierce three-day battle, 23–25 Nov. 1863, and sent Bragg's demoralized Army of Tennessee streaming back into Georgia. There, at last, Bragg was relieved of his command and was replaced by Joseph E. Johnston. Glenn Tucker, *Chickamauga: Bloody Battle in the West* (New York, 1961); Peter Cozzens, *This Terrible Sound: The Battle of Chickamauga* (Urbana, Ill., 1992); Longstreet, *Manassas to Appomattox*, 433–550; Sanger and Hay, *James Longstreet*, 200–276; Fairfax Downey, *Storming of the Gateway: Chattanooga, 1863* (New York, 1960); James Lee McDonough, *Chattanooga: A Death Grip on the Confederacy* (Knoxville, Tenn., 1984).

23. With his arm still in a sling from his Gettysburg wound, John Bell Hood arrived at Ringgold, Ga., on 18 Sept. 1863 and rode to his division, which was already engaged at Chickamauga. Longstreet placed him in command of four divisions in addition to his own, which Hood led during two days of Confederate attacks, achieving a breakthrough in the Federal line on 20 Sept. At about 2:30 P.M. of that day, he was shot in the right thigh, shattering five

inches of bone. The leg was amputated later that afternoon at his division's field hospital. For his aggressive handling of his troops and for their decisive role in the Confederate victory at Chickamauga, Longstreet recommended that Hood be promoted to lieutenant general. Having been "blessed with a good constitution,"

Hood wrote, he was able to resume his duties in the field by January 1864. Hood, *Advance and Retreat*, 61–65; Dyer, *Gallant Hood*, 205–10; Richard O'Connor, *Hood: Cavalier General* (New York, 1949), 159–66; Richard M. McMurry, *John Bell Hood and the War for Southern Independence*, (Lexington, Ky., 1982), 76–77.

1864. "UNTIL OUR INDEPENDENCE IS SECURED"

1. Following the battle of Chickamauga and during the opening stages of the siege of Chattanooga, Longstreet and Bragg quarreled over the direction of the campaign. In order to ease the tension in the Confederate command system, President Davis approved Longstreet's plan to take his corps out of Bragg's army to operate independently against Ambrose Burnside's little army at Knoxville. Longstreet left Chattanooga on 4 Nov. 1863 and reached the vicinity of Knoxville on the fourteenth. Alerted to the Rebels' advance, Burnside fell back into the defenses of the city and prepared to withstand a siege. On 29 Nov. the Confederates launched an assault on Fort Sanders, but due to the strength of the position and the heavy snow and rain, it failed with considerable loss. Immediately after the repulse of this attack, Longstreet learned that Bragg had been driven from Chattanooga and was retreating into Georgia and required his support. On 4 Dec., therefore, Longstreet's corps began its retreat out of east Tennessee. It established winter quarters in Russellville, Ga., where it remained until March 1864 when it returned to the Army of Northern Virginia. The Knoxville campaign was poorly conceived and badly executed, not only failing to perform its primary mission but depriving Bragg's army of badly needed manpower to maintain its siege lines as well, thus contributing to the Confederate disaster at Chattanooga.

Following the Knoxville campaign, Longstreet wrote to Adj. Gen. Samuel Cooper of his "desire to express my obligations to the officers of my staff," mentioning TJG by name, "for their usual assistance and attention." Longstreet, *Manassas to Appomattox*, 480–550; Marvel, *Burnside*, 324–43; *OR* I, 31, pt. 1:465.

2. Scrap, TJG's eighteen-year-old brother, Pleasant Kittrell Goree, traveled to Virginia in the summer of 1863 to join the army. Considering him too young, TJG turned him over to Dr.

Gabriel M. Baker who was returning to Texas. In Alabama, however, Scrap left Dr. Baker's company, remaining for a time in Marion with Governor Andrew B. Moore and his wife, Mary Ann Goree Moore, Scrap's first cousin. After several weeks he walked to Tennessee where the Texas Brigade was on duty with the Army of Tennessee. There he succeeded in joining Company H, Fifth Texas Infantry, the company of his brothers Edwin and Langston. Simpson, *Compendium*, 229, 545.

3. Cleveland was granted convalescent leave to Texas in February 1864 and was discharged for disability on 16 March 1865. Simpson, *Compendium*, 227.

4. Sarah Elizabeth King Goree was the daughter of Gen. Edwin Davis King and the wife of TJG's first cousin, John Rabb Goree, of Marion, Ala.

5. Robert Pulliam of Asheville, N.C., was SWKG's cousin.

6. James T. Hunter was elected first lieutenant of Company H of the Fourth Texas Infantry when the company—locally known as the Porter Guards in honor of its first captain, Procter P. Porter—was organized in Huntsville on 7 May 1861. After Porter's death on 20 July 1862, Hunter was elected captain. He was wounded at the second battle of Manassas and fought until the end of the war, surrendering with his company at Appomattox. He is said to have led the Fourth Texas on its return to Texas after the end of the war. Wright and Simpson, *Texas in the War*, 211; Simpson, *Compendium*, 146.

7. John Gregg (1828–1864), a native of Alabama, moved to Texas in 1852 where he was elected to the secession convention and to the Provisional Confederate Congress. Leaving his congressional seat after the first battle of Manassas, he recruited and was elected colonel of

the Seventh Texas Infantry. Gregg and his regiment were captured at Fort Donelson, but following his exchange he was promoted to brigadier general and given command of a brigade of Joseph E. Johnston's army. During the Chickamauga campaign Gregg and his brigade were transferred to Hood's division. He was severely wounded at Chickamauga and upon recovery was assigned to command of Hood's Texas Brigade. Gregg was killed leading an attack on Darbytown Road, 7 Oct. 1864. Webb, *Handbook of Texas* 1:733.

8. Peter W. Gray (1819–1874) was born in Virginia but moved to Texas in 1838 where he was elected to the state senate. He was a delegate to Texas's secession convention and a member of the Confederate House of Representatives where he was a friend and confidential adviser of Jefferson Davis. At the end of his term, he became a volunteer aide to John B. Magruder and served at the battle of Galveston.

9. Anthony Martin Branch (1823–1867) was born in Virginia but in 1847 immigrated to Huntsville, Tex., where he became closely associated with Sam Houston and was elected to the state senate. Although a Unionist, he enlisted in the Confederate army and was elected captain of Company A, Twenty-first Texas Cavalry. In 1863 Branch was elected to the Confederate Congress where he was an uncompromising exponent of states' rights.

10. Ball Wiley was a relative of Sarah Elizabeth Wiley Goree, the wife of TJG's half brother, Samuel Escridge Goree.

11. Charles William Field (1828–1892) of Kentucky accepted appointment as colonel of the Sixth Virginia Cavalry. Promoted to brigadier general, Field led a brigade in A. P. Hill's "Light Division" from the Peninsula to Second Manassas where he was grievously wounded. Returning to the army in 1864, he was assigned, over Longstreet's protest, to command of Hood's old division with the rank of major general. Field rendered distinguished service in the Wilderness campaign and the defense of Richmond.

12. On 7 Feb. 1864 a Union division under Truman Seymour landed at Jacksonville, Fla., and marched inland until checked at the battle of Ocean Pond on 20 Feb. In this engagement

on the Olustee River, Joseph Finigan with some 5,200 men delivered a stinging blow to the 9,400 raiders and sent them scurrying back to the safety of Jacksonville. Informed of this invasion of his department, Beauregard hurried south from Charleston, arriving at Camp Milton, near Jacksonville, on 2 March. There he took personal command of the tiny Confederate army and endeavored to draw the enemy out of the city into an attack on his siege lines. The enemy proved disinclined to venture out of the city, and Beauregard disregarded the War Department's orders to attack him there. Thus the siege dragged on until 20 March when Beauregard returned to Charleston, leaving James Patton Anderson in command at Jacksonville. Seymour's division, having suffered nearly 2,000 casualties, was withdrawn to Charleston as well. Roman, *General Beauregard* 2:184–91.

13. Mary Ann Goree Moore, the wife of former governor Andrew B. Moore of Alabama, was confined to an asylum in South Carolina.

14. Laura G. Goree Nelson, the wife of Gideon Nelson of Greensboro, Ala., was the daughter of John Rabb and Elizabeth King Goree and a cousin of TJG.

15. Mary Foster was the daughter of Protheus Jones.

16. In the spring of 1864 Ambrose Burnside was recalled to Virginia from east Tennessee and, once again in command of IX Corps of the Army of the Potomac, took part in Grant's overland campaign. For a time Burnside's corps was at least nominally an independent command due to his seniority over George G. Meade, the army's ostensible commander, but at no time did he conduct an independent operation against Richmond or Lee's army. Marvel, *Burnside*, 347; Edward Steere, *The Wilderness Campaign* (Harrisburg, Pa., 1960), 289; William A. Frassanito, *Grant and Lee: The Virginia Campaigns, 1864–1865* (New York, 1983), 36–37; Gordon C. Rhea, *The Battle of the Wilderness, May 5–6, 1864* (Baton Rouge, La., 1994).

17. Following the fall of Vicksburg, Shreveport, La., the headquarters of the Confederate Trans-Mississippi Department and the gateway to Texas, became an attractive target for Federal operations. Nathaniel P. Banks organized a task

force of 25,000 soldiers, twelve ironclad gun-boats, and four wooden steam transports to move up the Red River and rendezvous at Shreveport with a second column of 15,000 troops under Frederick Steele marching from Little Rock, Ark. Together they were to capture the city and move on into northeast Texas. Banks occupied Alexandria, La., on 19 March and pressed on toward Shreveport, but on the afternoon of 8 April, forty miles southeast of his objective, he was surprised by Richard Taylor and his 9,000 Confederates. Taylor sent his men surging forward, smashing two Union divisions in turn and capturing twenty cannon, scores of wagons, and hundreds of prisoners. By nightfall Banks had lost 2,235 men and was in full retreat downriver. The following day Banks made a stand at Pleasant Hill. Although outnumbered, Taylor felt confident that his men could drive Banks from the field. The Confederates attempted a double envelopment to cut the Federal route of retreat and complete the destruction that they had begun at Mansfield. Thomas J. Churchill's brigade achieved total surprise of the Federal left and drove it in with confusion. As Churchill's men were regrouping for an assault on the Federal rear, however, Banks's reserves struck them from behind and drove them back, demoralizing the rest of Taylor's army.

Although department commander Edmund Kirby Smith stripped most of Taylor's infantry to march to Arkansas to face Steele's invasion, Banks continued his retreat down the Red River. By 27 May Banks and his badly used command were back on the Mississippi River, having accomplished none of their objectives and having delayed Grant's intended campaign against Mobile by several vital weeks. Ludwell H. Johnson, *Red River Campaign: Politics and Cotton in the Civil War* (Baltimore, 1958); Parrish, *Richard Taylor,* 317–404.

18. Robert Michael Powell (1826–1916) immigrated to Texas from Alabama in 1849 and was elected to the legislature. He was elected captain of Company D of the Fifth Texas Infantry on 2 Aug. 1861, promoted to major on 22 Aug. 1862, and to lieutenant colonel on 30 Aug. 1862. Powell later became the commander of the Fifth Texas and the brigade's senior colonel. He was wounded and taken prisoner at Gettysburg and was not released until 2 Feb. 1865. At the end of the war, Powell was commander of the remnant of Hood's Texas Brigade. Wright and Simpson, *Texas in the War,* 103.

19. After Jeb Stuart's death on 11 May 1864 at the battle of Yellow Tavern, Longstreet wrote that his fall was a greater disaster to the Confederacy "even than that of the swift-moving General 'Stonewall' Jackson." Stuart, thought Longstreet, had held the Confederate cavalry together, "peerless in power and discipline," in a way that no other could have done. "After his fall their decline came swifter than their upbuilding had been accomplished by his magic hand." Although Stuart's death is often viewed as the beginning of the end of Confederate cavalry superiority in Virginia, his old corps continued to strike heavy blows at the burgeoning Federal horse. On 7 June 1864 Philip H. Sheridan left Grant's army at Cold Harbor with some 8,000 cavalry and four batteries of artillery with orders to join David Hunter in the Shenandoah Valley. On 11 June they were intercepted by Wade Hampton and some 5,000 Confederate cavalry near Trevilian Station on the Virginia Central railroad. As mounted infantry the two sides fought blindly through heavy underbrush, with each winning temporary local advantage. For a time Hampton's men surrounded George Armstrong Custer's Michigan brigade, which fought its way to safety only after sustaining heavy losses. On the following day the Confederates dug in behind the railroad embankment and repulsed charge after charge of Sheridan's dismounted troops. On the thirteenth the Federals withdrew to the James River, abandoning their goal of uniting with Hunter. On 22 June, Hampton's troopers turned back James Harrison Wilson's raiders at Reams Station, terminating a Federal attempt to extend Grant's siege line farther south and west of Petersburg. The Rebel cavalry harried the Federals back to Light House Point, inflicting heavy losses, forcing Wilson's command to abandon its artillery, wagons, and wounded, and several times threatening it with annihilation. During June, Hampton's division fought Grant's cavalry corps almost continually, marching more than 400 miles and capturing some 2,000 prisoners. On 2 July Robert E. Lee repaid Hampton's success with his recommendation that Hampton be promoted to chief of cavalry of the Army of Northern Virginia. The appointment was officially confirmed

on 11 Aug. 1864. Sanger and Hay, *Longstreet*, 279; Wellman, *Giant in Gray*, 144–52. For a discussion of the state of Confederate cavalry in spring 1864, see Robert K. Krick, "'The Cause of All My Disasters': Jubal A. Early and the Undisciplined Valley Cavalry," in Gallagher, *Struggle for the Shenandoah*, 77–106.

20. Richard Heron Anderson (1821–1879) was the first colonel of the First South Carolina Infantry. After participating in the bombardment of Fort Sumter, he was promoted to brigadier general, and his service under Longstreet on the Peninsula won him promotion to major general. When Longstreet was wounded at the Wilderness, Anderson was given temporary command of I Corps and a promotion to lieutenant general. With Longstreet's return Anderson was given command of a segment of the Richmond defenses, but on the retreat to Appomattox, his command was shattered at Sayler's Creek.

21. On the same field where Lee and Jackson had defeated Joe Hooker at the battle of Chancellorsville, the Army of Northern Virginia again met the Army of the Potomac on 6 May 1864. Almost one year to the day since Jackson received his fatal wound, Longstreet sustained a wound to his throat and right shoulder under almost identical circumstances. Longstreet learned that Grant's left extended but a short distance beyond the Plank Road and sent his adjutant general, Gilbert Moxley Sorrell, to lead three brigades around the unprotected flank and attack his left and rear. "They did this with perfect success," recalled Francis W. Dawson, "and the enemy fell back with heavy loss to a position about three-quarters of a mile from our front. It was the moment to make a bold stroke for victory." All of I Corps plus Anderson's division were in position to crush the crippled Union left, and Longstreet and his staff were at the head of the column ready to lead the attack. "Just then, General Jenkins, who commanded a South Carolina brigade in our corps, rode up, his face flushed with joy, and shaking hands with Longstreet, congratulated him on the result of the fight. Turning then to his brigade, which was formed in the road, Jenkins said: 'Why do you not cheer, men?' The men cheered lustily, and hardly had the sound died away when a withering fire was poured in upon us from the woods on our right. Jenkins, rising in his stirrups, shouted out, 'Steady men! For God's sake, steady!' and fell mortally wounded

from his saddle. Longstreet, who had stood there like a lion at bay, reeled as the blood poured down over his breast, and was evidently badly hurt. Two of General Jenkins's staff were killed by the same volley." Like Jackson, Longstreet and Jenkins were the victims of "friendly fire." Dawson, *Reminiscences*, 115.

22. Harry Thompson Hays (1820–1876) as colonel of the Seventh Louisiana Infantry earned promotion to brigadier general at First Manassas and in Jackson's Valley campaign. Given command of the Louisiana Brigade, Hays fought in every battle of the Army of Northern Virginia from Sharpsburg to Spotsylvania. In 1864 Hays was transferred to the trans-Mississippi where he remained until the end of the war. Edmund Kirby Smith assigned Hays to duty as a major general, but the appointment was never confirmed by Jefferson Davis.

23. Jubal Anderson Early (1816–1894) was appointed colonel of the Twenty-fourth Virginia Infantry and assigned to command of a brigade of Beauregard's army at Manassas Junction. He was promoted to brigadier general on 21 July 1861, to major general to rank from 17 Jan. 1863, and to lieutenant general on 31 May 1864. Temporarily assigned to the command of the II Corps, Early was detached to the Shenandoah Valley in 1864 to relieve pressure on the Army of Northern Virginia by threatening Washington. After initial success Early was bested in a series of running battles with Philip H. Sheridan that resulted in the destruction of his command. As the first president of the Southern Historical Society, he sparred with Longstreet over the blame for the Confederate defeat. Jubal A. Early, *War Memoirs: Autobiographical Sketch and Narrative of the War Between the States* (Philadelphia, 1912; rept., with introduction by Frank Vandiver, Bloomington, Ind., 1960); Millard K. Bushong, *Old Jube: A Biography of General Jubal A. Early* (Boyce, Va., 1955); Charles C. Osborne, *Jubal: The Life and Times of General Jubal A. Early, C.S.A.* (Chapel Hill, N.C., 1992).

24. David Hunter (1802–1866) was appointed a brigadier general and given command of a division of Irvin McDowell's army. Promoted to major general after First Manassas, Hunter relieved John Charles Frémont as commander of the Western Department and, in 1862, was given command of the Department of the South. As commander of the Department of West Virginia

in 1864, Hunter was brushed aside by Jubal A. Early, exposing Washington to the threat of capture. Hunter resigned from the army on 8 Aug. 1864.

25. After partially recovering from the wound sustained at the battle of the Wilderness, Longstreet recuperated at Lotus Grove, the plantation of his "cherished friend," Col. Jonathan D. Alexander, near Campbell Court House, some twelve miles east of Lynchburg, Va. There, on 13 June 1864, Longstreet and TJG barely missed capture by a Federal raiding party. Longstreet, *Manassas to Appomattox*, 572.

26. On 6 May 1864 Edwin King Goree was wounded in the right leg at the battle of the Wilderness and left for dead. Discovered by a burial party the following day, Goree was placed on a horse for transportation to a field hospital, but when he fainted and fell to the ground, he was once again thought dead and abandoned. Hours later he was again recovered and brought in for treatment, resulting in the amputation of his leg. Paroled at Lynchburg, Va., on 15 April 1865, Goree carved a crutch from the forked limb of a peach tree and walked back to Texas, arriving in May 1866 after a journey of thirteen months. Thereafter he was affectionately referred to as "Pegleg" or "Uncle Ed." He served as president of the Hood's Brigade Association as well as secretary and treasurer for life. Ironically, after all of his sufferings and almost miraculous recovery, he died of pellagra. Simpson, *Compendium*, 229, 526, 557; Yeary, *Boys in Gray*, 274; Chilton, *Unveiling and Dedication of Monument to Hood's Texas Brigade*.

27. Goree's first cousin John Bennett Ashford was shot and killed on the railroad station platform at Courtney near Navasota, Tex., by an eighteen-year-old station agent after an exchange of words over a misplaced passport.

28. The stricken Longstreet was first attended on the field by his personal physician, Dr. J. S. D. Cullen, and then removed to nearby Meadow Farm, the home of his friend Erasmus Taylor. From there he was transferred to Taliaferro Hospital in Lynchburg. After regaining enough strength to leave the hospital, he moved to the Lynchburg home of Samuel and Caroline Garland, relatives of Longstreet's wife and the parents of Brig. Gen. Samuel Garland, and later to the home of Jonathan D. Alexander. On 13

June a Federal raiding party swept through the area, so Longstreet moved to Georgia until October 1864. Wert, *Longstreet*, 390–91.

29. Goree's word were prophetic. Under pressure from President Jefferson Davis, John Bell Hood led his 53,000 men out of the defenses of Atlanta and into a series of attacks against William T. Sherman's 98,000-man army group. The battles of Peachtree Creek (20 July), Atlanta (22 July), Ezra Church (28 Aug.), and Jonesborough (31 Aug.–1 Sept.) only served to hasten the fall of Atlanta on 2 Sept. 1864 and to weaken Hood's army fatally. His subsequent ill-advised offensive into Tennessee resulted in the virtual destruction of the once-powerful Army of Tennessee at the disastrous battles of Franklin and Nashville. Hood, *Advance and Retreat*; Sherman, *Memoirs*; Stanley F. Horn, *The Decisive Battle of Nashville* (Baton Rouge, La., 1956); Albert Castel, *Decision in the West: The Atlanta Campaign of 1864* (Lawrence, Kans., 1992).

30. Dr. John J. Terrell (1829–1923) of Lynchburg, Va., trained as a physician at the University of Pennsylvania and at Jefferson Medical College. A Quaker and a pacifist, he was assigned by the Confederate medical service to Hospital No. 1, Division No. 3, in Lynchburg on 2 Aug. 1862 and served there as a surgeon until the end of the war. He was a brother of Brig. Gen. Alexander Watkins Terrell of Austin. Peter W. Houck, *A Prototype of a Confederate Hospital Center in Lynchburg, Virginia* (Lynchburg, Va., 1986), 52–58; Don P. Halsey, *Historic and Heroic Lynchburg* (Lynchburg, Va., 1935), 120; Rosa Faulkner Yancey, *Lynchburg and Its Neighbors* (Richmond, 1935), 187–90.

31. William Otway Owen was surgeon-incharge of the Lynchburg Medical Department. Minor may be Surgeon Henry Augustine Minor of the Ninth Alabama Infantry. Houck, *Confederate Hospital*, 58–61; "Paroles," SHSP 15(1887): 313.

32. This letter was addressed to Greensboro, Ala.

33. On 14 Aug. 1864 the Federals launched a strong demonstration against Charles Field's lines near the eastern end of the Confederate defenses of Richmond. In three day's fighting Field prevented a breach that would have imperiled the Rebel capital. Freeman, *Lee's Lieutenants* 3:588; Trudeau, *Last Citadel*, 150–53.

34. Field's adjutant, Maj. Willis F. Jones, was reportedly killed in battle in October 1864. No other member of the staff is listed as a casualty. Crute, *Confederate Staff Officers*, 60; Wright, *Staff Officers*, 89.

35. Richard James Harding (1842–1917) was born in Lynchburg, Va., and attended Virginia Military Institute. In 1852 he immigrated with his family to Texas and was elected first sergeant of Company B, First Texas Infantry, of Hood's Texas Brigade when the unit was organized on 28 April 1861. He was commissioned a lieutenant on 10 Oct. 1861 and promoted to captain on 16 May 1862. Despite being found guilty of "Deserting his command upon the march" on 13 Aug. 1863, Harding was promoted to major on 5 Jan. 1864 and to lieutenant colonel on 15 July 1864. He received a shoulder wound at the battle of Cold Harbor, 9 Nov. 1864, which caused him to leave the service. He later served as president of the Hood's Texas Brigade Association. Wright and Simpson, *Texas in the War*, 18, 207.

36. During the week beginning on 13 Aug. 1864, the Union army, hoping to divert Confederate attention from the defense of Petersburg, carried on a series of demonstrations east of Richmond at Fussell's Mill, White's Tavern, and elsewhere along the north bank of the James River. Fighting was especially heavy on 16 Aug. when Maj. Gen. Winfield Scott Hancock unsuccessfully attacked the Rebel fortifications at Fussell's Mill. Repulsed, the Federals withdrew to Petersburg and Bermuda Hundred. David M. Jordan, *Winfield Scott Hancock: A Soldier's Life* (Bloomington, Ind., 1988), 155–57; Trudeau, *Last Citadel*, 150–57.

37. Mobile, Ala., was one of the last and most important of Confederate ports. The city was defended by several forts and batteries, including the powerful Fort Morgan and Spanish Fort, which mounted a total of 400 pieces of artillery. The bay was strewn with mines and other obstacles to navigation. On 5 Aug. 1864 Rear Adm. David G. Farragut and his fleet of fourteen wooden ships and four monitors sailed into the bay. After losing the monitor *Tecumseh* to a mine, Farragut ran his fleet past Fort Morgan and faced the Rebel ram *Tennessee* under Adm. Franklin Buchanan. After a terrific battle at seventeen-to-one odds, Buchanan was forced to surrender. Now that the bay was in Union hands, Fort Morgan was compelled to surrender

as well. Nevertheless, Mobile held out until 12 April 1865 when E. R. S. Canby captured the beleaguered city. Arthur J. Bergeron, Jr., *Confederate Mobile* (Jackson, Miss., 1991), 138–92.

38. D. C. Farmer was elected third lieutenant of Company A, Fifth Texas Infantry, with the unit's organization. He was promoted to captain on 1 Nov. 1861 and was wounded at Gettysburg on 2 July 1863. Farmer was appointed acting major on 31 Oct. 1863 and acting lieutenant colonel on 31 Dec. 1863 before receiving a wound to the hip at the battle of the Wilderness on 6 May 1864. He then was assigned to recruiting duty in Texas for the duration of the war. Simpson, *Compendium*, 173.

39. Howards Grove Hospital, one of the twenty Confederate medical facilities in Richmond, was designated to receive the sick and wounded from Texas. During the winter of 1862–63 when a smallpox epidemic ravaged Richmond, the city secured three wards of the army hospital for black patients. Howards Grove was temporarily closed during the fall of 1864 for renovation and repair. Emory M. Thomas, *The Confederate State of Richmond: A Biography of the Capital* (Austin, Tex., 1971), 114; Cunningham, *Doctors*, 53, 64–65.

40. John I. Shotwell was elected third lieutenant of Company B, First Texas Infantry, on 29 April 1861, promoted to second lieutenant on 16 May 1961, to first lieutenant on 16 May 1862, and to captain on 5 Jan. 1864. In September 1864 he was acting aide-de-camp to John Gregg. Simpson, *Compendium*, 5, 20.

41. Jonathan Favel Slaughter (1808–1893) of Lynchburg, Va., took in Edwin Goree after his wounding at the Wilderness. Slaughter had married Mary Harker of Mount Holly, N.J., and was a kinsman of Brig. Gen. James Edwin Slaughter who commanded the Confederate forces in the last battle of the war, the action at Palmito Ranch, Tex., on 12 May 1865. Yancey, *Lynchburg*, 409.

42. Alexander Watkins Terrell (1827–1912) was born in Patrick County, Va., but moved to Austin, Tex., in 1852 where he established a law practice and entered politics, serving as judge from 1857 to 1862. In 1862 he was elected major of the First Texas Cavalry, Arizona Brigade. He was later elected lieutenant colonel of Terrell's Texas Cavalry Battalion and was promoted to

colonel in time to lead the unit in the Red River campaign. On 16 May 1865 he was assigned to duty as a brigadier general, but he was never appointed by Jefferson Davis. Webb, *Handbook of Texas* 2:725; Wright and Simpson, *Texas in the War*, 93.

43. Longstreet reported for duty in mid-October 1864. Although still "crippled," he requested of General Lee that he be reassigned to the Army of Northern Virginia or, if that was not possible, to any point where he could be of service. Sanger and Hay, *Longstreet*, 278, 280; Wert, *Longstreet*, 392–93.

44. On 7 Nov. 1864, in a last-ditch effort to forestall the collapse of his government, President Jefferson Davis called for the enlistment of black troops and the compensated emancipation of those who fought for the Confederate cause. Resistance to Davis's initiative was swift and intense, but with the South's military situation deteriorating daily, the Confederate Congress passed a black enlistment law on 13 March 1865. Recruitment began in Richmond and Lynchburg on 15 March, and some few companies of black volunteers were formed and began training. Within a month, however, Lee surrendered, rendering the question of blacks in gray forever moot. Edward Spencer, "Confederate Negro Enlistments," *Annals of the War*, 536–53.

45. On 19 Oct. 1864, in a desperate attempt to reverse the inexorable Federal advance up the Shenandoah Valley, Jubal A. Early launched his Army of the Valley in a predawn attack against the sleeping camps of Philip H. Sheridan at Cedar Creek. By 10:00 A.M. the Federals had been driven back three miles, and two of Sheridan's three corps had disintegrated before the fierce Rebel onslaught. The exhausted and famished Confederates failed to take full advantage of their success, however, pausing in the camps of the enemy to forage for food and luxury items. During this lull Sheridan, who had been away from his army attending a conference, returned, rallying scattered troops. At 4:00 P.M. Sheridan delivered his counterstrike, driving Early from the field and regaining all of the morning's losses. Although Sheridan's casualties amounted to 5,665 compared to Early's 2,900, the battle of Cedar Creek virtually destroyed the Army of the Valley and marked the end of Confederate control of the strategically vital Shenandoah. Wert, *From Winchester to Cedar Creek*; Gallagher,

Struggle for the Shenandoah; Thomas A. Lewis, *The Guns of Cedar Creek* (New York, 1988).

46. Nathaniel Prentiss Banks (1816–1894) served ten terms in the U.S. Congress and was chosen Speaker of the House of Representatives in 1856. In 1858 he was elected governor of Massachusetts, serving until his appointment as major general of volunteers in 1861. Although important to the Union war effort in terms of recruiting and fund-raising, Banks was continually humiliated on the battlefield: during Jackson's Shenandoah Valley campaign, in the siege of Port Hudson, La., and at the hands of Richard Taylor's Confederates during the Red River campaign.

47. Stephen Dodson Ramseur (1837–1864), after commanding a battery of artillery during the Peninsula campaign, was promoted to colonel in April 1862 as commander of the Forty-ninth North Carolina Infantry. Promoted to brigadier general in 1862, Ramseur took part in all of the major battles of Lee's army until 1 June 1864 when he was promoted to major general and detached to the Shenandoah Valley with Jubal Early. He was mortally wounded at the battle of Cedar Creek. Gary W. Gallagher, *Stephen Dodson Ramseur: Lee's Gallant General* (Chapel Hill, N.C., 1985).

48. Robert Daniel Goree married Melissa Hayes in August 1864. She died in childbirth in 1865, shortly after the end of the war.

49. In the autumn of 1864 a scandal broke regarding New York customs officials' complicity with Northern shipping firms trading with the Confederacy. In particular, Daniel Cady Stanton, the son of noted abolitionist Henry Brewster Stanton and feminist Elizabeth Cady Stanton, was accused of accepting bribes to allow U.S. merchant ships to sail directly to Southern ports. John Adams Dix dismissed Stanton from his position. Elisabeth Griffith, *In Her Own Right: The Life of Elizabeth Cady Stanton* (New York, 1984), 113–15.

50. Even before the Civil War, John Pope and Joseph Hooker had both earned reputations for their overendowed egos and had gained the enmity of many of their brother officers. As Union army commanders they earned the everlasting derision of the Army of Northern Virginia with ill-advised manifestos upon taking command of the Army of Virginia and Army of

the Potomac, respectively. Pope, fresh from some minor victories in Missouri, declared to his men that "I have come to you from the West, where we have always seen the backs of our enemies; from an army whose business it has been to seek the adversary and to beat him when he was found; whose policy has been attack, and not defense," an assertion that did not endear him to his new command. He further declaimed that from now on his "headquarters will be in saddle." To the latter pronouncement one Rebel wit replied that his headquarters were where his hindquarters should be. His thorough trouncing at the hands of Lee and Jackson at Second Manassas sent him packing back to the West, where he spent the remainder of the war on the Indian frontier.

Like Pope, Joseph Hooker had an unfortunate penchant for thumping his own chest. After taking command of the Army of the Potomac, he boasted that he had the "finest army on the planet; that he could march it to New Orleans; that he could cross the Rapidan without losing a man, and then 'take the rebs where the hair was short.'" On the eve of the battle of Chancellorsville, he announced to his officers that "if the enemy does not run, God help them" and further declared that "my plans are prefect, and when I start to carry them out may God have mercy on General Lee, for I will have none." Although such bombast might be excused as typical pregame locker-room rhetoric, Hooker's well-deserved reputation for insubordination and overweening ambition and his subsequent humiliating defeat hung those unfortunate words around his neck forever. Hassler, *Commanders*, 57, 59–60, 62, 130–34; John J. Hennessy, *Return to Bull Run: The Campaign and Battle of Second Manassas* (New York, 1993), 5–20; Ernest B. Furgurson, *Chancellorsville, 1863: The Souls of the Brave* (New York, 1992), 18–35.

51. With the fall of Atlanta on 1 Sept. 1864, Hood moved his army across northwest Georgia and into northeast Alabama, drawing Sherman after him. At last, unwilling to pursue Hood farther, Sherman returned to Atlanta, leaving George H. Thomas to watch Hood's army. After nearly a month of preparation, Hood drove north, hoping to defeat Thomas, reoccupy Tennessee, and draw Sherman back out of Georgia. The hope was a forlorn one, for Hood, although invincibly brave, was an unimaginative and unrealistic tactician. As he had

done before Atlanta, he hurled his depleted army against Federal entrenchments, first at Franklin, Tenn., on 30 Nov. when he lost 7,250 irreplaceable veteran soldiers and six generals killed, five wounded, and one captured and then at Nashville on 15–16 Dec., which virtually completed the destruction of the once mighty Army of Tennessee. James Lee McDonough and Thomas L. Connelly, *Five Tragic Hours: The Battle of Franklin* (Knoxville, Tenn., 1983); Stanley F. Horn, *The Decisive Battle of Nashville* (Baton Rouge, La., 1956); Hood, *Advance and Retreat*, 243–307.

52. Braxton Bragg (1817–1876) accepted appointment as a brigadier general in the Confederate army and was promoted to major general in September 1861, to assume command of II Corps of the Army of Tennessee. After Albert Sidney Johnston's death at the battle of Shiloh, Bragg was promoted to full general and assumed command of the principal Southern army in the West. His invasion of Kentucky in the fall of 1862 ended with the tactically indecisive battle of Perryville, and a drawn battle at Murfreesboro in January 1863 compelled him to evacuate all of Tennessee. He partially redeemed the loss with his victory at Chickamauga the following autumn, but in November, Grant raised Bragg's siege of Chattanooga and forced him back into Georgia. Blamed for the loss of Tennessee, Bragg requested that he be relieved of command, and Jefferson Davis, his old friend from Mexican War days, replaced him with Joseph E. Johnston. Davis thereupon called him to Richmond where he was given charge of the "conduct of the military operations in the armies of the Confederacy," an exalted job description with no real power. Grady McWhiney, *Braxton Bragg and Confederate Defeat*, vol. 1, *Field Command* (New York, 1969); Judith Lee Hallock, *Braxton Bragg and Confederate Defeat*, vol. 2 (Tuscaloosa, Ala., 1991).

53. In the fall of 1864, Sterling Price led 12,000 troops, only one-third of whom were armed, on a raid into Missouri, hoping to capture St. Louis and cross the Mississippi River into Illinois. The St. Louis garrison, however, caused Price to abandon his plan and turn west in an attempt to "liberate" the pro-Confederate counties in the central portion of Missouri. At Westport on 23 Oct., Price suffered a stinging repulse, forcing him to withdraw from the state. Albert Castel, *General Sterling Price and the Civil*

War in the West (Baton Rouge, La., 1968), 196–255; Robert E. Shalhope, *Sterling Price: Portrait of a Southerner* (Columbia, Mo., 1971), 263–80.

54. After Richard Taylor's repulse of Nathaniel P. Banks's invasion of Louisiana, Edmund Kirby Smith detached two divisions from Taylor's army and led them into Arkansas in hopes of destroying Frederick Steele's column, then marching on Shreveport. Steele reversed his line of march and attempted to regain the fortifications of Little Rock before Kirby Smith could overtake and overwhelm him. The Confederates pursued Steele to Jenkins' Ferry on the Saline River where, on 30 April 1864, Kirby Smith launched a series of uncoordinated assaults on Steele's entrenchments, taking a thousand casualties including two brigade commanders killed. Steele then marched into Little Rock without further molestation. Although Kirby Smith claimed victory, Arkansas remained firmly under Federal control. Robert L. Kerby, *Kirby Smith's Confederacy* (New York, 1972), 314–15; Johnson, *Red River Campaign*, 203–5; Edwin C. Bearss, *Steele's Retreat from Camden and the Battle of Jenkins' Ferry* (Little Rock, Ark., 1966).

55. In a critique of his plans for a campaign into Arkansas and Missouri, Jefferson Davis wrote to Edmund Kirby Smith, "If our forces on the west side of the river should allow the enemy to leave that section and . . . defeat those on the east side, your projected campaign could not fail to end in disaster." Despite this warning troops from Banks's XIX Corps were transferred to Virginia where they helped to repulse Jubal A. Early's drive on Washington in the summer of 1864, and the veteran division of A. J. Smith was attached to William T. Sherman's army group operating in Georgia and the Carolinas. *OR*, XLI, 1:102; Taylor, *Destruction and Reconstruction*, 229–31.

56. Soldiers serving east of the Mississippi River were typically contemptuous of those serving to the west. John C. Haskell, an artillery officer in Lee's army, for example, wrote after the Spanish-American War that "there was so much less fighting in the Trans-Mississippi area, that, like the one-eyed man in the country of the blind, anyone who was there was a great leader, and heroes were almost as cheaply made as in the Cuban War." Heavy fighting, however, did take place in Arkansas, Louisiana, and Missouri. Although not on the same scale as the battles in Virginia, Tennessee, and Georgia, the battles of Wilsons Creek, Pea Ridge, and Mansfield were in their own way decisive, and such small-scale fights as the Confederate recapture of Galveston in January 1863 and the repulse of an amphibious Federal invasion force at Sabine Pass, Tex., in September 1863 were of strategic significance, holding a vital grain- and livestock-producing area for the Confederacy and keeping open international trade across its only foreign border. John C. Haskell, *The Haskell Memoirs*, ed. G. E. Govan and J. W. Kivingood (New York, 1960), 19.

57. Maj. Robert Gould's Sixth Texas Cavalry Battalion (dismounted) was assigned to Horace Randal's Second Brigade of Walker's Texas Division. Gould, a native of North Carolina, immigrated to Texas in 1850 and by 1860, at age thirty-four, had become a prosperous Leon County attorney. A member of the state's secession convention, he voted for secession. *OR*, I, 22, pt. 1:903–4; Blessington, *Walker's Texas Division*, 45–59; W. D. Wood, *A Partial Roster of the Officers and Men Raised in Leon County, Texas, for the Service of the Confederate States in the War Between the States, with Short Biographical Sketches of Some of the Officers, and a Brief History of Maj. Gould's Battalion* (rept. Waco, Tex., 1963).

58. On 30 April 1864 Horace Randal was mortally wounded at the battle of Jenkins' Ferry, Ark. On 12 May 1864 Maj. Robert P. McClay of Walker's staff was promoted to brigadier general and assigned to the command of Randal's old brigade. His promotion, however, was never validated by the president or the Confederate Congress. Blessington, *Walker's Texas Division*, 261.

1865–96. "THE PRESERVATION OF THE HISTORY OF WHICH WE ARE ALL SO PROUD"

1. TJG's horse, Dick Turpin or Forrest, was placed in the care of William ("Bill") E. Duncan, a private in Company E, Fourth Texas Infantry, who had served as a courier for John Bell Hood and Charles Field. After receiving his parole at Appomattox, Duncan remained in Rappahannock County, Va. In a 16 Dec. 1865 letter to TJG, he wrote, "I think we will all have to secede again, or have you your fill of seceding?" Of Forrest, Duncan commented: "He is a perfect little mustang of a horse. . . . It is true he looks like a runt, but he shows some fine blood." Simpson, *Compendium*, 126; William E. Duncan to TJG, 16 Dec. 1865.

2. Maurice was Longstreet's black servant.

3. Edward Hopkins Cushing (1829–1879) was born in Royalton, Vt., but after graduating from Dartmouth in 1850, he emigrated to Texas where he became the owner of the Houston *Telegraph*. Despite his Yankee birth Cushing was an ardent Rebel, and so strong were his sentiments that Texas's Reconstruction governor, Edmund J. Davis, advised President Andrew Johnson against pardoning him and even suggested that he be hanged. E. B. Cushing, "Edward Hopkins Cushing: An Appreciation by His Son," *SWHQ* 25 (1922): 261–73.

4. Robert Burns enlisted as a private in Company A—the so-called Bayou City Guards—of the Fifth Texas Infantry but was detached as a clerk in the regimental adjutant's office on 4 Nov. 1861. On 7 May 1862 he was promoted to captain and appointed regimental commissary officer, and in August 1863 he was promoted to major and appointed brigade commissary officer. He returned to Texas on 15 Feb. 1865. Simpson, *Compendium*, 6, 169, 175.

5. William F. Ford enlisted as a private in Company B, Fourth Texas Infantry, but was promoted to second sergeant in 1863 and to third lieutenant in 1 April 1864. He was wounded on 6 May 1864 at the battle of the Wilderness and promoted to second lieutenant on 16 June. Ford was paroled at Appomattox. Simpson, *Compendium*, 104, 106.

6. Robert Frederick Hoke (1837–1912) entered the Confederate army as a second lieutenant of D. H. Hill's First North Carolina Infantry but quickly rose to colonel of the Twenty-first North Carolina. He was promoted to brigadier general in January 1863 and after Chancellorsville was transferred to North Carolina. Promoted to major general and recalled to Virginia, he assisted Beauregard in repulsing Benjamin F. Butler's thrust at Drewry's Bluff and took part in the battle of Cold Harbor. Hoke returned with his division to North Carolina in December 1864 and served under Joseph E. Johnston until the end of the war.

7. Joseph Walker (1835–1902) was elected captain of Company K, Fifth South Carolina Infantry—Micah Jenkins's regiment—on 13 April 1861. On 15 April 1862 he was promoted to lieutenant colonel and to colonel on 22 July 1862. Walker left the army in 1864 to become a member of the South Carolina legislature. After the war he became a bank president and six-term mayor of his native Spartanburg.

8. Augustus John Sitton served as quartermaster sergeant of the Palmetto Sharpshooters, Micah Jenkins's old regiment. "Paroles," *SHSP* 15 (1887): 127.

9. John Caldwell Calhoun (1782–1850), the most outspoken champion of Southern rights, was a member of the U.S. House of Representatives, secretary of war under James Monroe, vice president during the John Quincy Adams administration, and U.S. senator. After an unsuccessful run for the presidency in 1844, Calhoun was appointed secretary of state in the John Tyler administration. Charles Matrices Wiltse, *John C. Calhoun, Sectionalist, 1840–1850* (Indianapolis, 1951); Gerald Mortimer Capers, *John C. Calhoun, Opportunist: A Reappraisal* (Gainesville, Fla., 1960).

10. Miss Nelson was the daughter of TJG's cousin Laura Goree Nelson.

11. The Tallulah Falls was a well-known tourist attraction on the Tallula River, a tributary of the Savannah River, some fifty-five miles north of Athens. Between 1908 and 1920 the Georgia Power Company completed a series of dams along the Tallulah, impounding and diverting the river's flow so that today only a small stream trickles over the 1,000-foot precipice and

through the deep gorge below. *Georgia: A Guide to Its Towns and Countryside* (Athens, Ga., 1940), 402.

12. Robert Augustus Toombs (1810–1885) served in the Georgia state legislature, the U.S. House of Representatives, and the U.S. Senate before the war. In 1861 he was elected to the Provisional Confederate Congress and was nominated as president of the Confederate States. Losing to Jefferson Davis, he accepted an appointment as secretary of state but resigned to become a brigadier general. A wound suffered at Sharpsburg incapacitated him from further field service, and he resigned from the army and returned to his seat in Congress. There he became an outspoken opponent of the Davis administration. William Y. Thompson, *Robert Toombs of Georgia* (Baton Rouge, La., 1966).

13. The battle of New Hope, Ga., 25–27 May 1864, was the result of an attempt by William T. Sherman to outflank Joseph E. Johnston's army northwest of Atlanta. Sherman first misjudged Johnston's numbers and ordered an attack by Joseph Hooker's XX Corps that was handily repelled by A. P. Stewart's division. The following day, 27 May, Sherman ordered Oliver O. Howard's IV Corps to strike Johnston's right flank, but that attack was easily repulsed by Patrick R. Cleburne's division. Thereafter Sherman resumed his campaign of maneuver, ultimately forcing Johnston closer to Atlanta. Johnston, *Narrative of Military Operations*, 326–32; Sherman, *Memoirs*, 43–46.

14. This is likely either Maj. S. M. Bird, who was quartermaster on the staff of Brig. Gen. Dudley M. DuBose at the end of the war, or Maj. W. E. Bird, who served as quartermaster under Brig. Gen. Henry L. Benning. DuBose was colonel of the Fifteenth Georgia Infantry, and Benning was colonel of the Seventeenth Georgia Infantry when Wofford commanded the Eighteenth Georgia Infantry. Wright, *Staff Officers*, 14; Crute, *Confederate Staff Officers*, 18, 215.

15. William Tatum Wofford (1824–1884), a member of the Georgia legislature and secession convention, was commissioned colonel of the Eighteenth Georgia Infantry in 1861. After temporarily commanding Hood's Texas Brigade, Wofford was promoted to brigadier general and command of Thomas R. R. Cobb's Georgia brigade. At the battle of the Wilderness he pointed

out to Longstreet a route around the Federal left flank that resulted in I Corps's successful counterattack. In January 1865 he was transferred to command of the Department of North Georgia.

16. Henry Snow began the war as a private in Company F, First Texas Infantry, but was soon promoted to first lieutenant. He was wounded at the battle of Gaines' Mill on 27 June 1862 and was shortly thereafter reassigned to regimental headquarters as an assistant surgeon. He later returned to his company but resigned from the army on 18 June 1863. Simpson, *Compendium*, 12, 37, 45.

17. Gilbert Moxley Sorrel (1838–1901) left his job as a banker in Savannah to serve as a volunteer aide to Longstreet with the honorary rank of captain. He soon became Longstreet's adjutant and then his chief of staff, and as Longstreet rose in rank, so did Sorrel, receiving a lieutenant colonel's commission in July 1863. Sorrel led three of Longstreet's brigades in the crucial flank attack at the Wilderness that checked Winfield Scott Hancock's attack and saved the day for the Confederacy. So pleased was Lee by Sorrel's performance that he strongly urged his promotion to brigadier general and his appointment to a field command. He sustained a grave chest wound at Hatcher's Run on 7 Feb. 1865 but recovered in time to lead his brigade in the retreat to Appomattox. Although Francis W. Dawson found Sorrel to be "bad tempered and inclined to be overbearing," his memoirs, composed between 1899 and 1901, were considered by Douglas Southall Freeman to be "one of the most charming of all books on the War Between the States." Sorrel, *Recollections*.

18. J. S. D. Cullen, who had entered Confederate service as surgeon of the First Virginia Infantry, was appointed medical director of Longstreet's brigade at Manassas Junction in July 1861. In June 1862 he was named chief surgeon of Joseph E. Johnston's staff, but he returned to Longstreet's division later that month and remained his senior medical officer throughout the war. Cullen attended to Longstreet when he was severely wounded at the Wilderness. Cullen's 18 May 1875 letter to his former commander, absolving Longstreet of any blame for the Confederate defeat at Gettysburg, is reprinted in full in Longstreet's memoirs. Wright,

Staff Officers, 39; Longstreet, *Manassas to Appomattox*, 33, 383–84; Sorrel, *Recollections*, 117, 233.

19. Osmun Latrobe, a Marylander, was appointed adjutant to Joseph E. Johnston on 11 March 1862 with the rank of captain. In June he was transferred to the staff of D. R. Jones as adjutant and inspector general, and on 26 Oct. 1862 he assumed similar duties on Longstreet's staff with the rank of major. When G. Moxley Sorrel was promoted to brigadier general, Latrobe was appointed Longstreet's chief of staff and promoted to lieutenant colonel. Dawson, who was generally hypercritical of his fellow staff officers, found Latrobe "courteous enough at all times," about as high a compliment as he was capable of paying. Latrobe was painfully wounded in the thigh and hand at the battle of the Wilderness but remained with I Corps until the end of the war. His last days were spent in Baltimore in impoverished circumstances. Wright, *Staff Officers*, 95; Longstreet, *Manassas to Appomattox*, 581; Sorrel, *Recollections*, 118, 177, 231.

20. Peyton T. Manning was a resident of Aberdeen, Miss., when the war broke out. He was appointed one of Longstreet's aides in July 1861. During the Peninsula campaign he served as an aide to Joseph E. Johnston with the rank of major, and on 14 Oct. 1862 he was promoted to lieutenant colonel and chief of ordnance on Longstreet's staff. Francis W. Dawson found Manning to be "exceedingly kind and considerate" and "an exceedingly easy man to get along with. Unquestionably a gentleman in his tastes and habits, and brave as a lion." Unfortunately, however, "he knew comparatively little of his work as Ordnance officer, and was unable to write an ordinary letter correctly." Manning was wounded at the battle of Chickamauga and died at his Aberdeen home within four years of the war's end. Dawson, *Reminiscences*, 63, 101; Crute, *Confederate Staff Officers*, 104, 124.

21. John W. Fairfax was the owner of Oak Hill, the former estate of James Monroe in Loudoun County, Va. He became adjutant and inspector general on Longstreet's division staff in March 1862 with the rank of captain, and by 5 May 1862 he had been promoted to major. After a period as aide-de-camp to Joseph E. Johnston in June 1862, he returned to I Corps as inspector general and was promoted to lieutenant colonel on 17 Sept. 1862 and to colonel on 5 May 1864, after which time he served as Longstreet's adjutant. Moxley Sorrel described Fairfax as "tall,

courtly and rather impressive," while Dawson found him to be "clownish and silly." Brave and pious, he also was reputed to have a taste for whiskey and the finer things of life. Wright, *Staff Officers*, 52; Sorrel, *Recollections*, 29–30, 84–85.

22. September 1865 found Longstreet in New Orleans where many former Confederate generals—P. G. T. Beauregard, Braxton Bragg, Simon B. Buckner, Harry T. Hays, John Bell Hood, Dabney H. Maury, A. P. Stewart, Richard Taylor, and M. Jeff Thompson among them—were starting over. There, too, were Edward and William Miller Owen, both I Corps veterans. William Miller Owen had returned to Louisiana on 13 June "without a dollar in the world, emphatically and completely busted" but with the intention of taken up again "the broken thread of a business life" by reentering the cotton brokerage trade. At the Owens' urging Longstreet remained in the city and, as he was incapacitated from physical labor by his Wilderness wound, with them formed the brokerage firm of Longstreet, Owen & Company on 1 January 1866. Two months later, on 1 March, Longstreet was elected president of the newly formed Great Southern & Western Accident Insurance Company of New Orleans, which he ran concurrently with his brokerage business. In 1867 he and James F. Casey, U. S. Grant's brother-in-law, attempted to interest Grant in a railroad venture from New Orleans to Mazatlán, Mexico, but this promotional scheme bore no fruit. Sanger and Hay, *James Longstreet*, 320–23; Owen, *Washington Artillery*, 398.

23. William Miller Owen (1840–1893) was born in Cincinnati but moved to New Orleans in 1858. He joined the Washington Artillery as a private but was promoted to first lieutenant and appointed adjutant on 26 May 1861. He became the battalion's major on 10 Aug. 1863. After detached duty as commander of the Thirteenth Virginia Artillery Battalion in southeast Virginia, Owen returned to the Army of Northern Virginia in the spring of 1864. He was wounded at the battle of the Crater and promoted to lieutenant colonel early in 1865. His memoir, *In Camp and Battle with the Washington Artillery*, is a Civil War classic.

24. This letter printed courtesy Special Collections, James G. Leyburn Library, Washington and Lee University, Lexington, Va.

25. These are Pleasant Kittrell Goree, Norman Goree Kittrell, and Hugh Lawson Hayes

who in 1868 would marry TJG's sister, Susan Margaret Goree.

26. Edward Porter Alexander (1835–1910) resigned from the U.S. Army with Georgia's secession and accepted a commission as a captain of Confederate engineers. He served as Beauregard's signal officer at First Manassas and was subsequently promoted to lieutenant colonel and named chief of ordnance of the Army of Northern Virginia. In 1864 Alexander was promoted to brigadier general and named chief of artillery of I Corps. Maury Klein, *Edward Porter Alexander* (Athens, Ga., 1971); Gary W. Gallagher, ed., *Fighting for the Confederacy: The Personal Recollections of General Edward Porter Alexander* (Chapel Hill, N.C., 1989).

27. William Nelson Pendleton (1809–1883), educated at West Point, served as rector of Grace Episcopal Church in Lexington, Va., where Robert E. Lee was a vestryman. Although fifty-one years old in 1861, Pendleton was elected captain of the Rockbridge Artillery. His ability as an administrator quickly moved him up the ranks to become a colonel and chief of artillery under Joseph E. Johnston, a position that he maintained with the Army of Northern Virginia throughout the war. On 26 March 1862 he was promoted to brigadier general.

Longstreet's reference is to Pendleton's "Personal Recollections of General Lee: An Address Delivered at Washington and Lee University, at the Request of the University Authorities, on Gen. Lee's Birthday, Jan. 19, 1873." In it he thoroughly damns Longstreet, describing him in terms befitting Milton's Satan. Lee's plan for Gettysburg, Pendleton believed, was flawless and would have succeeded but for Longstreet's lack of cooperation; but "the animus of the slow-moving, jealous corps-chief was at the time unrevealed and unsuspected." Pendleton maintained that Lee had, in his own hearing, ordered Longstreet to attack Meade's left flank, below Gettysburg, "at sunrise next morning," 2 July, certain that his corps would sweep the enemy from the field. "Here, however, occurred the great, the fatal failure of the entire occasion." Longstreet delayed his attack until 4:00 P.M., the enemy was reinforced and fortified his position along Cemetery Ridge, and the opportunity was lost. Longstreet, in Pendleton's opinion, was "disastrously tardy in violation of explicit orders on an occasion of such supreme importance." The alleged delay, Pendleton told his audience, "was at the time lamentable, and

by the thoroughly examining will probably be always judged wholly inexcusable, if not unaccountable." Susan Pendleton Lee, *Memoirs of William Nelson Pendleton* (Philadelphia, 1893); William Nelson Pendleton, "Personal Recollections of General Lee," *Southern Magazine* 15 (1874): 603–36.

28. Benjamin Grubb Humphreys (1808–1882) was a member of the Mississippi state legislature. Although opposed to secession, he raised a company of the Twenty-first Mississippi Infantry in 1861 and was promoted to colonel of the regiment the following November. Promoted to brigadier general to rank from 12 Aug. 1863, he was appointed commander of the Mississippi Brigade of the Army of Northern Virginia. Incapacitated at the battle of Berryville on 3 Sept., he was appointed commander of a military district in Mississippi. Benjamin Grubb Humphreys, "Recollections of Fredericksburg, from the Morning of the 29th of April to the 6th of May, 1863," *Land We Love* 3 (1867): 403–60.

29. The original of this letter is in the Longstreet Papers in the Southern Historical Collection, Library of the University of North Carolina at Chapel Hill; a copy was presented to the Louisiana State University archives by Thomas Robson Hay, the coauthor of *James Longstreet, Soldier, Politician, Officerholder, and Writer*.

30. This letter is located in the James Longstreet Papers, Southern Historical Collection, Library of the University of North Carolina at Chapel Hill.

31. Lee's adjutant general, Lt. Col. Walter H. Taylor, charged in his memoir that Longstreet clearly admitted that "he assumed the responsibility of postponing the execution of the orders of the commanding general" on the first day of the battle of Gettysburg and was "fairly chargeable with tardiness" although urged to hasten his march to the sound of the guns. In a letter to Longstreet, dated 28 April 1875, however, Taylor denied any knowledge of Pendleton's article or of the purported order. Indeed, he wrote, "if such an order was given you, I never knew it, or it has strangely escaped my memory. I think it more than probable that, if General Lee *had had your troops available* the evening previous to the day of which you speak, he *would have ordered an early attack;* but this does not touch the point at

issue." Taylor went on to observe that the attacks on Longstreet's war record for present political reasons were "ungenerous" and met the disapprobation of "all good Confederates."

Likewise, Lt. Col. Charles Scott Venable, Lee's adjutant, in a note to Longstreet dated 11 May 1875, denied any knowledge of an order to attack Meade at sunrise on 2 July and did not believe any such order was issued. Lt. Col. Charles Marshall, Lee's aide-de-camp, too, had no recollection of such an order, and in a letter to Longstreet on 7 May 1875 he further observed that Lee's official report of the battle made no allusion to such an order. Walter H. Taylor, *Four Years with General Lee* (New York, 1877; rept., with introduction by James I. Robertson, Jr., Bloomington, Ind., 1962), 97–110; Longstreet, *Manassas to Appomattox*, 377–84.

32. Longstreet's reference here is apparently to J. William Jones, *Personal Reminiscences, Anecdotes, and Letters to Gen. Robert E. Lee* (New York, 1874).

Also of interest is John W. Daniel's contention in his address to the Virginia Division of the Army of Northern Virginia Association on 29 October 1875 that "the tardiness of General Longstreet's movements, and the prolonged absence of Pickett's division" caused the defeat at Gettysburg. "At any rate," Daniel told his audience, "the fault was not Lee's, for he was anxious to attack at dawn." But "lest injustice be done to General Longstreet," he concluded, "I forbear expressing an opinion." Major Daniel was Jubal Early's adjutant at the time of the Gettysburg campaign.

Probably closer to the truth is G. Moxley Sorrel's observation that "as Longstreet was not to be made willing and Lee refused to change or could not change, the former failed to conceal some anger. There was apparent apathy in his bearing on the battlefield. His plans may have been better than Lee's but it was too late to alter them with the troops ready to open fire on each other." J. William Jones, D.D., comp., *Army of Northern Virginia Memorial Volume* (Richmond, 1880; rept., with new introduction by James I. Robertson, Jr. Dayton, Ohio, 1976), 109–10; Sorrel, *Recollections*, 157–58.

33. J. A. Early, *The Campaigns of Gen. Robert E. Lee: An Address by Lieut. Gen. Jubal A. Early, before Washington and Lee University, January 19th, 1872* (Baltimore, 1872), 30. See also J. A. Early, "The

Gettysburg Campaign: Report of Major-General J. A. Early," *Southern Magazine* 4 (1872): 390.

34. Richard K. Meade, Sr., served on Longstreet's staff during the Peninsula campaign and the Seven Days battles. In his memoirs Longstreet referred to the incident on which he queried TJG. On 28 June, he wrote, Longstreet sent Meade across the Chickahominy River on a scouting expedition. Meade was the first to discover that George B. McClellan had abandoned his position south of the river and was retreating down the Peninsula. Meade took possession of a fortification that Lee had ordered Magruder to attack and then reported to Longstreet and Lee. The delighted Lee instructed Magruder "not to hurt my young friends, Major Meade and Lieutenant Johnson, who are occupying that fort." Crute, *Confederate Staff Officers*, 23, 97, 111, 124, 129, 151, 189; Longstreet, *Manassas to Appomattox*, 130, 148–49.

35. Erasmus Taylor of Orange Courthouse, Va., served as a captain on the staff of David R. Jones. After the retreat from Gettysburg, Taylor's home served as headquarters for Longstreet's staff. Sorrel referred to him as "a well-known gentleman" and remembered that "everything was done by him for our comfort and amusement. The house was spacious, well fitted for dances and entertainments, and being crowded with joyous, happy Virginia girls there was no lack of fun and gaiety." He accompanied Longstreet's corps to Tennessee in 1863 and following the death of Maj. S. P. Mitchell, Taylor was appointed as chief quartermaster. When Longstreet was wounded at the Wilderness, he was first taken to Taylor's home, Meadow Farm, where he was nursed by Taylor's wife. Living in Orange County, Va., after the war, Taylor corresponded with his former commander, offering his memories of wartime events as Longstreet was writing *From Manassas to Appomattox*. Crute, *Confederate Staff Officers*, 106; Longstreet, *Manassas to Appomattox*, 400, 557, 572; Sorrel, *Recollections*, 174, 196, 236.

36. Leonidas Jefferson Storey (1834–1909) served as captain in Xavier B. DeBray's Texas Cavalry Brigade. He was a member of the Texas state legislature from 1876 until 1880 when he was elected lieutenant governor. Webb, *Handbook of Texas*, 2:676.

37. James M. Goggin (1820–1889) was commander of Goggin's Battalion, Virginia Infantry,

and, after his battalion was consolidated with that of Edgar B. Montague, major of the Thirty-second Virginia Infantry. In June 1862 he became the adjutant on the staff of Lafayette McLaws and later served in the same capacity under Joseph B. Kershaw. He was appointed brigadier general to rank from 4 Dec. 1864, but his appointment was canceled. Crute, *Confederate Staff Officers*, 71; Crute, *Units*, 378; Sorrel, *Recollections*, 205.

38. E. P. Alexander, "Lee at Appomattox: Personal Recollections of the Breakup of the Confederacy," *Century Magazine* 63 (1902): 921–31.

39. TJG's memory is here at fault. The officer in question is Robert Moorman Sims, assistant adjutant general on Longstreet's staff. Of this incident Longstreet wrote: "As my troops marched to form the last line a message came from General Lee saying he had not thought to give notice of the intended ride to meet General Grant, and asked me to send his message to that effect to General Gordon, and it was duly sent by Captain Sims, of the Third Corps staff, serving at my head-quarters since the fall of A. P. Hill.

"After delivering the message, Captain Sims, through some informality, was sent to call the truce. The firing ceased. General Custer rode to Captain Sims to know his authority, and, upon finding that he was of my staff, asked to be conducted to my head-quarters, and down they came in a fast gallop, General Custer's flaxen locks flowing over his shoulders, and in brusk, excited manner, he said,—

"'In the name of General Sheridan I demand the surrender of this army.'" Wright, *Staff Officers*, 150; Crute, *Confederate Staff Officers*, 24, 68, 124; Longstreet, *Manassas to Appomattox*, 626–27.

40. John Irvin Gregg, major general of Union cavalry, was captured at the battle of Sayler's Creek on 6 April 1865 and held until Lee's surrender at Appomattox three days later. OR, XLVI, 1:1155, 1303; Stephen Z. Starr, *The Union Cavalry in the Civil War*, vol. 2, *The War in the East from Gettysburg to Appomattox* (Baton Rouge, La., 1982), 476; Richard Sommers, *Richmond Redeemed: The Seige at Petersburg* (New York, 1981), 192.

41. Jonathan Warwick Daniell (1842–1910), major and adjutant general of the staff of Jubal Early, was the author of *The Character of Stonewall Jackson* (Lynchburg, Va., 1868). He delivered an address to the Virginia Division of the Army of Northern Virginia at its annual meeting at Richmond on 28 Oct. 1875 that was published as *The Campaign and Battles of Gettysburg* (Lynchburg, Va., 1875). His oration on Robert E. Lee, read at the unveiling of the recumbent statue of Lee at Lexington on 28 June 1883, was published in Savannah in 1883. He delivered a memorial address on Jubal Early to the Association of the Army of Northern Virginia at Richmond on 13 Dec. 1894 published in the *Southern Historical Society Papers* 22 (1894): 281–335.

42. Reuben Lindsay Walker (1827–1890), a Virginia civil engineer and planter before the war, commanded the Purcell Battery at the first battle of Manassas. Promoted to lieutenant colonel and then to colonel, he became chief of artillery on the staff of A. P. Hill, serving in that capacity until Appomattox. Walker was promoted to brigadier general to rank from 18 Feb. 1865.

43. The Menger Hotel was opened on San Antonio's Alamo Plaza on 1 Feb. 1859 and after the Civil War became the best-known hotel in the Southwest. Among its more prominent guests and residents were writers William Sydney Porter (who mentioned it in several of his stories) and Sidney Lanier and generals Robert E. Lee, U. S. Grant, Philip H. Sheridan. Theodore Roosevelt is said to have used the barroom at the Menger, a replica of the taproom of the House of Lords, as a recruiting station for his First United States Volunteer Cavalry, the "Rough Riders." Webb, *Handbook of Texas* 2:174.

44. James Stephen Hogg, who was elected governor of Texas in 1890, determined to replace TJG as superintendent of penitentiaries. The Douglass of whom TJG wrote is most likely E. G. Douglas, a former sheriff and state senator, who was assistant superintendent of the Rusk unit of the Texas prison system under TJG. TJG's successor, Lucius A. Watley, placed TJG in charge of the Burleson prison farm where he remained until 1899 when he was promoted to head of the Harlem state farm. In 1907 Douglas was named assistant superintendent of the juvenile reformatory at Gatesville, but he died before the end of the year. Robert C. Cotner, *James Stephen Hogg: A Biography* (Austin, Tex., 1959); Walker, *Penology for Profit*, 148–49, 152.

45. "The Bonny Blue Flag" ranked with

"Dixie" and "Maryland, My Maryland" among the most popular of the battle hymns of the Confederacy. Written by vaudevillian Harry Macarthy to the tune of "The Irish Jaunting Car," this song was a roll call of the Southern states and a litany of their civic and martial virtues. The first verse, echoing Shakespeare's *Henry V*, encapsulates the Rebel cause:

> We are a band of brothers, and native to
>   the soil,
> Fighting for the property we gain by honest toil;
> And when our rights were threatened, the
>   cry rose near and far,
> "Hurrah for the Bonny Blue Flag that
>   bears a single star!"

Ironically, Longstreet is said to have made the comment, after attending a concert of Union music sometime after the war, that "if we had had songs like that, we would have won the war." Heaps and Heaps, *The Singing Sixties*, 54–56.

46. Sung to the tune of "The Bonny Blue Flag," "The Homespun Dress" expressed the Southern woman's pride in her cause and her willingness to make sacrifices for it. The second verse, written by Carrie Bell Sinclair, is typical:

> The homespun dress is plain, I know,
>   My hat's palmetto, too;
> But then it shows what Southern girls
>   For Southern rights will do.
> We send the bravest of our land
>   To battle with the foe,
> And we will lend a helping hand;
>   We love the South, you know!

Ibid., 348–49.

47. This is most likely Alexander Cheves Haskell, colonel of the Seventh South Carolina Cavalry. Haskell received wounds at Fredericksburg, Chancellorsville, Cold Harbor, and Darbytown Road but was with Lee's army when it surrendered at Appomattox.

INDEX